Nosh New York

ALSO BY MYRA ALPERSON

The Food Lover's Guide to the Real New York

The International Adoption Handbook

Dim Sum, Bagels & Grits

Nosh

New York

THE FOOD LOVER'S
GUIDE TO NEW YORK CITY'S
MOST DELICIOUS NEIGHBORHOODS

MYRA ALPERSON

ST. MARTIN'S GRIFFIN ♨ New York

www.stmartins.com

Photographs courtesy of the author.
Maps copyright © 2003 by David Lindroth Inc.

Book Design by Katy Riegel

ISBN 0-312-30417-X

10 9 8 7 6 5 4 3 2

I dedicate this book, with deep gratitude,

to the women and men,

from here and from many countries around the world,

who have made New York City

such a truly delicious place to live!

nosh
nosher
noshen

Rhyme respectively with "gosh," "josher," "joshin,"
German: *nachen*, "to eat on the sly."

(A) *Nosh*:
1. A snack, a tidbit, a "bit," a small portion.
2. Anything eaten between meals and, presumably, in small quantity: fruit, a cookie, "a piece of cake," a candy.
     Jews loved to *nosh* long before they ever went to a cocktail party or tasted tidbits.

(B) *Nosher*:
1. One who eats between meals.
2. One who has a sweet tooth.
3. One who is weak-willed about food and dieting.

(C) *Noshen*: (verb)
To *nosh* is to "have a little bit to eat before dinner is ready," or to "have a little something between meals." "I came in to find her *noshing*." "He's used to *noshing* after midnight."

Many delicatessen counters display plates with small slices of salami, or pieces of halvah, with a legend affixed to a toothpick: "Have a *nosh*." The *nosh* is not free, but cheap. In some Jewish delicatessens a lucky customer sees a little "flag" stuck into an open plate of goodies: "*Nem* (take) a *nosh* a nickel."

New York is full of the most extraordinary items and opportunities for *noshing*.

—from *The Joys of Yiddish*
     by Leo Rosten (New York: McGraw-Hill & Company, 1968)

Contents

Acknowledgments

The worst thing about writing acknowledgements is feeling certain that important people are being left out.

Let me begin with a mass acknowledgment to the many shop owners and restaurateurs in New York City neighborhoods who introduced me to their wonderful food—and sometimes provided considerable explanations (and tastes!) of what they make or sell. They are identified throughout this book.

I am also grateful to many other people who took me around the neighborhoods or provided insights into history and current trends. They include (with apologies to anyone I may have inadvertently omitted) Rena Appel and Martin Maskowitz of the Sephardic Community Center; Joann Billharz; Valerie Bradley; Jenny Cha; Joe Cicciu; Paul Engel; Lili Fable; Susan Fox and Margarita Kagan of the Shorefront Y; Renee and Tony Giordano; Yanghee Han; Lou Izzo and Maggie Krupka; Daniel Karatzas; Boris Kerdimun; Marc Crawford Leavitt; Man-Li Lin; Peter Madonia; Robin Marcato and Philip Cohen of the Tenement Museum; Christina McMullin; Dorothy Morehead; Erin Moriarty; José B. Rivera; Charles Sciberras; Wendy Shao; Bob Singleton of the Greater Astoria Historical Society, and John Tapper.

I am grateful to the many people who have loyally supported my newsletter, *NoshNews,* and to the many people who love taking and repeating the NoshWalks I lead, and who have also provided excellent suggestions on ways to improve them. Nach Waxman at Kitchen Arts & Letters Bookstore has been a tireless advocate!

Paul Messina of NY1 TV produced two wonderful stories about *Nosh-News* and NoshWalks when I was just starting out. Each captured exactly what I was trying to do—and gave me excellent visibility! Marian Lizzi, my editor at St. Martin's Press, saw Paul's story about my Nosh Walk in East Harlem and approached me about writing a book because, she said, she could see my passion for what I do. Gareth Esersky, my agent, deftly navigated the book contract. David Lindroth created the maps for the book.

A little girl named Sadie Zhenzhen Alperson (who would not want to see the word "little" before her name, because she's twelve days short of turning seven as I type this!) gets special mention for putting up with all the strange foods her mama brings home (even though she sticks her tongue out at most of them). She has also joined her mother on endless food explorations, and has helped her identify the best places for picky eaters—and where to find good bathrooms. This knowledge has been invaluable!

—Myra Alperson
September 2003

Introduction

I didn't want to finish this book. I was having so much fun researching and writing it that I knew I could have kept going forever. I had some valid reasons to stretch out the process: neighborhoods change; it is sometimes hard to keep pace, and if you're like me, you want to be current. Alas, deadlines loomed. But for you, this version of the book can be the beginning of an ongoing series of delicious journeys. I promise to continue to scout out new food adventures and to share them with readers. (I have excluded Staten Island from this edition of the book because it's a less popular area for exploration and food finds. Perhaps I'll include it in a subsequent edition.)

Nosh New York: The Food Lover's Guide to New York City's Most Delicious Neighborhoods is based on *NoshNews,* a newsletter I created in 1999 to indulge my passion for exploring the food and culture of New York City's ethnic neighborhoods.

Each issue of *NoshNews* profiles one, two, or sometimes more neighborhoods in depth and is packed with information. I choose the neighborhoods based on the diversity of the food, the richness of the local culture, and their accessibility.

Although some people may think my research consists of eating my way through a neighborhood, the task involves much more than that. Understanding food entails understanding culture and history. So, as I embark upon each neighborhood adventure, I try to do as much background reading and other research as possible. (The Internet is helpful for some neighborhoods but not for others.) To almost every chapter and side trip I've added information about local bookstores, organizations, and non-food shops that I find interesting. These shed light on the neighborhoods' cultures, including food.

I was already familiar with quite a few of these neighborhoods from my experience leading bicycle tours through a company I ran from 1983 to 1990 called Hungry Pedalers Gourmet Bicycle Tours. It has been fascinating to see how some areas have changed over the last twenty years—and how others haven't.

I also made contact with knowlegeable people within the communities, including real estate agents, business leaders, local historians, social service professionals, a theater manager, the developer of a community Web site, and, of course, the shop owners and restaurateurs themselves. These wonderful and generous individuals made a critical difference in helping me to get started and to understand and interpret what I was seeing and eating. Thanks to all of you!

In the summer of 2000, I launched NoshWalks to complement *Nosh-News*. Each NoshWalk is based on an issue of the newsletter, and I add new walks only as I finish the corresponding issues. The tours, like *NoshNews* and this book, combine local history with food.

Meanwhile, a boom of interest in world cultures has erupted all around us. People are more open than ever to sampling clothing, music, and literature from around the world. The ethnic-food explosion is visible on supermarket shelves, in restaurants in communities large and small, and in both cities and the suburbs. Ethnic cooking has become a major pastime, based on the extraordinary numbers of cookbooks and Web sites that promote it. Even our children now take quesadillas, biscotti, and dim sum for granted.

But there's nothing like going to "the source." And if you can't get to Italy, Guatemala, Senegal, Pakistan, or Poland, there's always New York City, where airfare is replaced by a MetroCard.

Back when Hungry Pedalers got started, we had a slogan:

> Nosh Your Way from Odessa to Bombay—
> . . . and Never Leave New York.

I use this slogan for *NoshNews*, and it certainly holds true for this book.

So . . .

Bon appétit—in any language!

Ready-Set-Nosh!

■

PREPARING FOR YOUR FOOD ADVENTURES

HOW THIS BOOK WORKS

GETTING AROUND

Preparing for Your Food Adventures

■

One of the pure pleasures of being in New York City is that you don't have to go far for an exotic culinary adventure. If you already love to travel and relish new tastes, sounds, and sights, and have an adventurous palate, you need little more than a MetroCard, an appetite, $15 to $20 (although you can get by with less), a backpack, and super-comfortable walking shoes to set out on a foreign journey close to home. Did I forget to add energy and imagination? (And you already have another useful tool: this book!) This chapter provides some tips to get you going.

On any trip you take using this book, I recommend just a few other items: a compact atlas of New York City (I like the *Hagstrom New York Atlas*—about $14.95—which is compact but easy to read), a collapsible umbrella or a poncho that doesn't make you sweat buckets in case of rain, a sun hat in case of glaring sun, and a credit card or an ATM card, just in case you find something extra that you absolutely *have* to have.

Extra cash comes in handy, of course: in neighborhoods where there are few banks, you may find an ATM in a supermarket or convenience store but you'll have to pay a fee of up to $2.00 for any transaction. And some restaurants in the neighborhoods I've written about take neither credit cards nor personal checks. Some folks also like to bring freezer bags in case they buy perishables.

Oh yes—don't forget your camera!

▪ An Ethnic Cornucopia

The diversity of New York City seems to increase each year. Neighborhoods, especially in Queens, Brooklyn, and the Bronx, continue to embrace newcomers from many lands. And in the past decade, these settlers truly have come to represent all continents (okay, except for Antarctica, unless you visit one of New York's zoos!) and, with them, new flavors and ingredients to discover in their restaurants and markets.

Neighborhoods such as Astoria, Elmhurst, Flushing, and Sunnyside, all in Queens, offer so much within their boundaries that an outsider trying to figure them out can easily experience information overload. So many young people from different countries have come to New York City with their families in recent years that the city's school system has created special programs just for them. One of these, Newcomers High School, was opened several years ago in Long Island City to help acclimate them to the United States and provide the basics for them to make a transition to a regular high school. (More than 100 languages are represented at Newcomers.)

Among the hundreds of business cards I've collected, a few have addresses in their home countries as well as New York. One for an African grocery in East Harlem also has an address in Dakar, Senegal. Another, for a shop in Bay Ridge, Brooklyn, which specializes in nuts and dried fruit, has a head office in Lebanon. And a Chinese shop selling Japanese-style sweets and dried snacks lists its counterpart in Hong Kong.

▪ When All This Started

Some folks date the dawn of New York City's ethnic food craze to 1973, when the then-new Ninth Avenue Association in Manhattan organized its first-ever ethnic food fair, scheduled for the third weekend of May. There were rainstorms that weekend, but several thousand people crowded the fair, which stretched over many blocks. (I remember, because I was there!) But in those days such an event was quite a novelty: street fairs of this type and on this scale were unheard of, though we take them for granted now.

And, in those days, that particular neighborhood—Ninth Avenue from about 37th to 57th Streets—was considered by some to be "Wild West" territory. You'd have to remember the bad old days, easily forgotten now, when Times Square was considered a crime zone after dark, when 42nd Street from Broadway to Eighth Avenue was lined with XXX-rated movie theaters. To get to Ninth Avenue it seemed necessary to wade through a considerable discomfort area. Businesses suffered—and that's why locals organized the association in the first place.

Nowadays the Ninth Avenue Street Fair is the mother of street fairs, drawing millions of visitors every May. Ironically, however, many of the exhibitors come from outside the neighborhood because the cost of setting up a booth is, sadly, too expensive for some local merchants, and competition for space is high, too. That's just one indicator of how times have changed. Now surrounded by luxury high-rises, Ninth Avenue (which itself is protected from overbuilding by local preservation regulations) has become a tourist destination, and its restaurants often fill up, especially before matinees at nearby Broadway and off-Broadway theaters.

I began preparing this book about two months after the events of September 11, 2001. It was a time of great mourning in New York City, and many of the small businesses I routinely cover for *NoshNews* suffered badly. So I've been very grateful to have the opportunity to promote these wonderful markets and eateries in my newsletter, walking tours, and this book.

If you're an adventurous cook, you will fall in love with many of the places you'll read about here once you visit them in person. A great way to take advantage is to have recipes in mind before you go. This book has a few, but you may want to stock up on more. An outstanding source for ethnic cookbooks is Kitchen Arts & Letters (1435 Lexington Avenue at 94th Street, 212-876-5550), the granddaddy of cookbook stores. If you can't find the book you think you want here, Nach Waxman and his staff will help you figure out what it is and then make sure you get it. The global food market Kalustyan's (123 Lexington Avenue between 28th and 29th Streets, 212-685-3888; fax 212-683-8458) has dozens of cookbooks with recipes from around the world and ingredients to make many of them at home. I have also found many recipe sources on line and have mentioned some in this book.

▪ Visiting the Neighborhoods: Bridging Language and Culture

I think it's important for us to make our trips with an open mind and an open heart. In visiting new neighborhoods, you may encounter cultural gulfs similar to those you may have experienced traveling in other countries. While these tours are hardly the equivalent of a Himalayan trek or an eco-tour of the Amazon, you will find some neighborhoods where stores have few signs in English and where few people speak English and are not prepared to accommodate your questions. For example, you might ask for more information about a particular item on a menu, and although the menu itself has been translated into English, you'll find that no one can explain what that item is. This can be frustrating, but it's also one of the more unique aspects of life in New York City.

It's important to remember, as well, that some of the neighborhoods I've written about are not geared up for tourists—and that's essentially what we are when we venture into them! These markets and eateries have been created to meet the needs of the local population, including many relatively recent immigrants, who seek out comfort zones where they can eat familiar food and speak their language—and not to attract intrepid food mavens like us!

Almost all of our families were part of this dynamic immigrant cycle at one time. Looking from the outside, we may wonder why the restaurants and markets aren't more welcoming to outsiders. At times you may even feel as though you're being regarded with suspicion—I have felt this myself. But with patience and respect, we can use these visits to gain more knowledge about our New York neighbors and, hopefully, begin to break down barriers.

Each time I prepare an issue of the *NoshNews* newsletter, I try to read up on whatever neighborhood I'm visiting so that I'm not walking into totally unknown territory. For some neighborhoods you can find Web sites that will provide good background material. (I've appended Web sites, when I've found them, for each neighborhood chapter and/or side trip.) A bibliography of recommended books is also included.

A very good overall resource for neighborhood background information is New York City's own Web site, which includes a section called "City Life." The URL is http://home.nyc.gov/portal/index.jsp?pageID=nyc_citylife&catID=803. (I wish I could include an instant link in this book!)

■ About the Food

Although you may think you know Chinese, Mexican, Indian, and other cuisines from restaurants you've visited close to home, you're bound to find ingredients, flavorings, and combinations that are totally new when you explore the neighborhoods described in this book. Part of the challenge of getting to know these neighborhoods is to be open (through sign language if necessary) and to have good will to be able to bridge gaps that may often seem unbridgeable. This guide will help, but it's inevitable that we will all encounter some challenges in understanding some of these new cuisines from time to time. (One woman who often participates in NoshWalks has suggested that I put together a glossary explaining all the foods I've seen. This is an interesting but daunting project, beyond the scope of this book, although we have developed a list.)

One of the best examples is a visit to Manhattan's Chinatown. This well-known area south of Canal Street and west of the Bowery has comfortably accommodated tourists for decades while continuing to feed throngs of Chinese families seeking the food they're familiar with. Here, especially in the better-equipped restaurants, you will find waiters happy to answer your questions and fulfill your particular needs.

But if you follow the famous Mott Street all the way south and then cross where it intersects with Chatham Square (you will see a statue of Lin Ze Xu, known for his role in ending drug trafficking in China), you will find yourself on East Broadway—and in another world. This is still Chinatown, but not the one you thought you knew. Here, in the heart of the Fujianese section of Chinatown, few people speak English, and you will see few tourists. Be adventurous—I confess to having been terribly daunted by this area of Chinatown when I began exploring. But it's now the area that I most love to visit because it just throbs with energy and has so much to experience, especially in the area under the Manhattan Bridge where, as I was writing this book, a whole new cluster of markets opened to accommodate this rapidly expanding community.

In these markets, I have seen unfamiliar fruits, greens, and seafood that I am eager to learn more about. And I would like to know more about the interesting-looking snacks that I see street vendors selling. I think I will need to find a Chinese guide to help me navigate this terrain, since I do not speak any Chinese dialect and am unable to ask even the most basic questions about some of the foods I've seen.

As you return to Mott Street from this area, you may well experience culture shock. It's as though you've just come back to the land of the familiar.

▪ Vegetarian Alert

From time to time I get queries from vegetarians about how useful my tours would be for them. The reality is that some neighborhoods will pose a challenge for people seeking a full-blown vegetarian meal and menu.

I do highlight vegetarian eateries when I find them, and many neighborhood bakeries also sell vegetarian snacks and appetizers. While it's true that some cuisines are heavy on meat—Latin American most immediately comes to mind—you will be surprised at the wide range of vegetarian side dishes and salads you can order to create a delicious, satisfying meal. So if you happen to stumble on a Brazilian *churruscarria* in Astoria or an Argentinian steak house in Jackson Heights, be creative. Salads of hearts of palm or Peruvian potato dishes can be combined with other sides—a pasta at the Argentinian place, or an avocado salad at the Peruvian one—to create a satisfying meal. I've described vegetarian options like these where I've found them.

Vegetarian cooks will find that produce markets in several neighborhoods outside of Manhattan offer outstanding quality and perhaps a greater variety of fruits, vegetables, cheeses, and various meat alternatives for a fraction of what you would pay in the costlier neighborhoods of Manhattan or Brooklyn, or in suburban areas, where access to a wide variety of fresh produce may be more limited. In Astoria, Queens, for example, I've seen at least four different types of dandelion greens. You'll be humbled by the varieties of eggplant, peppers, and tomatoes found in the produce stands in the famous indoor market in Belmont, Bronx; and in Brighton Beach, Brooklyn, whose shoppers are among the fussiest I've observed, you will find fresh fruit year-round at costs that more than make up for whatever parking fees or subway fares you paid to get there. (I once found a box of South African clementines in July for $2.99. Try to beat that!) In Middle Eastern shops (Bay Ridge and Atlantic Avenues in Brooklyn; and the Steinway Street area of Astoria, Queens) and in Turkish markets (Brighton Beach; Sunnyside, Queens; and Sunset Park, Brooklyn) you will find a daunting and satisfying selection of nuts, spices, and dried fruits that are likely to please vegetarian palates.

■ Greenmarkets

New York City has benefited immensely from the nationwide greenmarket movement, which brings locally grown produce to urban and suburban dwellers. Greenmarkets thrive in a number of the neighborhoods I've profiled in this book and play a particularly important role in areas where quality produce at good prices may be in short supply.

Although I do not routinely focus on greenmarkets here, you can find out whether your visit to a particular neighborhood coincides with a greenmarket day by consulting these two Web sites, which list the location and schedule for markets around New York City: the Council on the Environment, www.cenyc.org/HTMLGM/maingm.htm; and the Farmers Market Federation of New York, www.nyfarmersmarket.com/metro.html.

■ Smoking

As this book was being written, the City of New York enacted legislation to ban smoking in all city restaurants and bars. In some ethnic neighborhoods smoking is a fact of life and culture, so it will be interesting to see how this legislation affects these areas. (I am particularly curious to see what will happen in the Egyptian communities in Astoria, Queens, and Bay Ridge, Brooklyn, where smoking water pipes is an entrenched tradition.) I cannot at this time guarantee a smoke-free environment in many places; I've commented on this in some of the neighborhoods I've covered.

How This Book Works

As you'll see, the book is divided into sections by boroughs and then by neighborhoods. The larger, more self-contained neighborhoods have complete chapters. Mass-transit directions are included for all neighborhoods; driving directions are included for most. In some cases, I've also recommended which neighborhoods make good daylong journeys and which you can combine with others.

In general, the book excludes neighborhoods that are difficult to reach by mass transit in order to make the journeys as easy as possible. I also find that certain areas such as Northern Boulevard in Queens (which covers key areas of Woodside and Jackson Heights) that have interesting shops or restaurants but are car-oriented simply don't offer much neighborhood ambiance. You'll find a few exceptions, including Northern Boulevard in Flushing, which is more incorporated into the neighborhood.

In some cases, you will need to take both a subway and a bus to reach the destinations, but the transport is easy and if you follow the directions you won't have any problem figuring out where to go. (I cannot, however, assure you that subway or bus numbers or routes won't change, so you might want to consult a current transit map before you go.)

■ Side Trips

For each borough, you'll find side trips to neighborhoods that are intriguing but not large or significant enough to merit a full chapter. These neighborhoods include Elmhurst in Queens; Morris Park in the Bronx; and West

Harlem in Manhattan, which is part of a larger chapter covering Harlem as a whole (By contrast, East Harlem merits its own chapter.)

You may be surprised at some of the neighborhoods designated as side trips. The sprawling Washington Heights neighborhood in upper Manhattan covers a large geographic area but it lacks both variety and a critical mass of quality markets and eateries. So I've created two Washington Heights side trips. The first focuses on a stretch of Broadway in Washington Heights that has several good markets and interesting restaurants within a very-walkable twelve blocks. The other goes to a section of Washington Heights known as Hudson Heights (a designation invented by real estate agents), located near the Cloisters Museum. Within this geographic enclave are several fine markets and interesting places to eat that merit a visit. The Cloisters and Fort Tryon Park become part of the experience.

Bensonhurst, Brooklyn, well known for its Italian eateries and markets, has recently experienced an exodus of Italian families and the markets they patronize, so it's a side trip, too. It is, though, worth getting to know Bensonhurst more comprehensively because it has become the locus of much new immigration, and new ethnic neighborhoods—mainly Russian and Chinese—are emerging there.

Other side trips go to neighborhoods that are not normally destinations for folks who don't live in them, even for the most compulsive foodies. But I love exploring, so places such as Ridgewood, a neighborhood that straddles Brooklyn and Queens, and the Guyanese section of Richmond Hill, Queens, are included as side trips.

■ A Note About Inclusions and Exclusions

One of the key goals of this book is to identify excellent neighborhood places that are interesting, reflective of local culture, and inexpensive-to-moderate in price. The majority of my visits take place during the daytime, so, with a few exceptions, I omitted places that serve dinner only, unless their reputations are so strong or their neighborhood roles so important that I would be doing a disservice to readers to fail to mention them.

Some places are category-defying but deserved to be included anyway. Mehanata, located in Chinatown, is one. It's the only Bulgarian restaurant I know of in New York City, and is also noteworthy because of its peculiar location. Since it serves dinner only and is mostly a bar, I made a point of checking it out and reviewing it anyway, although arriving just as it opened at 6 P.M. and leaving by 7 P.M. meant that I completely missed the crowds that fill up the place until long after midnight.

In general, however, I didn't cover bars or pubs, although I've made sure to mention the neighborhoods in which they play an important role. The Irish neighborhood of Woodside, Queens, is a good example. Its many pubs serve a critical community purpose and some also host Irish traditional music nights that would appeal to visitors as well as locals.

I generally avoided reviewing markets or restaurants that are either parts of chains, very expensive, or so new (with some exceptions) that it's hard to know whether they will survive. In several issues of *NoshNews* I enthusiastically reviewed new places only to find that they weren't around the next time I visited. You will inevitably discover that some places I've written—and possibly raved—about won't be around when you read this book. I'm always sad to find this, though the corollary is that new establishtments crop up, too.

■ Making Contact

I have included phone numbers for almost all restaurants, but only occasionally for bakeries and markets. Regretfully, because of language barriers, you may find it difficult to call some of these places.

Most neighborhood markets in this book operate seven days a week. The exceptions are the kosher neighborhoods in the Brooklyn section as well as other kosher places mentioned (particularly on the Lower East Side of Manhattan and in Forest Hills, Queens), where all shops close from late Friday afternoon through Saturday (some restaurants open Saturday night but others don't reopen until Sunday), as well as Belmont, Bronx, where most stores close on Sundays. (Bakeries are open on Sunday but close early; most restaurants are open.)

I've also indicated some specific closings for individual shops and restaurants, particularly for the more popular destinations. For instance, the famous Sahadi food market on Atlantic Avenue has long been closed on Sundays, despite the fact that it's a busy shopping day in that neighborhood. The owners have always treasured Sunday as a family day.

Do be aware that some restaurants and shops may close for several weeks during the summer. Neighborhoods in which I've encountered long closings include Belmont, Bronx, and Williamsburg, Brooklyn, where the Hasidic families are known to head to the Catskills and Poconos for long family retreats. Since many of the businesses covered in this book are family-owned, they close up altogether when it's time to take a vacation—which is typically when business slows down anyway. (This may be particularly so during the last weeks in August and up to Labor Day, although of course many places will still be open.)

▪ Budgeting for Your Tour

Depending on the nature of your visit, you may get away with under $20 or find yourself spending much more. You'll find ATMs in most neighborhoods, although in some cases, as I mentioned earlier, you may not find a bank and will have to use an ATM in a convenience store, where fees are high. If you're planning to both eat and shop, you will, of course, want more cash on hand. The more established stores and restaurants take credit cards.

Getting Around

∎

I primarily rely on mass transit to get around New York City and I find it the best way to navigate most of the neighborhoods I've profiled. I've given driving instructions wherever possible, along with parking advisories. Some neighborhoods have good parking facilities, but you will still have to get back to your car when you're finished with your tour. The advantage of using mass transit is that you can wander off without worrying about having to retrace your steps.

∎ Bicycle Travel

I'm an avid bicycle rider, and many of the neighborhoods discussed here can be reached easily by bike. Using a bicycle can require considerable planning, though, but fortunately the New York City Department of City Planning has come out with a comprehensive, two-sided, user-friendly map of bicycle routes covering all five boroughs, which is a great service for bicyclists. These maps are informative, detailed, easy to read, and convenient for both recreational and commuter cyclists. The most current edition of the *New York City Cycling Map* is available at bicycle shops throughout the five boroughs or can be obtained from the Department of Transportation by calling 212-676-8476 or by downloading the map at www.ci.nyc.ny.us/html/dot/pdf/2003bikemapfront.pdf. The download is in PDF format; you will need Acrobat Reader to access the map, but Acrobat Reader (available at www.adobe.com) is a free download and easy to use. You can also get the map by joining Transportation Alternatives (www.transalt.org).

■ Mass Transit

New York City's mass transit system has been revolutionized in the last decade. Most of the subway lines have better, quieter trains and operate more efficiently than ever.

Mass transit has become much more user-friendly in recent years as a result of two great innovations: MetroCard and the free transfer between buses and subways (there's also the Fun Pass, which allows you to travel all day on buses and subways for less than the price of three full subway fares).

Internet Resources   You can get more information than ever on the Internet. The home page for the Metropolitan Transportation Authority (MTA), http://www.mta.nyc.ny.us/, will link you to information on the New York Transit Authority (New York City subways and buses, including express buses), Long Island Railroad, and Metro-North Railroad.

To link directly onto New York City transit, go to http://www.mta.nyc.ny.us/nyct/index.html.

For people who do not use the Internet, the contact phone numbers at the MTA are:

Travel Information Center (for all directions): 718-330-1234
Travel information for non-English-speaking people: 718-330-4847
Travel information for people with disabilities: 718-596-8585 or (TTY) 718-596-8273

An Important Advisory on Weekend Mass Transit   Most major subway-track renovation takes place on weekends. This means that parts of some subway lines may be closed off or some express trains might run on local tracks, or vice versa. Figuring this out can be confusing—or might come too late (i.e., you're on the train and it skips your stop!).

I advise you to check out weekend subway advisories just prior to the time you plan to make your visits. It's easy. First go to the home page of the MTA Web site listed above and click "Service Advisories." Then click "New York City mass transit," where you will see the letters and numbers of subway routes that have been changed for that weekend; and finally, click the subway you want to take, and you'll get the information. Updates are posted every Friday. (The URL is www.mta.nyc.ny.us/nyct/service/advisory.htm.) This Web site will also give you service-advisory information regarding changes to Metro-North, the Long Island Railroad and Long Island buses, and bridge and tunnel construction.

If you haven't gotten advance information and work is taking place on a route you want to take, you will be advised through subway announcements (on the train itself or on notices posted in subway stations) on alternate routes. Check before you go through the turnstile or ask the token booth clerk. In some cases shuttle buses will connect you from one stop to another.

I always tell people who are joining my NoshWalks to leave extra time to get to our meeting place. Weekend subway schedule changes are one of the more frustrating aspects of tour planning, and I have to confess to arriving late to one of my own tours, once, for this very reason.

If you plan to meet someone in a neighborhood, always allow extra time! Having a cell phone may not help if you're in an underground subway car and running late. (I always try to have the *New York Times* crossword puzzle on hand to allay any frustrations.)

BUSES

Buses are a great way to explore new neighborhoods, especially if you want to cover a large area in one day. With a MetroCard Fun Pass, you can hop on a bus for ten or twenty blocks, which will save you walking time and allow you to scope out an area or make a quick connection. This knowledge is particularly useful in neighborhoods such as the Hillside Avenue area of Jamaica, Queens, where interesting clusters of shops and restaurants are separated by stretches of apartments, stores, and offices.

Here's what to do:

- Have on-hand bus maps for each of the boroughs. Many public libraries have these maps, as does the New York Transit Museum (www.mta.nyc.ny.us/museum/index.html or 718-694-5100), which is based in Brooklyn with an additional branch in Grand Central Station.
- Travel with a pocket atlas, which will give you an idea of what the main roadways are, wherever you're going.
- When you exit a subway station in a new neighborhood, check in the station for:
  - A map of the immediate neighborhood—many stations have large wall maps close to the ticket booth that highlight local landmarks, and
  - A borough bus map, also posted on the wall in the subway station, often next to the large local street map.

Some buses cross boroughs and are useful for folks who don't like subways or have difficulty on stairs. Again, check bus maps and the MTA Web site for these buses. Unfortunately, some of these buses run infrequently and can be very slow, in part because they cross bridges where there might be a lot of traffic. I've found this particularly so on buses that run between Manhattan and Queens across the Queensborough Bridge (also known as the 59th Street Bridge), and these buses run even less frequently on weekends. One of the better lines is the M60, which travels through Morningside Heights in Manhattan and across 125th Street and the Triborough Bridge to LaGuardia Airport, passing Astoria and Jackson Heights en route. You can also inquire about express buses that cross boroughs, but they are more expensive than regular city buses and don't accept Metro-Cards. The MTA Web site will have information on these buses.

■ MetroCards—How They Work

When the MetroCard was first introduced, skeptics like me bemoaned the demise of the token. But I've since become a convert, especially as advantages to using a MetroCard have increased over the years.

Some MetroCards allow you to take a few rides at full fare. Others offer discount options, such as unlimited riding for a finite time (the one-day Fun Pass, the seven-day pass, the month-long pass) or eleven rides for the price of ten. Even with a full-fare pass, you can transfer free between two buses or between a subway and a bus in the space of two hours. You cannot get a free transfer on two separate subway rides.

THE 1-DAY METROCARD PASS

The Fun Pass is your best bet for one-day neighborhood touring, as it allows you the freedom to use as many buses or subways as you need in one day. (By the way, don't try to share this card with a traveling companion; it's a "smart card" with a built-in timer, which prevents the card from being used on the same bus or subway within eighteen minutes.) I advise you to buy something like an I.D. card holder sold at 99-cent stores for your MetroCard so you can keep it in one place that's easy to find. (It's possible to find yourself with two or three MetroCards that still have rides left on them, so you may want to mark your current MetroCard with a symbol in magic marker or ink to avoid mix-ups.)

The Fun Pass was originally targeted at tourists and was sold mostly in hotels and other tourist spots. But we New York City folks caught on pretty quick and started buying them for ourselves. The MTA realized that restricting Fun Passes to out-of-towners was a losing battle and started selling them at grocery stores and news shops along with their unlimited MetroCards. Now you can also buy them from subway station vending machines.

7-DAY UNLIMITED RIDE METROCARD

For tourists visiting New York City for up to a week who plan on taking lots of subway or bus rides, the 7-Day unlimited card is both a convenience and a money-saver. I used this card a lot when I was writing this book. A monthly card is also available, but this is recommended only for folks using mass transit very frequently (such as commuters)—and who won't lose them!

A Final Comment on Mass Transit   I have done my best to be as accurate as possible with subway and bus routes. However, the New York City Transit system is constantly rebuilding and upgrading. Routes will change over time. Please double-check maps and do be alert for the various weekend construction advisories that may involve route changes.

▪ Driving and Car Services

Although I don't drive, I know that many readers of this book prefer to use a car. I've recommended the most efficient driving directions, but unless you can make the tours during quieter weekdays or early in the day before the crowds descend, I cannot guarantee against traffic jams or that you'll find good parking place.

Summer weekends tend to be quieter as folks flee the summer heat, but I've been surprised to see some areas, such as Flushing, Queens, already jammed with shoppers early on a Saturday morning. I've listed municipal parking lots in these neighborhoods, but these can fill up, too!

Car services can be found in neighborhoods lacking medallion taxis. They are usually easy to identify, as they are often marked with the name of the company they represent. Keep your eyes peeled for a Lincoln Town Car, as this is the most popular model. Occasionally a car service driver may honk if he sees you walking and thinks you may be looking for a car.

You can hail a car service in the same way you hail a taxi, but with a few caveats:

- Sometimes the cars are in excellent condition, but I've seen others that look decrepit, and still others that lack seat belts. You do not have to take a car if the driver stops; wave it by if it looks uncomfortable or possibly unsafe.
- Car services do not have meters. So tell the driver where you are going—before you get into the car—and ask how much the fare

will be. A reasonable fare for short distances is $4 to $5, and up to $10 for longer distances. (If you call a car service from your home, ask for the fare in advance and be sure to get the dispatcher's name.)

- Tipping is acceptable—$1 for a short ride is customary; tip more for longer trips (assuming you had safe and efficient service).
- In areas of the Bronx, East Harlem, and other neighborhoods in which subway stations or other mass transit may not be convenient, some restaurants may be able to help you book a car for the trip home. This is recommended for evening visits only; during the day you will be fine if you follow the directions in this book.

■ Wheelchair Accessibility

Sadly, many of the places mentioned in this book are not wheelchair accessible, and unless you have access to good transportation you will have difficulty traveling to many of these neighborhoods because mass transit isn't adequate at this time. Shops and eateries in newer immigrant neighborhoods usually are not structured to accommodate wheelchairs, and some bathrooms are in narrow, inaccessible spaces or may be reached only by steep stairways. Whenever I've seen efforts by restaurants to be wheelchair-accessible I've mentioned them.

■ Some Last Tips Before You Go

Here are some final tips on planning your food tour.

Before you go, read through the neighborhood text first. Wherever possible, I've mentioned cultural landmarks—museums, theaters, libraries, architectural and historical sites, and other places you can visit as part of your tour. Make sure to check their schedules ahead of time so that you are not disappointed. (Some museums were closed for renovation at publication time but may have opened since, so call first.)

The neighborhood chapters and some of the side trips mention parks and other green space (playgrounds, community gardens, or public plazas) to which you can take food to eat in nice weather. If you're planning an outdoor meal, don't forget to bring extra napkins, forks, spoons, and other utensils.

You can sometimes combine two or more neighborhoods in one day, but you will first need to assess whether you really have the time and then figure out how to link them. For instance, several Queens neighborhoods—Sunnyside, Woodside, Jackson Heights, and Flushing—are accessible on the #7 subway line. But each neighborhood is so rich in delicious places to visit that you might put yourself on food overload if you try to do two—or more—in one day.

Finally, a note about the maps in this book. The borough maps give a broad overview, while each neighborhood map shows local streets, major landmarks, and subway stops. The shaded areas indicate tour routes covered in the book.

Are you ready?

Let's get started!

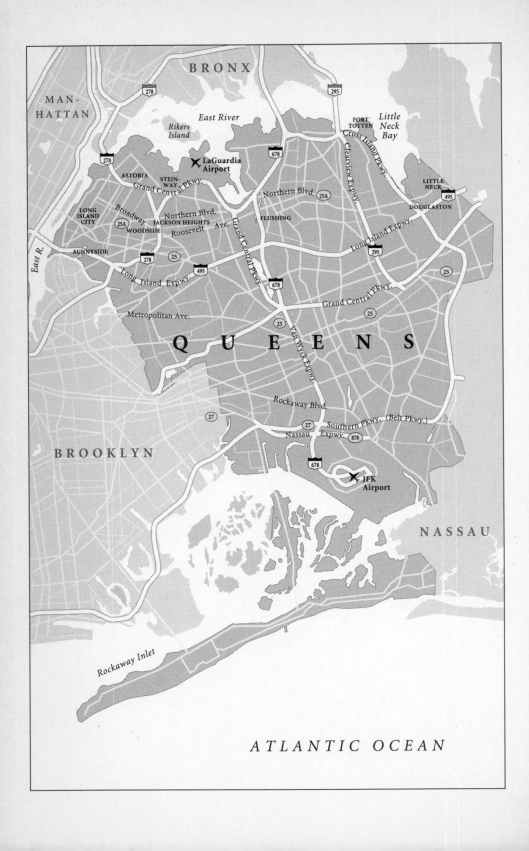

Queens

ASTORIA

FLUSHING

JACKSON HEIGHTS

SUNNYSIDE

WOODSIDE

SIDE TRIPS

■ *The Lemon Ice King of Corona*

■ *Elmhurst*

■ *Rego Park–Forest Hills–Queens Boulevard*

■ *Richmond Hill*

■ *Ridgewood*

...

Queens Notes

When 1990 census figures were published, Queens came out as the most diverse county in the United States. The 2000 figures just reinforce the observation that this borough is its own United Nations.

The #7 subway line, which links Flushing to Times Square, has been designated a national historical landmark because of the way in which its stops mirror the city's cultural diversity. It has been dubbed the International Express by some, but I call it the Immigrant Express. On a given ride you're as apt to hear a mariachi trio from Mexico as you are to make your way to your destination in the company of a Russian saxophonist.

The borough of Queens has another unique feature: it is the only one of the five in which the individual towns are used as the mailing addresses. It seems to be easier to associate certain neighborhoods with certain countries. Think Astoria and most people immediately think Greece (although, increasingly, they might also think Bangladesh, Brazil, Colombia, and Egypt). Think Flushing and it's China, Korea, and South Asia. Think Jackson Heights and it's Colombia, Ecuador, India, or Mexico. And Woodside might be the Philippines or Ireland. Imagine what a Woodside soccer team would look like! Say Elmhurst and folks will rattle off at least a half dozen countries.

While lower Manhattan was once the gateway to New York City because of its proximity to Ellis Island, perhaps Queens has taken over that role due to the fact that New York's two major airports are located there. Queens has housed New York's two World Fairs and was the original site of the United Nations. And when the New York City Board of Education created the Newcomers High School in 1998, it was, of course, located in Queens (in Long Island City, to be precise).

A good source of historic and current information related to Queens can be viewed at the Web site of the Queens Chamber of Commerce: www.queenschamber.org.

...

Astoria

Not Just Greek to Me!

Diversity sells, according to Astoria real estate salesman Charles Sciberras, and property values in the area have skyrocketed in recent years. Sciberras can tick off the various ethnic groups that now make Astoria home—the Egyptians a few blocks from his office on Steinway Street; the Bangladeshis, Brazilians, Mexicans, and Colombians who operate shops all over the place; the East European meat markets and private clubs that cater to an aging community (that is also welcoming some newcomers, for the most part from the remnants of Yugoslavia); and so on. Sciberras's parents emigrated here from Malta in the 1950s because there was already a Maltese enclave. As a real estate agent, he couldn't be happier that people of different backgrounds, including a particular ethnic group—young Manhattanites seeking more space and lower rent close to the City—are coming to Astoria.

Many people think of Astoria as a hub of Greek activity. The neighborhood indeed has had a large Greek presence since the aftermath of the Greek Civil War of 1945 to 1949, ballooning after immigration laws loosened up in 1962. Estimates of the number of Greeks here range from 60,000 to 200,000. Greek businesses, schools, and social institutions have flourished here, and some folks regard Astoria as the largest Greek city outside of Athens.

But in the 1980s, when I began leading bicycle tours through Astoria, the area was clearly far more than just Greek. Italian markets were everywhere, and Latin American and South Asian shops were starting to open. There's a nascent Little North Africa and a growing number of mosques (quite a few in storefronts or private homes) catering to Muslims from North Africa, the Middle East, and South Asia. One of the larger shops in the Acropolis building on Ditmars Boulevard is a halal market.

Rather than displacing the Greek establishments, Sciberras says, the newcomers are simply making the area more crowded and competitive. There is evidence of this everywhere; Zlata Praha, a Czech restaurant, is sandwiched between Opa, a Greek place, and Taste of Bengal, an Indian restaurant a few storefronts down from an Irish pub. And so on.

My challenge in profiling Astoria was to find a fresh approach to an area that has been covered extensively, and very well, by other writers. So I've focused on finding places about which very little or nothing at all has been written—or on taking an updated look at some that are well known. Some stores here have been at the same location for more than sixty years.

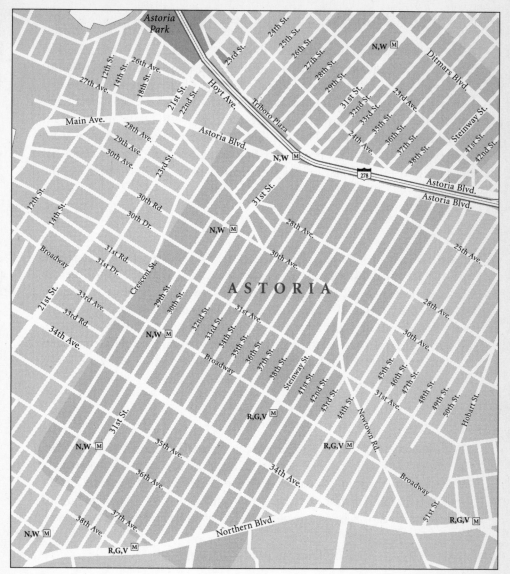

Their survival is due in part to adapting to both the changing needs of the existing community and the new waves of immigrants while continuing to offer quality service and products.

The Astoria chapter is divided into six sections, starting with 30th Avenue, which is its busiest and most varied area. The other sections are listed geographically, starting north at Ditmars Avenue and heading south to cover Astoria Boulevard, Broadway, and then 36th Avenue. A final section covers the newer Middle Eastern/Arabic area on Steinway Street.

■ Getting Oriented

Astoria has two commercial north–south spines—31st and Steinway Streets—and five commercial "ribs"—Ditmars Boulevard, Astoria Boulevard, 30th Avenue, Broadway, and 36th Avenue. Thirty-first Street, situated beneath the elevated train tracks, dotted with restaurants, cafés, and markets is the food spine. Steinway Street throbs with retail: major chain stores, banks, and offices. The long block between 25th and 28th Avenues (there's no 26th or 27th) is the only one that has significant international markets and restaurants, mostly Egyptian, Moroccan, and other Middle Eastern.

BY SUBWAY

Three subway lines serve Astoria: the N and W, which follow 31st Street, and the R, which weaves along the southeastern edge of Astoria before heading toward Forest Hills and Jamaica. There are five N and W stops in Astoria: 36th Avenue, Broadway, 30th Avenue, Astoria Boulevard, and Ditmars Boulevard; the W follows the same route but occasionally runs as an express and skips some of these stops. On the R train, the sole Astoria stop is Steinway Street, which has exits at 34th Avenue and Broadway. All take fifteen to twenty minutes from Times Square.

BY BUS

The M60 bus goes to Astoria Boulevard (en route to LaGuardia Airport) from the Upper West Side, heading across 125th Street and over the Triborough Bridge. Bus lines within Queens are very convoluted; contact the MTA at 718-330-1234 for information, or check www.mta.nyc.ny.us to download bus maps. Within Astoria, buses run along Steinway Street and the main avenues.

BY CAR

To drive to Astoria from Manhattan or points north, take the upper level of the 59th Street (Queensboro) or Triborough Bridge. Upon exiting from the 59th Street Bridge, bear right at the 21st Street exit, and at the light turn right and drive north on 21st Street. Watch the lights—depending on where you want to go you can make right turns at the key avenues. From the Triborough Bridge, bear right and turn right at the first exit (29th Street), where you'll immediately see a municipal parking lot. You can also drive along 31st Street (under the elevated tracks) until you find the avenue you want to explore. There is another municipal lot, smaller than the first, located on the east side of 31st Street just south of Broadway.

OTHER TRANSPORTATION

Astoria lends itself to good walking and bicycling, especially in search of food. An historic section of antebellum mansions and cottages can be found on its western edge, near Astoria Park (24th Avenue)—if you're interested in seeing it, track down a copy of the *AIA Guide to New York City* and bring it, along with a map!

■ History

Astoria takes its name from John Jacob Astor, the fur trader who became one of New York City's first developers and millionaires. The community developed in large part because of easy ferry access. The completion of the Astoria elevated line in 1917 spurred the building of six-story apartment complexes and the establishment of factories over the next two decades. The opening of the Independent subway line along Steinway Street in 1933 and the Triborough Bridge in 1936 led to further development. Astoria has long been an immigrant haven, initially for Italians, and, since 1962, as mentioned above, for thousands of Greeks. Now it's a virtual melting pot and a great start-off point for businesses.

In case you're wondering, Steinway Street *is* named for the founders of Steinway Pianos, and the factory is located at the northern tip of Steinway Street near 19th Avenue. (The landmarked Steinway mansion is located at 18-33 41st Street). Henry Steinweg immigrated to the United States from Germany and set up a flourishing family business in Manhattan in 1853. In the 1870s, manufacturing was moved to Astoria. Now privately owned by another family, the company has a staff of over 400 and manufactures about two thousand pianos per year. Factory tours can be arranged on an individual basis—to arrange one, call Steinway Hall in Manhattan at 212-246-1100. (And if you can, check out gorgeous Steinway Hall in person at 109 West 57th Street in Manhattan, where recorded piano music wafts through a room full of awe-inspiring statues and portraits of the great pianists.)

■ Green space

The nicest open space around the shopping hub is Athens Square on 30th Avenue and 30th Street. This Greek park in miniature covers just under one acre and provides ample seating for a leisurely snack. Designed by an architect of Greek descent and dedicated in 1998, it's the only decent open space in central Astoria and it has clean bathroom facilities. (On the northeast end of the neighborhood, Astoria Park has a pool and tons of amenities, but it's a schlep to reach.) In the summer, Athens Square is the venue for concerts of Greek and Italian music. Ironically, most of the stores surrounding this park are not Greek. Hoyt Playground, at Astoria Boulevard and 31st Street, near the traffic ramp to the Triborough Bridge, offers lots of seating—and lots of traffic noise. I recommend it only if you happen to be nearby and are utterly exhausted. (And I assure you that Astoria can be exhausting!)

QUEENS IL-LOGIC

New York City film buffs may recall a mediocre 1991 movie, *Queens Logic,* a working-class version of *The Big Chill* that was for the most part filmed in Astoria. I consider the area's street numbering to be its great illogic, and in Astoria it is especially confusing. Ditmars Boulevard is equivalent to 22nd Avenue. Then comes 23rd Avenue. Then, as you walk south on 31st Street, you'll come to 25th Avenue. Next is 28th Avenue. Yes, there's a 29th and a 30th, but after 31st Avenue comes Broadway, then 34th. The north–south numbered streets I've chosen for this trip generally are consistent (Steinway would be 39th Street). But walking west toward the East River, you'll run into roads, drives, and lanes, some a block long, and weird numbering. 23rd Street leads to 21st, and then 14th. If you plan to wander (and Astoria, with its idiosyncratic buildings and gardens, is lots of fun for wandering) bring a detailed map of your own.

· · ·

30th Avenue

(29th Street to Steinway Street)

Bangladeshi, Brazilian, Filipino, Greek, Indian, Mediterranean, Mexican, Thai

"It's the United Nations here" is how Charles Marino describes customers at the fish market his family has run since 1932; he's the fourth generation. To begin this tour you'll find a bit of almost everything on 30th Avenue.

Getting There   Take the N train (or the W on weekends) to 30th Avenue. The tour covers 30th Avenue from 25th Street to Steinway Street and includes some side streets. The best approach is to follow an eastward route toward Steinway Street. To start, go three blocks west from the subway exit to Crescent Street. Here you'll find a pair of Filipino businesses: a market called **Dun Fiesta Oriental Store** (23-25 30th

Avenue) and around the corner **Chapnoy Deli** (29-16 Crescent Street, 718-274-4141), which offers both take-out food and a sit-down café. Both establishments are owned by Nestor Dumlao, who says his is the only Filipino place left in the area. Its raison d'être is the Filipino staff at the hospital across the street. The deli offers an eclectic menu of hot Filipino specialties (served by a Peruvian counterman, who also helps prepare different dishes each day from a large menu). The day I visited, the Filipina cook was serving spring rolls she had just made, for free. The market has a large selection of Filipino packaged and frozen foods. I found (and bought) *double cheese* ice cream, which is made with real chunks of cheddar cheese and imported from the Philippines (made by Nestlé). And yes, it's sinful: I could just feel the calories settling in with each delicious swallow.

Across the street and due east is **Hidalgo Panadería y Cafetería** (25-22 30th Avenue, 718-726-4180), a beautiful and bright new bakery and restaurant owned by Carlos Sanchez, who also has two markets in Astoria. One visit was just before *El Día de los Muertos*—the Day of the Dead— a holiday that coincides with All Saints' Day in other cultures, and I bought a traditional sweet holiday bread. Their menu features unusual dishes such as *quesadillas con flor de calabaza*—quesadillas filled with both cooked pumpkin and pumpkin flowers. The cooked pumpkin has a smoky, fruity flavor and is quite nice. At 30th Street you'll come to **Plaza Café Patisserie** (29-02 30th Avenue, 718-726-2447), the first of many wonderful bakery/ cafés in Astoria. It's across the street from Athens Square, so if you visit on a warm day you can buy your coffee and pastries to go and head to the park.

Keep going and you'll come to **Trade Fair Supermarket** (30-08 30th Avenue). I rarely mention supermarkets here, but Trade Fair is a special case. There are nine or ten Trade Fairs in Queens, all in areas with heavily diverse populations (two or three others in Astoria, one or two in Jackson Heights, plus Elmhurst and Forest Hills, for instance), and the chain has an impressive inventory of packaged and fresh ethnic foods, including the best selection of Brazilian foods that I've seen anywhere in Queens. Just head toward the western section of the store, which is where the ethnic foods are located. You'll be surprised!

Across 31st Street you'll find produce, fish, and meat markets on almost every block, along with shops specializing in imported goods from Eastern Europe and the Mediterranean. You'll also see cafés and restaurants. **Athens Café** (32-07 30th Avenue, 718-626-2164) claims one of Astoria's best locations, at a strategic triangle of activity. It's here that I experienced sticker shock when I got the $4.35 tab for a double espresso. If I'd known in advance, I would have brought a novel, nursed the espresso, and indulged in one of the café's great pastries.

Meat lovers might want to check out **Akropolis** (31-04 30th Avenue), an Astoria mainstay. Specialties include *loukaniko,* sausage prepared in burgundy wine and mixed either with scallions or oranges. You'll find the freshest fish in several markets along 30th Avenue, but all except **Marino and Sons** (36-10 30th Avenue) are now owned by Koreans, according to Chuck Marino (Charles's father). So if you want a flavor of Astoria history with your fish, this is the place to go.

United Brothers Fruit Market (32-24 30th Avenue), in my view, sells the best produce for Greek cooking. You want to make a Mediterranean dandelion salad? Here you'll find four types of dandelion greens, including bitter, red, and sweet. You may also spot lichees from Israel. **Mediterranean Food Market** (30-12 34th Street) is an Astoria old-timer and a favorite from my bicycle-tour days. You could spend ages here. Some of my recommendations include fresh tahini bread, a wonderful olive pita bread with which you could choose a different cheese at each visit. The prices on feta cheese are lower than you'll see anywhere, and a domestic feta cheese costs just $1.99 a pound—about half what you'd pay elsewhere—and it's delicious. There are also chocolates from the Balkans and some beautiful *brikis* for preparing Greek coffee. Plus, of course, a variety of brands of Greek coffee. Because these specialty shops are so close to produce, fish, and meat markets, you may do better here for overall shopping than at Titan Foods on 31st Street (see pages 13–14), but you might want to comparison shop.

Mahmoud Abedlhamid displays just-baked pitas in Astoria.

Between 34th and 36th Streets is a cluster of Bangladeshi and Indian places. Bangladeshi breakfasts are as hearty as other meals, featuring meat curries and other spicy dishes in addition to eggs and *paratha* (a flaky Indian bread). You can also find typical South Asian sweets. At **Sonargaon Café and Sweets** (34-14 30th Avenue, 718-956-7655) you can eat a light meal and savor Mrinal Haque's evocative paintings of Bangladeshi life (see Jackson Heights for more on Haque); one shows a phalanx of soldiers with an Uzi-carrying leader. Across the street is **Sonargaon Tandoori** (34-11 30th Avenue, 718-956-9866). This non-Muslim restaurant offers wine and Indian beer. **Sabor Tropical** (36-18 30th Avenue, 718-777-8506) is a lovely Brazilian place with a great menu and an immodest ambition—a location in Manhattan. After trying one of their coconut-soaked dishes and the passion-fruit mousse I think he just might succeed.

Thai Pavilion (37-10 30th Avenue, 718-777-5546) is one of the most attractive Thai restaurants I've ever visited, and the service and prices are excellent.

. . .

Ditmars Boulevard

(29th Street to 33rd Street and 23rd Avenue)

Afghan, Czech, French, Greek, Italian, Peruvian, Spanish

The Ditmars area is cut off from the rest of Astoria by the Triborough Bridge. It's quieter and less hectic but still has a nice selection of markets and eateries, including more Italian holdovers than elsewhere. It has more Greek tavernas than other parts of Astoria and also has a new Czech restaurant.

Getting There   Take the N or W train to the last stop. Ditmars Boulevard is one block north of the exit.

Bakeries and Cafés   One of my favorite bakeries in all of Astoria is **La Guli** (29-15 Ditmars Boulevard, 718-728-5612), which opened in 1937 and is on only its second owner. The first owners were Italians and the current owners are Susana and Eduardo Lazzari, who are from Argentina but, like many of their compatriots, have Italian roots. La Guli is unpretentious and retains much of its original decor including rich wood paneling. Twenty-four flavors of outstanding gelato are available year-round. There's an enormous selection of cookies, and each tray is numbered so you don't have to point and haggle if you want a big mix. Some specialties include a terrific fig pastry called *cuccidata.* I also tried a packet of sugar-iced *taralli,* which are small, dense, lemon-flavored cakes. The house specialty is *cassata al forno,* a cake made of cannoli cream wrapped in cookie dough with pieces of citrus and chocolate chips. La Guli has a couple of tables and a small espresso bar. The Lazzaris also own **Chicken Festival,** a new fast-food/rotisserie place two doors down (29-19 Ditmars Boulevard), which specializes in Peruvian-style chicken. Around the corner, **Rose & Joe's Italian Bakery & Pizza** (22-40 31st Street) specializes in great Italian breads such as olive and lard breads, garlic and raisin toasts, and pizzas. **Ste. Honoré Patisserie** (33-18 Ditmars Boulevard), a marvelous French bakery with beautiful fruit tarts, croissants, rich cakes, and French jams is a nice surprise.

A number of Greek cafés can be found in this area of Astoria. The old-timer here is **Lefkos Pirgos** (22-81 31st Street), a bright place with coffees and outstanding, rich Greek pastries. I've described other Greek cafés elsewhere in the book. Note that when you sit in one of these cafés, prices will be about twice what they'd be if you were to get a pastry and coffee to go.

Markets   Good Mediterranean markets can be found all over Astoria. The very best Italian market is **Rosario's** (22-15 31st Street), a gorgeous place with just about everything. It has a butchery and sells lots of cheeses, fresh locally-made and imported pastas, olive oils, sauces, and more (I noticed chocolate from Ireland). It has been beautifully renovated and is a pleasure to shop in. For both Italian and Greek products under one roof, **J & T Greek Italian Deli** (31-12 Ditmars Boulevard, 718-545-7920) has a large inventory of fresh and imported goods. Lovers of fresh pasta should make a beeline for old-timer **Cassinelli** (31-12 23rd Avenue), in Astoria since the forties. Its owner is Tony Bonfigli, who started as a cleaner in 1960 and took it over in 1972. He recommends the spinach ravioli (which was delicious) and meat tortellini, but you'll find all kinds of fresh pasta every day.

Eateries   This part of Astoria is home to quite a few Greek tavernas, which can be described as less formal, more noisy, and more crowded than a restaurant with cloth-covered tables and napkins of linen rather than paper. I choose **Taverna Kyklades** (33-07 Ditmars Boulevard, 718-545-8666) over many of the others—there's something about this place that I find particularly appealing, despite (or maybe because of!) the noise of people having a good time. The ceiling is painted sky blue (complete with clouds) and marine images abound. You get the feeling that you might be looking outside onto a port but, in fact, this taverna is located in a building complex called the Acropolis, which includes a series of attached white brick apartment buildings that span 33rd to 34th Streets. What's interesting about them is their interior courtyards, lovely landscaped stretches of green that you wouldn't expect to see in the city, that can be seen by peeking through a fence near the entrance to Taverna Kyklades. You'll find more courtyards if you wander down 33rd Street and peek through the entryways. The taverna's entrées are a dollar or two lower than some of the fancier seafood places and there's a big selection of grilled lamb, pork, veal, and chicken entrées as well. **Stamatis** (29-12 23rd Avenue, 718-278-9795) is one of the most customer-friendly places in Astoria. For one, they recommend that you call in your order so it will be ready when you arrive. Like its sibling on Broadway (see page 16), many of the appetizers at Stamatis are ready-to-serve and are convenient as take-out dishes.

I had a spectacular lunch at **Balkh Shish Kabab House** (23-10 31st Street, 718-721-5020), a cozy Afghan place. Though most of the menu is meat-based, I chose *borani kadu chalow*—fried pumpkin with sauce and yogurt, accompanied by a serving of delicious brown basmati rice and Afghan bread. **El Olivo** (21-35 31st Street, 718-932-4040—it's a long walk down 31st Street to get there), offers Spanish cuisine and an inviting, soft-lit ambiance that suggests a long, slow meal—including wine and dessert. Go for the seafood entrées, especially the *paellas* (seafood with yellow rice) and *mariscadas* (seafood stew with mussels, clams, scallops, and shrimp) with a choice of sauces: garlic, creole (tomatoes, peppers, and spices), hot sauce, or garlic with onion and parsley. The *mariscada* in garlic sauce was rich and savory. How I would have loved to balance it with a dessert of Italian ice cream. (El Olivo, which opened in 1995, has a larger, newer sibling, Brisas de Espana, in Long Island City.) Although some South Asian places can be found in this neighborhood, the Greek and Italian presence generally remains stronger here than elsewhere in Astoria, and Greek cafés abound on 31st Street as you head along the elevated line. A relative newcomer to this area is **Koliba** (31-11 23rd Avenue, 718-626-0430), a Czech place that opened in 2001 that offers ready-made main courses that include beef goulash, boiled beef with dill sauce, and various spaetzle (a type of flour dumpling), including one version with sheep cheese and another with sauerkraut and bacon. (I tried spaetzle at a Slovak place in Brooklyn some years ago and found them incredibly boring.) It's best to choose an entrée with a combination of flavors such as Koliba's roasted chicken in garlic sauce. Most entrées are made-to-order, however, and you should prepare to wait twenty minutes for your food. For dessert you can try their strudel or crepes.

* * *

Astoria Boulevard and Nearby

Chilean, Czech, Greek

The Triborough Bridge and Grand Central Parkway bisect this area, so the immediate neighborhood lacks the cohesion of other parts of Astoria. But there are a few places worth checking out.

Getting There   Take the N train (or the W on weekends) to Astoria Boulevard.

Markets   **Titan Foods** (25-56 31st Street, 718-626-7771) is the Zabar's of Astoria. When I first encountered Titan in 1985 at its location two buildings north, it had been open less than two years. The space was large but dull. Co-owner Kostas Blafas and his partners relocated to the current site (which has its own parking lot) around 1996 and hired a Greek architect to give Titan its gorgeous Mediterranean feel. On entering, you first see—and smell—Domna's bakery (named after the mother-in-law of one of the owners), where you can get sweet and savory pastries (such as spinach pies) and different types of peasant breads. The choice of packaged goods is huge, as are the offerings of cheeses, meats, olives, and wonderful Greek dips. (I first tasted *kopanisti* here and I include the recipe below). At Titan I also found Total, the best commercial yogurt I've ever tasted. It's sold plain or with honey or preserves. You can find Total in other Greek and gourmet markets, but Titan is its principal importer, so it's cheaper here. Other products include umbrellas in the shape of the Greek flag and T-shirts for the 2004 Athens Olympics.

Eateries   A classic here is **Elias Corner** (24-02 31st Street, 718-932-1510), a seafood place that has no menu but always has lines (unless you can get there at 4 P.M. during the week or on Sundays at 3 P.M.). Fresh fish is made-to-order, but there are also some menu staples including grilled shrimp and some meat dishes.

KOPANISTI CHEESE DIP

Courtesy of Dimitrios Kosmidis of Titan Foods in Astoria, Queens

Serves 4

> 1 pound feta cheese (A soft and sharp feta such as Arahova or Parnassos is recommended)
> 3 pounds olive oil
> 1 long green hot pepper, finely chopped
> 1 teaspoon dried oregano
> Freshly-ground black pepper to taste

1. Place the feta and oil in a blender and purée.
2. Add the chopped pepper and blend again.
3. Transfer the dip to a serving bowl and stir in the spices. Serve with delicious Greek bread.

Note: I rarely see kopanisti at Greek restaurants, so I asked Dimitrios Kosmidis why. In southern Greece, he said, mainly on the islands, kopanisti is considered a tasty cheese but one that smells bad—and thus restaurants don't like to serve it. The dip is popular in northern Greece, and at Titan it is described as Macedonian cheese dip. It's also called tirosalata.

At 29-19 24th Avenue you'll find **Bohemian Hall** (718-728-1718), the last authentic beer garden in New York City. (At one point there were more than 800.) Nowadays it also houses a senior center for the small Czech and Slovak community. In the seventies and eighties I attended folk music festivals at Bohemian Hall, and the musicians came from Queens—via Albania, Bulgaria, Greece, and other parts of Eastern Europe. In warm weather, the beer garden opens at 5 P.M. during the week and at noon on weekends. Call to check for their hours before you go.

I stumbled on **San Antonio Bakery #2** (36-20 Astoria Boulevard, 718-777-8733) on my way back to the N train after visiting the wonderful Egyptian, Moroccan, and Middle Eastern shops and eateries on Steinway Street. This combination luncheonette (serving meat stews) and bakery with a small selection of Chilean imports was the first Chilean place I'd found within the five boroughs, although I have since discovered Pomaire, a dinner-only Chilean place at 371 West 46th Street (along Restaurant Row) in Manhattan, El Guaton in Woodside, and a Chilean-owned pizzeria on Amsterdam Avenue in the West 70s. Try San Antonio's *milogas*, a rich, layered, custard-filled pastry. Another specialty is the "Chilean hot dog," with lots of trimmings. (By the way, there *is* a San Antonio Bakery #1 in Valley Stream, Long Island.)

. . .

Broadway

(23rd Street to Steinway Street)

Brazilian, Colombian, Cypriot, Greek, Japanese, Pakistani,
Peruvian–Chinese, Ukrainian

If you love art, combine your visit to Broadway's cafés, markets, and restaurants with a side trip to the Isamu Noguchi Museum and Socrates Sculpture Garden (see page 23). It's a fifteen-minute walk from the subway and will add spice to your other culinary adventures.

Getting There   Take the N train (or the W on weekends) to Broadway.

Restaurants   Al Beraka (23-18 Broadway, 718-956-7115), at the corner of 23rd Street, is an inexpensive Pakistani place worth visiting. Although there was a bit of a wait for the *bhindi masala* (okra curry), *mooli paratha* (stuffed bread), and mango *lassi* (yogurt drink) I ordered, it was worth it. The meal was delectable. The decor—paintings of seascapes and flowers—seemed a bit odd, but the Pakistani videos playing in the background put me in the mood for a great South Asian meal. **Shima** (29-13 Broadway, 718-721-5566; dinner only), a Japanese restaurant next door to the

Japanese Family Market, offers an elegant setting and an excellent menu of teriyaki and grilled dishes as well as dumpling entrées and great sashimi. Prices are reasonable—you'll pay between $3 and $7 for appetizers and just $9.50 to $12 for most entrées. **Aliada** (29-19 Broadway, 718-932-2240) is a fairly new Cypriot place with a toned-down elegance and some unusual dishes, including some that make use of grilled vegetables in combination with *halloumi* (traditional Cypriot) cheese and marinated minced pork, that offer an alternative to more traditional Greek cuisine. For instance, *dolmades* (Cypriot stuffed grape leaves) include pork with the rice, unlike the Greek version that generally uses herbed rice only. **Stamatis** (31-14 Broadway, 718-204-8968) has an older sibling of the same name at 29-12 23rd Avenue, and is a great classic Greek eatery. It's a heaven for vegetarians, as you can create a great meal out of their appetizers and side dishes. I had an excellent dish of peppers and tomatoes stuffed with herbed rice and elephant (fava) beans in tomato sauce. I heartily recommend the shrimp *saganaki* (shrimp in feta cheese and tomato sauce). **Roumeli** (33-04 Broadway, 718-278-1001), a popular taverna in the neighborhood which has been around just about forever, has an extensive menu. Among its attractions are the dishes that are ready to be served, including many of the vegetarian and some meat appetizers, so it's possible to order food to go without a wait. Orzo in tomato sauce, fried vegetables with garlic dip, and meatballs in lemon sauce are just a few that I've tried. Roumeli also has a busy grill. I was put off by the cigarette smoke during my last visit and it kept me from eating in. If you're up for a bit of noise and a crowd, aren't in a hurry to get served, and perhaps have insomnia, **Uncle George's** (33-19 Broadway, 718-626-0593) is the place to go. As you enter, you'll see rotisseries of lamb, beef, pork, and chicken spinning around, with a whole lamb near the entrance. This is particularly off-putting to vegetarians, but it lends an air of authenticity. The restaurant, which operates twenty-four hours, is big, but it's the type of eatery that would fill up no matter how big it was. It's truly non-smoking, which is a plus. While Uncle George's is not expensive, service tends to be slow, but if you're with pals, that shouldn't be a big deal, and you'll always find good bread on the table.

If you look for the Brazilian restaurant **Alho & Oleo** at its address (31-18 Broadway), don't be alarmed if you don't find it. It's actually tucked away on 32nd Street a few storefronts south of Broadway (718-777-8484). I first knew it as an excellent Brazilian take-out place. Now it also has a pleasant, informal dining area where you can savor Brazilian steak, pork, seafood, and chicken specialties with sides such as collards, plantains, and yucca. I always enjoy Brazilian appetizers such as spicy cheese patties or chicken pieces fried with garlic and parsley. I love *palmito* (hearts of palm). Entrées range from $6.95 to $9.50—truly a bargain—and

Brazilian desserts such as passion fruit mousse and various puddings and pastries are also available. **Tierras Colombianas** (33-01 Broadway, 718-956-3012) is a big, pricey Colombian restaurant that serves heavy meals best enjoyed as supper. (See the Jackson Heights chapter for more on Colombian food.) Two blocks away, **Caravan Chicken** (35-01 Broadway, 718-545-3980) is one of a growing number of Peruvian-Chinese chicken places that have become popular in Queens. The specialty here is marinated chicken, but you can get a variety of combinations such as fried rice and lo mein to go with your chicken, and wonton soup is included on the menu. **La Fonda Atioquena** (32-25 Steinway Street, 718-726-9857), another Colombian place in this part of Astoria, is far more informal than Tierras Colombianas. Here I had a modest and inexpensive meal (about $6) of creamed crabmeat soup and a side of yucca. The place was packed.

Bakeries and Cafés   Several Greek cafés are clustered on Broadway at 33rd and 34th Streets. The large (and possibly intimidating) **Omonia** (32-20 Broadway, 718-274-6650) is the old-timer of the bunch—more than twenty-five years old—and the only one I spent time in. The others were too small and smoky. Omonia has a no-smoking section, but the aroma of tobacco did waft uncomfortably to my area. I asked a waitress about it and she shrugged, replying, "Greeks smoke." It does have a lovely ambiance, though, and great Greek music (live music on weekends) to accompany an espresso and *tiramisù*. For a non-smoking alternative, the much smaller **Patisserie Dumas** (25-21 Broadway, 718-932-2894) is a fun place to indulge in pastries and coffee. It has plush old chairs and a sofa and fabulous Greek (and a few French) specialties. I suspect you'll be charmed by **Your Neighborhood Bakery** (33-09 Broadway, 718-777-5044), a Greek bakery whose Greek name I could not possibly pronounce. Owner Harry Pappous, who opened the place in October 2001, says he prepares a lot of the breads and other traditional pastries using baking methods that have fallen out of use with the larger bakeries. You'll find breads, croissants, and some fancier pastries here, but what Your Neighborhood Bakery specializes in is understatement.

Markets   Several old-time butchers operate on Broadway. **Astoria Meat Market** (35-09 Broadway) specializes in *kielbasa* (Ukrainian and Polish sausage) as well as packaged products from Eastern Europe. At **Plaza Meat Market** (30-07 Broadway), which has been around since the forties, you'll find popular Greek specialties such as baby lamb (they sell 400 to 500 each Greek Easter) and a homemade pork sausage cooked in Greek spices. (Chris Papogeris, the son of owner Vasilis Papogeris, would not divulge the recipe!) Indian shoppers can speak in Punjabi or Hindi with counterman Jimmy Singh, an ex-seaman from India who spent a few years in Greece before coming to the United States. Newest on the scene is **Family Market** (29-15 Broadway, 718-956-7923), a Japanese grocery that opened in 2001 to accommodate the growing community of young Japanese in Astoria (and the many non-Japanese who also like the food).

• • •

36th Avenue and Nearby
(31st Street to 34th Street)

Bangladeshi, Brazilian, Cuban, Greek, Mexican, Spanish, Thai

If you could wander through all of Astoria in a day, you'd notice Brazilian markets and eateries scattered throughout the area, but this small section features Astoria's largest critical mass of Brazilian businesses. You may be confused by some of the addresses because this stretch is on the cusp of two neighborhoods—some places may claim to be in Astoria and others in Long Island City. This mostly residential and industrial area is close to the American Museum of the Moving Image and I find it particularly interesting precisely because it's not touristy. Some of the most interesting places are on 31st Street, surrounded by industrial shops.

Getting There   Take the N train (or the W on weekends) to 36th Avenue.

Restaurants   Starting on 31st Street and 34th Avenue, you'll find one of the newest and most gracious places in Astoria: **El Boqueron** (31-01 34th Avenue, 718-956-0107), a Spanish *tapas* bar and restaurant that opened in mid-2001. It has a lot of great seafood *tapas* such as shrimp in garlic sauce, Galician-style octopus, and scallops in asparagus sauce, many types of ham and sausage, and a variety of vegetarian combinations. The *tapas* cost $4.50 to $9.25, and you really must go with a friend or two, or more, to make the most of it. The menu features some house special *tapas*, including roasted quail in fruit sauce ($6.95) and Spanish sweet roasted peppers with asparagus and pepper sauce ($7.95). Lunch and dinner entrées are much higher-priced, with chicken starting at $14.95 and seafood at $18.95. A *paella* for one is $17.95, $28.95 for two. Moving south toward 36th Avenue, you'll find a couple of more low-key places: **El Sitio de Astoria** (35-55 31st Street, 718-278-7694) is a cozy Cuban restaurant that serves great, cheap breakfasts as well as a modest but authentic menu of chicken and beef dishes. On one of my earlier visits to Astoria, I stopped there with a friend and for a hearty breakfast special. His platter of eggs, bacon, toast, and a strong cup of *café con leche* was just under $3, tax and tip included. Next door, **Taqueria Xochimilco** (31-06 36th Avenue) serves hearty Mexican breakfasts, including a so-called executive breakfast, which apparently includes *huevos* (eggs) *rancheros,* refried beans, rice—the works. The appetizers, including sautéed calamari with jalapeños, are also tasty.

Heading east, you'll hit a cluster of Brazilian shops. **Copacabana Pizza** (31-13 36th Avenue, 718-545-3685) sells standard pizzas, hamburgers, and sandwiches along with Brazilian pizzas and *salgadinhos* (appetizers) such as patties and fried dough filled with cheese, potato, yucca, chicken, and beef. Luiz de Souza's uncle owns the place, but Luiz, whose family comes from Fortaleza in northern Brazil, is there much of the time, and made a pizza for me with a topping of *palmitos* (hearts of palm), olives, and chicken. The crust on this pizza is thin and crunchy and the topping is not at all oily. Luiz de Souza recommends the Portuguesa pizza, which is topped with eggs, olives, ham, *palmitos,* onions, and peppers. One pizza I wish I'd tried was made with *catupiri* (Brazilian white cheese) and shrimp. You can't buy slices of the Brazilian pizzas, so buy a whole one to take home. The *salgadinhos* are tasty, filling, and portable.

Further east and around the block is a Bangladeshi place called **Dhaka Café Jhill** (35-55 33rd Street, 718-937-4200). Whether you get a biriyani, kebab, or fish entrée, you get a lot more—a big side of rice and bread—for no more than $6.75. Breakfasts—smaller portions of curry and one *paratha* (spelled *porota* here)—are also available. Back on 36th Avenue, **Arharn** (32-05 36th Avenue, 718-726-4463), a Thai eatery, offers menus both in Thai and in English, and has the most extensive Thai menu I've ever seen. I had time to go just once and ordered *goong masaman,* an excellent curry of shrimp, peanut, potato, and onions cooked in coconut milk. Arharn is best visited with a group of friends.

There are two Greek places with a big presence in this neighborhood. **Greek Captain** (32-10 36th Avenue, 718-786-6015) is a neighborhoody, informal fish place where you can either buy fish to take home or order it broiled, fried, or grilled. You can eat at the counter or in the adjacent new dining area. Greek Captain draws a large Spanish-speaking clientele, so the menu is in both English and Spanish. Although the overall setting is plain,

One of Copacabana Pizza's delicious Brazilian-style pizzas, fresh from the oven.

the dishes are not—this is serious fish. Don't expect to pay less than $20 for a dinner with soup, although if you make a meal out of an appetizer such as baked clams, grilled octopus, or shrimp cocktail you can get away with less. Shrimp and lobster soups are $5. The large **Galini Seafood Restaurant** (33-12 36th Avenue, 718-729-3474, which translates to "Say-Fish"), reminds me of the restaurant palaces my parents used to take me to when I was little. This place, set up with red carpeting, fancy tablecloths, and menus on large round tables, gets packed with family gatherings on weekends and the menu, unlike Greek Captain, includes a full complement of Greek dips and a nice selection of seafood combinations, brochettes, and broiled or fried dishes. Because I'm a feta cheese fan, I chose the shrimp *Santorini,* which is prepared in tomato sauce with feta. Galini's distance from Central Astoria probably plays to its advantage because parking is easier to find (but a valet parking service is also available).

· · ·

Steinway Street

Egyptian, Moroccan, Middle Eastern, North African

Although Gus Kobleck of the Greater Astoria Development Corporation had told me about the Egyptian places clustered along lower Steinway Street and *Newsday* dubbed the area "Little Egypt," I hadn't anticipated how extensive the area would be. And to call the area Little Egypt is a misnomer— the area is fast becoming home to immigrants from several North African and Middle Eastern countries. Between 24th and 28th Avenues (there's no 26th or 27th), in addition to markets, restaurants, and coffee shops, you'll find the Al-Iman Mosque, an Islamic school, and shops that sell the Koran, tapes, and other religious and decorative items used by Muslims, including a clock that sounds five times a day to signal prayer time. Remember that alcohol is off-limits at many restaurants here.

Getting There   Take the N train to Astoria Boulevard or the R to Steinway Street. From the N, walk east on Astoria Boulevard (on the south— right-hand—side) to Steinway Street and turn right (south, as the numbers get *higher*). From the R, exit at Broadway and walk north. The avenue blocks along this route on Steinway are *very* long.

Restaurants   You'll find several Egyptian and Moroccan restaurants here. **Kabab Café** (25-12 Steinway Street, 718-728-9858), which has been here for almost a decade, feels like an import from the Village of the 1960s—small, dark, crowded, and filled with the idiosyncratic designs and *tchotchkes* of owner Ali El Sayed, who smokes and kibitzes while he cooks at the front.

When I visited he was playing the soundtrack to the *Buena Vista Social Club*—Ali adores old Cuban music—and he produced delicious platters of *mahshi* (grilled vegetables and stuffed zucchini). On the hot day of my first visit, Ali served iced mint tea—a treat. If you love Moroccan food, check out **Aya's Café Restaurant** (25-60 Steinway Street, 718-204-6040). The sign outside might still say Mamounia's—it had been there for months after the restaurant changed owners, and it's so attractive that perhaps the new ones decided to keep it! Inside, the atmosphere evokes the type of eatery you might find in a Moroccan market—dark, with narrow aisles between the tables and seating near the front with cushions and a low table. The menu includes traditional Moroccan *tagines*—long-cooked stews that combine chicken, meat, or fish with various vegetable (and some fruit) combinations—couscous dishes, kebabs, and *bastillas* (phyllo pies). Nothing's terribly expensive—vegetarian dishes are about $7.95 and most tagines and couscous entrees are $9.95, while a seafood bastilla, with layers of shrimp, calamari, and swordfish, is $11.95. You can also make a meal of appetizers, such as Moroccan "cigars" (long, thin, phyllo-wrapped pastries with beef or other fillings), *zalouk* (a slow-cooked eggplant appetizer), and hearty soups, for about $4 or $5. The popular *harira* soup has a chick-pea base with meat and amazing spices.

If you didn't know beforehand, you might not realize that the peculiar storefront with mystical eyes and embedded mirrors at 25-22 Steinway Street is actually **Mombar** (718-726-2356), a restaurant that serves Egyptian specialties (dinner only) in an eccentric setting similar to that of Kabab Café. The owner, Mustafa El Sayed, who happens to be Ali El Sayed's brother, has decorated the place with all sorts of found items such as mirrors, glass, and tiles. The restaurant's name refers to a type of stuffed sausage, usually lamb or beef (or both combined) made with cardamom, rice, and parsley. You can get it at Mombar, but you'll also find great dips, fish entrées, grilled vegetables, and spectacular desserts oozing with honey. At first glance, **Balbaa** (24-25 Steinway Street, 718-932-0607) looks like an Egyptian version of your friendly not-quite-greasy-spoon. It's an informal place with about a dozen tables, semi-fast service, and a menu familiar to folks who love Mediterranean food. They serve great dips, salads, and kebabs (shish, kofta, chicken, lamb, and veal) in addition to Egyptian specialties such as stuffed dove, which is $14 (I haven't tried it!); *molokhia*, a stew of grilled rabbit meat with rice ($10); and meat pies, which cost $6.99. The pie list also includes shrimp pie and pastrami pie and wonderful dessert pies with custard, nuts, or cream. They also have honey-covered pastries. If you want to keep it light and simple, you can make a decent meal out of appetizers (this is, for me, often the best way to get different tastes at one place without becoming too full). I've had stuffed grape leaves along with pieces of eggplant and tomato marinated in a hot pepper relish with fresh pita bread. Each piece is just $1 and quite substantial. (By the way, Balbaa has a larger branch at 6823 Third Avenue in Bay Ridge, Brooklyn; see page 104.) There are also Thai, Italian, and Argentine restaurants along this restaurant row.

Bakeries   The star here is the gorgeous **Laziza of New York Pastry** (25-78 Steinway Street, 718-777-7676), which opened in early 2002. The owners, who are Jordanian, have made true art out of their Middle Eastern pastries, offering miniature baklavas of various shapes and with various fillings and other honey-soaked delectables including a farina pudding called *borma* that is both simple and spectacular. "Laziza," by the way, is Arabic for "delicious."

Some places clearly are a male domain. **Egyptian Coffee Shop** (25-09 Steinway Street) is packed with men smoking water pipes; the smell of the

CHICKEN PAPRIKASH

Courtesy of Zlata Praha Restaurant in Astoria, Queens

Serves 4

2 tablespoons butter
½ cup chopped onions
1½ tablespoons Hungarian paprika
1 teaspoon salt
¾ cup chicken stock
1 3-pound broiler-fryer chicken, cut into pieces
¼ cup flour
¼ cup half-and-half
½ cup sour cream

1. Heat the butter in a large, heavy saucepan over medium heat. Add the onions and sauté until light brown. Add the paprika, salt, and stock. Cover and cook 3 minutes.
2. Add the chicken, cover, and cook until tender, about 40 minutes. Take the chicken pieces out of the pan and remove the skin from the chicken breasts and thighs and return the chicken to the pan. Add water or extra chicken stock, if necessary, to make 1¼ cups broth.
3. In a small bowl blend the flour with the half-and-half. Add it to the pot and cook, stirring constantly, until thick.
4. Add the sour cream and cook until it's heated through. Do not let it boil. Serve over noodles or rice.

fruity tobacco mixture wafts outside. I've found people in this area to be quite friendly, and once when I was leading a tour of students from Penn State through the area, a man beckoned the group into one of the larger shops and let some of the students try a pipe!

Markets   Al-Iman Food Market (24-31 Steinway Street) is packed with inventory from all over North Africa and is in high demand locally, according to Algerian co-owner Abelnour Djenas. Among its many specialties is a lovely *fatir* bread, made of layers of phyllo, which is nice to eat with a dry cheese that some folks call *turki* and others *rumi,* and mint tea. You can also buy halal toothpaste, which is made without any animal by-products. **El Manara** (25-95 Steinway Street) is a large and very well-put-together Lebanese market that also sells prepared dishes such as *kibbee* (spicy meat patties) and its own baked *zataar* and other Middle Eastern breads. I had a fabulous *fattoush* of rice, onions, and lentils and my first ever sautéed dandelion salad. El Manara also sells a beautiful fruit cup, layered in green, yellow, and red, which is made by blending individual fruits (kiwi for green, banana for yellow, and strawberry for red), adding pieces of whole fruit to the blends, and then layering the blends. **Old City Market** (25-17 Steinway Street) is an area anomaly that you might think refers to Jerusalem. But actually it sells products from Eastern Europe, as well as smoked meats. It's worth a visit to see neighborhood contrasts, and the many interesting products are yet another sign of Astoria's magnetic draw on new communities from around the world.

· · ·

Astoria Diversions

Socrates Sculpture Park and Isamu Noguchi Garden Museum

It was raining the day I set out for **Socrates Sculpture Park** (31-42 Vernon Boulevard) and the **Isamu Noguchi Garden Museum** (32-37 Vernon Boulevard)—no matter. The visits were worthwhile and I recommend that you include both places in your Astoria tour.

From the Broadway stop on the N or W train, walk west on Broadway for about fifteen minutes to the end, which is Vernon Boulevard. (You can also get a bus on Broadway.) Don't be daunted by the street numbers—21st Street leads to 14th Street, and the last street here is 8th. You will see a big Costco across the street. For Socrates Sculpture Park, turn right on Vernon for a brief moment, cross the street, and you'll soon come to the entrance. This space was set up by sculptor Marc di Suvero, and it is the largest outdoor sculpture exhibition area in New York City, having been integrated formally into the network of New York City parks in 1999. Visit www.socratessculpturepark.org or call 718-956-1819 for more information.

The Noguchi museum is a treat. It's peaceful and inspiring, and represents the scope of Noguchi's work. Video clips of dance sets he designed for Martha Graham and photo retrospectives of his monumental plazas around the world can be seen. The café displays some of his lovely *akari* lamps, inspired by Japanese lanterns. For more information, call 718-204-7088 or check the Web site at www.noguchimuseum.org. (Note: At this writing, the museum was closed for renovation. Check its Web site or call for updates.)

American Museum of the Moving Image

The closest subway lines are the R train (Steinway Street stop, exit at 34th Avenue) and the N train (36th Avenue).

Astoria has had a film culture since the Astoria Studios complex opened in the 1920s to produce feature films. As Hollywood became dominant Astoria Studios declined and in 1942 the U.S. Army took it over to create propaganda and, after the war, training films. It closed in the 1960s and reopened in the mid-seventies and put out feature films including *The Wiz, All That Jazz,* and *Radio Days* and TV shows such as *Sesame Street* and *Cosby.*

In 1988 the American Museum of the Moving Image opened in one of its buildings on 36th Street at 35th Avenue. The museum has ongoing screenings, seminars, and permanent and rotating exhibits, many of which are interactive, and a special display of licensed merchandise tied to popular films. The gift shop is lots of fun, and doesn't require museum entry to get in.

The hours are Tuesday through Friday from noon to 5 and Saturday and Sunday from 11 to 6. Admission is $8.50 for adults, $5.50 for students and senior citizens. For more information call 718-784-0077 or visit www.ammi.org.

Elsewhere in Astoria . . .   Around the corner from the museum is **Café Bar** (32-90 36th Street, 718-204-5273). This new hangout is what I'd call "Greek chic," with floppy sofas and old stuffed chairs, trunks as tables, vintage movie posters, heavy curtains, and lots of *tchotchkes,* plus a light Greek menu of sandwiches with fillings such as cucumbers and *halloumi* cheese. It was slow the afternoon I was there but I gather it picks up steam up at night. On the far border of Astoria is **Rio Bonito** (32-86 47th Street, near 34th Avenue), the largest Brazilian supermarket in New York City. When I visited in October 2002, it had just opened and much of the inventory was not in yet but many products (including pepper sauces, cheeses, cookies and chocolates, beverages, soup mixes, big bags of beans for *feijoada,* Brazilian shampoos and cosmetics, CDs) could be found in its aisles. There are plans for a bookstore and travel agency. Anyone who adores Brazilian food (count me in!) will appreciate this store.

▪ Off the Eaten Path . . .

Among the greatest joys of exploring New York City's ethnic neighborhoods are the unexpected discoveries. On numerous explorations of Astoria I would pass **Byzantion Woodworking Company,** a storefront at 37-20 Astoria Boulevard. Their display window would be full of beautiful carved religious items such as podia, tables, doors, pews, and icons. One day while I was leading a tour, I saw that the workshop was open, and I stopped in to inquire about it. Owner Konstantinos Pilarinos welcomed us inside to observe his Greek and Romanian carvers at work, and also to proudly display the National Heritage Award certificate he received in 2000 from President Bill Clinton. This award honors individuals who play a role in the preservation of unique crafts, and this type of hand-carving has not only become very rare in the United States but is in decline in Greece as well.

▪ ▪ ▪

Flushing

Where East Meets East

"This is Main Street, U.S.A. Have a nice day!" says the conductor on the #7 subway as we pull into its last station, in Flushing, Queens. Most of us chuckle and I look around: it's mid-afternoon on a weekday and the train isn't very crowded. I am probably the only Caucasian person in the car. Most of the other passengers appear to be of Asian origin and perhaps another handful are Latin American. I head toward the escalator as the recorded voice reminds me to "please face forward while riding this escalator." There is a pause and then a second recorded voice follows, presumably repeating the same words, in Mandarin. Then, "Have a great day," followed by, I gather, the same thing in Mandarin.

Welcome to Flushing. As you take the #7 train here from Times Square it will be pretty obvious why this line is dubbed the International Express. But by the time you reach Main Street, you'll understood why it is also referred to by its other nickname: the Orient Express.

Flushing has been home to a substantial Asian community for more

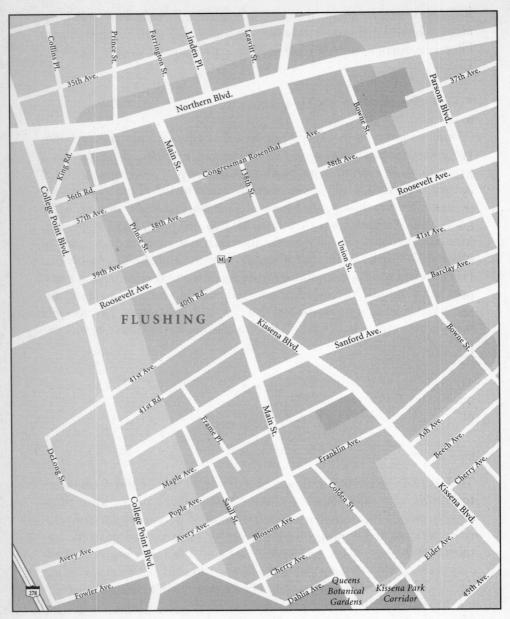

than thirty years. But its numbers simply have exploded over the last ten to fifteen years. In the 2000 census, nearly 55% of Flushing's 80,000 residents were described as Asian, with Chinese making up about 25%, Koreans 15%, and Asian Indians about 9.4%. (Latinos make up almost 22% of Flushing's population.) In 2001, Flushing elected John Liu, who was born in Taiwan and is only in his mid-thirties, as New York City's first Asian New York City Council representative. Short of having its own mayor, Flushing surely is one of the most cosmopolitan urban communities in the United States.

▪ Getting Oriented

Downtown Flushing is divided into several axes. The key north-south axis is Main Street and the key east-west axis is Roosevelt Avenue. Main Street, especially south of Roosevelt Avenue, is mostly Chinese. Some older chain stores can be found north of Roosevelt Avenue but more and more Chinese-owned stores and markets are moving in. The area south of Roosevelt Avenue until Franklin Avenue is heavily Chinese, and then it becomes South and Central Asian, specifically Indian, Pakistani, Bangladeshi, and Afghan. Union Street, the parallel north-south block east of Main Street and north of Roosevelt Avenue, is Korea Central and is packed with stores, restaurants, bakeries, and markets. Several major Korean restaurants and markets line three or four blocks of Northern Boulevard east of Main Street (see pages 33–36).

Typical of Queens, numerous shorter blocks such as 40th Road and 41st Avenue fall in between the long blocks. But it isn't difficult to figure out, and it's hard to get lost. The only diagonal road you need to be aware of is Kissena Boulevard, which meets Main Street at 41st Avenue.

BY SUBWAY

The Flushing tour is one of the easiest ones to get to: just take the #7 train to the last stop, where Main Street meets Roosevelt Avenue. From Times Square, the #7 local takes about forty minutes; the express train, which runs weekdays to Flushing from 12:30 P.M. to 10 P.M., takes twenty-five to thirty minutes.

BY BUS

Many bus lines run through Central Flushing. The Q25 and Q34 connect Jamaica and Flushing along Kissena Boulevard and Parsons Boulevard, and the Q44 crosses the Bronx-Whitestone Bridge, starting at the Bronx Zoo. The Q48 enters Flushing from western Queens along Roosevelt Avenue and the Q65 and Q66 come from western Queens along Northern Boulevard. Queens bus maps are available at many public library branches and on line at www.mta.nyc.ny.us, or by calling 718-330-1234.

BY CAR

Northern Boulevard leads directly into Flushing from points east and west. A municipal lot is located in a two-block area bounded by 37th and 39th Avenues and 136th and Union Streets. It often fills up on weekends and it can be difficult to find street parking. Parking is also available near the Flushing Mall (see page 33).

BY TRAIN

Take the Port Washington line of the Long Island Railroad to the Main Street, Flushing, stop. The train lets you off downtown, so it's a great alternative to driving. For schedule information see www.mta.nyc.ny.us/lirr/ or call 718-217-LIRR.

■ Tips for Touring

You'll shortchange yourself if you try to do Flushing in a day. I suggest you organize separate visits to each of the three areas I describe. Although the South Asian stretch on Main Street is small, you can add to the experience by including a visit to the Queens Botanical Gardens as well as the Hindu section, which is about ten minutes away on foot (see pages 40–41).

■ Landmarks

Several historic sites spotlight Flushing's role in promoting religious freedom and tolerance in the New World (see pages 39–40). The **Flushing Public Library** (718-661-1200), an excellent resource, is located at the intersection of Kissena Boulevard and Main Street—it's impossible to miss. Its periodical room is filled with newspapers from all over the world, and on the Main Street side you'll see carved into the front steps titles and names of authors of famous books from around the world, many in their original alphabets. The Flushing Public Library is said to be one of the busiest in the world! **Flushing Meadow Park,** the site of the 1939 and 1964 World's Fairs, houses the **Queens Museum of Art** (www.queensmuse.org, 718-592-9700). This museum displays the amazing New York City Panorama, the world's largest scale model of New York City, which was built for the 1964 World's Fair. (The replica World Trade Center remains.) To get there, take the #7 train to 111th street.

■ Food Resources and Supplies

Asian Greens by Anita Loh-Yien Lau (New York: St. Martin's Press, 2001) and Charmaine Solomon's *Encyclopedia of Asian Food* (North Clarendon, Vermont: Periplus Books, 1998) are two excellent books that were a tremendous help to me. Both feature great recipes with photographs and provide a thorough explanation of Asian ingredients. The newsletter *Flavor & Fortune* (King's Park, New York: Institute of the Science and Art of Chinese Cuisine) is a wonderful resource on Chinese cuisine. To find a copy go to www.flavorandfortune.com or send an e-mail to flavorandfortune@hot mail.com.

Sunrise Kitchen Supplies (42-05 Main Street) has a huge selection of cookware for Asian cuisine including gigantic woks, microwave steamers, and various utensils and appliances.

...

Chinese Flushing

Flushing has had a significant Chinese presence—mainly Taiwanese—since the mid-sixties, but vast changes have taken place over the last decade as new businesses appear to serve the influx of people from Hong Kong and the mainland. This has meant more variety—and greater scale—for lovers of Chinese food. Chic tea shops offer peanut butter on toast while bakeries serve exotic tea concoctions and fruit shakes. A 13-restaurant food court has opened, and huge buffets offer diners much greater choice, and more calories to worry about.

Getting There   You're practically in the heart of Chinese Flushing when you exit the #7 train at Main Street—the core area runs along Main Street and Roosevelt Avenue west of Main Street, with some spillover onto the side streets.

Markets   For first-timers, the vast and modern **Hong Kong Supermarket** (37-11 Main Street) is a good starting place—it's easy to negotiate and everything is marked in English. (Elsewhere in this book I've referred to branches of the Hong Kong Supermarket chain in Manhattan's Chinatown; Sunset Park, Brooklyn; and Elmhurst, Queens.) The supermarket also has a good selection of products from Japan, Thailand, Indonesia, Malaysia, and the Philippines. On the aisles furthest to the right as you enter you will find inexpensive prepared dishes and further down you'll see cuts of meat such as cleaned duck uteri, blood, tongues, intestines, and brains that you may not have encountered before. You'll find frozen dumplings and a vast assortments of noodles, sauces, and just about any other ingredient and condiment you can think of, plus Chinese ices in lichee, durian, and longan flavors. **A&C Supermarket** (41-41 Kissena Boulevard), near the Flushing Public Library, has the best layout of these supermarkets featuring terrific produce and seafood sections, a variety of packaged and frozen foods, and a busy take-out counter of prepared dishes at very low prices ($2 to $3 for heaping containers). Be forewarned that if you don't know what something is and don't speak Cantonese, you'll have a nearly impossible time getting an explanation. If you have a weak stomach and are not familiar with the some of the varieties of seafood used in Chinese cooking, you may have a hard time as you encounter buckets of turtles that are not being sold as pets. Fourteen cashiers enable traffic to move amazingly fast even when the store is packed, which is often. **A&N Supermarket** (41-79 Main Street) has an excellent kitchenware and appliances section located behind the very large grocery area. It also has a great selection of cookbooks featuring Taiwanese, Vietnamese, Szechuan, Shanghai, and other regional cuisines and volumes on subjects such as noodle dishes and one-pot cuisine. Most of them are illustrated with color photos and are good buys at $14 to $20.

You will notice many herb stores interspersed among the food markets of Flushing. **Shun An Tong** (135-24 Roosevelt Avenue) is one of the best for a first-timer—its owners will do their best to help you find what you need, or merely answer questions. One of the owners has written the illustrated *Oriental Herbal Cook Book for Good Health* (C. H. Image, 1993), which is on sale at the store for $20. You can buy seasonings for the book's recipes in the shop.

Not quite a market, but not really an eatery either, **Aji Ichiban** (41-51A Main Street), a Japanese-style "snackery," is a must-see. They sell an assortment of fish and vegetable snacks that taste delicious because of one common ingredient—sugar. My favorites are licorice-lemon and seven-scented olive. Aji Ichiban is a growing chain that actually is based in Hong Kong and at this writing has five outlets in Manhattan's Chinatown.

Bakeries   Chinese bakeries—mostly Taiwanese-inspired—are scattered throughout downtown Flushing, with a Bakery Row on the south side of Roosevelt Avenue between Main and Prince Streets. These bakeries tend to be similar, selling inexpensive pastries (60 to 80 cents each) along with coffee, tapioca tea drinks, fruit shakes, and iced desserts. Many also serve salads and hot snacks. I've bought Chinese birthday cakes for my daughter for the last few years. Their cakes ($7 to $12) tend to be light and spongy with frostings embellished with pieces of melon, kiwi, berries, and other fruits and sometimes have chopped fruit in the layers as well. Manhattan's **Ten Ren's Tea Time** has a Flushing branch at 135-18 Roosevelt Avenue (718-461-9305) as does **Fay Da** (135-16 Roosevelt Avenue) next door. I especially like Fay Da's checkerboard cakes. (Fay Da also owns a big seafood place on

41-60 Main Street, 718-886-4568.) Do check out the mod **Sago Tea** (39-02 Main Street, 718-353-2899), a popular youth hangout that serves drinks, pastries, and light snacks. At another popular spot, **Tapioca Express** (41-96 Main Street, 718-445-1989), you can get fruit-flavored "icys" (similar to slushes), flavored teas, and fruit shakes similar to Caribbean *batidos*. The setting—bright with Asian rock music playing—is great for kids.

Restaurants "Daunting" is the first word that comes to mind. Your food choices range from street stands (including three near the Flushing post office), where you can buy warm tofu or scallion pancakes, to fancy multicourse buffets. Eateries reflect the cuisines of mainland China, Hong Kong, and Taiwan as well as Malaysia and Vietnam.

A young customer enjoying Bubble Tea at Ten Ren's Tea Time in Flushing.

A popular budget option that will allow you to sample a variety of Chinese dishes can be found at one of the many places that advertise four dishes and soup for $3.99. One such place, **Echiban Chinese Fast Food** (135-32 40th Road, 718-539-0002), claims to serve over eighty dishes every day, although I counted only forty-seven when I was there. I had delicious sautéed string beans, spicy bean curd, sautéed kale, and sesame chicken. The soup was a forgettable fish broth.

For a step up, check out **Chao Zhou** (40-52 Main Street, 718-353-7683) and **Wen Zhou** (135-15 37th Avenue, 718-888-9388). Aside from the large bowl and chopsticks on the roof and the fact that Hillary Clinton ate there while campaigning for senator, Chao Zhou attracts a following for its huge and eclectic Cantonese menu (although I ordered chicken curry with potatoes on one visit). Go early! Wen Zhou, named for a seaport in Zhejiang province, specializes in seafood in an elegant setting that gives the sense of eating in a large dining room. Despite the fancy-for-Flushing decor, most entrées are just $5.95 to $10.95.

If you love juicy buns, **Joe's Shanghai** (136-21 37th Avenue, 718-539-3838) and **Guo Bu Li** (135-28 40th Road, 718-886-2121) are two great places. The same folks run Joe's on Pell Street in Manhattan's Chinatown, but this is the original. The friendly Guo Bu Li is known for its Tianjinese steamed dumplings. You can watch as fresh buns and noodles are prepared in a kitchen visible from the main dining area.

On 38th Avenue east of Main Street you'll find a pair of *chi-chi* Taiwan-style restaurants popular with young folks (but grown-ups needn't be shy—I wasn't). **Minni's Shabu-Shabu** (136-17 38th Avenue, 718-886-9815) specializes in Taiwanese hot pot. You order raw seafood or thinly sliced meats, cook them in a boiling chicken or spicy broth, and then embellish them with peanut, soy, chili, garlic, or other sauces. Before you place your order, you'll get an appetizer plate of greens, sprouts, and bean curd—enough for a meal! The experience is fun and slightly exhausting. At **Sweet 'n Tart** (136-11 38th Avenue, 718-661-3380) you can order dessert only, choosing from a menu of elaborate fruit shakes, ice cream concoctions, hot and cold tea drinks, and lots of snacks. Peanut butter on toast is one of the more popular choices. There's also a cappuccino bar. Most items, except for house specials, are $5 or less.

Going out with friends? Check out **East Bistro & Café** (42-07 Main Street, 718-358-9810). Climb the grand marble stairs into a vast dining room and get set for an all-you-can-eat buffet with dozens of choices, including even sushi and Italian dishes. The best bargain is the $8.99 weekday lunch, and weekday dinner is $19.99. On weekends, lunch jumps to $15.99 and dinner to $23.99, although kids get discounts. The nearby **East Lake** (42-33 Main Street, 718-539-8532) is a former Greek-American diner with a formal restaurant on the main floor, which is up a flight of stairs; a take-out place and bakery are on the street level. This Hong Kong–style place serves dim sum much of the time but also has excellent seafood specialties. Both East Bistro & Café and East Lake have parking lots.

VEGETARIAN OPTIONS

For vegetarians wondering where to go, there's just one exclusively vegetarian (Chinese) option: **Buddha Bodai** (42-96 Main Street, 718-939-1188), one block from the Queens Botanical Gardens. It's also kosher-certified.

▪ Mini-Mall Mania

The Chinese are very entrepreneurial and love to run their own businesses. So it's common to see large spaces divided into mini-malls packed with small shops. These can be found in Hong Kong and China, and in Manhattan's Chinatown and Chinese Flushing. Some large supermarkets also contain small businesses such as travel agencies, locksmiths, and insurance brokers. My favorite of these malls is the **Mayflower Plaza** (40-46 Main Street), with two small jewelry stores, a place to buy phone cards, a shop with bamboo and other plants, a bun shop, a sushi bar, a Taipei noodle shop where you can watch experts make noodles and buns on the spot, a $3.99 cafeteria, and the **Mayflower Bakery** itself. In addition to its baked goods the bakery has a bin of cold teas as well as fresh juices—watermelon, papaya, mango, taro, lichee, longan, and more. A mezzanine eating area enables you to take in the rhythm of the crowds. One day, a television set above the noodle shop was blaring a Taiwanese staging of *Mary Poppins*. When I heard the familiar melody I realized it was the song "Just a Spoonful of Sugar Makes the Medicine Go Down" sung by a Chinese Mary Poppins.

The modern **Flushing Center Mall** is part of the Sheraton LaGuardia East Hotel (135-20 39th Avenue), which towers over Flushing. It's a much more formal place catering to sophisticated travelers, and merchandise is pricey. A gorgeous gown shop where you can order custom garments is located on the street level as you enter the mall from the rear entrance on Roosevelt Avenue. Inside the mall you can check out the attractive **La Cascade** restaurant, which offers both Continental (European) and Chinese menus, but I have never tried it.

Further down on 39th Avenue (en route to the Oriental Cash & Carry—see pages 34–35), you'll pass the **Flushing Mall.** The main entrance is at 133-31 39th Avenue, and there's adjacent parking. The mall's food court is impressive: thirteen eateries share the same roof and offer various regional Chinese cuisines along with sushi, Korean food, dim sum, hot pots, tapioca teas and desserts, and, yes, pizza, bagels, and Mexican food. It's great for families with picky eaters! All are managed by the Manhattan-based noodle place Ollie's.

* * *

Korean Flushing

In Manhattan, the single block of West 32nd Street between Fifth Avenue and Broadway has become known as Little Korea. It's jammed with restaurants, markets, shops, and all sorts of services; if you look at the upper floors of the street's office buildings, you'll see signs in Korean for many types of businesses. Korean Flushing is 32nd Street times ten. As you turn onto Union Street from 39th Avenue, Korean markets, twenty-four-hour barbecue restaurants, luncheonettes and bakeries, department stores, boutiques, and dozens of service shops will gradually unfold before you, some crammed, like layer-cakes, into three-story buildings—inventive setups such as a church on top of a nail salon on top of an Internet café. But you'll see only one chunk of Korean Flushing; unlike Manhattan's Chinatown, which is crowded into a single dense downtown area, there are numerous clusters of Korean shops in Flushing (including one further east on Northern Boulevard and southeast on Kissena Boulevard). Other Korean areas are scattered around Queens in Sunnyside, Bayside, Woodside, Elmhurst, and Jackson Heights. Approximately 13% of Flushing is Korean, compared to a Chinese population of at least 25%.

Here are some words on Korean cuisine from a relative newcomer: Chinese and Japanese occupations of Korea have had a lot of impact on its cuisine. Almost all of Flushing's sushi places are Korean-owned and some Chinese eateries specifically cater to the Korean palate. I love how the textures, flavors, and spices used in Korean cooking combine to create a fascinating new set of tastes and sensations. Korean cooking involves a lot of fresh and dried roots, mushrooms, and wild greens. (I saw pickled fiddlehead ferns at a Korean take-out place.) Noodle dishes, especially buckwheat vermicelli, are staples, and common garnishes include pine nuts, sesame seeds, and chile threads. Seafood dishes often make use of expensive ingredients such as sea cucumber, large shrimp, and abalone, and beef is favored over pork. I find Korean dishes beautiful to look at, with colors as rich and varied as their tastes.

Getting There   Take the #7 train to Main Street, and head east on Roosevelt Avenue (Macy's will be across the street on your right) and turn left at Lippman Plaza, a wide pedestrian passageway. You'll emerge on 39th Avenue, where, turning right, you'll pass several bright, busy shops that cater to Koreans and some video arcades populated by teenagers. Then you'll reach Union Street, the heart of Korean Flushing.

Markets   There are three worth visiting within walking distance of the subway. If you can't read Korean (there's no English sign to lead you there), you might pass the large **Han An Reum** supermarket (141-40 Northern Boulevard, between Bowne Street and Parsons Boulevard). It occupies a former Chevrolet showroom, and its large inventory makes it a worthwhile stop. Then walk east on Northern Boulevard from Union Street for 1½ blocks and you'll see the ramp to a parking area and a covered produce market on the right. Most products here have English labels. **Jahnchi Jahnchi** (138-28 Northern Boulevard, 718-321-2575) has a terrific selection of prepared vegetarian, meat, and seafood take-out including sushi and porridges at reasonable prices. It's a good place to try new dishes because servings are not too big and there are many choices. The owners and staff don't speak English well but are friendly and try to be helpful. The warehouse-sized **Koreatown,** also known as **Oriental Cash & Carry** (131-01 39th Avenue), is a few blocks west from downtown and has a parking lot. Restaurant-size packages of seaweed, sauces, noodles, spices, and other ingredients used for Korean cooking are sold here along with fresh seafood and produce. This store targets shoppers who want to buy in quantity, although regular-size packaging is also available. I found pine nuts imported from China for just $3.99 a pound and a twenty-pound bag was only $25. A deli section sells prepared foods and a snack bar offers noodles, soup, and other simple dishes. Tasty Korean ices are also available. There are several other shops and excellent bathrooms on the top floor.

Bakeries   Korean bakery-cafés are very popular, but for some reason they are much more expensive than their Chinese counterparts. I like them for their unique teas and (in some cases) ambiance. At the large **Koryodong Café** (39-02 Union Street, 718-762-0369), you'll feel like you're in Seoul, watching giggling high school kids meet after school and families gather to enjoy cakes and drinks, especially the popular *phat bing su* made with shaved ice, red beans, fresh fruit pieces, and whipped cream. I had a wonderful quince tea made with delicious pieces of fresh quince. (Koryodong has a branch at 156-19 Northern Boulevard, driving distance from the subway.) Around the corner, at the smaller **Wien Bakery** (136-58 39th Avenue), I tried two very good teas: a strong ginger tea with pine nuts, and *jujube* (red date) tea flavored with pieces of date. At the entrance to Koreatown (see page 34) you'll see the small **Kyoto Bakery,** which sells delicious breads including a bean paste loaf and a yummy "chestnut morning" bread. Kyoto is for take-out only—there's no seating.

Restaurants   The vast **KumGangSan** (212 967-0909 Northern Boulevard, 718-461-0909) occupies a former Ethan Allen Furniture store and features a waterfall in the back. (Its Manhattan counterpart, Kum Kang, on 32nd Street, between Broadway and Fifth Avenue, has a small waterfall in the front.) Marinated barbecues that you cook at the table are popular, as are grilled fish and beef or seafood casseroles, although they are a bit expensive. Also offered is a seven-mushroom casserole for $35 cooked in a hot pot at the table. Most dishes are not so expensive, though, and lunch specials—Japanese as well as Korean—run $6 to $8. More typical is the smaller **San Soo Kap San** (38-13 Union Street, 718-445-1165), where you also can order barbecue at the table, and lunch specialties including Korean *bibimboap,* a casserole of shredded spicy vegetables with meat and a fried egg, range from $5 to $9. Mix them all together before eating.

My most interesting experience was at **Uncle King's Chinese Restaurant** (136-75 Roosevelt Avenue, 718-353-2261), an unassuming place east of the subway station's escalator exit. I had taken their menu early in my Flushing explorations but didn't think of eating there. A Korean friend surprised me when she suggested we go. As we walked in we found the place packed with Koreans. My friend said a few words to the waiter and the soup noodles and duck sauce on the table disappeared and were replaced with *kim chee* (pickled cabbage), sliced onion, and a dipping sauce. My friend ordered a seafood casserole in white sauce—no rice—from a Korean menu and we finished our meal with vermicelli in a delicious brown sauce with onions. My friend informed me that this fabulous selection was a typical Chinese-Korean dish, adapted over time by Chinese cooks in Korea.

. . .

South Asian Flushing

Afghan, Indian, Iranian, Pakistani

The stretch of Main Street from Franklin Avenue to Dahlia Avenue features the enticing aromas, textures, and colors of South Asia in the form of green and red chiles, ginger, purple or white eggplants, fuzzy or sleek squash, papayas, pomegranates, persimmons, and mangoes and all sorts of nuts, spices, teas, sauces, rice, and legumes. Unlike Jackson Heights, which focuses on the food of India, Pakistan, and Bangladesh, the scope of Flushing is broader, including products from other areas such as Afghanistan and Iran. Since this area does not cater to tourists, with the exception of the new Patel Brothers store (see page 37) you won't find cookbooks and you may find that the staff at some restaurants does not speak enough English to answer questions. But I've had some wonderful experiences here, and I'm sure you will too.

Getting There   From the intersection of Main Street and Roosevelt Avenue at the end of the #7 subway line, head south on Main Street, passing through Chinese Flushing. You'll see a Bank of India on your right one block before the tour begins, at Franklin Street. The last block of shops faces the Queens Botanical Garden (see pages 40–41).

Markets   I found **Ariana Afghan** market (42-49 Main Street, 718-445-4922), which carries products mostly from Afghanistan, Iran, and Pakistan, to be the most intriguing market. The market carries products from Afghanistan such as *bair,* a dried fruit that looks like a date; a type of super-long green raisin that I had never seen before, at $4.99 a pound; a type of pine nut called *jalghoza,* at $5.99 a pound; and dried black mulberries, at $5.99 a pound. The Australian ginger, at 25 cents a piece, is sweet and spicy. Check out the sweet round *roat* bread, which is eaten with Afghan black tea, and other sweet pastries. Ariana also carries many Persian products such as the Sadaf-brand sauces and various herb mixtures used in Persian cooking. They also sell some beautiful tea sets and cookware. **Chand** (43-37 Main Street, 718-886-2117) is the last of the South Asian stores on Main Street and carries a great variety of products, from Persian sweets to Indian spices, and it's big enough to explore comfortably. Cousins Girish Patel and Mahendra Patel run two Flushing branches of the **Patel Brothers** grocery chain—the smaller, older one is located at 42-79 Main Street and a newer one (which replaced an Indo-Pakistani market) is almost directly across the street at 42-92 Main Street. The new, larger space has allowed them to create wide aisles for shopping and to add a huge selection of produce, spices, and legumes, and other packaged and frozen foods used in South Asian cooking. There's also a large downstairs area with a selection of housewares, cookware, religious items, and some crafts. You'll also find several brands of Indian toothpaste and a few cookbooks. It's a beautiful store to shop in, and one you can easily lose yourself in!

Restaurants   Most eateries here are fairly modest Pakistani or Afghan kebab places and Indian restaurants. None significantly cater to a tourist crowd as do many of the places I've covered in Jackson Heights (see pages 41–57). **Shere Punjab** (42-87 Main Street, 718-358-1999) did not look inviting from the outside, but its menu is vast and impressive, offering, among other things, more types of *paneer* (vegetarian cheese stew), made with combinations of curry, cream, chili, and nuts, and a greater variety of sauces than are usually seen on Indian menus. Most dishes range from $6.50 to $10, with shrimp and seafood dishes running a little higher. Their tandoori mixed grill is great, at $10.95. **Shamiana** (42-47 Main Street, 718-445-2262) is a stark, bright place serving excellent vegetarian food and their front counter is full of sweets and spicy hot snacks. The staff speaks little English and I found the service to be indifferent, but the food is good. Their *mysore masala dosa,* a huge crepe filled with vegetables and cashews, at $4.75, was very hot. A good follow-up is the *falooda,* a fruit shake with vermicelli noodles, at $3.50. I also recommend three kebab places—**Kabul Kebab House** (42-51 Main Street, 718-461-1919), **Chathkhara Kebab House** (43-11 Main Street, 718-353-1227), and **Choopan Kebab House** (43-27 Main Street, 718-539-3180). Despite its name, Kabul Kebab House specializes in Persian dishes—*koresh* (fluffy rice dishes) and kebabs marinated in special spices. I had a Cornish hen kebab, which was under $10. They also serve hummus and some other Middle Eastern dishes. Chathkhara is Pakistani and Choopan is Afghan. It's fun to compare similar dishes in these different restaurants, as some foods, such as *samosas,* seem to cross cuisines.

A Glimpse at Hindu Flushing

A ten-minute walk from South Asian Flushing will bring you to one of the largest Hindu temples in northeast America, quite an amazing sight and well worth the trek. The **Hindu Temple Society of North America** occupies a complex of buildings along Bowne Street that's capped by what is usually referred to as the **Ganesh Temple** (45–57 Bowne Street, at Holly Street), named for the image of this elephant-headed god, its centerpiece. The society was established in 1970 and its first piece of property—a former Russian Orthodox Church—was purchased in 1972. The temple opened in 1977 and more properties were acquired from the mid-eighties through the late nineties. In 1997 a large community center with a canteen, a shop, classrooms, and an auditorium opened next to the temple. (There are several restaurants nearby, but most are small and undistinguished. **Thai Food House** [144-20 45th Avenue, 718-961-3094], around the corner from the temple, specializes in Burmese, Chinese, and Thai food. It is quite pretty, and conveniently located a block from Flushing Hospital. Since there are so few restaurants in this area, Thai Food House must cater to a lot of hospital personnel.) For more information, go to www.nyganeshtemple.org.

To get there from the front of the Botanical Gardens (see pages 40–41), walk east on Elder Avenue, then turn right (south) on Kissena Boulevard to Holly Street, about four blocks. Turn left, go one block to Bowne Street, and you're there.

PANEER TIKKA MAKHANWALA

Courtesy of Ramesh Kumar of Shere Punjab Restaurant in Flushing, Queens

Ghee or vegetable oil for frying
2 pounds paneer (an Indian white cheese), cubed
3 pounds tomatoes, diced
2 teaspoons salt
2 teaspoons chili powder
¼ cup heavy cream
1 teaspoon garam masala
2 teaspoons kasturi methi

1. In a large saucepan fry the paneer in hot ghee or vegetable oil on both sides until it turns light brown. Remove from pan and set aside.
2. Place the tomato pieces in the hot oil and cook for 20 minutes, until tender.
3. Add the paneer along with the rest of the ingredients, and cook 5 minutes.

Flushing's Freedom Mile

As mentioned earlier, Flushing has played an important historic role in the development of religious diversity and tolerance in the United States. The Freedom Mile tour enables you to see some of these landmarks as well as a few other places I've added to make the tour complete.

Flushing Town Hall (137-35 Northern Boulevard) is a good starting point. This beautifully renovated Civil War–era building that served as Flushing's town hall until Flushing merged with New York in 1898 is used as a cultural center these days. Across the street, the **Friends Meeting House** (137-16 Northern Boulevard), built in 1694–1695, is still in use by Quakers. From there, head east on Northern Boulevard to Bowne Street, just 1½ blocks away, and turn right (south). You'll soon reach the head-quarters of the **Queens Historical Society** (143-35 37th Avenue), located in a park that you can't miss. For more information go to www.preserve. org/queens/. It's located in the Kingsland Mansion, which was built in 1785. The large Weeping Beech Tree, fenced in in a park near the mansion's entrance, was brought to the United States from Belgium in 1847 and is the only living historic monument in this country. Near the "mansion" (the term is relative!) is the **John Bowne House** (37-01 Bowne Street), built in 1661. Bowne was a Quaker who fought for religious tolerance at a time when such views were in the minority.

Although not formally on the Freedom Mile, some other sites show-case Flushing's amazing religious diversity. If you walk one block east on 38th Avenue from Bowne Street to Parsons Boulevard, you'll come to the **Sikh Center of Flushing** (38-17 Parsons Boulevard), which sits opposite **Gates of Prayer Synagogue** (38-20 Parsons Boulevard), Flushing's oldest synagogue. It was founded in 1900 but the current building is relatively new. Back on Bowne Street, keep walking south and you'll reach the Ganesh Temple complex at 45-57 Bowne Street at Holly Street (see page 38).

By the way, this part of the walk will allow you to see a Flushing that the rest of this chapter doesn't cover. Although the community is quite diverse, the Latin American, Eastern European, and other markets catering to greater Flushing are located off the main roads. En route to the temple you'll see a lovely Salvadoran restaurant, a Colombian market, and a Russian deli.

From the Ganesh Temple, head west on Holly Street for one block to Kissena Boulevard. There you'll see the **Hindu Center** (45-52 Kissena Boulevard), and if you backtrack one block on Kissena Boulevard you'll see the **Muslim Center of Flushing** (137-58 Geranium Street). Continue back on Kissena Boulevard heading downtown. At Maple Avenue, on your left, you'll see the **Free Synagogue of Flushing** (41-60 Kissena Boulevard).

Founded in 1917, it was the first Reform Jewish congregation in Queens and is noted for the leadership role played by women. At Main Street and 38th Avenue, in the heart of downtown, you can't miss **St. George's Episcopal Church** (135-32 38th Avenue). Originally founded in 1702, its current building dates to 1854. Several dozen tombstones, many dating from that era, fill the modest lawn around the church. Cross Main Street again and head east on 39th Avenue. You'll soon see the huge **China Buddhist Association** (136-12 39th Avenue). Continue on 39th Avenue and turn left on to Union Street. Pass the municipal parking lot and you'll come to your last stop: the **A.M.E. Macedonia Church** (37-22 Union Street) in the heart of Korean Flushing. This church was once a stop on the Underground Railroad.

An amazing mile (and then some)!

▪ Off the Eaten Path . . .

I highly recommend a visit to the neo-Georgian **Flushing Post Office** at Main Street and Sanford Street, built in 1932. The walls are covered with fanciful murals envisioning early Queens painted by Vincent Aderente. The images are wonderful.

▪ Queens Botanical Gardens

A brisk twelve-minute walk from the #7 train will take you to the **Queens Botanical Gardens** (43-50 Main Street), and a world away from the bustle of downtown Flushing. It provides both a colorful and calm respite and offers a wonderful opportunity for Flushing explorers to learn more about the botanical history of the area (the nation's first nurseries were in Flushing) and the ethnic origins of the plants and produce available here.

To get there by subway, take the #7 train to Main Street and walk south, through Chinese and South Asian Flushing. (You'll pass the glass-sheathed Flushing Public Library en route.) For driving directions, call 718-886-3800 or go to www.queensbotanical.org.

For several years now, the gardens have supported a gardener-in-residence, whose responsibilities include researching the cross-cultural culinary, health, and religious significance of the plants, produce, herbs, and spices available at local markets. The gardener-in-residence also maintains a diverse herb garden, helps run educational programs, and participates in community outreach, developing links to local markets. I was fortunate enough to be able to work with one of the gardeners, the talented

Erin Moriarty, who has since gone on to study landscape architecture at Cornell. We developed and led a Flushing NoshWalk together.

...

Jackson Heights

Revisiting Jackson Heights, Queens, for the first time in a decade, I was impressed by the staying power of the neighborhood. Its ethnic mix of mostly South Asian and Latin American areas has remained intact, but it is more intense now, more exciting—and more diverse.

The economic boom has made its mark. In the early 1990s, Patel Brothers market on the west side of 74th Street crammed huge inventory into a claustrophobic space. In 1998, Patel opened a huge, modern super-market across the street. Jackson Diner was really a diner—with some Indian dishes—when I first visited in 1985 (you could get scrambled eggs and other diner fare along with *samosas* and *roti*); today it's in a new, larger space up the street and offers an elaborate menu of Indian specialties. Only the name has remained the same.

Colombian cafés, restaurants, and markets are everywhere, from sim-ple snack bars to full-service restaurants. The presence of the cultures of Ecuador, Peru, Mexico, and Uruguay is strong.

While Jackson Heights revels in its ethnic diversity, it also celebrates a fine architectural history: in 1993, residents won landmark status for

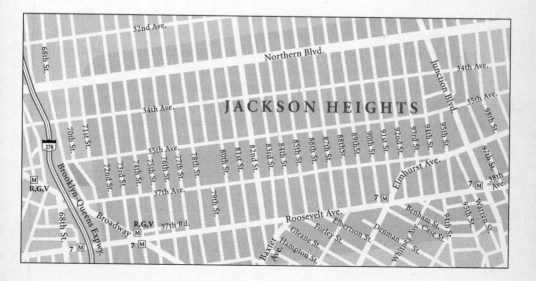

several clusters of housing. It's a great place not just for eating and shopping, but also to live.

I sometimes wonder how the area balances the old and the new. From my readings and conversations I gather it has not been easy—but somehow it appears to be working. Visit the Jackson Heights library at 35-51 81st Street or watch parents waiting to pick up their kids weekday afternoons at P.S. 69 (37th Avenue, between 77th and 78th streets), and you'll see the world in a few blocks. It's a great sight: Welcome to New York!

■ History

How did Jackson Heights get its name? I wondered. Unlike communities named after early settler families or Native Americans who had lived there previously, the naming of Jackson Heights was evidently a political plum for John Jackson, president of the Hunterspoint and Flushing Turnpike Company. Jackson's firm built the road that became Northern Boulevard and helped create the grid of this community-to-be whose growth was sparked by the opening of the Queensborough Bridge in 1909 and hastened by the completion of the elevated train in 1917.

Folks credit the rise of Jackson Heights itself to developer Edward Archibald MacDougall, head of the Queensboro Corporation. In 1909 he began buying land and in 1910 started building one- and two-family brick houses, later adding garden apartments with interior garden courtyards along with playgrounds, tennis courts, a golf course, a community newspaper, and a family clubhouse.

In the 1920s, a number of the Queensboro apartments were converted into cooperatives, long before co-op living had become popular. By the time of the Depression, however, a number of the co-ops failed. (Sunnyside Gardens witnessed some parallel patterns.) In one account I read, a resident recalled how her family moved from a $125-a-month apartment to a top-floor $75-per-month rental, and then short time later the rent fell to just $55.

The next major wave of development came after World War II, with the construction of large apartment complexes for growing families at the start of the baby boom. Some of the open space left from the MacDougall era was filled in with buildings. Gradually Jackson Heights, previously almost all white—largely Irish and Italian—began to become more racially and religiously diverse.

By the 1960s, new development on Long Island prompted upwardly-mobile families to leave Queens for Nassau County. These people gradually were replaced by immigrants from South America and Asia and, later, Eastern Europe. This process has continued into the present, with Mexicans as the most recent arrivals.

In 1988, long-time residents committed to community preservation, focusing on the area's best housing, formed the Jackson Heights Beautification Group. In 1993 it succeeded in winning designation of a portion of Jackson Heights as Queens's second historic district by the New York City Landmarks Preservation Commission. The core of this area spans 34th and 37th Avenues between 77th and 88th Streets (mostly the side streets). You can see two beautiful examples at the Chateau Apartments (34th Avenue between 80th and 81st Streets) and the McAvoy Tudor-style houses (87th and 88th Streets between 35th and 37th Avenues). You also can check out the so-called English Convertible Country Homes of 84th to 86th Streets.

For more information on Jackson Heights, go to the Jackson Heights Beautification Group's Web site, www.preserve.org/jhbg/jhbg.htm or call 212-439-8784 for the brochure "Historic Jackson Heights." For more neighborhood history, you can order a copy of *Jackson Heights: A Garden in the City*, written by Jackson Heights Beautification Group member Daniel Karatzas. Send a check or money order for $15 to Jackson Heights Beautification Group, P.O. Box 253, Jackson Heights, New York, 11372.

■ Getting Oriented

The boundaries of Jackson Heights go west to east, 72nd Street to Junction Boulevard (96th Street), bordered on the north by 32nd Avenue and on the south by Roosevelt Avenue. (The south side of Roosevelt Avenue is still Jackson Heights, but shops on the side streets to the south are in Elmhurst.) This tour focuses on a narrow area of Jackson Heights, as indicated by the map: Roosevelt and 37th Avenues, which go east-west, and the north-south boundaries of 72nd Street on the west and Junction Boulevard on the east, which forms the boundary with Corona. I've planned this section for walkers using mass transit, so I've omitted Northern Boulevard, which has many restaurants and shops but is a bit far for pedestrians and not nearly as much fun for wandering and window-shopping.

BY SUBWAY

As I mentioned on the Flushing Tour (see page 25), the busy #7 subway line is often referred to as the International Express because it truly takes you on a multicultural journey. Four of its stops are in Jackson Heights: 74th Street, 82nd Street, 90th Street, and Junction Boulevard. The E, F, G, and R trains all stop at 74th Street and Roosevelt Avenue but then veer off toward Elmhurst, Forest Hills, and Jamaica. I prefer the #7 because it's elevated, but be aware that *some* Flushing-bound #7 trains runs express weekday afternoons and evenings, skipping 74th, 82nd, and 90th Streets. So if you're traveling during the week at these hours, check first before you get on.

BY BUS

Queens bus routes tend to be convoluted, but a number of routes (the Q33, Q47, Q66, Q72, and Q198) go to or through Jackson Heights. The Q32 links Jackson Heights to Manhattan's Penn Station. Many public libraries have bus maps, and you can also check www.mta/nyc.ny.us for more information or phone (718)-330-1234.

BY CAR

Drive at your risk. On weekends the area is maddening for drivers (and for pedestrians trying to cross streets). But, if you must drive, there's a big parking lot at Broadway and 78th Street in Elmhurst. Here are some directions, courtesy of the Jackson Heights Beautification Group: from elsewhere in Queens and Long Island, take the Grand Central Parkway west to the Marine Air Terminal exit. Turn left onto 82nd Street, to 37th Avenue. From Brooklyn, take the Brooklyn-Queens Expressway (278) east to the Northern Boulevard exit. Turn right onto Northern Boulevard and proceed to 82nd Street. At 82nd Street, turn right to 37th Avenue. From Manhattan, cross the Queensboro Bridge and take Northern Boulevard to 82nd Street, and follow instructions above. From the Bronx and Westchester, cross the Triborough Bridge to Queens (left toll lanes) and proceed east on the Grand Central Parkway to the Marine Air Terminal, and follow instructions above.

BY TRAIN

If you take a Long Island Railroad train that stops in Jamaica you can connect to a train that stops in Woodside, Queens, where you can connect directly to the #7 train by walking up a flight of stairs or taking the elevator. Call 718-217-LIRR for schedule information or check www.mta.nyc.ny.us/lirr.

▪ Tips for Touring

You can walk the neighborhood in a day, but I suggest dividing it into three separate day trips instead:

- One to the South Asian area
- One focusing on the Latin American (and other) areas

■ One exploring the historic district, stopping for a delicious lunch and shopping expedition in either of the first two areas

Be careful in your wanderings, especially on Roosevelt Avenue, where traffic can be treacherous and drivers often turn abruptly at intersections. Jaywalking can be dangerous in this area and definitely is not recommended.

Another great pleasure of this tour is the non-food shopping you can do. Quite a few markets sell crafts such as Mexican blankets or wall hangings and there also are some great music stores.

■ Green Space

The section of Jackson Heights profiled here has almost no easily-accessible green space—not even a playground—close to the shopping and eating areas. You can find some farther away near the more residential areas of 34th and 35th Avenues, but it's a long walk. Thankfully, the café culture in the Latin American areas is alive and well, so you can nurse a cup of coffee or tea or a *batido* and pastry while resting your tired feet.

■ Off the Eaten Path . . .

The **Jackson Heights Historic District** contains some of the most lovely apartment dwellings in Queens. They are not so much historic—the best buildings came up in the 1920s and thirties—as they are excellent examples of how high-density urban living can still be spacious and humane. Apartments here are taller and more densely constructed than those in Sunnyside Gardens, where many of the homes and apartments are two or three stories only, and where many blocks are made up of attached single-family dwellings. The loveliest blocks in Jackson Heights reflect a style and quality of life that is hard to find in neighborhoods of this density, which explains the neighborhood's continued appeal. Bear in mind that originally the area had much more open space, with tennis courts and parks, but this space was soon filled in and the texture of the area began to change greatly.

...

South Asian Jackson Heights

According to Kenneth Jackson's *Encyclopedia of New York City*, South Asians began to settle in Jackson Heights in the mid-1970s, following the lead of Sam and Raj (37-08 74th Street) the area's first Indian-owned business. The location of this electronics store, near excellent transport and halfway between Manhattan and Long Island, began to attract more Indian entrepreneurs and eventually other South Asians.

I decided to check out Sam and Raj, and met Sam—Subhash Kapadia—who still presides over the operation. (His partner, Raj Gandhi, went into the real estate business some time ago.) Once the only Indian-owned business in the neighborhood, now it is surrounded by jewelry shops, music stores, beauty parlors, sari emporiums, groceries, travel agencies, bakeries, and, of course, restaurants catering to palates in search of the cuisines of South Asia.

Sam is grateful for the opportunities he has had here, but times have changed. He once owned more stores, but as electronics have become more readily available in India, the demand here has decreased, and he cut back. But the area remains a healthy place to do business, especially as it has further diversified. The Indian presence is still large but now there is also a large community of Pakistanis and Bangladeshis that, Sam estimates, represents about half of the community. This influence can be seen in stores that stock Muslim religious goods and in some restaurants that do not serve alcohol.

Getting There   The South Asian section of Jackson Heights is concentrated in a crowded area of 74th Street between Roosevelt and 37th Avenues and along 37th Avenue from 72nd through 75th Streets, with some spillover onto other side streets and a little further. I highly recommend that you don't drive here, especially on weekends, as traffic moves slowly and is often clogged. Mass transit is far better!

Markets   **Patel Brothers** (37-27 74th Street, 718-898-3445) is the superstore of Indian Jackson Heights, occupying what was once a Key Food supermarket. You'll find everything here—fresh produce, packaged and frozen goods, cooking utensils, spices, and toiletries from India. Although it lacks the character of the two markets listed below, it doesn't get too crowded and is very efficient, so if you're in a hurry, shop here. For produce (and everything else) your best bet is **Apna Bazaar Cash and Carry** (72-20 37th Avenue). Next door busy **Subzi Mandi** (72-30 37th Avenue) carries much of the same inventory but seems less crowded. Check out the tiled murals by Mrinal Haque (see page 48), located along the 73rd Street side of the store, that depict the twenty-one-year war that led to the creation of Bangladesh.

Restaurants The selection here is daunting, from basic snack bars to fancy dining, with several fine vegetarian places. All-you-can-eat lunch buffets for $5.99 (more on weekends and holidays) are popular weekday attractions. They will usually include rice pudding for dessert—if you have any room left. I visited just a few of the many places that offer this buffet. I had to revisit **Jackson Diner** (37-47 74th Street, 718-672-1232), which is known as much for its unusual name as its fine food at good prices. Few folks remember when it was really a diner at 37-03 74th Street. A Pakistani place called **Al-Naimat** (718-476-1100) now stands at this location. I am one of the people who does remember—and I mentioned it back then in my previous book *The Food Lover's Guide to the Real New York*. Most impressive—aside from the lovely decor—is the extensive menu that offers ten different *tandoor* dishes baked in a traditional clay oven, a *tandoori* deluxe, a large vegetarian selection, and nine *tandoori* breads. Even the buffet has more choices than those I've seen elsewhere, offering about ten entrées along with various chutneys and other complements. **Kabab and Curry—Eat In/Take-Out** has two neighborhood locations: 72-18 37th Avenue (718-476-2300) the nicer of the two, and 37-66 74th Street (718-429-0505). The 37th Avenue spot has some of Mrinal Haque's artwork and a lovely buffet, with a *tandoori* fish specialty. Another specialty is *tandoori* quail. **Kabab King Palace** (74-16 37th Road; entrance also at 74-15 Roosevelt Avenue; 718-205-8800) advertises halal Chinese dishes and Nepalese cuisine in addition to *tandoori,* and *tawa* (grilled) dishes and many curries. And you can see still more murals by Mrinal Haque there. I had a fine lunch there but was put off by the plastic forks and glaring fluorescent lights that make the place feel like a factory cafeteria. For the same price but with nicer ambiance, try either **Ashoka** (74-14 37th Avenue, 718-898-5088) or **Delhi Palace** (37-33 74th Street, 718-507-0666). Ashoka offers a great mixed grill appetizer for two for $7.95, along with *tandoor* specialties and several kebabs. Delhi Palace has a huge menu and is one of my favorite places.

VEGETARIAN OPTIONS

Anand Bhavan (35-66 73rd Street, 718-507-1600) occupies a space that once belonged to Udupi, a vegetarian place that specialized in *uthappam,* a type of pancake. (The owners of Delhi Palace also owned Udupi, and now include four types of *uthappam* on their menu.) Anand Bhavan serves six types of *uthappam* and bargain-priced lunch specials, from $5 to $7, which include a variety of tastes. The setting is attractive and Indian music plays in the background, but be warned—service can be slow. I was told that the Lunch Express would be ready in thirty minutes. Next door is **Dimple** (35-68 73rd Street, 718-458-8144; also at 11 West 30th Street in

ALOO GOBI (CURRIED CAULIFLOWER)

Courtesy of Manjit Singh of Jackson Diner in Jackson Heights, Queens

6 tablespoons cooking oil
1 ½ teaspoons cumin seeds
1 tablespoon ginger paste
1 tablespoon finely chopped garlic
½ onion, chopped or diced
1 tomato, diced
Salt and hot chili powder to taste
1 teaspoon turmeric
1 teaspoon garam masala
1 large potato, peeled and diced
1 head cauliflower, cut into small pieces
Chopped cilantro for garnish

1. Heat the oil in a deep frying pan over medium heat.
2. Add the cumin seeds and cook until they start to brown, about 1 minute.
3. Add the ginger paste, garlic, and onion and cook over medium heat until the onion starts to brown.
4. Add the tomato, salt, and spices and cook 5 minutes under a medium-low heat.
5. Add the potato and cook, covered, over a low heat, for about 8 minutes, stirring occasionally.
6. Add the cauliflower and cook, covered, over a low heat, stirring occasionally, for 10 to 15 minutes.
7. Garnish with the cilantro.

Manhattan, 212-643-9464), a crowded and informal fast-food place. I enjoy both places, but prefer Dimple for its quick service and wide array of choices.

Most Indian restaurants also offer delicious traditional milk or honey-soaked sweets. My favorite place for sweets is **Rajbhog Sweets and Snacks** (72-27 37th Avenue, 718-458-8512), an unpretentious, busy, fast-food vegetarian eatery. If you don't mind the lack of ambiance, you'll find inexpensive, complete meals and desserts here, and you also will be able to select from a large variety of hot, crunchy lentil, chickpea, and other snacks from bins near the back. Rajbhog manufactures and sells frozen foods and ice cream as well. Frozen entrées usually cost $2.50 each but on one visit I bought three for $7. You can also order their products from www.rajbhog.com.

▪ Good Reading

Don't miss **Butala Emporium** (37-46 74th Street), an amazing bookstore (and much, much more), or check out their Web site, www.indousbooks. com. This two-story treasure trove offers a large selection of books, incense, jewelry, textiles, clothing, and musical instruments, and it's a joy to explore. (In 2002, Butala opened a shop in Manhattan's Curry Hill at 108 East 28th Street.)

Also ... As you explore South Asian Jackson Heights, you might notice elaborate tile murals in front of some markets and restaurants. You'll see some of the same style of murals inside the restaurants, along with paintings and stained glass depicting daily life in Bangladesh or the revolutionaries who helped secure that country's freedom. These are the works of Mrinal Haque, a Bangladeshi artist who moved to New York in 1996 and has created paintings and murals in dozens of restaurants and retail shops in New York City and Long Island. Working in many media—painting, stained glass, sculpture, and mosaics crafted from basic bathroom tile—Haque is unique in this community. And few in Bangladesh have been as prolific as he. When he was just in his twenties he received commissions from major businesses, governmental agencies, and foreign diplomats. His work can be seen today at embassies, private estates, and public places in Bangladesh.

▪ ▪ ▪

Colombian Jackson Heights

Of the Latin American countries represented in Jackson Heights, Colombia dominates by far. Colombian restaurants, bakeries, and markets, and other Colombian-owned businesses dot Roosevelt and 37th Avenues. Many places also advertise Colombian-Ecuadorian cuisine. *Arepas,* cornmeal cakes that are a specialty of Colombia, are eaten at any time of the day, sometimes as an accompaniment to a meal, sometimes as a stand-alone snack. The popular *arepas con queso* (*arepas* with melted cheese) are quite filling. Or you can have dessert *arepas* served with a sweet spread. Colombian rotisserie chicken is also very popular. A whole chicken can be had for as little as $5.50 at La Estancia Antioqueña (86-20 37th Avenue). Many of the restaurants have live music on weekends.

Getting There   Go to 82nd Street on the #7 elevated line. All sorts of eateries can be found in this area—Roosevelt Avenue from 72nd Street through 96th Street—from informal fast-food places to those with waiter service and a slower pace. Then there are the bakery-cafés that serve meals and the juice bars that provide drinks and snacks for folks on the run.

Markets   The produce and packaged products sold in the large supermarkets in Jackson Heights target Latin American shoppers. But it's more fun to visit the smaller markets, which sometimes double as social venues. These markets also sell cooking utensils, CDs, videos, and newspapers from home. The Colombian markets have large meat sections and may be referred to as *carnicerias* (butchers) but they actually offer a full range of food products. My two favorites are on 37th Avenue: **La Risaralda Corp.** (91-02 37th Avenue) and **Carniceria HispanoAmericana** (89-22 37th Avenue). La Risaralda has the bigger inventory, featuring frozen fruit from the Andes used to make some of the more unusual juices found in juice bars, frozen potatoes and corn from Peru, and a variety of types and sizes of *arepas,* to name a few.

Juice Bars/Snackeries   Fresh tropical fruit and vegetable juices can be found all over Latin America and the Caribbean, sometimes in combinations with unusual names such as *Amor Prohibido* (forbidden love), which is a brandy, honey, milk, and egg combination popular in Colombia. Colombian juice bars, some freestanding, some inside bakeries, can be found all over Jackson Heights. And many restaurants also offer a large selection of juices. **Los Chuzos** (79-01 Roosevelt Avenue, 718-651-7709), with a second branch in Woodside at 64-14 Roosevelt Avenue, offers vegetable juice combos with choices such as spinach, *apoi* and *remolacha,* carrot and orange, and carrot, beet, and orange. Los Chuzos also features snacks such as *arepas,* sausage, chicken nuggets, and fancy hot dogs called "Lucky Dogs." At the popular **Tropigood!** (90-31 37th Avenue, 718-507-2208) you can order sandwiches, juices, empanadas, and desserts, and nothing is more than $5. Service is fast and informal and it's a hangout for neighborhood kids. **Casa Latina** (90-02 37th Avenue) is a Colombian supermarket that ordinarily wouldn't stand out if it wasn't for its *choladeria,* or cholado bar, that sells this wonderful Colombian iced drink that's a cross between a thick fruit shake and an ice cream sundae. It's made with shaved ice, sweetened condensed milk, fruit syrups, and fresh fruit and whipped cream, and is big, beautiful, tempting, and loaded with delicious, scrumptious, fabulous calories. All this for $3, and no one I know can drink (or eat—you really do need a spoon!) a whole one on his or her own.

Bakeries/Restaurants   La Gata Golosa (89-01 37th Avenue, 718-651-0788) is a typical, cute neighborhood place where you can get snacks or complete meals without much of a wait. I ordered a *batido* made with the wine-tree tomato, which is a typical Colombian fruit. I didn't think it would taste like a real tomato, but sure enough, the drink was the closest to a ketchup milk shake I've ever had! **Cositas Ricas** restaurant-bakery (79-19 Roosevelt Avenue, 718-478-1500) is bright, large, modern, and always packed. They serve pastry and cappuccino at the counter and full meals at the tables. They make seven types of *arepas,* with fillings such as chicken and guacamole, shrimp, and pork sausage. Italian-style gelati are available year-round. One patron likened it to places she knew in Medellín. **Aquí Colombia** (86-10 Roosevelt Avenue, 718-478-9502) serves *antojitos* (snacks), baked goods, and full meals at its four tables. No one there speaks English but they were friendly and patient during my attempts to describe what I wanted—an *arepa* with cheese.

Restaurants   These are two selections from a long list of choices. The family-friendly **Casa Colombia** (86-23 Roosevelt Avenue, 718-779-6459) is a sunny, attractive, 24-hour place with excellent service. I had an enjoyable light lunch there of a hearty mashed plantain soup and a mixed fruit *batido.* The entrée-size soup comes with rice and a shredded lettuce-and-vegetable salad. All this was under $9. Be forewarned, though, that what may seem to be a vegetarian dish often is not; the plantain soup had meat. **La Boina Roja,** or Red Beret (80-22 37th Avenue, 718-424-6711) may be the most upscale Colombian restaurant in Jackson Heights. I had a delicious chicken in orange sauce, which came with rice and salad and carrot-orange juice, for less than $13. A second branch, **La Boina Roja II,** at 77-05 A 37th Avenue (718-429-2500) opened in 2002. A Colombian taxi driver I met recommends **Listo El Pollo** (86-02 37th Avenue, 718-779-7595) and a local artist I met likes **Tierras Colombianas** (82-18 Roosevelt Avenue, 718-426-8868), which has an excellent menu and also has a larger counterpart in Astoria.

■ ■ ■

Argentinian Jackson Heights

Restaurants   For great Argentinian cuisine in Jackson Heights, check out **La Cabana Argentina** (95-51 Roosevelt Avenue, 718-429-4388, with another location at 86-07 Northern Boulevard). You can see their menu at www.laca-banaargentina.com. They serve the usual *parrillada* (mixed grill) with prices ranging from $3.50 to $17.50. Chicken entrées are all $13.50 and pasta dishes are from $8.95 to $13.50. Though prices may seem low, everything is à la carte, so most side dishes are extra. At the bar at **La Porteña** (74-25 37th

Avenue, 718-458-8111; www.paradero.com/laportena) an autographed photograph of Donald Trump reminds you that he's a Queens native. The place is attractive and busy, the prices are very Queens ($3 for sausage, $15 for a mixed grill, and $13 to $15 for chicken entrées), and there is an ample choice of salads and pastas for a vegetarian to eat well in the Argentinian meat culture.

Bakeries   Confitería Buenos Aires (90-09 Roosevelt Avenue, 718-672-4046, with a branch on Flagler Street in Miami) is a small, crowded place specializing in miniature European-style pastries. No place to drink coffee, alas, but you can sit down for a cup at **El Hornero** bakery (96-08 Roosevelt Avenue, 718-651-0400), which primarily sells Argentinian and Uruguayan specialties—*dulce de leche, maté,* and *alfajores* (wafers). The owners actually are a Colombian-Dominican couple, so you'll also find Colombian and Dominican pastries and breads. (To learn more about the Argentinian and Uruguayan presence in Queens, go to www.caminito.com.)

Markets   Don Francisco 2000 (85-17 37th Avenue, 718-505-5892) is a new Argentinian meat market and grocery that features all the makings for mixed grill as well as pastas from Argentina and other imports. In addition to Argentinian products (including several flavors of "yerba mate," the popular herbal tea drunk in that part of the world, such as lemon, orange, and apple), I noticed Peruvian pepper pastes, mineral water from Uruguay, and other interesting imports, along with the beef required to prepare Argentinian parrilla.

• • •

Ecuadorian Jackson Heights

Restaurants   I've tried three places in this area: **Hornado Ecuatoriano** (81-10 Roosevelt Avenue, 718-651-6162), the fanciest of the three, with a large menu, **Gus** (80-26 Roosevelt Avenue, 718-396-9890), which is very basic, with paper plates and plastic forks, but reliable and popular, and **La Picada Azuaya** (84-19 37th Avenue, 718-424-9797), somewhere in between. I love the shrimp *ceviche,* which comes with *tostados* (salted, toasted kernels of corn). The kernels of Ecuadorian corn are large, which allows you to really taste their nutty centers. The specialty here is *hornado,* a shredded pork dish that's marinated in a special sauce.

Snackeries   An office building on Roosevelt Avenue with lots of small shops on street level is home to a couple of Ecuadorian places. They are quite different from one another, and both are terrific. **Sabor Típico** (86-10 Roosevelt Avenue) has a homey atmosphere and six tables, and features many Ecuadorian specialties such as *morocho,* a vanilla-custardy type of dessert, and *tostados*. A few doors down in that same building, **El Pequeño Coffee Shop** is just that—a small coffee shop that happens to be Ecuadorian and serves some Ecuadorian specialties.

Markets   I was delighted to discover **Los Paisanos market** (79-16 Roosevelt Avenue, 718-898-4141), which has the best selection of imported foodstuffs from Ecuador and Peru that I've found in Jackson Heights. They sell beans, dried potatoes, several types of large corn including the purple corn used in Peruvian dishes, and *maiz* for *tostados,* along with cooking utensils. They also carry *Famosa* beer from Guatemala, *Cuzco* beer from Peru, and *Baranquilla* beer from Colombia.

• • •

Salvadoran Jackson Heights

Restaurants   **Tierras Salvadoreñas** (94-16 37th Avenue, 718-672-0853) is one of the larger, more colorful Salvadoran restaurants I've seen in New York City, and the only one I know of in Jackson Heights. They boast a substantial menu of *platos típicos* such as *pupusas,* which are corn cakes similar to Colombian *arepas; tamales;* and various beef and seafood specialties). I enjoyed a platter of *pupusas* topped with spicy slaw and salsa, served with sweet plantains and refried beans with cream. Not great if you're on a diet, but it was delicious. I had *horchata*, a cinnamon-flavored almond drink, to go with the meal. Try a tasty Salvadoran quesadilla, a type of corn bread made with sweet cheese, much different from the Mexican version.

• • •

Mexican Jackson Heights

Markets and Bakeries   Check out **Natella** (94-27 37th Avenue) for produce and **Susana's** (94-25 37th Avenue) next door for packaged goods—they have everything! **Mi Bello Mexico** (87-17 Roosevelt Avenue) is a new market featuring Mexican and Peruvian products. Here I found Peruvian *huincana* sauce mix, a mix to make a Peruvian purple corn drink, and *chipotle*-flavored *tostados*. **Cholula Bakery, Panadería and Pastelería** (88-06 Roosevelt Avenue, 718-533-1171) sells Mexican pastries as well as sandwiches, breakfasts, *tamales,* and *empanadas,* typical of Cholula in the Mexican state of Puebla.

Restaurants   Since I was focusing on food that I wouldn't find elsewhere, I tried just one Mexican restaurant in Jackson Heights, **Plaza Garibaldi** (89-12 Roosevelt Avenue, 718-651-9722), an animated, popular family place that sells Plaza Garibaldi T-shirts and Mexican toys including harmonicas, wooden airplanes, tops, and dollhouse miniatures along with your meal. I was drawn in part by the children's menu—a rarity in neighborhoods I research. Two kids from our group ordered *hamburguesas y papas fritas* (hamburgers and French fries) while the grown-ups had excellent fajitas, enchiladas, tacos, quesadillas, and avocado salads.

. . .

Peruvian Jackson Heights

Restaurants   **La Casa del Pollo** (87-07 Roosevelt Avenue; closed Mondays) is part of a small chain of Peruvian chicken places owned by Percy Tan, who has a Chinese background and grew up in Peru. The menu combines Peruvian dishes ("The marinade is secret!" Percy warns) with Chinese specialties, so you'll find Chinese fried rice, spare ribs, and lo mein alongside the yucca and plantains. This is more or less a fast-food place— you order at the counter but then you're seated and your meal is brought to you. Soups include *aguadito* (rice and giblets) and wonton. Don't call— there's no delivery and they don't take reservations, but there *are* lines! **Don Alex** (95-04 37th Avenue, 718-424-5187; closed Tuesdays) is a small, quiet, and friendly place. I had two appetizers there: potatoes *a la huinicana* (a spicy sauce) and seafood *ceviche*, followed by a purple corn drink, which at $15, made a hearty lunch. In 2001, Mr. Tan got a little competition when a larger place, **NYS Best Peruvian Chicken** (84-10 37th Avenue) opened, featuring an outstanding menu of Peruvian and Chinese specials. **El Rey del Buffet** (86-22 Roosevelt Avenue, 718-396-2206) is Peruvian owned but offers a Latin American buffet of chicken, pork, rice and bean dishes, side dishes, and a salad bar at $3.99 a pound. They also sell bottled drinks from Colombia, Ecuador, Peru, and the Dominican Republic.
Markets   Check out **Los Paisanos** (see page 53), **Mi Bello Mexico** (see page 53), and **La Risaralda** (see page 50).

...

Uruguayan Jackson Heights

Bakeries   La Nueva 2000 (86-10A 37th Avenue) is a large, modern, and energetic café specializing in Uruguayan, Argentinian, and Colombian pastries and snacks and Mexican breads. Try the *arrollados*: rolled sandwiches on a sweet challah-like bread with heart of palm, tuna, olives, greens, and tomatoes. In 2003, a second branch opened at 85-05 37th Avenue.

Restaurants   El Chivito d'Oro III (84-02 37th Avenue, 718-424-0600) is one of my favorite places in Jackson Heights, offering excellent and inex-

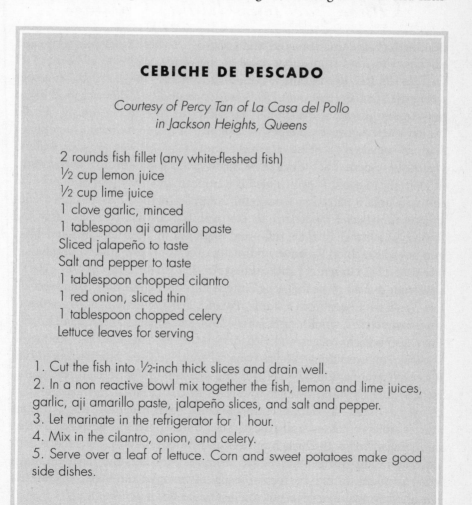

CEBICHE DE PESCADO

*Courtesy of Percy Tan of La Casa del Pollo
in Jackson Heights, Queens*

2 rounds fish fillet (any white-fleshed fish)
½ cup lemon juice
½ cup lime juice
1 clove garlic, minced
1 tablespoon aji amarillo paste
Sliced jalapeño to taste
Salt and pepper to taste
1 tablespoon chopped cilantro
1 red onion, sliced thin
1 tablespoon chopped celery
Lettuce leaves for serving

1. Cut the fish into ½-inch thick slices and drain well.
2. In a non reactive bowl mix together the fish, lemon and lime juices, garlic, aji amarillo paste, jalapeño slices, and salt and pepper.
3. Let marinate in the refrigerator for 1 hour.
4. Mix in the cilantro, onion, and celery.
5. Serve over a leaf of lettuce. Corn and sweet potatoes make good side dishes.

pensive take-out in a lovely atmosphere. In addition to the usual mixed grill, the menu includes Italian pastas, salads, and seafood and you can make a meal out of appetizers. I enjoyed half-servings of octopus salad, Russian salad, and shrimp, with thick-cut, spicy potatoes, for just $8. *Chivito* itself is a popular Uruguayan steak sandwich, sometimes served as a platter, prepared with lettuce, mayonnaise, tomato, ham, eggs, olives, cheese, and other accompaniments.

...

Other Jackson Heights Cuisines

Besides the Latin American and Asian places listed here, you'll find shops and eateries with food from other areas of the world. With the addition of **El Castillo del Rey Restaurant** (78-23 37th Avenue, 718-426-7272) in a spot where the Spanish restaurant Las Brasas once stood, Dominican food is just now becoming part of the culinary landscape in Jackson Heights. El Castillo del Rey's new owners have kept some Spanish dishes on the menu, including a Spanish *manchego* cheese appetizer and a pasta with mixed seafood (*mariscada*) sauce, but the extensive menu specializes in the wonderful range of Dominican cooking, which blends European and Caribbean influences. A simple plantain patty is a wonderful example: mashed plantain filled with spicy ground beef, wrapped in a banana leaf. The flavors blend delectably, and for just $2.50 you'll be quite full—and that's just to begin! El Castillo del Rey also has a branch on Broadway near City College of New York in Manhattan (see page 227). **Gourmet Fantasy Food** (75-28 37th Avenue, 718-446-4169) is a Russian-owned place that sells Eastern European and some Asian specialties. You'll find beer from Estonia, Poland, and Ukraine, many varieties of cheese, appetizers, smoked fish, jams, jellies, and Russian and Afghan breads. They also sell chocolates and rich desserts. They offer a 10% discount on Tuesdays, on everything except caviar, cake, and cookies. **Tibetan Yak** (72-20 Roosevelt Avenue, 718-779-1119) is one of a handful of Tibetan restaurants in New York City and is worth a visit for its calm ambiance, music, and, of course, its food. Vegetarian entrées include vegetable dumplings, various sautées, spicy potatoes, and pastas. Meat entrées include steamed or fried dumplings filled with chicken or beef and various curries. The food is delicious and inexpensive—entrées are no more than $12, and most are much less. You might want to try the *bocha*, lightly buttered and salted Tibetan tea. It is often an acquired taste, but you just might like it.

As you wander through Jackson Heights, you will see quite a few fortune-telling places and *botanicas* (shops selling Christian, African, and indigenous religious supplies). For a price they will offer solace and advice for whatever financial, personal, or other problems you may face. Several *botanicas* in Jackson Heights describe themselves as Mexican or Brazilian. **Indio Atahualpa** (84-28 37th Avenue) is a Mexican/Colombian/Peruvian *botanica* and **Botanica El Trebol** (90-12 37th Avenue) is a Brazilian *botanica.* On Roosevelt Avenue, you will pass two large and busy *botanicas,* both known as **El Indio Amazonico** (86-26 Roosevelt Avenue and 88-05 Roosevelt Avenue). A third storefront opened on 37th Avenue while I was working on this chapter. This operation looked more intriguing, and I've tried to set up a meeting with El Indio himself, but have not yet been able to do so.

•••

Sunnyside

When I began planning *NoshNews,* I wanted the very first issue to focus on a neighborhood with several specific qualities. First, it should be quite diverse, so a range of eating opportunities could be showcased. Second, it should be easy to get to. Third, it should be easy to explore and understand. And fourth, it should be a place that hadn't been covered everywhere else.

Sunnyside clearly fit the bill. Its ethnic range is amazing, it's close to Manhattan, the area is compact and doable in a day, and it's pretty, friendly, full of surprises, and rich in history. Yet for some reason, Sunnyside receives little attention in guidebooks.

■ History

Like many communities in New York's outer boroughs, indigenous peoples (in this case the Lenape, or Delaware Indians) originally inhabited the area of Queens and Long Island that is now known as Sunnyside.* (Indian objects estimated to be 5,000 years old have been discovered in Bayside!) When Dutch settlers bought the colony of New Amsterdam in 1626, the western portion of Queens became part of it. Newcomers from Holland, France, and England settled there and began naming towns, which are now known as Maspeth, Flushing, and Jamaica. By 1664, some Dutch names, including Kings County (Brooklyn) and Queens County, were changed to represent English royalty.

---

*Historical material in this section comes from *Small Town in the Big City: A History of Sunnyside and Woodside* by Pam Byers and the Local History Committee of the Sunnyside Community Service Center (Local History Committee of the Sunnyside Community Service Center, New York, 1976).

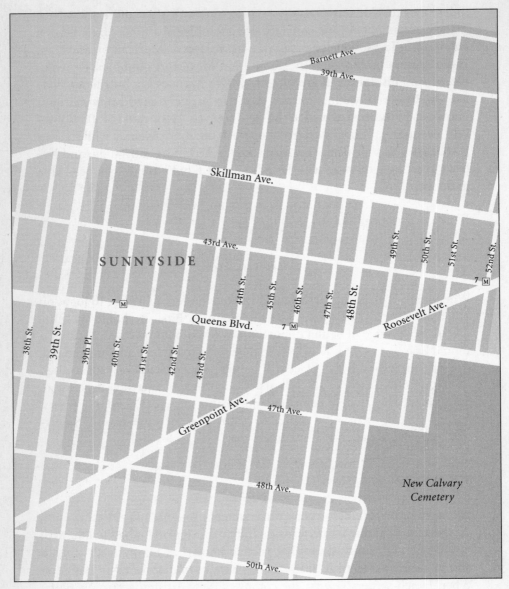

In the nineteenth century the communities of western Queens began
to develop rapidly. Proximity to ferries prompted the development of the
coastline areas of Astoria and Long Island City. The laying out of roadways,
then of railroads (reaching Woodside in 1861), offered housing speculators
plenty of opportunities to build. By 1891, maps of Sunnyside showed grids
marking streets and lots, although no real development would take place
until a few years later. During the first decade of the twentieth century the

quiet of Sunnyside was to change radically: subway construction began in 1903 and a huge rail yard was established in the area. The Queensborough Bridge opened in 1909, the Long Island Rail Road tunnel opened under the East River, and the #7 subway line from Manhattan (elevated in Queens), reached Long Island City by 1915, and further destinations over the next several years.

In the 1920s apartment buildings, mostly the three- to six-story buildings we see today, were being built throughout Sunnyside. But the landmark development of Sunnyside Gardens was the area's crown jewel. The great architecture critic and city planner Lewis Mumford was a major influence in the creation of Sunnyside Gardens in northern Sunnyside. Inspired by British gardens, he brought the idea of creating a humane urban environment for middle-class families, including common green space, light, and shared amenities (to maintain economies of scale), to New York builders who wanted to develop Sunnyside farmland. The seventy-seven-acre complex of low-rise attached houses and some apartment buildings was completed in 1924, and Mumford's family was among the first to move in. Just two miles from Manhattan, its tranquility and modest rents attracted a core of families that included so many artists and writers that it was dubbed "the maternity ward of Greenwich Village."

Although the Gardens represent just one part of Sunnyside, they're emblematic of the area's overall scale and appealing intimacy, which prompted historian Pam Byers to refer to it as "the small town in a big city." Sunnyside has managed to sustain both its small-town feel and its polyglot character without resulting in the acrimonious displacement of any one group. Sunnyside's Irish community remains vibrant as single young men and women keep arriving to kick-start their careers while others return home as they start families. And at the same time, the community is being transformed by newcomers from Southeast Asia, Latin America, the Middle East, and Turkey.

Yet within all this diversity some traditions hold fast. Joann Billharz, whose family's plumbing business has operated here since 1947, notes that Sunnyside sponsors New York City's only Flag Day parade.

How do people of so many backgrounds coexist so well? Lawyer Marc Crawford Leavitt, a longtime Sunnysider who practices in the neighborhood, attributes it to a tradition of tolerance and community involvement and perhaps an above-average number of ethnically or religiously mixed families, including his own. As he rattles off the nationalities and religious backgrounds of his immediate neighbors, each is different: Irish, Colombian, Trinidadian, and Orthodox Jew, for example. Rather than a melting pot, however, Sunnyside is closer to the "magnificent mosaic," a term used by former Mayor David Dinkins to celebrate the city's diversity.

▪ Getting Oriented

Queens Boulevard is the dividing line between two distinct neighborhoods. Northern Sunnyside is older, more settled, and a bit more affluent. Southern Sunnyside is more dynamic, with more activity and a larger turnover of shops and restaurants as many businesses move and expand within the neighborhood, the older stores being quickly replaced with newer bakeries and markets.

Sunnyside's northern boundary is Barnett Avenue and its southern boundary extends to 51st Avenue parallel to the Brooklyn-Queens Expressway. For some reason, there are no even numbered avenues in this area until 48th Avenue, so if you walk north or south from the elevated train station, the next avenues will be 43rd (due north) and 47th (due south). Greenpoint Avenue moves at a gentle diagonal through southern Sunnyside and creates little triangles of activity and some tricky intersections. Some do not have traffic lights, so cross carefully!

BY SUBWAY

Sunnyside can be reached by taking the #7 train to the 40th and 46th Street stops, about twenty minutes from Times Square. The area runs along Queens Boulevard (equivalent to 45th Avenue if you follow a numbered grid). The ride is lovely—much of it is elevated, with spectacular views of the Manhattan skyline.

BY BUS

The Q32 bus links Manhattan to Queens Boulevard, but it often gets caught up in traffic over the 59th Street Bridge.

BY CAR

Take the 59th Street Bridge (Queensborough Bridge) to Queens Boulevard, which heads directly into Sunnyside. The expressways skirting Sunnyside (Brooklyn-Queens Expressway and Long Island Expressway) also have Queens Boulevard exits. Sunnyside is located on Queens Boulevard between Van Dam Street (near 33rd Street) and 48th Street. You'll find ample parking under the subway overpass along Queens Boulevard.

...

Northern Sunnyside

Anchored by the landmark Sunnyside Gardens residential complex, northern Sunnyside provides a sense of settled-ness rare in neighborhoods where immigration is such a vital factor. It could be because the trees planted when the Gardens were built in the 1920s are now mature. They are generous shade trees that give this neighborhood an almost timeless feel. Yet here you'll find about as much variety as you'll see along Queens Boulevard and south of it: markets, restaurants, and a fancy sit-down bakery catering to Armenian, Indian, Bangladeshi, Pakistani, Turkish, Mexican, Lebanese, Romanian, and Ecuadorian tastes—and you.

Getting There   From the 40th or 46th Street subway stop on the #7 train walk along Queens Boulevard to 43rd Street and turn north (to your right if you're facing Manhattan, which you can't miss, with the Chrysler Building glistening in the distance) toward 43rd Avenue.

Markets   On your left you'll pass the small **Sunnyside Meat Market** (43-10 43rd Street), whose Romanian owner giggled when I bought a bottle of Drax Beer (with a fanged Dracula, blood dripping from his mouth, on the label). The bottle is marked "Brewed in Transylvania" and it is apparently produced for export only. Turn left toward **Massis** (42-20 43rd Avenue, 718-729-3749), a huge store catering mainly to Armenians, Lebanese, and Romanians. Named after a mountain in Armenia, the store was opened in 1991 by Raffi Bezdjian, who was raised in Lebanon by Armenian parents. You'll find a terrific selection of foods from all over the Mediterranean, and in super sizes. You can choose from huge tins of olive oil, jars of grape leaves, vats of tahini, and many types of feta cheese in big slabs. A specialty is a type of sausage called *basterma.* They also sell gift boxes of pastries and sweets and Romanian audio and video cassettes and CDs. I was tempted by an Armenian tango CD. Massis has a mail-order business and a Web site under construction (www.Massis.com). Heading west from Massis, just across the street, you'll find **El Shater** (43-62 43rd Avenue, 718-392-2702), an attractive, large Lebanese market that offers an excellent selection of meats and baked goods; fresh, prepared, and packaged foods; and an international selection of spices, nuts and dried fruit, syrups, and cheese. Some of their products, including pastas and juices, are organic. The prepared foods here include *kibbee* (Lebanese meatballs), terrific falafel (chickpea patties) and *baba ghanoush* (smoked eggplant dip), *tabboulleh* (bulgur salad), and *mujaadarah,* a lovely mixture of rice, onions, and lentils. Don't miss their honey-dipped, phyllo-wrapped pastries. Try the *halwat el-jouben,* an incredible pistachio-crusted cheese pastry with honey syrup, or the *basbousa,* honey-soaked squares made from farina, sesame oil, and honey, and covered with pistachio nuts. El Shater also sells cookware and gift items.

Continuing west toward 46th Street you'll come to **Sunny Grocery** (45-26 43rd Avenue, 718-937-6256), one of several Turkish markets in Sunnyside. (Turkish immigrants began settling in Sunnyside in the early 1980s, according to Nigar Evren, Sunny's proprietor.) Here you'll find a great selection of packaged foods and beverages, plus nuts and spices, even a packet of thirteen spices used for Turkish recipes. You'll also find some take-out foods, such as *gozleme,* the Turkish equivalent to a grilled cheese (or spinach or meat) sandwich, made with Turkish cheese and a type of flat bread, and mini-pies with spinach or cheese fillings. You can also indulge your sweet tooth with a vast selection of baked goods, including baklava. They also sell Sarelle, a delicious hazelnut cream often eaten on soft bread for breakfast.

Bakeries   Now head north (left) on 46th Street to Skillman Avenue, cross the street, and turn right to the lovely **Zoita's Bakery** (46-11 Skillman Avenue, 718-433-0339). It's a beautiful Romanian bakery-café that opened in early 2002, which adds something important to this neighborhood—a place to sit down and nurse a cappuccino while savoring a fabulous pastry. Continuing one block east you'll find **La Plaza Mexico** (47-19 Skillman Avenue), a Mexican grocery that has a few tables for *tamales* and *tortas.* At 47-31 Skillman Avenue you'll see **Turkieyem**. It has a fantastic Turkish Delight flavored with mint, rose, and lemon and *tulum peynir,* a spectacular cheese that starts off bland but gradually grasps your tongue with a marvelous tang.

A bit further (technically in Woodside), the French bakery **La Marjolaine** (50-17 Skillman Avenue, 718-651-0495) offers a great selection of breads made on the premises and pâtés, but I recommend the sinfully delicious cassis, pear, and passion mousse tarts, which melt in your mouth, or a packet of madeleines. Dunk them in cappuccino from Nancy's (see page 63).

Restaurants   One of the oldest restaurants in northern Sunnyside is the Romanian place **Transilvania** (43-46 42nd Street off Queens Boulevard, 718-786-9401), which offers an ample menu of seafood, veal, poultry, and beef stews. There also is entertainment—it's a nightclub on weekends. My first visit was on Christmas Eve of 1989, during the uprising in Romania. I found the dishes to be generous, the noise deafening, and the optimism of the crowd palpable. More recently I've gone at lunchtime, when business is slow, but it's best to make this an evening excursion so you can enjoy the crowds and music.

One block away, **Haji's Biriyani and Sweets** (43-45 43rd Street, 718-706-9718), a Bangladeshi, Indian, and Pakistani restaurant, specializes in *tandoori* dishes. Though mainly a fast-food place, the new owners have upgraded the interior. Curries are good and reasonably priced, and you can get a big box of Indian sweets for $5. On 43rd Avenue, walk six blocks to 49th Avenue and you'll find **Nancy's Trattoria and Grill** (49-07 43rd Avenue, 718-651-6802), an Argentinian restaurant which is actually in Woodside, as Sunnyside stops on the west side of 49th Street. Owner Tito Del Gobbo used to serve fantastic cappuccino from his nearby market, Flor de Cuba, in the 1980s, then set up an outdoor grill in 1991, and then opened a full-fledged restaurant in 1994. (He closed the market.) Here you can find the typical Argentinian *parrillada* (mixed grill) along with more conventional chicken and steak dishes. Argentinians traditionally eat supper *very* late, so unless there's a big soccer game on TV, the restaurant is often quiet during the early part of the day but busy later in the evening. **Rincon Latino** (48-18 Skillman Avenue, 718-424-8169) is a friendly, inexpensive Ecuadorian restaurant that offers traditional dishes such as plantain soup and many chicken and seafood dishes (with *ceviche* specialties). Most orders, except house specials, are between $4.50 and $6.50, and they include side dishes and one beverage.

   Romanian Garden (46-04 Skillman Avenue, 718-786-7894) was known as Cornel's Place in its original small space on Greenpoint Avenue. It moved here and changed names in 1999 and expanded from a handful of tables to seat twenty people to a large space for 120, and then changed owners. Skip the regular menu and go for the specials, such as stuffed cabbage with *mamaliga,* a luscious dish of polenta with cottage cheese and sour cream. I also recommend their terrific hardy winter vegetable soup, which comes with homemade bread.

- - -

Queens Boulevard

If you wander along Queens Boulevard between 39th and 47th Streets, you'll find a United Nations of small businesses—markets, restaurants, barbershops, storefront law offices—and an amazing diversity of tastes, sounds, and smells. There also are some terrific thrift shops.

Getting There   Exit at the south side of the #7 train's 40th Street elevated train stop and walk east toward 39th Street. (You'll see the Empire State Building in the distance.)

   Your first stop is **Casa Romana** (39-20 Queens Boulevard, 718-784-4768), a Romanian restaurant that offers a nice selection of cold and hot appetizers and meat stews. I made a vegetarian meal out of a few appetizers and salads. There's weekend music, for which you need to make a reservation. A half block up, **La Vienesa** (39-44 Queens Boulevard, 718-786-2924), a Colombian bakery which looked tired when I had visited it for my first issue of *NoshNews,* now has a spiffy new look and is busy and friendly. Its *arepas* (corn cakes) are delicious served warm with *queso blanco,* a mild white cheese. **The Butcher's Block** (41-12 Queens Boulevard, 718-784-1078) is the area's major Irish grocery, which sells both wholesale and retail. You can find Irish imports (including many more variations of Cadbury chocolate than I've seen anywhere else in the United States), delicious Irish breads and mustards (some flavored with beer), and locally made dishes such as black-and-white pudding and kidney stew, plus Irish periodicals, cassettes, and videos. **Sidetracks** (45-08 Queens Boulevard, 718-786-3570) is a popular gathering place for lunch, dinner (when it becomes a nightclub), and drinks. Its wood paneling, plush booths, and upholstered easy chairs placed around an old central bar offer a warm, homey setting that evokes an old-time railroad station. The walls are adorned with black-and-white photographs of vintage movies and railroad scenes. When I met owner Andy Breslin I had expected to see a patriarch whose family had been in Sunnyside for generations. But Andy is in his early forties and arrived in the United States from County Meath only in 1981. He's a true model of how hard work can lead to success: he now co-owns, with two brothers, two other Sunnyside restaurants and the Red Lion on Bleecker Street in Manhattan. And (though he's modest about this) he has been a generous donor to local civic groups. He told me that Sidetracks often hosts farewell parties for Irish families returning home.

The **Oasis Express Bakery** (45-18 Queens Boulevard) offers espresso and a large selection of traditional Mediterranean pastries. I recommend the *mousto kouloura* cookies, which are flavored with grape juice, a subtle complement to your espresso. Oasis is tiny and has a counter overlooking the boulevard with three stools—good for a quick snack before heading to the #7 train, which is across the street.

Cross Queens Boulevard at 47th Street and you'll find **Empire of India** (46-15 Queens Boulevard, 718-472-4100), one of Sunnyside's fancier restaurants, which has a great selection of curries and Indonesian dishes. I ordered a stunning *por ayam* (chicken in coconut cream sauce) with pineapples and nuts, served with *nasi goren* (Indonesian fried rice). One block down I found **El Buen Sabor** (45-07 Queens Boulevard, 718-361-8714), one of Sunnyside's nicer Colombian bakeries.

Continuing west, you'll find that the block between 42nd and 43rd Streets mirrors the area's diversity. **P. J. Horgan's** (42-17 Queens Boulevard) is an Irish restaurant with a traditional pub menu, and **Chips Mexican Grill and Rotisserie** (42-15 Queens Boulevard) serves what you might call Mexican "nouvelle cuisine" (or should I say *nueva cocina*?), with a nice menu of steak, chicken, pork, and seafood dishes. Next door, **Kim's Fish Market** (42-13 Queens Boulevard) sells fresh fish as well as sushi and sashimi. **Bucovina International Grocery** (42-07 Queens Boulevard) offers Eastern European and Mediterranean specialties including cheese, yogurt, and other dairy products, honey from around the world, various packaged goods such as cookies, syrups, and jams, and meat. **Mavi Turkish Cuisine** (42-03 Queens Boulevard, 718-392-3838) is very popular and is often packed. Here you'll find a full range of meat and vegetarian Turkish cooking, including Mediterranean dips, eggplant and yogurt appetizers, phyllo dough pies and dumplings, and various kebabs and grilled entrées of chicken, lamb, or ground beef, followed by baklava, rice pudding, or Turkish custard. Vegetarians can do fine with appetizers but there's also a vegetarian casserole entrée and a fresh-baked *karshari* cheese pita. You'll be hard-pressed to spend more than $20 for your meal. **Malik Grocery and Halal Meat Market** (42-01 Queens Boulevard) on the corner specializes in produce and other products from Southeast Asia. Are you out of breath yet?

Near the 40th Street elevated station, **Baruir's Coffee** (40-07 Queens Boulevard, 718-784-0842) has been selling coffee and Eastern European imports since Romanian-born Baruir Nersesian opened it in 1966. His son, Mike, runs it now, and you'll hear mostly Romanian spoken here—you can even buy a Romanian newspaper. You can see coffee beans roasting in the window—and smell them from the nearby train entrance—and sip espresso alongside a homemade pastry. I recommend their walnut crescents, which Baruir buys from a local Hungarian woman.

Dazie's Italian restaurant (39-41 Queens Boulevard, 718-786-7013) is a Sunnyside landmark. In contrast to the area's newcomers, Dazie's earthy, carpeted ambiance evokes an older Sunnyside, reminiscent of the restaurants my parents took me to as a treat when I was little and would get to wear my black patent-leather strapless shoes. Owner Lily Gavin welcomes you in as if this were her home, and, in a way, it is. She bought the place nearly thirty years ago and had been a waitress at its predecessor, Mazie's. (Most of her five grown children work here, too.) You can dress up if you like, or not, and kids are welcome; the service is attentive; and you can relax while a pianist plays jazz standards on the baby grand by the wood-paneled bar or while the Sinatra classics are piped in during his break. It's also, I'm told, a meeting place for local politicians and business leaders, which is no surprise because it's one of very few area restaurants of this caliber. The menu offers a traditional selection of pasta (mostly home-made), seafood, poultry, and meat entrées, but we chose from the specials: black ravioli in a wine-flavored seafood sauce and swordfish with asparagus and artichokes. We shared an enormous, luscious fruit tart from the mouthwatering dessert tray. Dazie's has provided a good living for Gavin, who has become very involved in the community. She's now benefiting from the area's new luxury residential development and the Citibank office tower in nearby Long Island City as well as the Museum of Modern Art, a few blocks away, in its Queens incarnation.

Carry on and you'll find the large **Harmony** (39-23 Queens Boulevard at 39th Place, 718-786-8383), the fanciest Romanian eatery in Sunnyside, which replaced a Chinese-Japanese place with the same name and phone number. The wait staff here wears traditional clothing and the decor is heavy on glass and mirrors. I didn't eat there, though—the cigarette smoke kept me away. And **Turkish Hemsin Bakery & Restaurant** (39-17/19 Queens Boulevard, 718-937-1715) is a wonderful, friendly, moderately-priced place where I went with a group of friends. As with many Mediterranean restaurants, you will do well with a group because you can share combination appetizer plates (dips and grilled vegetables), breads, and main dishes, mostly various types of kebab. The fresh-baked herbed bread is worth a special stop! A loaf to take home is just $1.

. . .

Southern Sunnyside

Southern Sunnyside is a busier and more dynamic area than northern Sunnyside. At least a half dozen Latin American (mostly Colombian) bakeries and markets are clustered on and off Greenpoint Avenue between 41st and 47th Streets. Most shops are *carnicerias* (butchers), but they all carry groceries, cookware, and other products.

Getting There   If you're taking the subway, take the #7 train, exit at the 46th Street stop, and turn south toward the Sunnyside Arch at 46th Street and Queens Boulevard. Continue for a short block to Greenpoint Avenue and then bear right (taking you southwest) along Greenpoint Avenue. On the first block, you'll find several excellent Colombian grocery stores with major meat counters. It's amazing how many interesting shops are packed into a small area!

Markets   **Carniceria las Americas** (45-12 Greenpoint Avenue), which offers excellent variety, is owned and managed by brothers Ricardo and Carlos Lopez, who have been in business here for more than twenty years. If you can catch them during a quiet moment (which is rare, as the store is very busy), the Lopezes will explain what the different products are. While most customers come mainly for the meat, you'll also find a large selection of fresh and packaged goods from all over Latin America. On my visit I bought a Peruvian pepper sauce; marmalade made of boroja, a fruit that only recently has been introduced to North American markets; Brazilian cashew juice concentrate; *dulce de leche,* a caramel dessert served in a gourd; and gelatin made with lula, a fruit similar to kiwi. You can also buy fruit pulp to make *batidos* (fruit shakes), common in Latin American and Caribbean restaurants, and *helados del parque* (tropical ices), which are more apt to be found in Mexico City's Chapultapec Park than Central Park. The store moved to its current location in 2000 and now has a pizzeria/*piquetadero*, where you can get pizza and Colombian dishes along with your groceries.

A couple of doors down is **Carniceria el País** (45-10 Greenpoint Avenue), which offers a wider variety of groceries, including packaged goods from all over Central and South America. I especially enjoy looking at the lovely crafts from many countries in that region on display in the rear of the store, which are, regretfully, for decorative purposes only, not for sale. I find it easier to shop here than in **Las Americas.** Walk one block down Greenpoint Avenue to **El Huerto** market (44-12 Greenpoint Avenue), a newcomer that specializes in produce, packaged goods, and cookware, including pottery and pans, for Colombian and Mexican cooks and also has a large section of Peruvian products. In warm weather you can order a refreshing *champus,* a sweet corn-based beverage, or *salpicón,* a delicious fruit cocktail made with watermelon, canteloupe, kiwi, grapes, apples, and papaya. (The term *salpicón* in general refers to a food that is diced and mixed, and you'll see references to *salpicón* as a salsa or a flavored chicken or other dish.) A nice spicy snack you can buy here is a packet of *pepitas con chile y limón,* which is chile-spiced pumpkin seeds with lime.

Bakeries   Unless you're on a radical diet, don't miss **Nita's European Bakery** (40-10 Greenpoint Avenue, 718-784-4047). John and Theodora Nita opened this shop in 1982, a year after moving to this country from Bucharest. Specialties include luscious chocolate cream concoctions (some dipped in rum), but I chose a vanilla mousse pastry flavored with chopped fruit. Check out the spectacular chocolate porcupine cake (the "quills" are made out of almonds) with a liqueur-flavored filling.

Restaurants and Eateries   Southern Sunnyside is packed with family-style restaurants and informal eateries, mostly Latin American. Don't go for the decor, as most are quite plain—the ambiance is created by the people and music. **Pecas y Más** (44-20 Greenpoint Avenue, 718-589-4443) is a Colombian juice bar specializing in *cholados* (loosely translated as "snowglass fruit"). A *cholado* is a cross between a fruit shake and an ice cream sundae, a rich, refreshing beverage made with crushed ice, fruit syrup, and fresh fruit such as melon, pineapple, papaya, and banana and coconut and condensed milk, and it is very sweet. Some of the beverages served here are described as aphrodisiacs! One is known as *Amor Prohibido* ("Forbidden Love") and another is called *Morir Soñando* ("To Die Dreaming"). For a fun snack in Sunnyside I used to enjoy the snug Colombian snackery

El Triangulo, so-named because it sat on a triangular site at 44-08 Greenpoint Avenue. It was renovated and is now called **Seba Seba** (718-786-5919)—"Yum Yum"—with a menu of *hamburguesas* (not your typical Big Macs), *perros calientes* (special hot dogs), and shish kebabs with *arepas* (Colombian corn cakes). It's still informal, fun, and very inexpensive. **El Refugio** (43-20 Greenpoint Avenue, 718-752-5652), a new and attractive Ecuadorian place, has a long list of house specials including hen or goat stews, tripe, and *hornado,* Ecuador's national dish of roast pork with corn. Its very long seafood menu includes various types of *ceviche* (marinated fish platters) and interesting mixtures such as *escudo*—tripe, goat stew, shrimp *ceviche,* and fish in onion sauce—for just $12. They also serve a special daily lunch for just $6. One block up, do be sure to check out **La Union** (42-18 Greenpoint Avenue, 718-392-0493), which has a full Chinese menu as well as Peruvian dishes; it's the first Peruvian-Chinese place in Sunnyside. **La Pollera Colorada** (41-20 Greenpoint Avenue, 718-729-8580) is a bustling Colombian eatery with specialties including *pollo a la brasa* (rotisserie chicken), but I relished a creamy, rich *sopa de mariscos* (seafood soup), which is a meal in itself. **El Comelón** (41-04 Greenpoint Avenue, 718-392-7822) is an attractive Salvadoran and Colombian eatery that replaced Cornel's Place when it moved to Skillman Avenue. It offers specialties such as Salvadoran and Colombian breakfasts (the former has eggs, rice, beans, two tortillas, cream, and avocado; the latter has two eggs, an *arepa,* and rice and beans); Salvadoran *pupusas* and Colombian *empanadas*; various steak, chicken, and pork entrées; and some seafood. I recommend ordering *horchata,* a cold almond and cinnamon beverage, with a Salvadoran meal. The menu also includes *marañon,* a cashew juice drink that is more likely to be seen on Brazilian, not Salvadoran or Colombian, menus. **Mario's** (43-04 47th Street, 718-729-0834) is an old-time Italian restaurant that serves dinner only and makes all dishes to order. I mention it because it represents the old Italian side of Sunnyside that most folks aren't aware of. Local folks give it raves. There is one Bolivian restaurant in Sunnyside, **Mi Bolivia** (44-10 48th Avenue, 718-784-5111), which features *lechón,* a spicy baked pork dish available weekends only, and *sopa de mani,* a peanut-based short ribs stew. It's one of just a handful of Bolivian places in Queens, and I know of no others in New York's other boroughs.

For something different, try **Tricolorii Café** (47-53 43rd Street, 718-391-0098), a delightful Romanian restaurant with a substantial menu offering main courses of chicken, grilled fish, pastas, and steaks that range from $7.50 (for Romanian skinless sausage) to more than $16 (for filet mignon). Lunch specials are $6.95. I prefer to order a variety of appetizers, which include *mamaliga* (polenta) with a porcini mushroom and blue cheese sauce, a personal favorite, and an eggplant spread served with homemade bread. The outdoor café looks like a European student hang-out, oddly situated in the middle of Queens! Last but not least, you'll have some happy surprises at **Yerevan** (47-57 41st Street, 718-784-4651) with an Armenian and Middle Eastern menu featuring a range of kebabs (chicken, pork, and beef) and familiar dips. But I went for their baked smoked salmon on pita bread and an Armenian vegetable salad of toma-toes, cucumber, green pepper, onions, and olives. Chicken breasts served with bulgur is a house specialty. (You can find a variety of types and sizes of bulgur, a Mediterranean grain used to make *tabouli,* in the shops in this area.) Yerevan's hours are on the late side, so call first.

• • •

Sunnyside Walking Tour

Don't miss Sunnyside Gardens (located approximately between Skillman and 39th Avenues and from 43rd to 49th Streets), one of the great delights of this neighborhood. "Gardens" is accurate in every way, as the area is filled with foliage and flowers. Wander around and check out the block-long (east-west) walkways, where you'll see the common gardens and yards. Don't be put off by gates; they're often unlocked. Some gardens are quite large and reflect the idiosyncratic tastes of the residents. Halloween is a good time to appreciate the small-town feeling of this neighborhood, with the intimacy and humor in the variety of decoration on display. Lewis Mumford (see page 59) lived at two addresses here: 41-12 48th Avenue (1925–1927), then 40-02 44th Street (1927–1935). As an amenity, the Gar-dens contain a 3½-acre community park and garden at 39th Avenue and 48th Street, which is for residents only. There also is a day-care center, which Mumford's wife, Sophia, cofounded under the name Sunnyside Pro-gressive School (47th Street at Queens Boulevard), now called Little Friends, and a central parking tower at 48th Street and Barnett Avenue.

In southern Sunnyside, check out the Jehovah's Witness Temple at Greenpoint Avenue and 45th Street. If you can't get in (it's usually locked), peek through the glass in the front doors to see rococo murals of nature and spiritual scenes on the lobby walls and ceiling. This site was once one of Sunnyside's several movie theaters and still has remnants of its Egyptian-inspired ornamentation; now only one multiplex remains on Queens Boulevard.

Along 48th Avenue between about 45th and 48th Streets, you'll see a few churches that reflect the area's ethnic diversity, including a Greek Orthodox church with a small, layered spire and an Armenian church next

door to a Korean church. The area's architecture doesn't have the flavor, cohesiveness, or history of Sunnyside Gardens, but I enjoy wandering the avenues and side streets, which vary widely in architecture and character.
Parks/Picnic Sites   I always like to find out where I can eat outside on a nice day. Sunnyside has few such spaces, and they're small. The best is the Thomas Noonan playground, where 42nd Street, Greenpoint Avenue, and 47th Avenue meet. It has lots of benches and tables, which are packed on balmy days with elderly folks. Vincent Daniels Square at 52nd Street and Roosevelt Avenue is attractively landscaped, but sits in the rumbling shadow of the 52nd Street stop of the #7 train. A playground with benches on Skillman Avenue between 41st and 43rd Streets is not especially picturesque but is convenient if you're shopping on 43rd or Skillman Avenue.

▪ Sunnyside Arch

One of Sunnyside's more unusual features is the art deco–style arch standing at the southern intersection of Queens Boulevard and 46th Street. It was built as part of the economic redevelopment effort of the late 1980s, as neighborhoods citywide were being revived in an effort to attract new business investment. According to Antonia Dosik, former executive director of Sunnyside's Gateway Community Development Corporation, the arch was designed and built by ArtKraft Strauss, the company that created the Times Square Ball. It is meant to be illuminated at night but local folks say it hasn't been lit up in years, and the pedestrian mall below, with its widened sidewalks and extra benches, has deteriorated from neglect. Nonetheless, this intersection is always busy in warm weather. The benches are usually packed and a pet shop and two large markets teem with customers. "Sunnyside always felt like a small town," says Dosik, who moved to Ohio in 1988 to take a new job but still keeps in touch with friends here.

The renovation of the eighties included a brick promenade on the underpass area at the 46th Street elevated subway entrance, an intersection where north–south traffic is barred. There, vendors sell belts, wallets, souvenirs, and toys. This walkway and the activities that take place here provide the only real link between south and north Sunnyside along Queens Boulevard.

▪ Sunnyside's Thalia Theater

Manhattanites "of a certain age" (like me) may recall the old Thalia movie theater on West 95th Street between Broadway and West End Avenue, which offered a repertory of rare foreign and eccentric modern films and was a landmark to many film buffs. (In 2002, a renovated Thalia opened on that site as part of the Symphony Space cultural complex.)

Sunnyside has had its own Thalia, a showcase for Spanish-language theater, since 1977. Located in a former discount store at 41-17 Greenpoint Avenue between 41st and 42nd Streets (718-729-3880), it was founded in 1969 in Manhattan but moved to Queens because of the growing Spanish-speaking population there. It's intimate and attractive, with just seventy-five seats, and its weekend shows, which specialize in classic Spanish and Latin American dance including zarzuelas and tangos, are usually packed. The company also produces Spanish-language dramas and sponsors outreach programs to non-Spanish-speaking audiences. Each May it hosts an outdoor festival in the playground located across the street.

The Thalia's founders were truly prescient when they relocated to Sunnyside; the thriving and ever-growing Spanish-speaking community in Queens has generated a more friendly demographic profile for theater attendance at a time when the traditional theater-going audience is graying. According to Kathy Giaimo, Thalia's administrative director, their core audience is between twenty-five and fifty-six—and 70% female. Corporate supporters are now more receptive to the Thalia than they have been in the past, and its reputation is growing. The Thalia's production of *Tango* has had a hit run at Lincoln Center.

* * *

Woodside

Woodside takes its name from a series of articles called "Letters from Woodside" written by a nineteenth-century journalist named John Andrew Kelly, whose father had built a mansion there. In 1867 a rail line was extended to Woodside and the first developer began buying up land and laying out plots for houses. By the time New York City Transit—the #7 subway line today—reached Woodside in 1917, the community had already been laid out. Full-fledged apartment construction then followed. The Brooklyn-Queens Expressway, which has an exit in Woodside, contributed to the perception of this area as a transportation crossroads.

After World War I, Irish families were among the first to take Woodside as their next stop on the Immigrant Express from Manhattan. The area around 61st Street between Roosevelt and Woodside Avenues is hard-core Irish. Further east on Roosevelt Avenue you'll find yourself in New York City's Little Manila, which, although it takes up just one full block and a few side streets, has so many shops and eateries that it can transport you briefly to the Philippines.

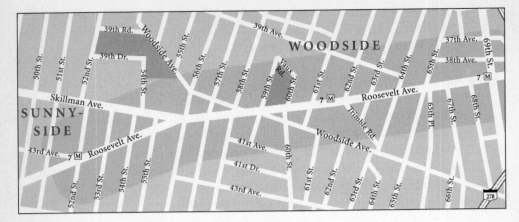

While you're wandering around, you'll see a variety of other places—a Venezuelan restaurant, one of New York City's few Chilean eateries, an Uruguayan/Paraguayan bakery, a Chinese market, a Korean supermarket, Colombian and Salvadoran eateries, an old-fashioned Italian bakery, a Thai grocery, and, next door to it, a restaurant often described by folks who *know* Thai food as New York City's best Thai restaurant. If you wander even more, you'll find a wonderful Mexican-owned café featuring both Mexican and Soho cuisine (think tacos and latte). It's not really such an unlikely combination—Woodside, like other borough neighborhoods close to Manhattan, has begun to attract a growing community of Manhattanites who no longer can afford Manhattan rents. And Woodside has a lot to offer close to home in addition to its fast transportation to Manhattan.

■ Getting Oriented

I recommend that you start with Woodside's Little Manila, which occupies slightly more than one block along Roosevelt Avenue. Filipino settlement in New York City is relatively recent, having started in critical mass during the 1960s economic boom when hospitals were recruiting doctors and nurses. Other professionals soon followed to take advantage of the economic opportunities—and freedom—in the United States, particularly during the Marcos dictatorship of the 1970s. These days you'll still see Filipino markets near many hospitals but many second-generation families have settled in suburbs. But, for eating out and entertainment, many still come to Woodside!

(NOTE: Woodside is far larger than the area described in these pages. Some places profiled in the Sunnyside chapter are technically in Woodside, but are there because they're much closer to the Sunnyside tour I've put together.)

BY SUBWAY

Take the #7 train to 52nd, 61st, or 69th Streets; 69th Street takes you into the heart of Little Manila and 61st Street to the Irish area. A fast, but far less scenic way to get there from Manhattan is to take the E or F train to 74th Street and Roosevelt Avenue and to walk west along Roosevelt. It's just five relatively short blocks to get to Woodside.

BY BUS

For Queens bus information, contact the Metropolitan Transit Authority at 718-330-1234.

BY TRAIN

The Long Island Railroad's Woodside station stops at 61st Street and connects to the #7 train (which is elevated here).

■ ■ ■

Little Manila

Take the #7 train to 69th Street, then walk back to 70th Street. You'll see **Phil-Am Foods** (40-03 70th Street at Roosevelt Avenue, 718-899-1797), the best Filipino grocery store I've seen in Queens. (I've also seen excellent ones near Montefiore Hospital in Norwood, Bronx, and in Manhattan on 14th Street between First and Second Avenues, near Beth Israel Hospital.) Among other things, I bought *Mama Sita's Cookbook* for just $3.99; it's inexpensive, in part because it's published by the manufacturer of the Mama Sita Filipino food brands, and every recipe calls for one Mama Sita ingredient, but you can use substitutes. Nestlé makes an ice cream especially for Filipinos in several flavors you don't normally see in the United States: double cheddar, containing chunks of cheese; avocado; and purple yam. If you're interested in trying out some Filipino recipes now that you know where to buy the ingredients, you can check out a great recipe Web site called asiarecipe.com/phimain.html.

Within this block you'll find several Filipino restaurants that offer a wonderful variety of foods. For fairly fancy eating, **Perlas ng Silangan** (69-09

Roosevelt Avenue, 718-779-3272), a large, classy place, offers grilled and sizzling hot plate specials. Chicken, pork, steak, and a wide range of seafood are available. Filipino food, like its culture, is a mixture of many influences, and you'll recognize an intersection of East and South Asian as well as Spanish flavors such as coconut, garlic, ginger, peanut, papaya, and tamarind. A popular dessert is *halo-halo* (*halo* means mix), which is as interesting to look at as it is to eat. It combines tropical fruits with crushed ice, ice cream, and condensed milk, rather like Colombian *cholados.* The dishes here are surprisingly inexpensive with everything on the menu less than $8.50 (except for seasonal seafood entrées), and servings are generous. **Ihawan** (40-06 70th Street, 718-205-1480) brags of having "the best barbecue in town," and you can get take-out from its ground-floor store or eat in a large upstairs dining room decorated to look like a patio. Barbecue sticks of pork and chicken are just $2 per stick or $4.50 for two sticks with side dishes. Noodle dishes, listed as *merienda* (Spanish for snack), combine a variety of noodles with shrimp and chicken or shrimp and eggs, served with vegetables. Among the house specials is *ginisang ampalaya* (sautéed bitter melon with shrimp). These delectable dishes are no more than $5, although, as at Perlas, sizzling plates and seafood will set you back more, depending on the seasonal price. For something faster, **Krystal's Café** (69-02 Roosevelt Avenue, 718-898-1900) is a crowded and fun restaurant and pastry shop. It's quite informal and quick, rather like the Chinese bakeries in Manhattan and Flushing where you can order inexpensive hot dishes as well as great pastries and other desserts from its extensive menu. By the way, the upstairs dining room features a rotating weekday "All You Can Eat" lunch special for $6.10, including beverage and dessert. An interesting dish you'll find here (and at the other places in this tour) is oxtail cooked with peanut sauce. **Renee's Kitchenette & Grill** (69-14 Roosevelt Avenue, 718-476-9002) is a homey place that has a similar menu to the others but more of a family-style ambiance, and has been described as "home of Pampanga's Best Cuisine." **Only 2 Go** (69-05 Roosevelt Avenue, 718-899-9162) is a little storefront that sells bubble drinks for $3, soups, and Filipino snacks including steamed chicken, pork, sausage, and egg buns for $1.25 to $2. A special Filipino beverage flavor is *buko pandan* (green coconut).

Leaving Little Manila and continuing west on Roosevelt Avenue (as the street numbers descend), you'll find stores and eateries reflecting many nations. **El Sitio Restaurant** (68-28 Roosevelt Avenue, 718-424-2369) is a popular Cuban restaurant that shares the same owner as El Sitio de Astoria (see pages 18–19). At **La Uruguaya Bakery** (68-24 Roosevelt Avenue, 718-672-1919), you can nurse strong espresso (or *yerba maté*, an herb tea popular in Argentina, Brazil, and Uruguay) with pastries. The shop sells different brands of *dulce de leche* (caramel cream) and also uses it in many of its small cakes. I once tried a *chipa,* a type of Paraguayan bread, which was, frankly, dry and boring. More interesting was a *cañone de dulce de leche*—a cross between a croissant and a cannoli filled with *dulce de leche*. **El Guaton Pizzeria and Amasanderia** (68-14 Roosevelt Avenue, 718-478-1199) sells pizza, calzones, South American *empanadas*, and Chilean sandwich specialties made with *pan amasado*, a typical Chilean bread. Two examples are the sandwich *completo*, which contains frankfurters, sauerkraut, tomatoes, avocado, and mayonnaise and the *chacarero*, made with beef, avocado, string beans, and tomatoes.

Los Chuzos (64-14 Roosevelt Avenue, 718-476-2017) offers delicious Colombian-style fresh juices as well as smoothies and *batidos* (tropical milk shakes) and snacks such as fried chicken, sausage, *arepas*, fancy frankfurters called "lucky dogs," and patties. It has a counterpart at 79-01 Roosevelt Avenue in Jackson Heights.

People who love Thai food rave about **Sripraphai** (64-13 39th Avenue, 718-899-9599), especially its papaya salad and catfish dishes. It's the one Thai restaurant I've heard invoked time and again by different people who *know* Thai food. To try preparing it yourself, go next door to **New Bangkok Grocery** (64-11 39th Avenue) to pick up the ingredients. **Izalco** (64-05 Roosevelt Avenue, 718-533-8373) is a fine and friendly Salvadoran place which has been in Woodside for many years. (There also was an Izalco Restaurant in Jackson Heights, which is now Tierras Salvadoreñas; see page 53.) **Fish World** (62-24 Roosevelt Avenue, 718-426-2835; open Monday through Saturday 10 A.M. to 10 P.M., Sunday by appointment) is a lovely Korean-owned fish market and sushi bar; it was just a fish store for a long time, but when the adjacent space became available, the owners expanded it beautifully. They have a great price on sashimi—a regular portion is just $8.95. **La Fina** (62-08 Roosevelt Avenue, 718-426-7902) is a pretty, new Colombian bakery that serves all sorts of fresh breads as well as Colombian *antojitos* (small snacks) including tamales, stuffed potatoes, *arepas*, and patties.

I enjoy walking around Woodside. Once while I was getting out at the 69th Street station in the late afternoon, when many people were coming home from work, I saw a man selling coffee that was coming out of a type of backpack contraption. I'm sure this is something one sees in Mexico or Colombia, but it was the first time I'd seen it in New York. One of the great things about neighborhoods like Woodside is how they can transport you to another culture in such an immediate way!

...

61st Street Area

When you get to 61st Street you'll be in the heart of Irish Woodside. **Shane's Bakery** (39-61 61st Street, 718-424-9039) is a handsome little place that was opened in 1998 by Shane Moynagh, originally from County Cavan, that sells tea and scones and traditional Irish breads as well as soups and snacks. A few doors down, **61st Street Deli** (39-67 61st Street, 718-457-3182) sells a full complement of Irish products and Irish newspapers. There are also about six Irish pubs within a few blocks of 61st Street and several feature live Irish music. The one I recommend is **Saints & Sinners Bar & Grill** (59-21 Roosevelt Avenue, 718-396-3268), an open, easy-going, real neighborhood place with many Irish specialties and a children's menu. (During the day you're likely to see young moms with their stroller-bound kids.) I had a hearty cabbage and bacon soup ($3) as well as a grilled chicken salad ($7). The **Stop Inn** (60-22 Roosevelt Avenue, 718-779-0290) looks like a typical Greek-American diner, which, with its large menu and nice setting, it basically is, but the menu also includes many Irish specialties. A traditional Irish breakfast of bacon, eggs, sausage, grilled tomatoes, black or white pudding, and coffee or tea is $7.25 and the Irish special— four Irish sausages, French fries, Irish beans, and toast (Watch the cholesterol!) is $6.50. Irish mixed grill—lamb chops, liver, bacon, sausage, one egg, fried tomatoes, and pudding—is $11.

A branch of the Korean supermarket chain **Han An Reum** (59-18 Woodside Avenue) is not nearly as large as its Flushing flagship or the Manhattan branch, but its presence here indicates a significant Korean community, and you'll see many other Korean stores, restaurants, and churches in Woodside, as well as in nearby Jackson Heights and Sunnyside. Continuing on Roosevelt Avenue, you will eventually come to the lovely **La Flor Bakery and Café** (53-02 Roosevelt Avenue, 718-426-8023). La Flor has deservedly gotten very good press since it opened a few years back, not only for its very good food but for its lovely setting: it's an intimate café where you can loll over a cup of cappuccino—there's no pressure to buy anything more—and read or write at your leisure. Its Mexican owners have created a menu of *tortas* (Mexican sandwiches), tacos, and quesadillas with decidedly gringo dishes such as Caesar salad, grilled chicken and roast turkey sandwiches, and hamburgers. The home-baked bread includes baguettes, sourdough, multi-grain, and sweet Mexican *pan dulce*. As Woodside, with its reasonable housing and quick access to Manhattan, continues to attract both Manhattanites and people from other countries, places like La Flor with its ethnic mix and crossover appeal will continue to appear.

Continuing toward the 52nd Street entrance to the elevated train, you'll come upon one of New York City's smallest restaurants, **Warteg Fortuna** (51-24 Roosevelt Avenue, 718-898-2554; closed Monday), a treasure of an Indonesian eatery that serves several kinds of curry ($3.75 a platter) and a handful of other tasty specialties. It's a delicious marvel that you could easily pass, but don't! Then, for a last interesting taste of Woodside, cross the triangular park by the station (misnamed Vincent Daniels Square), where you'll find **La Chanita** (51-29 43rd Avenue, 718-458-1947), a Mexican coffee shop that serves Mexican breakfasts side by side with Irish breakfasts. One intriguing specialty is a *nopale* (cactus) omelet ($5).

A bit off the beaten path is **Sapori d'Ischia,** an Italian grocery and trattoria nestled among factories and warehouses (55-15 37th Avenue, 718-446-1500). It began as a wholesaler, then added retail and, later, a restaurant serving lunch and dinner, plus a wine bar specializing in small labels. There's music during the week. To get there from Roosevelt Avenue, you'll have to walk north on 58th Street for three long blocks, then turn left (west) for three shorter blocks. It's a schlep, but worth it for the prices and quality—and to see this gourmet marvel in this location!

Queens Side Trip

The Lemon Ice King of Corona

Bordered by Jackson Heights, Elmhurst, and Flushing Meadow Park, Corona, Queens, comes off as ragged at the edges. It is a place undergoing change. Some folks describe Corona as one of the next frontiers for new immigration. Once solidly Italian, it now also has large Mexican, Bangladeshi, and Ecuadorian communities. Perhaps indicative of how Corona is changing, a landmark church is now a mosque. And it's crowded: the yard of the local public school on Roosevelt Avenue is filled with trailer classrooms to accommodate the overflow.

Getting There   Mass transit users (unless, of course, you live in Corona) will need to take a subway and bus. Take the #7 train to 103rd Street and then wait for the Q23 bus at the northeast corner of 104th Street and Roosevelt Avenue. The bus eventually turns onto 108th Street and stop a half-block from the store. (Keep your eyes peeled for 52nd Avenue.)

Corona is also known for the **Lemon Ice King of Corona** and for **Louis Armstrong,** whose rather simple house at 34-56 107th Street is in the process of being turned into a museum. (The Armstrong archives are based at Queens College. For more information, see www.satchmo.net.) The Lemon Ice King of Corona is one of those food institutions that I'd be castigated for overlooking, so here goes. It's located at 52-02 108th Street, where 52nd Avenue meets Corona Avenue and 108th Street, and its sign looks unchanged from when I used to bicycle by in the 1980s. Although the immediate neighborhood is quiet and nondescript, it's within walking distance of the Queens Hall of Science in Flushing Meadow Park (walk three blocks east on 52nd Avenue and you're just about there). They carry about two dozen flavors (imagine licorice ice!), and the place is open year-round. A small ice costs 80 cents, two scoops are $1.15, and on up, and NO, THEY WILL NOT COMBINE ICES, so you choose your flavor, and that's it. The Lemon Ice King uses real fruit to make its classic Italian ices and there are three sugar-free options: lemon, orange, and chocolate. It's nice to know that this place is here (it's been franchised, so you'll see others at street fairs and on Long Island) but these days, with so many new and interesting types of ice cream, ices, and gelati out there, the Lemon Ice King doesn't quite ring as unique as it used to. For unusual iced desserts, I generally point people to places such as the Indian markets for their ultra-creamy fig, rose, and saffron-flavored ice creams; or to Sunset Park's Sundaes and Cones, where you can choose from sesame, ginger, lichee, red bean, and the (to some folks utterly awful but to others stupendous) durian flavors; or to Cositas Ricas in Jackson Heights, which sells Colombian-style fruit ices; or to Villabate Bakery in Bensonhurst, which has the most outstanding gelati I've tasted . . . and I'm sure I've missed a lot of good ones. But for nostalgia and a taste of old Queens, the trek is worth it!

Queens Side Trip

Elmhurst

Several years ago a National Public Radio profile of Elmhurst found it to be the "most entrepreneurial community" in the United States, and when you get off the subway at Elmhurst Avenue (see page 79) you'll see why. Looking up at the windows of the shops and the two- and three-story office buildings on Broadway, you'll see signs in almost every window offering every kind of service you could want, and in many languages. This is just one indicator of what makes Elmhurst so vibrant.

It is also—and this is perhaps Elmhurst's greatest selling point—one of New York City's most diverse neighborhood. Within its borders you'll find an Indonesian Baptist Church, a Thai Buddhist Temple, a strip of Malaysian, Thai, Chinese, and Vietnamese restaurants, and an Indian-owned pizza place. There's an Argentinian steak house and numerous Colombian and other Latin American restaurants and markets catering to the Spanish-speaking community that also calls Elmhurst home. And for the growing Pakistani and Bangladeshi population, you'll see markets and kebab houses.

When the media is focusing on the diversity of the United States, Elmhurst is an easy place to prove their point. Census data for 2000 indicate that about 44% of Elmhurst residents are Hispanic or Latino, hailing from many countries in Central and South America, and another 40% are Asian. The 4,300 students at Elmhurst's Newtown High School represent 110 countries and speak some forty-one languages. One-fifth of its students have arrived in the United States within the last three years. The density is striking and the community positively vibrates with activity and energy.

What has attracted so much activity to Elmhurst? Imagine, first of all, what Elmhurst was like more than twenty years ago, when many storefronts were empty or just getting by. For immigrants who don't speak English well, one of the only possibilities for economic success is to open a business. As in Flushing and Brighton Beach, where immigrants revitalized communities that were in bad shape, immigrants have also turned Elmhurst around.

The location of several historic sites (including a now-multicultural Presbyterian church that dates back to 1652) in this neighborhood make for quite a novel community rolled into one relatively contained geographic area.

One of Elmhurst's advantages is its proximity to excellent mass transportation and roadways—Queens Boulevard intersects with Broadway here. A number of the larger markets have parking lots, and unlike neighborhoods where parking is a problem, this is one where a motorist will be happy.

Getting There   Take the G, R, or V train to the Elmhurst Avenue stop, which lets out at a busy intersection of 82nd Street, 45th Avenue, and Whitney Street. You can use any of the several exits at this busy intersection. You can also take the #7 train to 82nd Street and walk north on Baxter Avenue.

As you emerge you will find yourself in the thick of what I would call New York City's fourth Chinatown (after those in Manhattan, Flushing, and Sunset Park). The branch of **Hong Kong Supermarket** that I found here (82-02 45th Avenue) looks even larger than the one in Manhattan at 109 East Broadway (at Pike Street). (See pages 29–30 for Flushing's Hong Kong Supermarket and page 162 for the one in Sunset Park.) This one also has a parking lot and sells more Western groceries than the other markets and the clientele appears to be far more mixed than in Chinatown, lured perhaps by the low prices and convenience as well as the huge inventory. This may be in part a result of the active competition just a couple of doors down at **New Century Supermarket** (82-22 Broadway), an equally vast place teeming with activity. (I laugh when I go—it's an amazing sight!) While both supermarkets have large produce sections, **Favoured Produce** (82-02 45th Avenue—same as Hong Kong), a skinny market sandwiched between the two stores, has even more. Across Broadway, **New/Top Line Supermarket** (81-37 Broadway) has a large selection of products from Indonesia, the Philippines, and Thailand, and it's the first store I've visited that sells rice steamers from Laos. (How did I know? Because the steamers were set in baskets in which the words Lao, using the Roman alphabet, was woven.)

Within this area you will also see quite a few Chinese bakeries and other types of shops similar to those in Jackson Heights, Flushing, and other neighborhoods with large Asian communities interspersed with halal markets that serve people from Bangladesh and Pakistan. One place I found here that I haven't seen elsewhere is a Thai snackery called **Sugar Club** (81-20 Broadway), which sells crunchy Thai snacks and sticky fruit sweets as well as versions of the popular Thai basil seed and tea drinks that have been cropping up in Asian markets. As at other ethnic markets, you will see the Thai versions of well-known American-brand items such as Fanta sodas. This corner of Elmhurst has the closest equivalent I can find to a "Little Thailand." In addition to two restaurants close by—Takrai Thai (see below) and **My Thai** (83-47 Dongan Avenue, 718-476-6743), which you'll pass as you continue along Broadway I had an interesting mussel omelet as a lunch special for $6.95—you'll also find **Dok Bua** (83-04 Broadway, 718-335-5959), a Thai bookstore that sells Thai snacks and about three dozen cookbooks. About five or six are in English and have great photos, but they're a bit pricey: $25 for a small paperback. You'll also find Thai videos and music CDs.

Heading further southeast Broadway, past the large markets, you will come to a mini-mall of Asian chain restaurants that have branches elsewhere in Queens and in Manhattan. If you're driving, you'll find ample parking. The restaurants include **Joe's Shanghai** (82-74 Broadway, 718-639-6888), **Takrai Thai** (82-80 Broadway, 718-898-7996), **Penang Malaysian Cuisine** (82-84 Broadway, 718-672-7380), and a Vietnamese noodle place, **Phô Bǎnc** (82-90 Broadway, 718-205-1500), which has several branches in Manhattan's Chinatown and one in Flushing, with outlets in Houston, New Orleans, Phoenix, and Philadelphia.

Further down, you'll come to **Kam Lun Food Products** (86-18 Broadway), a Taiwanese market with a bakery. The bakery has ample seating and serves hot dishes, too—a serving of kung pao chicken is $4. This place is good for a quick, fairly light meal.

▪ Latin American Elmhurst

If you take the #7 train to the 82nd Street stop, you'll be in the Latin American area of Elmhurst. If you walk first on 82nd Street and then along

Baxter Avenue, you'll pass several Colombian and Ecuadorian places. My favorite is **La Fusta** (80-32 Baxter Avenue, 718-429-8222), an attractive Argentinian restaurant. Their very large menu includes the usual *parrillada*—grilled specialties, including a *parrilla* (mixed grill) for two for $28.50. They also have a great seafood selection including dishes such as an Ecuadorian-style shrimp *ceviche* appetizer for $13.50. A personal favorite is the *canelone* (which is like a crepe) filled with salmon for $15.50.

Vegetarians can do surprisingly well here, which is rare for an Argentinean restaurant. You can choose from a large selection of pastas with vegetable fillings or sauces and salads. The desserts also are special, featuring banana crepe, flambéed with rum.

Also . . .   If you follow Broadway in Elmhurst you'll see a number of historic churches that have adapted to the present—and future—and offer services in several languages. **The First Presbyterian Church of Newtown** (54-05 Seabury Street) was founded in 1652, making it the oldest church in Queens. Nowadays, like many other churches in Elmhurst, it has also become multicultural, and the old St. John's Church at 86-02 Broadway is now known as the **Bethel Indonesian Christian Reformed Church**, which is next door to Kam Lun Food Products (see page 80). **The Ch'an Buddhist Meditation Center** is at 90-56 Corona Avenue. A Thai Buddhist temple is at 76-16 46th Avenue.

Queens Side Trip

Rego Park–Forest Hills–Queens Boulevard

Queens has its own version of the Silk Road connecting Europe to China. It moves along 63rd Road, Queens Boulevard, 108th Street, and several side streets in Rego Park and Forest Hills. Here, amid clusters of faceless 1950s brick apartments and the crush of traffic, you'll find a fascinating assortment of bakeries and markets and several restaurants offering specialties from Eastern Europe, the Middle East, and Central Asia.

Their common thread is that they cater to relatively new Jewish (including Israeli) communities in Queens, although some older, more traditional places coexist among them. A first wave of Jews from Central Asia arrived in the United States in the mid-1970s when the former Soviet Union loosened immigration laws, easing the way for Jews to leave. A second wave occurred after the Soviet Union fell in 1991. Among the Russian and Bukharan (Central Asian) Jews are many who did not grow up with Jewish traditions, so some of the stores sell pork products and some have signs indicating that they sell kosher and non-kosher foods, while others are strictly observant.

In addition, you will see some cultural crossover. Among the kosher markets specializing in products from the Middle East, I found one—whose owner is from Iran—that also sold the Koran. One Forest Hills restaurant specializing in the food of Uzbekistan is named after a historic plaza whose centerpiece is a majestic fifteenth-century mosque.

An interesting time to visit this area is on a Friday afternoon several hours before sundown as people are doing their last-minute shopping for Sabbath.

Getting There   The G, R, and V trains stop at 63rd Road and Queens Boulevard in Rego Park. Exit on the north side of Queens Boulevard. Within Queens, the Q60 bus runs along Queens Boulevard and stops at 63rd Road.

The road grid in this part of Queens is confusing—on one angle are numbered streets that include avenues, roads, and drives and some of the street numbers repeat (as in 63rd Drive, 63rd Road, and 63rd Avenue). The numbered streets do not run consecutively, either. After 99th Street comes 102nd Street, then Yellowstone Boulevard, and then 108th Street. I suggest you start at 63rd Road and follow an approximate triangle that goes to 108th Street and then heads back to Queens Boulevard along 65th Avenue. There's a considerable amount of walking involved, but you can also catch buses on 63rd Road (the Q38) and 108th Street (the Q23), but they don't run often.

▪ 63rd Road

To begin, take the V or R train to 63rd Drive stop (Rego Park). Take the south exit and walk to 63rd Drive, where you'll turn left. You'll find two markets worth visiting here. Start with **A&D—The Best European Delicatessen** (93-07 63rd Drive, 718-997-0501), owned by brothers Ariel and Daniel Kandhorov. It's an attractive store with everything from soups to blintzes to fish to sausages to elaborate cakes that come from two Brooklyn bakeries: Kiev Bakery on Coney Island Avenue and New Style Bakery, which specializes in the Uzbek Market, on McDonald Avenue. The Kandkhorovs are originally from Tadzhikistan, but their market, like others in this area, offers the gamut of Eastern European, Russian, and Central Asian products. Across the street, closer to Queens Boulevard, you'll find **Queens Bazaar Food** (94-02 63rd Drive, 718-459-5536), a market with Israeli as well as Persian products. It attracts a younger crowd than the two other Persian markets described in this side trip. Middle Eastern or Persian Jewish music is usually playing in the background. There's a great selection of nuts, dried fruit, spices, flavored waters, and other ingredients for Persian as well as Israeli cuisine.

Now cross Queens Boulevard and follow 63rd Road. The first place of note will be **Ristorante Micelli** (97-26 63rd Road, 718-275-0988), which offers kosher Italian and Eastern cuisine, and a split personality: one menu, for the Italian dishes, is in English, and the East European dishes are in English and Russian. Micelli was known previously as Da Mikelle I and was owned by the operators of the two Da Mikelle places (see pages 85–86).

A&D—The Best European Delicatessen (97-28 63rd Road, 718-896-0617), also known as Tadzhikistan, sells packaged products from the former Soviet states, Israel, and Eastern Europe. You'll see some of these items in other Russian stores, but what you really need to look for here are the specifically Central Asian home-baked specialties and salads including Georgian *hachapuri* (patties, usually stuffed with meat) and Uzbek *bourekas*, another type of stuffed bread closer to phyllo dough filled with meat, potato, cheese, or vegetables. My favorite salad is called *shuba* ("mink coat"), a herring concoction layered with potatoes and beefs. A walnut-honey pastry called *chakchak* is typical of what you'd find in Dushambe, Tadzhikistan's capital.

Keep going and you will soon come to a small Uzbek restaurant called **Tandoori** (99-04 63rd Road, 718-897-1071), which is pleasant and inexpensive and well-known for the bread they bake. Their menu includes shish kebabs ($1.50 to $3.50), salads, hardy soups, *pelmeni* (small Russian dumplings, often described as ravioli), and meat entrées. While I waited for both my meal and an order of bread to take home, other people would rush in to pick up their own orders of bread, sometimes four or five loaves at a time. As each new batch would come out, people would line up for the warm, heavy, brown bag containing their loaf. A loaf of bread is just $1, and they sell out fast.

■ Forest Hills (108th Street)

Continue up 63rd Road until you reach 108th Street. This will take you about ten minutes if you walk briskly and maybe less if you're lucky enough to catch the bus. Turn right on 108th Street—you can't miss it, it's the first bustling shopping area you'll hit after several quiet residential streets.

The first place you'll see is **Salute** (63-42 108th Street, 718-275-6860), a pretty and homey

A few of the home-baked goodies you'll find at A&D—The Best European Delicatessen in Rego Park.

Kosher Uzbek place, with kebabs for as little as $1.75 and not more than $3, and you can get a filling meal for under $10. The service is friendly and easygoing, and a TV with Uzbek videos in the background adds real ambiance!

A&R International Food Delicatessen (63-46 108th Street, 718-459-3956) is a gorgeous, mostly Russian market that sells everything from soup to nuts and whatever comes before, after, and in between as well as imports from Eastern Europe. You'll find fresh bread, lots of prepared dishes, tons of chocolates and cakes, and meats and fish. The presentation itself is special— it's a smaller version of the best Russian markets you'll see in Brighton Beach, but sunnier because of its big picture window.

Nagila Market (63-69 108th Street, 718-268-2626) truly represents a global crossroads—it's owned by Iranian Jews and sells products from India, Pakistan, Iran, Afghanistan, Israel, and elsewhere. There are lots of dried fruits and nuts, grains, curries, spices, jams, rose water, and other flavorings. They also carry condiments for Central Asian and Mediterranean cuisine and packaged Sadaf-brand herbs for Iranian cooking. I noticed a number of foods such as dried blueberries and dates and the long pine nuts that I also found at Ariana Afghan Market in Flushing (see page 36). Especially appealing are the beautiful gift packages of mixed dried fruit. Owner Chai Frouz is obliging with easy Persian-Jewish traditional recipes.

Abrahams L&L Kosher Cake Land (64-17 108th Street, 718-997-1008) will remind you of that dying breed of old-time Jewish bakers that has just about vanished from the Lower East Side (although you can still find good bakeries of this type in Borough Park and Williamsburg). You'll find good rugalach, *babkas,* and heavy, oozy cakes here.

One of the great attractions of **Carmel** (64-27 108th Street, 718-897-9296), an international market specializing in Israeli and other Mediterranean products, is the coffee roaster, which gives off a seductive aroma. Carmel is owned by Romanians and has fascinating inventory including, in the freezer section, jute from Egypt, phyllo dough, *bourekas,* and other products to prepare Middle Eastern specialties. **Monya & Misha European Deli** (64-46 108th Street, 718-459-0180) is a lively, large market with lots of prepared dishes in front. **Beautiful Bukhara** (64-47 108th Street, 718-275-2220) is a small Uzbek bakery-restaurant that produces the popular *tandoori* bread as well as a type of matzoh-like bread that's baked in a wok-shaped pot. Go on a Friday when the bakers are working quickly to produce the utterly warm and fresh bread that shoppers eagerly await.

Turning right on 65th Avenue toward Queens Boulevard to 99th Street, you'll see a small cluster of shops including several kosher places. One of these is **Registan** (65-37 99th Street, 718-459-1638), an Uzbek restaurant named after Registan Square, a fifteenth-century historic plaza in Samarkand, Uzbekistan's capital. The restaurant itself is a simple place, and the first thing you'll see on entering is a sink so you can, in the Orthodox Jewish tradition, wash your hands (and say a blessing) prior to ordering your meal. (Okay, so you should wash your hands anyway, but you'll see sinks like these in many Orthodox Jewish eateries.) The modest menu includes a few kebab dishes, soups, *pelmeni,* and salads. The food is better at Tandoori (see page 83) and Salute (see pages 83–84) but Registan is an interesting example of the crossover of the Jewish and Muslim communities of Central Asia.

▪ Queens Boulevard

Between 65th and 68th Roads you'll find a number of kosher and non-kosher Asian, Russian, and Israeli markets and restaurants. A word of caution: crossing Queens Boulevard at almost any intersection can be treacherous and the blocks can be very long. Even if you don't see traffic coming, obey the crossing signals rigorously and if necessary walk an extra block or two in order to cross safely. Don't even *think* of jaywalking!

You'll need to cross the boulevard for the first two stops. **Andre's Hungarian** (100-28 Queens Boulevard at 67th Road, 718-830-0256) is a thirty-year old bakery with perfect strudels, tiramisù cakes, rich sacher tortes, and the other multilayered sweet pastries and cakes for which Hungarian bakers are renowned. As a counterbalance, Andre's also offers a low-carbohydrate, sugar-free rugalach made with soy flour. Next door, at the corner of 67th Road, you'll find **Knish Nosh of Forest Hills** (100-30 Queens Boulevard, 718-897-5554), a huge knish bakery. If you find New York City prices high (knishes are $1.95 at Yonah Schimmell's on East Houston Street), you'll be happy to find large knishes here for $1.50 each if you order them hot, and you also can buy cold knishes to take home for $1.30 apiece. They don't make any fancy cheese or fruit knishes here—just potato, spinach, kasha, broccoli, and meat, and they're all kosher.

Now walk to 68th Road. Here you'll find **A & A Middle East Foods Inc.** (102-30 Queens Boulevard, 718-997-7371), a small, crowded market that specializes in the foods of the Persian Jews including spices, nuts, dried fruit, and jams from Iran. One happy discovery was brown rock sugar that a friend of mine had been relentlessly looking for. I was surprised to see a Koran and some other Muslim items at the front of the store, especially since the owner wore a yarmulke. I suppose my surprise was a result of being unaware of how the Muslim and Jewish communities of Central Asia traditionally have worked and lived together. Chancing upon a place like this is one of the delights of urban exploring!

Now cross back—at the light—to the glatt kosher **Da Mikelle II Restaurant** (102-39 Queens Boulevard, 718-997-6166), which is incredibly over-decorated with bright chandeliers, mirrors, paintings, and floral displays. If you go in jeans you'll be underdressed. Come hungry, as the lunch platters are served on plates the size of cafeteria trays. The cuisine is Italian and French and you can get a terrific $7.95 lunch special (Sunday through Friday), which includes soup or salad, an entrée of grilled salmon, filet of sole, or chicken marsala, and coffee or tea and dessert. You also can get a $13.95 dinner special (Sunday through Thursday) until 9 P.M. The à la carte menu includes a good selection of appetizers and salads, several main-dish crepes (with fish, meat, tofu, or vegetable fillings), a variety of fish, meat, and chicken entrées, and fancy desserts including chocolate mousse and tiramisù. Owner Michael Savorunov and his son, Ilya, also operate a large catering hall around the corner, **Da Mikelle Palace** (102-55 Queens Boulevard, 718-830-0500), which occupies what had been Troyka, a Russian restaurant. (Ilya insists that restaurant service is far better here than in Brighton Beach because all the wait staff speak English.) As a last stop en route to the subway, **Kosher Palace** (103-27 Queens Boulevard at 68th Drive) is a small Bukharan market selling European and Middle Eastern products. It's a good place to stock up as you leave the neighborhood. If you continue along Queens Boulevard for several more blocks, you'll come to the 71 Street subway entrance where you can get the E and F express trains.

Also . . . If you want to learn more about Uzbek culture in New York City, you can check out the **Uzbekistan Culture Center** at 120-35 83rd Avenue, which is south of Queens Boulevard in Kew Gardens. This address also houses **Uzbekistan Tandoori Bread** (718-850-3426), which features owner Isak Barayev's freshly made bread and soups. To get there, take the E or F train to Kew Gardens/Union Turnpike and catch the Q10 bus to 83rd Avenue. (See Richmond Hill side trip for bus details, pages 87–88.)

Queens Side Trip

Richmond Hill

For a country with just under 700,000 people, Guyana has had an amazing influence on New York City. An estimated 70,000 Guyanese live just in Richmond Hill, Queens, New York's "Little Guyana," and many more are scattered throughout Queens, the Bronx, and Brooklyn. (For more information on Guyana and Guyanese cuisine and immigration, the Web site www.guyanaonline.net/c-recipes/ contains Guyanese recipes, and go to www.fuzion.com/directory/us/liberty/libertyave.htm for Guyanese recipes and a bibliography of books about Guyana and Guyanese immigration.)

The twenty-plus-block stretch of Liberty Avenue in south Richmond Hill, from about 110th to 130th Streets and beyond, teems with markets, *roti* shops, Chinese-Guyanese eateries, and other stores catering to this community. Interspersed with these shops you will find many different houses of worship, including a Hindu temple, a mosque, and mainstream and independent Christian churches. As you walk, you also will hear music—the throbbing rhythms of Indian "chutney" as well as Jamaican and Trinidadian reggae. You will smell incense as you pass some stores and curry as you pass others—a truly sensuous experience! The area is home to a diverse community, which also includes Indians from Punjab and people with Indian roots from throughout the Caribbean, particularly Trinidad, who have much in common with the Guyanese who live here. There also are many Afro-Caribbean Guyanese and Central Americans here—you'll find an Ecuadorian eatery around the corner from the elevated train.

Most commercial buildings in this neighborhood are just two stories and most homes are detached dwellings, some for one family, others subdivided into apartments. Closer to the intersection of Liberty Avenue and Lefferts Avenue you will see more mainstream institutions including a few banks and major chain stores. Only a few blocks in either direction, however, the commercial landscape changes to smaller locally based businesses. A few are family-owned chains, such as Sybil's Bakery (which also has outlets in Flatbush and Jamaica) and Singh's Roti, which has three shops on Liberty Avenue.

Richmond Hill covers a much larger geographical area than the one described in this side trip, and its historical and ethnic mix are also much broader. For a more complete view, the Richmond Hill Historical Society (www.richmondhillhistory.org/quickinfo.html) maintains an historical archive of the area including some great photographs of old Richmond Hill; it also lobbies to preserve some of the neighborhood's best architecture.

Getting There   For mass transit users, the A train marked "Lefferts Boulevard" takes you directly there—it's the last stop on the line and the train runs fairly quickly from Manhattan, especially during weekdays when it skips the local stops (about fifty minutes from the Times Square/Eighth Avenue stop—make sure you're on the downtown platform). Sit in the back of the train (which will become elevated during the trip) and exit at 116th Street. An alternative subway route (which I prefer) is via the E train to Kew Gardens/Union Turnpike, which you also can catch from Times Square/Eighth Avenue—on the uptown/Queens platform; then to transfer to the Q10 bus to JFK Airport. Finding the bus stop can be tricky. Follow the signs in the subway station for the Q10. The stairs out of the station will take you onto Queens Boulevard, a very busy, multilane roadway transversing Forest Hills. You will see signs for the Q10 on Queens Boulevard, but they're wrong! What you need to do is turn right under an arcade at the newsstand near the subway entrance, which will take you to the parallel road. This is where the Q10 leaves from. (If you can't find it, ask someone waiting for the other buses on Queens Boulevard.) The bus leaves frequently because it's used by airport employees. It will take you through some attractive areas of Forest Hills and Kew Gardens and then will head through parts of Jamaica before reaching Richmond Hill. You will see one elevated subway line (the end of the J line) on this route, but don't get off there—in another ten minutes you'll reach the Liberty Avenue stop. A lot of other people will get off here; you also can ask the bus driver or other passengers to confirm when you've arrived.

By car, take Queens Boulevard to Lefferts Boulevard and turn right toward Liberty Avenue. I didn't see any parking lots, but you will probably find parking on a side street.

From 116th Street and Liberty Avenue, walk west just one block and your tour will begin. The first stop is **Guyana Oriental Garden** (115-20 Liberty Avenue, 718-323-2453), one of several Guyanese-Chinese restaurants in the area. What makes this menu interesting is the Guyanese-Chinese fusion dishes such as jerk chicken fried rice. The menu also features West Indian curries and lo mein and chow mein.

Walk one block west to **Little Guyana Bakery** (116-04 Liberty Avenue), where in addition to the iced cakes and sweet pastries you'll also find a good selection of spices and packaged products for Guyanese cooking. Cross the street and walk west again to **Fish World** (117-09 Liberty Avenue), a huge new market with an amazing selection of seafood used in Guyanese cuisine including butterfish, cuffum, gilbaker (or gilbaka), Guyanese black shrimp, luckanam, buck graf, patwa, and houri. For less adventurous palates, there's fried chicken and fried fish to go plus a huge selection of packaged goods and some produce.

For a better selection of produce, walk further west on the same block to **Liberty Fruit and Produce** (117-19 Liberty Avenue). This enormous place has West Indian specials such as cherry peppers, swan grapes, and *bodhi* (or *phodi* or *bhodi*), which are long beans. Here you'll also find a Guyanese lime rickey and a very good ginger beer. In this store I bought Karibbean Flavoured Extra Hot Lime Sauce, made in Trinidad. Richmond Hill is paradise if you love super-hot foods!

The next block is fun for the non-food items you will see, particularly **Neena Jewelers** (118-01 Liberty Avenue), which sells gorgeous and intricate statues of Hindu gods and goddesses and elaborate jewelry. Just next door is **Choji's** (118-03 Liberty Avenue), a shop that sells clothing and musical instruments. **Eatwell West Indian Bakery** (118-15 Liberty Avenue), further along, is a modest place compared to its neighbors, but in addition to the basic buns and spice cakes you'll find here you can also buy special cooking utensils for preparing Guyanese dishes.

Cross the street and you'll come to **Singh's Roti Shop #3** (118-06 Liberty Avenue, 718-835-7255). *Rotis*—wraps filled with various spicy combinations of vegetables, meat, or seafood—are often substantial enough to be a meal, but they usually come with side dishes of pumpkin, okra, cabbage, and other vegetables or starches such as chickpeas or pigeon peas. This busy place is one of several Singh's in the neighborhood; the largest, Singh's Big Roti (see below), is about twelve blocks away and has a dance floor with a live band on weekends.

At 120-23 Liberty Avenue, you'll come to **Hot & Spicy Restaurant** (718-641-1901). I used to find this place unfriendly, but under new owner Savi Singh and her sons, Ram and Shazar, and Shazar's wife, Meriam, it's a lot more welcoming and is already drawing a following. (Come in on a Saturday and you'll see the kitchen area to the rear, which is open, teeming with cooks.) Here you can get all sorts of *roti* combinations, curried vegetables, patties with various fillings, baked goods (including fried breads such as *puris*), and more. The Singhs originate from Tortola, in the British Virgin Islands, so theirs is perhaps New York City's only Tortolan restaurant!

By the time you have reached 121st Street, you will have gotten an excellent sampling of the cuisine and food products of this area. But I recommend that you keep going a few more blocks. I had a meal of goat curry and eggplant at **Sandy's Deli and Roti** (121-10 Liberty Avenue, 718-659-8000). Sandy's seems to have several functions—it also has a travel agency and a CD shop on its premises. It's busy, fast, and friendly. As I waited for my order, a man eating his meal came up to the counter, said a few words, and one of the counterpersons handed him two Scotch Bonnet peppers, which are among the hottest around. The counterperson wore rubber gloves—handling these peppers can burn your hands—but the customer proceeded to bite into the peppers as he ate his meal. Trinidadian food combines Caribbean and Indian influences in such interesting ways, and I enjoy reading Sandy's menu with its many cross-cultural beverages, curries, Trinidad-style Chinese food, aloo pies (curried, potato-stuffed bread with chickpeas), and desserts. A newcomer to Richmond Hill is **Patel Brothers** (124-10 Liberty Avenue), a new branch of the Indian grocery chain headquartered in Chicago, with others in Flushing and Jackson Heights. With state-of-the-art technology, a gorgeous set-up, and great prices, Patel may well challenge some of the grim-looking competition in the immediate area. **Singh's Big Roti** (described above) is at 131-14 Liberty Avenue (718-323-5990). Unless you plan to make a trek to Richmond Hill for the music, it's not necessary to go this far down Liberty Avenue to find great *roti* and other Guyanese and Trinidadian dishes. **Sybil's Bakery** (132-17 Liberty Avenue) feels more off the beaten track—it's just on the border

VEGGIE DELIGHT

*Courtesy of Meriam Singh of Hot & Spicy Restaurant
in Richmond Hill, Queens*

One 4-pound pumpkin
Vegetable oil (enough to sauté the onion, garlic, and pepper)
1 medium onion, chopped
3 cloves garlic, minced
1 green pepper, chopped
2 teaspoons salt
2 tablespoons sugar
Curry powder to taste

1. Peel the pumpkin, cut it in half, and remove the seeds. Then cut the halves into small pieces and wash them. Set aside.
2. Heat the oil over medium heat and sauté the onion until it begins to brown. Then add the garlic and green pepper and sauté until tender. Add the pumpkin, salt, and sugar and cook, covered, over low heat until the pumpkin is soft.
3. Mix in curry powder to taste.

of the area, but it's a popular destination and the food (mostly take-out) is great. Sybil Bernard-Kerrut (now deceased) opened her first place in 1978 on Hillside Avenue in Jamaica and followed with another—now her flagship—on Church Avenue in Brooklyn. This is the smallest.

This neighborhood is great for vegetarians. Guyanese food offers many non-meat options, as it is influenced by Hindu traditions and the versatility of West Indian produce. You can pull together quite a few side dishes to create a delicious, complete vegetarian meal.

If you love rum, by the way, you might want to check out **Lefferts Wines & Liquors** (103-55 Lefferts Boulevard), which sells El Dorado brand rum from Guyana, including a fifteen-year-old rum for $27.99.

Also ...   Richmond Hill has many different religious institutions. At 104-14 127th Street, you'll come to one of the local mosques, **Masjid Al-Abidin** (which you can see from Liberty Avenue), and just up Liberty Avenue one more block is the **Shri Narayan Mandi Hindu Temple** (128-04). It's open on Sundays. Richmond Hill also has a large Sikh community; the **Sikh Cultural Center** (95-30 118th Street), established in 1965, is one of the oldest and largest Sikh temples, or *gurdwaras,* on the East Coast.

Queens Side Trip

Ridgewood

I first read about Ridgewood in the early 1980s when the *New York Times* article touted its charms and local residents were trying to turn it into the next Park Slope. Real estate prices were soaring throughout the city and families who could no longer afford to stay in Manhattan were moving into Brooklyn.

Despite its attractive row houses built of a distinctive golden-yellow brick (which won awards as model housing in their time) Ridgewood never took off. It's not difficult to figure out why. For one thing, it's relatively hard to get to, and it's not near any of the amenities of the brownstone neighborhoods of Brooklyn Heights and Park Slope such as Prospect Park, the Botanical Gardens, the Brooklyn Museum, and quick transport into Manhattan. It doesn't have the convenience of neighborhoods such as Kensington and Ditmas Park, which are close to the Q train, excellent shopping, and the beach. Today Ridgewood is a solid working-class neighborhood that appears to have changed little architecturally but has been affected by shifting immigration patterns, originally German and Italian, then Romanian and Yugoslavian, and, more recently, arrivals from the Dominican Republic, Mexico, China, and Vietnam. Bordering with Bushwick in Brooklyn, Ridgewood has the feel of a village, which is one of its appeals. Ridgewood essentially has remained a low-rise bedroom community, with some factories scattered along its perimeter.

On my bicycle tours, the influence of German settlement and subsequent new waves of immigrants from Eastern Europe, especially Romania, could be seen in neighborhood markets and cafés such as Dracula Café, which has since closed. As I explored Ridgewood for this book, I found a large Dominican community. The canopy of Ridgewood's community resources center is marked in English, Spanish, Chinese, and Vietnamese. Blocks of Myrtle Avenue have been upgraded and beautified and some streets are closed off to create triangular plazas. It's an attractive place to explore, but most of the retail stores here are parts of chains and nothing much stands out as unique.

Since Ridgewood is not a tourist area by a long shot, its markets truly cater to the locals. So if you see a Romanian restaurant (and there aren't many), there probably will be no English menu and no one who can speak to you easily. If you're adventurous give it a try, but if you want to find Romanian food in a more tourist-friendly setting, check out Sunnyside. (The Sunnyside chapter of this book lists five Romanian eateries.)

So why visit? You should go if you want to see a totally different neighborhood and if, like me, you're compulsive about exploring new areas of New York City.

Getting There   By subway, take the L train to Myrtle Avenue/Wyckoff Street or the M (elevated) train to Seneca Avenue, which crosses over the Williamsburg Bridge, providing fabulous views of the Manhattan and Brooklyn skylines and the East River. If you take the L, which runs frequently, from the exit follow the elevated train north on Palmetto Street. The Seneca Avenue exit served as a location for the film *Brighton Beach Memoirs* because it resembles the way the Brighton Beach Avenue stop looked in the 1930s. The tour follows Seneca Avenue from Palmetto Street to Myrtle Avenue.

Markets, Bakeries, and Restaurants   **Muncan Food** (676 Seneca Avenue at Gates Avenue, 718-418-2212) is filled with Romanian sausage hanging from the ceiling and all sorts of Romanian cheeses and packaged products including jams, dessert wafers, and chocolates. Several shelves are allocated for Goya food products, which cater to Ridgewood's growing Spanish-speaking community. **Jorge's Restaurant** (689 Seneca Avenue, 718-456-3900) is an attractive Dominican eatery right by the stairs to the elevated train. At 749 Seneca Avenue at Woodbine Street you'll come to **International Bakery** (718-366-9550), a Romanian place with cheesecakes, phyllo-dough pastries filled with meat and cheese, strudels, coffee cakes, and breads. Just after you pass Madison Street, you'll come to **Le Georgette European Cuisine** (778 Seneca Avenue, 718-366-2243), a small Romanian restaurant with about five tables and a counter—and no one who speaks English. The menu isn't very large—mostly a few chicken and meat dishes and some salads and stews. You may have to get a customer to translate for you, and it can be a frustrating experience. You'll do far better shopping at **Seneca Pork Store** (801 Seneca Avenue at Putnam Street), an old-time market packed with all sorts of delicatessen items such as meats, cheeses, and salads plus beverages, syrups, jams, and other products from the Slavic countries. Occasionally there is produce in the front such as yellow peppers, which are used in much Eastern European cooking. Just before you reach Myrtle Avenue, you'll come to **Rudy's Pastry Shop** (905 Seneca Avenue), which has been in Ridgewood for seventy-five years. The traditional German pastries have been replaced with a more general selection of baked goods and cookies, a little bit of everything.

Turn right onto Myrtle Avenue and begin your walk back to the subway. If you're still hungry, **Castillo Restaurant** (54-55 Myrtle Avenue at St. Nicholas Avenue, 718-386-0387), a former diner, features excellent Dominican cuisine. It's located at a triangle along Myrtle Avenue that has been made into a landscaped park by closing off a block-long side street.

Brooklyn

■

BAY RIDGE
BRIGHTON BEACH
GREENPOINT
KOSHER BROOKLYN

- *Borough Park*
- *Crown Heights*
- *Kings Highway*
- *Midwood*
- *Williamsburg*

SUNSET PARK

SIDE TRIPS

- *Atlantic Avenue*
- *Bensonhurst*
- *Caribbean Crown Heights and Flatbush*
- *Coney Island*
- *Greenwood Heights*
- *Sheepshead Bay*

...

Brooklyn Notes

Brooklyn stalwarts often will evoke the era when Brooklyn was a separate city, as if they might like this status to be restored. After all, Brooklyn has a little bit of everything—some say the best of everything—and, possibly, the world's most famous bridge. Why should it still be part of greater New York City?

To support this argument, one need only invoke some of the things that make Brooklyn great: a park—Prospect Park—that rivals Central Park for its grace, design, and amenities; a world-famous art museum; one of the world's best-known amusement parks; fabulous architecture; an active port area; excellent beaches; universities; libraries; a burgeoning cultural district anchored by the Brooklyn Academy of Music; the highest elevation in all of New York City (it's in Green-Wood Cemetery, and the second highest elevation is in Brooklyn, too, in Sunset Park); and tons of delicious food to be found everywhere.

Indeed, the Brooklyn food profiles in this chapter go a long way in supporting the argument for independence—Brooklyn has its own Chinatown, more kosher places than in all Manhattan, a thriving Caribbean community, the only real Polish neighborhood in New York City, and an expanding Mexican and Latin American district in Sunset Park, to name a few.

Brooklyn probably couldn't claim to be as diverse as Queens, nor could it claim the "Comeback Kid" award due to the Bronx. And while it still aches from the loss of the Dodgers (the minor-league Brooklyn Cyclones just don't compare), Brooklyn retains a richness that comes from being old and established yet resilient in the face of many changes. Queens may be recognized for its thriving immigrant cultures and the constant influx of newcomers but it is still relatively young. Brooklyn, on the other hand, enjoys a real sense of establishment—its beautifulhistoric brownstone districts in Brooklyn Heights, Park Slope,

Bedford-Stuyvesant, and elsewhere, and some of its gracious residential neighborhoods of turn-of-the-century single-family homes hark back to a time when Brooklyn was, as architect and historian Elliot Willensky neatly puts it, "the world."*

...

Bay Ridge

Years ago a friend of Norwegian descent exhorted me to visit Bay Ridge in mid-May to watch the Norwegian Independence Day Parade on Third Avenue. I never made it then, and my friend has since moved away. The parade still takes place, ending at the aptly named Leif Ericson Park, even though the population of Norwegians—and Scandinavians overall—descendants of sailors who once settled here, has shrunk. Today there's just one market exclusively dedicated to Nordic products and another that offers some, along with products from Ireland, and for both, much of the business is mail-order.

The truth is that I not only missed the parade but also never made it to Bay Ridge at all until I began working on this book. Was I in for some surprises! I was unaware of how beautiful some sections are. West of Third Avenue are some of the loveliest streets you'll see within the five boroughs, lush with greenery and regal architecture, stretching out to scenic views of the Narrows, with the Verrazano Bridge framing the neighborhood in the distance. After you have a meal in one of the eateries of Bay Ridge, walk a few blocks west to lovely Shore Road Park—this will be your dessert! (One of its features is a spectacular running and bicycle path along the water.)

Bay Ridge is far more cosmopolitan than I had thought. I had envisioned a small-town corner of the city and, instead, found an almost global array of markets and eateries. Once the heart of Scandinavian New York (a group that was never prominent relative to other ethnic groups in New York City), it now has a significant Arabic community, represented by people from Egypt, Morocco, Lebanon, Turkey, and other countries of the Middle East and North Africa. But there are also shops and markets catering to people from Greece, Poland, and Ireland, and from China, Korea, Vietnam, and Russia, too. The latest waves of newcomers include Chinese spilling over from Sunset Park and Russians moving here from Brighton Beach, Bensonhurst, and other neighborhoods. Some old-time places hang on, too.

*Elliot Willensky, *When Brooklyn Was the World, 1920–1957* (New York: Harmony Books, 1986)

Shore Pkwy.

(Leif Ericson Dr.)

2nd Ave.

278

Gowanus Expwy.

Owls Head
Park

4th Ave.

68th St.

3rd Ave.

Gowanus Expwy.

5th Ave.

66th St.

67th St.

Senator St.

Bay Ridge Ave.

68th St.

R M

BAY RIDGE

Ovington Ave.

72nd St.

73rd St.

Bay Ridge Pkwy.

4th Ave.

74th St.

R M

76th St.

77th St.

Colonial Rd.

Ridge Blvd.

3rd Ave.

78th St.

79th St.

80th St.

5th Ave.

81st St.

Gowanus Expwy.

82nd St.

McKinley
Park

83rd St.

84th St.

6th Ave.

86th St.

R M

85th St.

87th St.

88th St.

Monastery
Square

90th St.

4th Ave.

Fort Hamilton Pkwy.

Gatling Pl.

Dyker Pl.

7th Ave.

10th Ave.

278

FORT
HAMILTON

Third Avenue, with a cornucopia of restaurants, cafés, and markets, reminds me of a smaller scale, quieter version of Manhattan's Ninth Avenue. For the visitor unfamiliar with the neighborhood, its diversity and quality are surprising. I'd heard years ago that many families that had established successful businesses in downtown Brooklyn along Atlantic Avenue had settled in Bay Ridge, and that a Middle Eastern/North African community had grown up there. But until I saw it, I had no idea of its scope. Now, along more than ten blocks of Fifth Avenue are all sorts of markets, clothing stores, cafés, restaurants, gift and book shops, and services catering to this growing community. These stores serve not just the families that have lived here for generations but a new community of immigrants who also feel at home here.

Bordered on the west by the Narrows, by 86th Street to the south, by the Gowanus Expressway to the east, and by 65th Street to the north, Bay Ridge includes some blocks of large (for New York City) private homes and many attractive attached homes with small lawns. A striking feature of Bay Ridge is the gracious trees that give the neighborhood a very leafy look—what a difference trees make! (Bay Ridge even has its own Botanical Gardens, with its entrance at Shore Road and 71st Street.)

The Verrazano Bridge looms in the distance from many vantage points, almost like a picture frame, while many side streets look as they have for many years—like the quintessential urban village.

■ Getting Oriented

Although you might expect that Fourth Avenue, where the subway runs, would be the most commercial area of the neighborhood, the places to explore are actually along Third and Fifth Avenues, from about 68th Street to 86th Street. Eighty-sixth Street interrupts the reverie, with its vast chain stores and traffic jams. With several bus lines running here, it links Bay Ridge to the rest of Brooklyn.

The eateries and markets of Bay Ridge are concentrated along Third and Fifth Avenues, starting at 68th Street and stretching south to 86th Street. Crossing south on 86th Street takes you to the Fort Hamilton neighborhood, which includes a pocket of nice Italian places on Third Avenue. Be aware that some restaurants in Bay Ridge are closed Monday night; call first if that's when you're thinking of visiting.

BY SUBWAY

The R train heads straight to Bay Ridge, where it terminates. Stops in Bay Ridge include Bay Ridge Avenue (equivalent to 69th Street), 77th Street, and 86th Street. Although the R train runs in Manhattan, it is slow. I recommend taking the W train, which is an express in Manhattan and makes just two stops in Brooklyn before 36th Street. Change there for the R.

BY BUS

The B37 runs from downtown Brooklyn toward Third Avenue, where it runs the length toward Shore Park. The B63 runs along Fifth Avenue. The B1 runs along Bay Ridge Avenue and links the neighborhood to Brighton Beach.

BY CAR

Exit the Gowanus Expressway at 90th Street. A municipal parking lot is located on the east side of Fifth Avenue between 85th and 86th Streets; enter on 85th Street.

If you want to explore Bay Ridge in a day (start early!), start at 86th Street and Fourth Avenue at **Karam Lebanese Restaurant** (8519 Fourth Avenue, 718-745-5227). It's a small, simple, and friendly place with inexpensive dips, breads, shish kebabs, and spicy vegetable dishes. One extra-hot day I had fresh lemonade there ($2.50). It tasted slightly different from any other lemonade I'd ever had—the secret ingredient was rose water!

• • •

Fifth Avenue
(68th Street to 86th Street)

In the next seventeen blocks between 68th and 86th Streets, you will encounter a remarkable range of markets and eateries, but as you walk north you will see a growing number of Arabic signs marking shops and eateries representing Egypt, Morocco, Lebanon, and other Arabic-speaking countries.

Getting There   If you follow the route below, exit the R train at 86th Street and walk one block east.

Restaurants   Start at **Hinsch's** (8518 Fifth Avenue, 718-748-2854); it's an old-fashioned eatery of a type that's rare today. Also, the owners sell chocolates in all sorts of shapes—there's even a miniature computer-shaped chocolate—that they make in a factory on Third Avenue in Bay Ridge. **Sunflower** (8020 Fifth Avenue, 718-491-9050) is the only Mexican-Japanese restaurant I've ever seen, and you can get sushi, teriyaki, tacos, and other Mexican goodies here. **Mazza Plaza** (8002 Fifth Avenue, 718-238-9576) is the first of the Middle Eastern places you'll see. It's a large, newish place that was opened by the Karam family that previously owned Karam (see page 101). Somewhat ruefully, the manager told me that the Karams sold the name when they sold the restaurant, and can't use it now. Mazza Plaza has a rich list of specialties, including *zataar* (thyme, sesame, and olive oil), cheese and meat "pizzas" (with varied meat or cheese toppings over Middle Eastern pita bread), roast chicken and chicken, lamb and beef kebabs, and the dips and salads that draw so many foodies to Middle Eastern eateries. The key to many of the dishes is how they are herbed, and Mazza does an amazing job flavoring its dishes. **La Maison du Couscous** (484 77th Street, 718-921-2400) has found a terrific niche in Bay Ridge by offering variations of lamb, vegetarian, and chicken couscous, as well as dessert couscous flavored with sugar, almonds, and cinnamon. They are economical at $7.25 (for the vegetarian couscous) to $9 (for the couscous royal made with chicken, lamb, and vegetables). You can also get *tagines*—Moroccan stews—here. A truly authentic *tagine* (which also refers to the clay pot in which the stew is prepared) usually would have to be ordered ahead of time because of the hours required for preparation, but that's not the case here. There are *tagines* of chicken or lamb with various combinations including, for instance, prunes and almonds (I've had this one with lamb), onions and raisins, and olives and lemons. Mouth-watering! There is also a fish *tagine* and a fish brochette. **Bahry Fish Market & Restaurant** (484 Bay Ridge Avenue, 718-680-8135) is an informal Egyptian place where you can either buy fresh fish to take home or have a meal on the premises. The menu includes fish sandwiches (all $5, served with pita and salad) and entrées of fried fish (whiting, shrimp, or calamari) and grilled fish. You'll pay $10 to $13 for the main meals.

Lola Bell's Café (7428 Fifth Avenue, 718-921-6200) is located in a former bank, and one waitress described for me how the kitchen still has some of the original vaults. You won't see those, but what you will see is a large, personable place where you can get a meal or a drink and make yourself at home. Part of the draw of Lola Bell's is the book exchange, where you can bring in old books and buy some others at a deep discount. They also sell some new books. The setting is like a gigantic living room, with couches, plush chairs, and dark wood tables. Live jazz is played Saturday nights at 9 P.M. (no cover charge), and the café has the advantage of being located on a corner where the sidewalk is just a bit wider than elsewhere, so in warm weather tables are set up outside. The cuisine is contemporary American— grilled portobello mushrooms, mozzarella and arugula, *panini* sandwiches, appetizers, soups, and salads.

Siwa Grill (6915 Fifth Avenue, 718-748-3271) was one of the newer places I visited in Bay Ridge. You'll see the *tagines* (clay pots to prepare Moroccan stews) lined up in front, but the menu is both Moroccan and Egyptian and includes such Egyptian specialties as baked dove—a waitress pointed them out to me (but they weren't listed on the menu). The menu includes many vegetarian dishes—stews of okra, spinach, zucchini, and vegetarian combinations are $6, including rice and salad.

Markets   As you make your way south on Fifth Avenue, you will pass many markets as well as eateries. One of the first worth visiting is **A&D Turkish Halal Meat & Grocery** (7919 Fifth Avenue), which has a wonderful selection of Turkish nuts and dried fruit, and also sells halal marshmallows. One of my favorite markets in Bay Ridge is **Al-Amir Moroccan Market** (7813 Fifth Avenue), which has an awesome window display of Moroccan coffee urns and other bronze and copper items. In the store, in addition to foodstuffs (there's also a butcher, and a whole lamb was advertised at just $2.98 when I was there), you'll find elaborate glass tea sets as well as spices and pastries. There are shelves of *tagines* if you're thinking of learning how to make this dish yourself. Among the Egyptian markets in the area is the large **Zahran** (7618 Fifth Avenue), which is packed with fresh and packaged goods and also sells Egyptian water pipes and the fruit-flavored tobacco smokers use.

Mejlander & Mulgannon (7615 Fifth Avenue, 718-238-6666) specializes in Irish, Scottish, and Norwegian products. You'll find Norwegian fish cakes and brown goat cheese (which I bought—it didn't taste like anything I'd expected, but I'm not sure what I *should* have expected), plus Swedish lingonberry jam, Finncrisps from Finland, and so on.

Pyramid Gifts (7219 Fifth Avenue) is a remarkable place. In front of the store is a table packed with miniature pyramids and images of King Tutankhamen and other Egyptian icons. Inside, it's a coffee shop and gift shop, where you can see men smoking water pipes, sipping tea or coffee, and playing board games. I saw some marvelous wood tambourines for sale, as well as embroidered pillow covers and other items. **Al-Halabi Nuts** (7207 Fifth Avenue, 718-833-5900) is part of a Beirut-based chain that sells nuts, dried fruit, and sweets from Lebanon. The one in Bay Ridge is fairly new—and it's a child's (and adult's) dream.

At **Albeddawi Shopping Center** (7128 Fifth Avenue, 718-748-8944), loose coffee is just $3.99 a pound, and you can buy it with cardamom ground into it. The cardamom is in an adjacent bin and is $12.99 a pound, but you truly will want a small amount, and the owner will help make the blend. I've always loved the Najjar brand of coffee, especially the one that has cardomom mixed into it, that you can find in many Middle Eastern neighborhoods, but buying the coffee and cardamom fresh is sensational. The store also has a general inventory of products from Egypt. The number of Egyptian coffee shops, markets, and gift shops grows as you approach the Islamic center. One nice, friendly place is **Delta Trading** (6815 Fifth Avenue), which has very good produce, water pipes, and more.

Bakeries   The first to visit is **Leske's Bakery** (7612 Fifth Avenue, 718-680-2323 open 7 A.M. to 6:30 P.M., Sunday 7 A.M. to 3 P.M., closed Mondays), the only Scandinavian baker left in Bay Ridge. Specialties include Danish *kringlers*, large pretzel-shaped pastries covered with custard or raspberry jam, and Swedish *lempe* bread, which is a type of rye bread. **Jean Danet French Pastry** (7526 Fifth Avenue, 718-836-7566) is simply amazing. Look at the meringues in the shop window, as well as the various fruit tarts, pastries, and pieces on display. Prices aren't that high: small pastries are $2.25 to $2.50, a fabulous mixed fruit tart is $12.25, and pineapple, blueberry, and cherry cheesecakes are $10. **Arayssi** (7216 Fifth Avenue, 718-745-2115) is a Lebanese bakery that has been in Bay Ridge for years. In addition to the traditional baklavas and other recognizable products, you can get Lebanese-style ice cream here. It's actually made in Warren, Michigan, but there aren't many places to buy it, the manager explained, because it's expensive—$7 a quart—and many people balk at paying that price until they understand that the $7 also covers the expensive shipping of refrigerated dairy products. The two flavors are pistachio and *achta* (pronounced "ashtta"), which is made of what the manager described as "heavy milk" (and he insisted that it wasn't cream!).

. . .

Third Avenue

(68th Street to 86th Street)

If you're still standing after Fifth Avenue and want to explore some more, turn west on 68th Street and walk the two long blocks to Third Avenue and begin the trek south (as numbers ascend). Or save this walk for another day. **Getting There**   To follow this route, follow the above directions or take the R train to Bay Ridge Avenue and walk one block west.

Restaurants   One of the first eateries you'll encounter on this stretch of Bay Ridge is **Balbaa** (6823 Third Avenue, 718-680-3366), an Egyptian place that also has a counterpart on Steinway Street in Astoria (see pages 21–22). It's informal, with a menu offering a range of Mediterranean appetizers and entrées that includes kebabs, grilled chicken, lamb, and other Egyptian specialties. Across the street, **Anopoli Ice Cream Parlor & Family Restaurant** (6930 Third Avenue, 718-748-3863) is a 1950s-type place (with some of the original woodwork from when it first opened in the 1920s), which appeals to families wanting a night out and nothing too challenging. The menu is mostly diner-plus, but the appeal is the old-fashioned sundaes and "fancy frappes" you can get here. **Polonica Restaurant** (7214 Third Avenue) offers the usual Polish fare of pierogis, blintzes, and meat entrées, with a good choice of side dishes—prices are in the $8 to $10 range. Yasser Madbouly opened **King Falafel** (7408 Third Avenue, 718-745-4188) about twenty years ago, one of the first Middle Eastern arrivals to Bay Ridge. Although the menu will seem familiar to fans of Middle Eastern food, the quality and scope are exceptional. When I asked Madbouly, who's Egyptian, to describe what makes his place different, he mentioned the fact that his style, combined with that of co-owner Salwa Baydoun, who is Lebanese, offers a fusion of versions of Middle Eastern food. For instance, there are two types of spinach pie—a Greek version made with phyllo and feta cheese ($2.50) and a Syrian version baked in dough ($1.50). A special rice pilaf features pine nuts, green peas, raisins, and almonds. They've updated the menu with Middle Eastern gourmet wraps. Prices are low for everything on the menu; the most expensive dish is charbroiled lamb chops, for $12.95. You can also get fresh juices here. **Sancho's** (7410 Third Avenue, 718-748-0770) has been in Bay Ridge for years, serving Spanish *paellas* (just $13.95), shrimp entrées, crab meat, and more. The menu is surprisingly reasonable, and the setting is warm and welcoming. Some restaurants derive their appeal from the personality of the owners, and that, I think, is what draws a lot of people to **Tanoreen** (7704 Third Avenue, 718-748-5600). Opened around 1999 by Rawia Bishara as a second or third career, Tanoreen seems more like her living room, as she welcomes you—and just about everyone—with an expansive invitation to share her specialties, which you can take out or eat in. You'll find dishes here that are slightly different than what you're used to, including a popular vegetarian stuffed cabbage; cauliflower salad with pomegranate syrup, tahini, mint, and olive oil; an olive spread with capers, garlic, and spices; a cheese salad; and pickled eggplant; plus plenty of grilled chicken, lamb, and ground meat entrées, of which the most expensive is just $13. (Appetizers range from $3.50 to $7.50.) I usually don't think of the word "sweet" to describe a French eatery, but it works with **Provence-en-Boite** (8303 Third Avenue, 718-759-1515), a friendly place that features $7 ham, chicken, and mushroom crepes on its lunch menu and a $13.50 prix-fixe Sunday brunch (although the menu lists lots of options that have supplemental costs). Dinner entrées, which range from $15 to $18, include braised rabbit, monkfish, Coquilles St. Jacques in whiskey sauce, and a fine bouillabaisse provençale—fish soup with saffron *rouille* (garlic paste). If you love French food and don't want to spend too much, the setting here and service are just fine.

NOTE: Quite a few restaurants in this area are open for dinner only, and I did not cover them.

Bakeries and Cafés   Omonia Café (7612 Third Avenue, 718-491-1435) is
a smaller version of the Greek café of this name on 30-20 Broadway in
Astoria (see page 17). You can get all kinds of coffees and rich Greek pastries to savor with them. **Arachne Antiques & Café** (7922 Third Avenue) is
an eccentric space that sells antiques and offers beverages and snacks. It's
interesting to see but hard to spend much time in because smoking is
allowed and the space is small.

Markets   Perhaps the block on the east side of Third Avenue between
69th and 70th Streets best summarizes Bay Ridge. **The Family Store** (6905
Third Avenue, 718-748-0207) specializes in high-quality Lebanese products—nuts and dried fruit, prepared foods such as *kibbee* (Lebanese meatballs), fried zucchini and other vegetables, dips, and Lebanese pastries, and
breads and packaged goods. Owner Minerva Dabas, who is Palestinian,
drew on family recipes to get started. Just next door is **Nordic Delicacies**
(6909 Third Avenue, 718-748-1874), which, in addition to loads of Norwegian fish and homemade codfish cakes, cheeses, jams, and other products,
also sells Norwegian troll dolls, T-shirts, and mugs. Helena Bakke and her
daughter, Arlene Rutuelo, opened the store in 1987 to make sure Norwegian items remained available. Now a lot of their business is done by mail
order through the Internet around the United States. **Cangiano's Third
Avenue** (6931 Third Avenue, 718-836-5521) specializes in Italian food
products, although it also sells a wide range of general groceries. For non-
food items, **Village Irish Imports** (8505 Third Avenue) helps round out the
ethnic mix of Third Avenue.

■ A Taste of Italy South of 86th Street

I found an interesting cluster of Italian restaurants and a couple of markets
around Third Avenue between 89th and 93rd Streets (and also a Starbucks). This area is technically Fort Hamilton, but I do want to mention
two impressive places here, including **Piazza Mercato** (9204 Third Avenue,
718-513-0071), a high-level market that opened two weeks prior to my
first visit during the summer of 2002. Besides the Italian meats, cheeses,
pastas, and other products for sale, Piazza Mercato lists over 100 sandwich
combinations that can be made on your choice of four breads baked in-
house. The owners of the Piazza also operate a nearby café called **Paneantico** (9124 Third Avenue), an attractive sit-down place that serves
sandwiches, soups, quiches, and desserts. Both are owned by **Royal Crown**
(6512 14th Avenue), which operates another Paneantico at 6308 14th
Avenue. At Piazza Mercato, I bought a delicious *scamozza con burro,* a
semi-soft cheese with a chunk of sweet butter. It's made for grilling on a
slice of country bread and is nothing short of divine.

By the way, Bay Ridge has two nice independent bookstores. **Bay Ridge Book Store** (8506 Fourth Avenue, 718-680-5137) is the smaller of the two, with a nice selection of books on New York City and children's books. **A Novel Idea** (8415 Third Avenue, 718-833-5115) is a big, homey place with plush chairs where you can park yourself for a good read.

■ Elsewhere in Bay Ridge . . .

At 6807 Fifth Avenue you can check out the **Islamic Center of Bay Ridge.** Next door you'll find **Islamic Books & Tapes** (6805 Fifth Avenue), where, among other things, I saw Saudi black seed honey for sale for $10.

Not all Bay Ridge residents of Arab descent are Muslim; not far from the mosque, at 345 Ovington Avenue, is the **Salam Arabic Lutheran Church** for Christian Arabs, and many Arabs also attend mainstream churches.

Although the Scandinavian population in Bay Ridge has declined, its tradition is being upheld locally through the **Scandinavian East Coast Museum** (formerly the Norwegian American Collection in Brooklyn), which opened in December 1996. It's primarily a "virtual museum" that its founder and president, Victoria Hofmo, is developing, although she also puts together traveling exhibits. For more information call 718-748-5950, or see www.scandinavian-museum.org.

. . .

Brighton Beach

The old Soviet Union was never like this—imagine a Ukrainian night club around the corner from an Uzbek kebab joint, and a Georgian restaurant almost toe-to-toe with a Russian sushi place. At another place, specialties from Azerbaijan evoke a crossroads between Asia and Europe—and a touch of nouvelle cuisine. A short walk away, in Sheepshead Bay, is an Armenian café, and down the street is a fine Turkish restaurant. Almost all these places have music playing in the background—sometimes contemporary rock from the countries whose food is being served, sometimes the rich traditional music that evokes another place, another time.

Go into the M&I International Market, very possibly the crown jewel of Brighton Beach, Brooklyn—amid its crowded shelves you'll be goggle-eyed as you see just about everything under this roof that all the restaurants around here serve up. It's a gastronomic journey that can put you on overload.

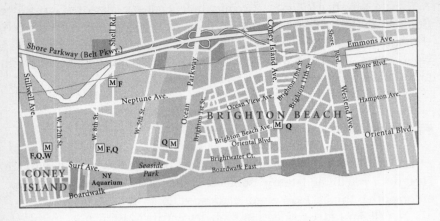

I approached Brighton Beach expecting the much simpler task of writing up restaurants and shops reflecting a relatively small region of the world. After all, compared to Flushing, Queens, I wouldn't have to face the vast challenges of many different cultures, languages, and boundaries—or so I thought. Rather, I found a neighborhood that was much more complex and layered than I'd imagined. For in addition to the many confluences of food, languages, customs, and culture of the various Russian communities in Brighton Beach, I had to acknowledge that the neighborhood is also Turkish, Pakistani, Mexican, and more—although these are a bit hidden. I took that journey, too.

■ Getting Oriented

The area known as Brighton Beach is bordered on the south by the Atlantic Ocean, on the north by Neptune Avenue, and from Ocean Parkway on the west toward Brighton 15th Street to the east. The main commercial strip is Brighton Beach Avenue, which stretches from Ocean Parkway to Corbin Place. The core commercial area runs under the elevated tracks from Ocean Parkway to Coney Island Avenue. Several café/restaurants and smaller food concessions run along the boardwalk parallel to Brighton Beach Avenue between Brighton 4th and Brighton 6th Streets, and many side streets now also have commercial businesses, including cafés and markets. This is a relatively new development.

A smaller commercial area runs along Neptune Avenue from Brighton 4th Street to Coney Island Avenue. This is of interest mainly as a contrast to the dense Russian area—you'll see Mexican, Turkish, Pakistani, and Indian shops here.

Two communities on either side of Brighton Beach—Sheepshead Bay to the northeast (see pages 179–181) and Coney Island to the west—are worth visiting for their food, culture, and history. Manhattan Beach, just east of Brighton Beach, merits a visit if you prefer a smaller, less crowded beach. It can be reached by foot (fifteen to twenty minutes) from Brighton Beach or via the B1 bus on Brighton Beach Avenue.

BY SUBWAY

The Q train from Times Square takes about forty-five minutes to reach Brighton Beach, stopping at Brighton Beach Avenue and Ocean Parkway. The Q goes over the Manhattan Bridge and is elevated for much of the ride. A Q express train runs weekdays, saving ten minutes, and ends at Brighton Beach Avenue. From Grand Central Station, take the #4, 5, or 6 train downtown to Union Square and switch to the Q. From Queens, it's a very long ride without a car! The F train goes to Coney Island, where you can switch for the Q to Brighton Beach.

BY BUS

The B68 runs north-south on Coney Island Avenue, and the B1 crosses the outer edge of Brooklyn, from Manhattan Beach through Brighton Beach, and then through Gravesend and Bensonhurst, ending in Bay Ridge. Many subway stops link up with this bus along 86th Street.

BY CAR

Take the Belt Parkway to Exit 7S (Ocean Parkway) or Exit 8 (Coney Island Avenue). There's a municipal parking lot between Brighton 3rd and Brighton 4th Streets at Brightwater Court.

▪ Tips for Touring

The areas covered here are eminently walkable: Brighton Beach itself is quite compact, and you can walk to Coney Island along the boardwalk and to Sheepshead Bay within fifteen minutes. You might also visit Manhattan Beach, east of Brighton Beach. It's an affluent residential neighborhood whose dominant institutional presence is Kingsborough Community College. Its beach is smaller and much less crowded than Brighton Beach.

Also, some neighborhoods I've written about have posed real challenges because of language difficulties. In some ways, Brighton Beach has been the most difficult. Many stores have signs in Russian only. Eateries often have menus in English, but the servers may not speak it.

■ History

Long before Brighton Beach drew folks in search of gastronomic pleasures, it was a vacation destination. First developed as a resort in the 1870s, it had a large inn, amusement park, and racetrack. But the beach was the draw, and summer bungalows offered refuge from urban heat. Clusters of these bungalows, now winterized, remain, and you can see some by heading north on Brighton First Place and wandering in and out of the paths and walks (marked by signs such as Brighton 1st Walk, Brighton 1st Way, and so on).

The completion of the elevated train in the 1920s prompted developers to pack the neighborhood with six-story apartment buildings. Huddled masses, mostly Jews from tenement-choked East New York, Brownsville, and the Lower East Side, filled them—and provided the setting for Neil Simon's autobiographical *Brighton Beach Memoirs*. Brighton Beach Baths, a beach club, eventually replaced the inn. At its peak in the 1960s the baths had 13,000 members.

In the 1970s the population shifted—after the Soviet Union relaxed immigration laws tens of thousands of Soviet Jews arrived in the United States. As older American-born Jews left, agencies assisting these newcomers placed many of them in Brighton Beach. (During the 1970s, by the way, the only McDonald's in Brighton Beach closed!)

But the dominance of this group was threatened by yet another change: in the mid-1990s developers began to replace the now-closed Brighton Beach Baths with up-market condos, many with spectacular ocean vistas. A new wave of immigrants, including New Yorkers from other neighborhoods, bought in, some paying over a $1 million for a condo. And many second-generation Russians left for affluent areas such as Manhattan Beach to the east or to suburbs.

The history here is rich, but so is the contemporary culture. It takes time to "get" it, but it's worth it! Sadly, there are no hotels in Brighton Beach. A bed-and-breakfast would be nice. I love it at dusk and can imagine how nice it would be at dawn, with the sun rising over the ocean. . . .

On the Boardwalk
(Brighton 4th Street to Brighton 6th Street)

I still remember when the Brighton Beach boardwalk was dotted with cheesy fast-food stands. The transformation over the last fifteen years has been startling, and now the stretch from Brighton 4th to Brighton 6th Street is occupied by restaurants offering Russian and French cuisine, and even sushi. To some extent, they're all similar, with traditional Russian appetizers and entrées—*blinis*, herring, caviar, "dough" entrées (*vareniki*, *pelmini*, and *hachapuri*—stuffed Georgian patties), plus soups and a long list of seafood and meat entrées. Tatiana Varzar owns two of them—**Tatiana Café** (3145 Brighton 4th Street, 718-646-7630) and **Tatiana Restaurant and Nightclub** (3152 Brighton 6th Street, 718-891-5151), which features an aquarium built into the dance floor. (They take credit cards if you spend at least $25.) Another is **Volna** (3145 Brighton 4th Street—same address as Tatiana Café, but it's next door; 718-332-0501; cash only). The manager, Igor, was the best English speaker among all I spoke with there. **Winter Garden Restaurant** (3152 Brighton 6th Street—same address as Tatiana nightclub; 718-934-6666) features a $10.99 lunch special: soup, salad, lox and potatoes, an entrée, beverage, and dessert—a generous meal that will carry you for the day. Winter Garden also runs **Moscow Café,** a low-key version of the other places. At all, you also can buy ice cream and sodas to take to the beach.

At Tatiana's I savored a shrimp kebab in pomegranate sauce one early evening on the beach ($17.95) and enjoyed reading the menu—how about a black caviar crepe for $70? Or crepes Tatiana (breast of duck sautéed in apples and wine) for just $18? I also saw quail and fillet of ostrich. Meals are artfully put together, and you're paying not only for the creativity and unusual combinations of flavors but the luxury of enjoying them at the beach. For instance, an "apple salad" turned out to be a salad *caprèse*, with very fresh cut tomatoes and slices of mozzarella cheese. But they were sliced to look like an apple—pieces of tomato alternating with mozzarella and an artfully placed basil leaf to look like the leaf on a just-picked red apple. Go mid-week if you can because it's so much quieter and you can linger without out pressure.

• • •

Brighton Beach Avenue

(Ocean Parkway to Brighton 14th Street)

From Ocean Parkway on the west to Brighton 14th Street on the east, Brighton Beach Avenue bustles. Within this area you'll find all the varied cuisines of the former Soviet states: Eastern European fish and meat dishes and "dough" entrees as well as spicy shish kebabs and an intriguing fusion of styles (such as *dolmades*—grape leaves—wrapped not in rice but in spicy chopped meat). Baklava is sold next to rum-soaked Hungarian pastries. Several Turkish markets and one kosher shop complement the food festival.

Markets   Produce is of very high quality and generally inexpensive in Brighton Beach—look for luscious and varied tomatoes, plums, cherries, and nectarines for a bargain. The best market is **Fancy Farm** (224 Brighton Beach Avenue), which is slightly more expensive than the rest but has the highest quality and most beautiful presentation. The owners are Russian-speaking Koreans and their inventory includes fruit, vegetables, nuts, and melons not seen many other places. Russians love sushi as well as more traditional herring and other smoked fish dishes, and there are several fish markets. My favorite is **Fish Palace** (244 Brighton Beach Avenue), the nicest-looking of the area's fish stores. Two excellent Turkish markets, **EFE** (243 Brighton Beach Avenue) and **Vintage** (287 Brighton Beach Avenue), sell nuts, dried fruit, crackers, imported candies, chocolates, preserves, and juices. Quart bottles of pomegranate juice, $4 or more elsewhere, cost $2 here. The only remaining kosher establishment in Brighton Beach is **Melrose Glatt Kosher** (282 Brighton Beach Avenue), a small, crowded place with unspectacular prepared and packaged dishes and grumpy service. The must-go market in Brighton Beach is **M&I International** (249 Brighton Beach Avenue, 718-615-1011), the Zabar's (and then some) of Brighton Beach. This epitome of excess teems with dozens of types of sausage, smoked fish, cheeses, yogurts, salads, sweets, and teas, and the inventory covers the breadth of Eastern and much of Western Europe, though I've also seen products from Southeast Asia and even honey from Australia. Like many of us, its girth has expanded over time, as the twenty-plus-year-old store run by the Vinokurov family (who also own National Night Club—see page 114) has taken over more space on the street and upstairs levels. There's also a downstairs café for Russian fast food—cold salads, chicken, fish, and dumplings—and a dessert café upstairs, which extends onto a roof area. Upstairs you can buy boxed chocolates, preserves, and other confections from around the world for about half what you'd pay elsewhere, and pastry slices that would cost $2 or $3—or more—are $1 or less here. Meat and fish counters fill the front area on the ground floor; beverages and breads are in the center followed by cheeses and then, in the back, are the yummy prepared dishes that prompted my guide, Boris Kerdimun, to say: "When you come here, you never have to cook!"

By the way, during the course of covering Brighton Beach I became acquainted with *tkemali* sauce, a Georgian condiment that you'll see everywhere. I *had* to buy it because the name intrigued me. It's made of plums and spices and is used with chicken, other meats, or whatever food you want to flavor—I suppose it's the Russian version of ketchup, but it's a lot tastier. It comes in red and green versions, and I confess to having become addicted. A sixteen-ounce bottle generally runs $2.50 to $3.50.

Bakeries   You'll find pastries and breads galore in all the big markets; there are just a few distinct bakeries. Some fun places to visit for baked goods are **The Russian Bread Shop** (129 Brighton First Walk) and **Gold-field Bakery** (358 Brighton Beach Avenue), which has luscious pastries and breads. I'm told that many of these actually come from **Kiev Bakery,** whose factory is on Coney Island Avenue. Kiev has a retail outlet at 1611 Kings Highway (718-627-5438) and I took a detour one day to visit it. It's about a block east of the Kings Highway exit on the Q train, and beware—the window display alone is enough to undo any daydreams of abandoning rich cakes.

Restaurants   There are roughly three levels of eateries in Brighton Beach. The most basic are what I would call the daytime cafés (even though they're open late). Their decor is simple, the dishes budget-priced, and there's no entertainment (although Russian videos are ubiquitous). You can have a meal, with beverage, for $7 or less, and some places have lunchtime specials. Places I've tried include **Varenchnaya** (3086 Brighton 2nd Street, 718-332-9797), which specializes in *pelmini* (sometimes called Russian ravioli) and *varenicki* (also called pierogi), with fruit, cheese, or meat fillings. They have soups and other dishes here as well, and you also can buy packages of frozen *pelmini* and *varenicki* to take home. **Ocean View Café** (290 Brighton Beach Avenue. 718-332-1900) is unusual for Brighton Beach as it had a no-smoking policy that worked even before smoking was banned everywhere. Service is quick, professional, and friendly, with a nice selection of salads and seafood dishes plus a hefty meat menu. I especially like the shrimp in white sauce. Sadly, the only time it has an ocean view is in the evening, when tables and chairs are set up on the sidewalk. **Chio Pio** (3087 Brighton 4th Street, 718-615-9221) is a relatively new Uzbek place where you can get salads and shish kebabs, with mystical Central Asian music playing in the background (on video). Salads cost more than the kebabs and are hearty and delicious. The popular **Gina's Cappuccino Café** (409 Brighton Beach Avenue, 718-646-6297) has an almost Manhattan feel (appealing to a younger crowd, I think). Wanting something filling but low-cost, I had the herring appetizer, which filled the bill, and me, for $4.50 I got several thick chunks of herring with potatoes boiled in garlic butter and dill, and brown bread. I drank the popular com-pote, a fresh fruit juice with sour cherries. I visited the popular **Café Shish Kebab** (414 Brighton Beach Avenue, 718-368-0966) on an off day—the manager was gone and two frazzled waitresses were having a hard time managing the impatient lunch crowd. Feeling frustrated, I knocked on the kitchen door and was able to get a waitress to take my order, although it then took ages to get served. (I felt a little better when I saw a Russian cus-tomer do the same thing.) All I got was a salmon shish kebab—no side dishes—and it was so-so at $5.50. Meat kebabs range from $3.50 to $5 and fish kebabs are higher (shrimp kebab is $8.50). Low prices explain the appeal—entrées are $4 to $6.50 (for a fish dish).

The next notch up is restaurants that also have evening entertainment, usually live music, and they often have lunch specials. **Café St. Petersburg** (233 Brighton Beach Avenue, 718-743-0880) has a $6.99 late lunch special available from 3 P.M. to 6 P.M. (These meals usually include soup—borscht or another choice—a salad, shish kebab or herring, and French fries or rice, plus coffee.) Late at night the café becomes a nightclub, with a prix fixe starting at $65! I particularly like **Primorski** (282 Brighton Beach Avenue, 718-891-3111), one of the oldest restaurants in Brighton Beach. Its extensive menu includes a $4.99 lunch special, but whether you get that or try the banquet, the food will be delicious, with many Georgian specialties. It's odd eating lunch at a place set up for evening, though!

Nightlife   Brighton Beach is famous for its nightlife. Add a stroll on the Boardwalk and you'll be in heaven! Prices at nightclubs, where stage shows start at 10 or 11 P.M., start at $60 for a prix fixe banquet, but that's before taxes and a 10% service charge. With extra drinks and substitutions to the meal, it's unlikely you'll leave for under $80. I brought friends to Primorski, where there was live music and a banquet. The $35 Saturday night banquet ($30 on Fridays and Sundays, $25 other times) began with delicious Georgian bread and dips. Cold meats, pickled vegetables, and *dolmades* soon followed. Then came smoked fish and herring, and then *blinis* with jam, followed by shish kebab and chicken Kiev. Oh—and chocolate and vanilla *milles feuilles* for dessert! And you get all the seltzer and Coca-Cola you want and one bottle of wine or vodka for four people. (We chose an Inglenook chablis that wasn't bad.) When the musicians weren't singing Ricky Martin or Russian rock as folks crowded the dance floor, we heard Yiddish karaoke (sung by a woman celebrating her seventieth birthday) and learned from the headwaiter that the table of thirty exotic-looking people nearby was a clan of Polish gypsies. The table behind had celebrants from the Mermaid Parade held earlier that day in Coney Island. More elaborate still are the nightclubs that have prix fixe menus (with variations if you ask for more) starting at $60 or $65. One of the oldest is the **National Night Club** (273 Brighton Beach Avenue, 728-646-1225).

Also . . .   Shopping in Brighton Beach is fun, with new upscale boutiques, housewares stores, and Russian gift shops. Don't miss the extraordinary **St. Petersburg Bookstore** at 230 Brighton Beach Avenue. **Kalinka's Gifts** (402 Brighton Beach) and **Russian Gifts** (292 Brighton Beach Avenue, even though it's west of 290) are worth a visit. **Zuckerman's Pharmacy** at 701 Brighton Beach Avenue has many Russian toiletries for sale. It's fun to look at the packaging of the various soaps, shampoos, and skin lotions—some are made to look like the popular Russian *matroushka* (nesting) dolls.

...

Brighton Beach Avenue

(Coney Island Avenue to Brighton 14th Street)

Coney Island Avenue is the dividing line between Brighton Beach Avenue "under the el" and a four-block stretch that lacks the throb of the previous section of Brighton Beach Avenue—probably because it doesn't have the vibrations of the subway tracks overhead and has stores just on the north side!

Markets   The large **Gourmet Plaza Supermarket** (1007 Brighton Beach Avenue, 718-769-1700) usually isn't busy yet has a surprisingly large staff. I come here to buy strawberry and apricot-raisin cream cheese and prepared dishes such as chicken in mushrooms, salad *olivie* (Russian potato salad), and various slaws. There are many fish dishes, cakes, and an exceptional selection of preserves from all over Europe. **Gastronom Arkadia** (1079 Brighton Beach Avenue) has a large self-service Russian salad bar from which you can choose among many salads and cooked fish and chicken preparations. There aren't many self-service opportunities in Brighton Beach, and this is definitely the best. Most salads and dips are $2.99 a pound; meats and fish are $3.99 a pound. A disadvantage (as at most area markets) is that signs are in Russian and few staff speak much English. So take your chance, but chances are you'll do well! You can't mix dishes together, so you'll see customers stacking up six or more containers of the goodies they're taking home for the night—or the week! Always-crowded **Golden Key** (1064 Brighton Beach Avenue and addresses nearby) occupies several storefronts, with one specializing in meat, one featuring seafood (actually on Brighton 12th Street, although it has a Brighton Beach Avenue address), and others. The Golden Key supermarket has a modest self-serve salad bar. **EFE** Turkish market (1081 Brighton Beach Avenue) is a counterpart to one I mentioned earlier near Brighton First Place. **M&A Liquors** (1109 Brighton Beach Avenue) has wines from Moldova and Georgia and many vodkas, including Ukrainian honey pepper vodka, new on the scene.

Bakeries   **La Brioche** (1073 Brighton Beach Avenue, 718-934-7709) is like an overflowing toy box, offering a tantalizing selection of cakes, halvahs, chocolates, and pastries at remarkably low prices (they average $3.49 a pound) and you can buy slabs of baklava, cake rolls, and pastries for 50 cents or $1. In the middle is a long wooden table set up for folks to drink coffee (several flavored coffees are available—it's self-service) while indulging in a trillion-calorie delight. (Too bad the owner tends to smoke inside—but go anyway!)

Eateries   At the busy intersection, you'll come upon **Mrs. Stahl's Knishes** (1003 Brighton Beach Avenue), which shares its address with an Uzbek kebab place called **Eastern Feast.** Mrs. Stahl's, which has been around for decades, strikes me as tired; the knishes were soggy and boring. Eastern Feast has an intriguing menu and brusque service. For similar cuisine I recommend the friendlier **Chio Pio** (see page 113). Heading west, the newish **Art Café** (1005 Brighton Beach Avenue) is beautiful to look at and ranks high on the daytime café menu list.

Nightlife   At 1031 Brighton Beach Avenue you'll find two local institutions: **Millennium Theater** on the second floor, which seats 1,200, is Brighton Beach's venue for major acts. Ray Charles, adored by Russians, played here in May 2001; there was not a peep about this sold-out show in the English-language press. On the ground floor is the restaurant/nightclub **Atlantic Oceana** (718-742-1515), which is decorated to create the atmosphere of a cruise ship. Its multicourse banquets feature East European, Israeli, and Central Asian dishes. Want gaudy? See the rococo statues in front of twenty-five-year-old **Odessa Nightclub** (1117 Brighton Beach Avenue, 718-332-3223). Its prix fixe of $60 for a show and banquet includes two shots of vodka. The owners also operate a large market next door.

Neptune Avenue

Another Side of Brighton Beach

If you're as compulsive an explorer as I am, check out Neptune Avenue between Brighton 4th Street and Coney Island Avenue, where you'll see the non-Russian face of the neighborhood—the large Mexican, South Asian, and Turkish population.

To get there, head north on Coney Island Avenue from Brighton Beach Avenue to the busy intersection with Neptune Avenue and turn left (west). The **Mosque of Brighton Beach** is at 230 Neptune Avenue at Brighton 7th Street.

The nicer places in this area include **Yatan Turkish Market** (201 Neptune Avenue at Brighton 8th Street) and **El Jarochito,** a Mexican bakery and grocery at 195 Neptune Avenue (near Coney Island Avenue). The canopy at **New Eastern Market** (229 Neptune Avenue at Brighton 7th Street) notes that it caters to American, Pakistani, Indian, Russian, and Mexican tastes. **Anandal Halal Grocery** (225 Neptune Avenue at Brighton 7th Street) serves mainly Muslim customers from Pakistan. **Chinantla Imports** (205 Neptune Avenue at Brighton 8th Street) down the block sells Mexican goods.

■ Elsewhere in Brighton Beach . . .

MOTHER JONES IN BRIGHTON BEACH

Imagine my surprise to discover an apartment building (3102-16 Brighton First Place) called Mother Jones. To me, she's Mary Harris Jones (1837–1930), the firebrand who organized miners and other workers to stand up for their rights. So what's she doing in Brighton Beach? I figured the owner might know, but residents I approached to ask for his name only spoke Russian. *The Neighborhoods of Brooklyn* (New Haven: Yale University Press, 1998) mentions that a number of apartment buildings erected in the 1920s and 1930s were named after socialist leaders, but this was the only one I saw.

COOKBOOK ALERT

I always look for good cookbooks when I visit any neighborhood, but it's rarely easy when English is definitely the second language. The best I found in Brighton Beach was *Russian Cuisine* (St. Petersburg, Russia: P-2 Art Publishers, 2000), $16.99 at the **St. Petersburg Bookstore** at 230 Brighton Beach Avenue, although the translations are sometimes unwittingly funny.

■ Beyond Brighton Beach Avenue

As I researched this area, people I met recommended places they love that aren't in the thick of Brighton Beach but are worth a visit. One of these is the terrific **Café Glechik** (3159 Coney Island Avenue, 718-616-0494), a short walk north on the long block of Coney Island Avenue from Brighton Beach Avenue. This friendly Ukrainian café has lovely down-home décor and music and constant crowds. Opened in 2000, its owners had turned a profit within two months, and you'll see why crowds pack in when you go: platters of *pelmini,* shish kebab, salads, and whatever else you order are huge, delicious, and very fresh. (A *glechik,* by the way, is a clay pot used to prepare traditional Ukrainian dishes.) I had a spectacular salmon shish kebab platter (with salad and French fries) for just $12.50 and took half home because it was too much.

You also should definitely try **Baku Restaurant** (2718 Coney Island Avenue, 718-615-0700) between Avenues X and Y. It's about a ten-minute walk beyond Glechik, and may be the only Azeri (as in Azerbaijan) restaurant in New York City. Owned by Azeri Jews, its cuisine fuses the influences of Eastern Europe, Central Asia, and the Middle East—dips, smoked fish, kebabs, and *blinis,* and (surprise!) crabs, mussels, and shrimp. Try the *lula* *kebab* in *lavash*: kebabs of ground lamb wrapped in a thin bread resembling Indian *roti*. A filling bean salad called *lobio* is made of red kidney beans, finely chopped walnuts, oil, and parsley.

For shopping I was directed to the huge **NetCost Market** (which Russian speakers call *baza* from the Russian equivalent to bazaar). It's at 2257 East 16th Street at Gravesend Neck Road (with a second location at 2339 65th Street in Bensonhurst, where many Russians live). Take the Q train one stop from Brighton Beach to Gravesend Neck Road—it's around the corner from the subway entrance. You'll find almost everything you'll see in Brighton Beach. The difference is that it's self-service and slightly cheaper, and there's good parking. Although it has a modest selection of salads, it's missing the wonderful variety of prepared specialties that are available within Brighton Beach.

■ ■ ■

Greenpoint

In contrast with multi-ethnic neighborhoods such as Jackson Heights and Sunset Park, Greenpoint has long been known for one particular ethnicity and cuisine—Polish. When I set out to explore Greenpoint in 2001 for the first time in many years, I was curious to see if this image still held, especially amid gentrification.

At that time I hadn't been there for over ten years. I was intrigued to see how much the area had changed, and how much it hadn't. Some of the same markets and bakeries were still in business and looked unchanged. But I also saw a number of new places—Polish and not—that had sparked up the place. During a second visit more than a year later, I counted five Thai restaurants on Manhattan Avenue and two new sushi places.

As I explored, I came to realize how little I'd understood Greenpoint. Helena Zubrovich, a gift-shop owner who grew up there, put me straight. "Most outsiders think it's just Polish, but that's not it at all," she said. She, for instance, is Slovakian, and much of the area for years was (and, she says, remains) Irish and Italian. (She stocks many Irish-themed gifts.) And these days, in addition to more families from Latin America, especially Mexico, there has been an influx of artists, some spilling over from Williamsburg, others who have come for the loft space and arts community at Greenpoint's north end. And, finally, there are refugees from Manhattan, seeking in Greenpoint more space, cheaper housing, easy parking, proximity to Manhattan, and the particular quiet one can find in this "urban village."

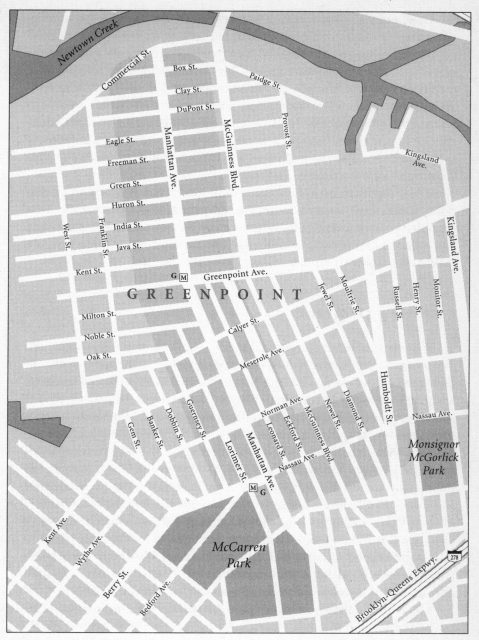

And there *is* a feeling of village here. Few buildings rise above six stories, and few, it seems, were built after the 1920s. Its isolation—it's bordered on three sides by water and on the fourth by the Brooklyn-Queens Expressway—keeps Greenpoint apart and perhaps explains why so little development has taken place here. Blocks of nineteenth-century architecture remain intact.

Greenpoint's Polish roots are deeper than I'd realized: the first families settled here more than a century ago. These days, estimates of the Polish population range from 50% to 80% of its 180,000 residents. Folks "in the know," including businessman John Tapper and Christine McMullan of the Polish National Alliance, say the numbers are falling off as rising rents are pushing out Polish working-class families. But most stores and many restaurants remain Polish (and Greenpoint's 99-cent stories carry Polish goods). I sense that a younger generation of Polish-Americans is choosing to stay here because the quality of life is good and you can always buy Grandma's food from the corner market.

There seems to be a real push-pull between old and new in Greenpoint. Once there were many movie theaters; now there are none. New shopping centers several subway stops away have lured away business and entertainment. You make a deliberate choice when you decide to move here. And to come to explore and eat. So—take the trek!

■ Getting Oriented

There are basically two commercial axes in Greenpoint: a north-south axis along Manhattan Avenue, which could be described as the spine of Greenpoint, and an east-west axis along Nassau Avenue. The visual centerpiece on Manhattan Avenue is the Church of St. Anthony of Padua, which sits slightly elevated at the intersection of Milton Street and Manhattan Avenue. (The clock on its spire is always working!) To the east is busy McGuinness Boulevard which connects Queens and Brooklyn. It creates a physical dividing point between the two key sections of Greenpoint. The centerpiece of the Nassau Avenue axis—though not actually at the center—is Monsignor McGolrick Park, a lovely, leafy place for a picnic. Greenpoint has a handful of chain shops—a Burger King can be found next to McDonald's, and you'll also see a Rite Aid and some large supermarkets. But for the most part, this is a neighborhood of small business. Greenpoint's historic landmark district centers around Kent, Milton, and Noble Streets west of Manhattan Avenue. Crimson-colored signs in the area mark the historic district.

Once upon a time, you could take a ferry to Greenpoint from Manhattan and be there in minutes. Now it takes two or three subways from Manhattan and two from almost anywhere else. (If you live in certain parts of Queens or Brooklyn, you might be in luck and be able to get there on one.)

BY SUBWAY

The two subway stops in Greenpoint (Nassau Avenue and Greenpoint Avenue) are on the G line, which connects Brooklyn and Queens. From mid-Manhattan you can connect to the G from the E, F, and R trains at Queens Plaza *on weekends, holidays, and at night.* At Queens Plaza, climb the stairs and go down to the *opposite* platform for the G train headed toward 9th Street, Brooklyn. It's three or four stops to Greenpoint. If you're lucky with connections, you'll be there in just twenty minutes; otherwise plan on twenty-five to thirty minutes. (Reductions in the G line during the week have made the midtown connection more difficult. See the recommendation from lower Manhattan for easier access.) You also can take the #7 train, which runs along 42nd Street in Manhattan with stops at Times Square, Fifth Avenue, and Grand Central Station, to the first stop in Queens (Vernon Boulevard/Jackson Avenue) and then walk over the Pulaski Bridge at Jackson and 12th Street into Greenpoint. Take the stairs down to Ash Street at the northern tip or a ramp further south at Eagle Street. It's a fifteen-minute walk.

From lower Manhattan, take the L train (which runs along 14th Street) to Lorimer Street and switch for the G (where the stop is called Metropolitan Avenue) headed toward Forest Hills. It's one stop to Nassau Avenue, two stops to Greenpoint Avenue. The Bedford Avenue stop on the L train (the first stop in Brooklyn) leaves you off at the trendier area of Williamsburg. If you get off here and walk north (actually northeast) on Bedford toward its end, you'll come to an intersection with Lorimer Street and Nassau Avenue. It's an interesting walk that takes just ten to fifteen minutes.

BY BUS

The B61 runs from Queens Plaza in Long Island City into Greenpoint.

BY CAR

The Pulaski or Greenpoint Bridges in Queens cross into Greenpoint. From the Brooklyn-Queens Expressway exit at Meeker-Morgan, Metropolitan Avenue, or McGuinness Boulevard. You should be able to find parking on sidestreets.

▪ History

The name "Greenpoint" comes from the name Dutch settlers gave it in the 1600s when they sighted a neck of grasslands jutting into what is now Newton Creek. Although you won't find many signs of gardens nowadays, you will find beautiful nineteenth-century architecture and many interesting places that combine charm and history, and some quirks.

There are spectacular vistas from several intersections, especially if you walk along Franklin Street, where, at various turns, you'll see the Citicorp Center, the Chrysler Building, the Empire State Building, and lower Manhattan. (There used to be a clear view of the World Trade Center from here.) At the intersection of Franklin and Dupont Streets is Greenpoint Playground, an adequate play area with a sensational Manhattan skyline view, which is, alas, marred by Dumpsters, parking lots, barbed-wire fencing, and ugly industrial buildings along the Greenpoint perimeter. The India Street Pier is in ruins—if people once fished here, they cannot do so now. The block-long Astral Apartments at 184 Franklin Street between Java and India Streets were built in 1886 by oil magnate Charles Pratt (after whom The Pratt Institute is named) to provide airy, humane housing to local workers; it has a central court but no dark airshafts. The six-story complex once had a settlement house and social programs. Despite its size, it retains a humble presence in keeping with the tone of the neighborhood. Many warehouses and small factories still operate here. Don't miss the former Eberhard Faber Pencil Factory at the northwest corner of Greenpoint Avenue and Franklin Street, where you'll see one-story-high pencils (the #2 yellow kind) adorning the façade.

In terms of green space, Monsignor McGolrick Park is the nicest around. The sprawling McCarran Park at Greenpoint's southwestern edge is frayed and unappealing. Slightly north of McCarran Park is the small, nicely landscaped Father Jerzy Popieluszko Square—really a triangle—across the street from Monsignor's Restaurant, where you can pick up a picnic meal.

. . .

Manhattan Avenue

Getting There   I recommend you start at the north end of Manhattan Avenue. Take the India Street exit from the Greenpoint Avenue station of the G train or descend the stairs at Ash Street if you're entering Greenpoint along the Pulaski Bridge from Long Island City. Work your way south.
Markets   Greenpoint is loaded with small markets. The traditional meat markets specialize in *kielbasa* (Polish sausage) and usually also sell bread, condiments, and prepared foods—pierogi (dumplings), salads, and soups. A typical market is **Staropolsky,** which has branches at 1053 Manhattan Avenue (a new arrival, near Freeman Street) and 912 Manhattan Avenue in the heart of Greenpoint. I also like **Europa Delicatessen** (650 Manhattan Avenue, near Nassau Avenue) because it's very hands-on, easy-going, and friendly, and somewhat chaotic in a way I find

quite comfortable. (The folks at the otherwise nicely laid-out Polski Market nearby were not helpful during several visits.) **Fresh Point Market** (854 Manhattan Avenue, near Milton Street) specializes in produce. You'll see an appealing selection of peppers, potatoes, dill, cabbage, cherries, and other fresh ingredients used for Polish cooking, as well as many packaged products. The classiest liquor store in Greenpoint is **Z&J Wine & Liquor** at 761 Manhattan Avenue near Meserole Street. The decor itself is beautiful and the selection of East European cordials, vodkas, and Polish specialties is substantial.

Restaurants   **Christina's Restaurant** (853 Manhattan Avenue between Milton and Noble Streets, 718-383-4382) is my favorite in this area. A sweet, homey place with a counter and comfortable booths, it offers a nice selection of Polish and American specialties and, more to the point, it's friendly and accessible to non-Polish speakers. You'll find traditional Polish cuisine—*kielbasa* and *babka*—along with French toast, blintzes, potato pancakes, and pierogi (a complete platter is $4.25; a half-order is $2.50). Check out the soups—various types of borscht (Ukrainian, white, and red) and cucumber soup. A really great blintz is filled with cheese and plum butter. You can also get more traditional diner entrées and sandwiches. **Stylowa** (694 Manhattan Avenue, south of Norman Street, 718-383-8993) is a newer place with a more contemporary look but it has much of the traditional cuisine found at other Polish eateries and an accommodating staff. There are homemade soups (three different types of borscht, cucumber, and others); pierogi, blintzes, and pancakes; and veal entrées, dumplings, and shish kebab—the second most expensive dish on the menu at $7. The most expensive, at $8, is chicken *devolaille*—chicken breast roll stuffed with butter. For a contrast, try **Polonia Restaurant** (631 Manhattan Avenue at Nassau Avenue, 718-383-9781). Upon entering this place I thought I'd trespassed into someone's family room. The wood-paneled walls are adorned with flags and photographs of Polish soccer teams, and two women engage in a lively banter (in Polish) while dishing out heaping portions of stews, potatoes, and vegetables side dishes. I felt like a real tourist here. There is no take-out menu but if you can point your way to the dishes you want you will have a hardy meal—and you'll struggle to spend more than $6 for it.

Bakeries   There are quite a few in Greenpoint, but I've narrowed my preferences to three. Two are on Nassau Avenue, mentioned below. On Manhattan Avenue I love **Chocolatiere Bakery** (615 Manhattan Avenue, south of Nassau Avenue, 718-383-8450). This sit-down café offers low-cost espresso and cappuccino—I paid just $2.95 for a cappuccino *and* a poppy seed pastry—half the going rate at any Starbucks or Greek café I've written about in Astoria—and at least as good!

Sweets Don't miss mouthwatering **Stodycze Wedel** (772 Manhattan Avenue at Meserole Street, 718-349-3933), a beautiful shop with a vast selection of Polish and other imported chocolates, candies, and cookies.

. . .

Nassau Avenue

As I noted in "Getting Oriented" (see pages 120–121), Nassau Avenue is Greenpoint's east-west commercial axis. McGuinness Boulevard, a six-lane roadway east of Manhattan Avenue, bisects the area. It's a noisy, unpleasant road that links Greenpoint to the Pulaski Bridge leading into Long Island City. Once you walk past it, though, you're in a quiet, friendly neighborhood. **St. Stanislaus Kostka Church** on 607 Humboldt Street at Driggs Avenue has New York City's largest Polish-Catholic congregation. Pope John Paul II visited this church when he was still a cardinal.

Getting There At the Nassau Avenue stop on the G train, exit at the south end (Nassau Avenue; the north exit is at Norman Street). To get oriented, when you leave the station look for the spire and clock tower at St. Anthony of Padua Church, which is several blocks north of the stop up a modest hill. Go east (right) to start the tour.

Markets **Podlasie Meat Market** (121 Nassau Avenue, at the corner of Leonard Street, with a counterpart at 65-47 Myrtle Avenue in Glendale, Queens) is a traditional market where you'll have a hard time communicating if you don't speak Polish, and it's often crowded. There's a large selection of *kielbasa*, Polish hams, and other meats, and a refrigerator stocked with prepared soups (borscht, *shav*, and others) and various salads and dips. There's also an impressive selection of breads (baked elsewhere—many markets buy from the large Syrena Bakery on Norman Street).

Steve's Meat Market (104 Nassau Avenue) is a popular stop for *kielbasa* fans. One of its appeals is that Steve himself—who grew up in Greenpoint—is glad to describe to non-Polish speakers the different types of *kielbasa* (more than a dozen), which is their specialty. They range from the thick, dry *krakowsky* (the leanest—it's fat-free with no fillers or additives—and most expensive at $4.80 a pound) to *zwyczajna* (barbecue sausage, ground fine and with ample fat for cooking), *kabanosy* (like a Slim Jim, just right to take to a baseball game), *biala* (fresh, not smoked—good for breakfast), and *mysliwska* (hot dog–sized sausage flavored with juniper berries). There's also an "Original Greenpoint" *kielbasa*—specially made for Steve's—which is a long sausage in a fiber casing with a smokey flavor.

Rachel's Garden (122 Nassau Avenue between Eckford Street and McGuinness Boulevard) opened in 2000 and offers high-quality produce and a nice but not overwhelmingly large selection of appetizers (various types of herring and cheeses), sweets, frozen Polish specialties (about six different types of pierogi), and assorted imported delicacies, as well as dried fruit. No meat here, so vegetarians needn't worry about being overcome by the aroma of smoked meat. In 2002 the owner opened **Rachel's Corner** (116 Nassau Avenue at Eckford Street), offering pizza, sandwiches, and salads, plus a salad bar that includes pierogi, roast chicken, noodles, and other Polish specialties. (When I inquired about Rachel, I was told she's the daughter of the owner—who is Turkish.)

Young's Fruit & Vegetables (192 Nassau Avenue) is a Korean-owned produce market that has one of the best selections of Polish dairy products in Greenpoint including one of my favorite products: chocolate cheese spread. Yum!

Restaurants   I saw about a half dozen Polish eateries along Nassau Avenue. None are fancy, but my favorite is **Old Poland Bakery & Restaurant** (190 Nassau Avenue at Humboldt Street, 718-349-7757), which has one of the area's largest menus, including eighteen soups, seven different types of blintz, a large selection of meat dishes, and enough side salads or vegetables to please a non-meat eater. Not everything is served every day, but you'll still have a good choice. A nice feature here is an entry ramp (helpful for the many young moms with strollers, shoppers with carts, and older people in the area). There's a homey bakery counter near the entry. The setting, in keeping with the low prices, is very informal. Old Poland also has a wholesale bakery outlet in Williamsburg that can be reached at 800-GO-POLAND.

Maybe it's the name, but I just have to mention **Relax Restaurant** (68A Newell Street, just south of Nassau Avenue, 718-389-1665), a small, homey place with a very large *jadlospis*—menu.

Cafés   **Baron's Café** (97 Nassau Avenue, 718-389-5050) is an example of a "new wave" Polish establishment. It was founded in 1998 by Israeli Alon Cohen, who moved to Greenpoint more than twenty years ago with his Polish wife. He has had other businesses here but opened Baron's because he felt Greenpoint needed something like it, and he's right. There isn't anything else around with the space and ambiance, and where you can come in for dessert only or have a full meal. It appeals equally to long-time residents wanting something fancier than the norm and to newcomers to Greenpoint who may be used to something like this. It's modern, artsy, and relaxed, with brick walls and ceiling fans. And it offers an eclectic mix of typical Polish dishes—pierogi and blintzes—along with guacamole and chips, buffalo wings, and grilled chicken breast salad (and other salads) and fajitas. The desserts are baked elsewhere but the Polish specials—which

Cohen has been adding over time—are prepared in the open kitchen area in the back. I took a group of folks here for lunch one day and everyone was delighted with their meals. The bill for everything was just over $51—a great bargain! I had the *fasolka* (bean stew with *kielbasa*) cooked in a very tasty tomato sauce—it was wonderful. There's also a nice garden.

Bakeries   My two favorites on Nassau Avenue are next-door neighbors. **Jaslowiczanka** (163 Nassau Avenue) offers a rich palette of colorful multi-layered tortes, strudels, and other pastries, most at $7 a pound. The baked goods at **Jubilatka Bakery & Deli** (161 Nassau Avenue) are not as fancy (and they're cheaper), and the store also sells fine breads (baked elsewhere) and take-out foods including pierogi, cabbage and beet salads, soups, and several meat dishes. There are a few tables for on-site noshing. These shops are between Diamond and Newel Streets.

■ And Elsewhere . . .

Norman Avenue is one long block north of Nassau Avenue and has a few small delis. It is notable for the **Greenpoint Library** as well as **PS 34** at the intersection of Norman Avenue and McGuinness Boulevard—it's the oldest operating public school in New York City. The **Islamic Center of Greenpoint** is on Leonard Street south of Norman Avenue. **Antek Restaurant & Deli** (105 Norman Avenue, 718-389-6859) is a very pleasant small eatery with many of the dishes you'll find at other typical Polish restaurants.

■ ■ ■

The "Other" Greenpoint

Not Just Polish

Gentrification is coming to Greenpoint in the form of higher-priced housing, converted lofts, and fancier, pricier restaurants catering to a new type of clientele. At the same time, Greenpoint continues to absorb new immigrants from Eastern Europe and South America, especially Mexico, Peru, and Ecuador. "Hispaños Unidos de Greenpoint" holds an annual festival every July in the neighborhood's north end. An alternative art/political culture coexists among all these. Several galleries operate on Manhattan Avenue and Franklin Street and many artists and artisans work here. This section lists restaurants and markets representing these other sides of Greenpoint that you'll see amid the Polish places I've described.

Restaurants   **Acapulco Deli & Restaurant** (1116 Manhattan Avenue at Clay Street) has a varied and appealing menu offering Mexican and American specialties including an extensive selection of "crunch" French toast, American and Mexican omelet platters, and pancakes. It's pleasant and inexpensive—a shrimp burrito is just $5.75. **Budo-En Sushi** (1013 Manhattan Avenue, near Green Street, 718-389-1071) would seem to be an anomaly here, but it's quite an "in" place for the arts and alternative crowds. One door south is the equally anomalous **Java & Wood** (1011 Manhattan Avenue), a custom woodshop that serves coffee, tea, and soy beverages, as well as muffins and cakes. Customers play chess or checkers while they sip. **Divine Follie** (929 Manhattan Avenue, north of Kent Street, 718-389-6770) is simple and stunning. Opened in 2000, this sweet establishment owned by a Colombian couple, Segundo Heras and Luz Dary, offers an eclectic selection of Italian specialties and their own creations. Two interesting appetizers are poached pear salad with arugula, walnuts, and gorgonzola ($6.50) and tower of Follie—stacked portobello mushrooms, mozzarella, tomato, peppers, and basil oil ($6). Main courses are very reasonable—for example, chicken parmigiana is $10 and red snapper sorrentina is $12.50. Pastas are even less—for just $5.50 you can have a basic penne with tomato and basil, but you'll have to pay $9.50—still a deal—for fettuccini *ai gamberi*—red-beet fettuccine with spinach, shrimp, cherry tomatoes, and capers. The place is small and unpretentious and rather unique. **Monsignor's** (905 Lorimer Street at the intersection with Nassau and Bedford Avenues, 718-963-3399) specializes in Italian cuisine, but some years ago the Italian owner sold to a Mexican family from Puebla, so the menu now has a fine selection of Mexican dishes. I've tried both—pasta dishes, a delicious *camarones Cancun* (shrimp in garlic, onions, peppers, tomatoes, and cream), and a chicken quesadilla. Lunch specials are $5. The setting is simple—white walls, ceiling fans, big picture windows, and black-and-white photographs of Humphrey Bogart in his film roles. **My Place** restaurant bar (109 Franklin Street at Greenpoint Avenue, 718-349-6865; Tuesday through Friday, noon to 5 P.M.) is the only appealing eatery I've found on Franklin Street. With daytime hours only, it caters mainly to the employees of nearby factories. It's a handsome little place with a $3.95 lunch special and an idiosyncratic cuisine that includes Spanish-American dishes and some Thai specials.

Amazingly, there are *five* Thai restaurants on Manhattan Avenue. **Thai Café** (925 Manhattan Avenue, corner of Kent Street, 718-383-3562) is very popular and has a substantial menu that features eleven vegetarian dishes, each $5.95; chicken entrées from $6.50 to $6.95; noodles from $5.95 to $6.95; and seafood entrées from $6.95 to $7.95. Near the south end of Manhattan Avenue in Greenpoint is **Amarin Café** (617 Manhattan Avenue between Driggs and Nassau Avenues, 718-349-2788). **Moon Shadow** (643

Manhattan Avenue at Bedford Avenue, 718-609-1841), which opened in 2000, is an offshoot of Williamsburg's popular Planet Thai. Newer-comers include **Bangkok Thai** (681 Manhattan Avenue, 718-349-8215, the newest branch of several in Brooklyn, including two in Williamsburg) and the very pretty **OTT** (970 Manhattan Avenue at India Street, 718-609-2416). Two new sushi places arrived in 2002 on lower Manhattan Avenue close to the border with Williamsburg. Something's happening in Greenpoint!

Lite Bites II Deli & Bakery (700 Manhattan Avenue at Norman Street, 718-383-2820) offers popular light meals—quesadillas and grilled chicken sandwiches—and other types of sandwiches and salads. (There's another Lite Bites on East 55th Street in Manhattan, but it isn't as nice.) I chuckled when I saw it as a backdrop for the TV series *Third Watch* while I was working on this chapter. **Socrates Restaurant** (651 Manhattan Avenue, north of Nassau Avenue, 718-389-2752) is popular with a number of long-time Greenpointers I spoke with, including one man who says he eats there daily. A few notches above a typical American diner-restaurant, it has a huge menu and modest prices. Among its features is a garden patio that looks directly into neighbors' backyards, so you might dine to the view of someone's laundry hung out to dry.

Markets   The Garden (921 Manhattan Avenue at Kent Street) is a beauti-ful and large natural-foods market that owner John Tapper opened in 1994. It was one of my biggest surprises when I first started exploring Greenpoint but it became clearly less of an oddity as I got to know the neighborhood better. There's a large selection of prepared foods including Polish special-ties, plus gourmet coffees, cheeses, lots of organic goods, and organic soaps and cosmetics. I found several flavors of non-fat *kefir* (drinking yogurt) that I couldn't find elsewhere in Greenpoint. The Garden is also a good place to pick up fliers listing local political and cultural activities.

▪ Elsewhere in Greenpoint . . .

One of Greenpoint's great food treasures is tucked into a tiny street away from the key food places listed in this chapter. If you're free on any Friday between 8 A.M. and 1 P.M., you can buy retail at **Acme Smoked Fish Com-pany** (30 Gem Street, 718-383-8585). Now run by the fourth-generation member of the founding family—Henry Brownstein launched the business from a pushcart—Acme offers all sorts of salmon specialties, as well as cod, trout, mackerel, tuna, and whitefish, plus salmon and whitefish spreads, which are distributed to gourmet markets and restaurants. To get there, take the G train to Nassau Avenue, exit at Norman Street (north end of the station) and walk north on Manhattan Avenue for one block to Meserole

MIXED VEGETABLE SALAD (SALATKA JARZYNOVA)

*Courtesy of Horst, chief chef of The Garden
in Greenpoint, Brooklyn*

½ cup dill pickles, diced
1 cup carrots, diced
1 cup apples, diced
1 cup cooked potatoes, diced
1 cup canned sweet peas, drained and rinsed, diced
1 cup hard boiled eggs, diced
1 ¼ cups mayonnaise

In a large bowl, combine all the ingredients and toss with the mayonnaise.

Street. Then turn west (left) and walk five short blocks, as the neighborhood morphs from residential to industrial. You'll see the Acme sign just before you reach Gem Street.

■ ■ ■

More About Greenpoint

■ Reading About Greenpoint

For more information about Greenpoint, see *Greenpoint Neighborhood History Guide,* which was published in 2001 by the Brooklyn Historical Society as part of a series of profiles of waterfront communities. With text by Marcia Reiss, the guide provides a lively pictorial retrospective beginning before Dutch settlement and has an excellent map of landmarks. For more information, check out www.brooklynhistory.org.

▪ Web sites

There are several useful Greenpoint Web sites. Go to www.polishnation-alhome.com, a clever site representing an institution at 261 Driggs Avenue that is being converted into a local cultural and arts center for the new arts community in Greenpoint and Williamsburg, although traditional Polish arts also are supported. For Greenpoint nostalgia go to www.greenpt.com, which is maintained by Frank Dmuchowski, who grew up there, and www.greenpointusa.com, which has excellent historical information and interesting local anecdotes but has not been updated in a while. The Greenpoint Waterfront Association for Parks and Planning, a coalition of neighborhood groups, hosts www.gwapp.org to organize around environmental and community issues, including proposals to build a power plant in the community (they're opposed), and to protest proposed subway cuts. (When G train service was to be reduced, they created www.savetheg.org.)

▪ Gift-Shopping

Charming little shops abound in Greenpoint. Many, especially along Manhattan Avenue, have been here for decades, selling costume jewelry, vintage clothes, old cameras, and an eclectic array of other goods.

Don't miss **Zakopane** (714 Manhattan Avenue, north of Norman Street), in Greenpoint for thirty-five years. Owner Mr. Strug, who is in his mid-nineties, sold me a carved-wood diorama depicting a room in an old-fashioned cottage for just $20. Traditional Polish dolls, clothing, clocks, painted eggs, spoons, and bowls, religious icons and other religious items fill his shop.

You won't find a gift shop more different from Zakopane than **Oaza** (Oasis), a few blocks north at 928 Manhattan Avenue. Owner Stenia-Stislawa Krakówka, who is more than a half-century younger than Mr. Strug, also sells religious items, but you'll see Hindu symbols and Buddhas alongside Christian icons. Her selection is international, including Chinese wind chimes, candlesticks, mobiles, and picture frames; Indian incense; statuettes from Africa; and ceramics from Mexico.

Helena of **Helena's Gifts** (211 Nassau Avenue at Russell Street) calls her shop "Greenpoint's answer to the country store, right here in the heart of the city." I'm not sure "heart of the city" aptly describes her place, but it's certainly near the heart of Greenpoint, facing the leafy setting of Monsignor McGolrick Park. You'll find cards, toys, housewares, and T-shirts and caps with the Greenpoint logo. You can also visit **Mit Music** (661 Manhattan

Avenue, www.mitmusic.com) for Polish CDs and videos, **Manhattan Furrier** (685 Manhattan Avenue), which, despite its name, specializes in Native American jewelry and western boots, and **Netta** (688 Manhattan Avenue), which features leather sandals, handbags, and briefcases made in Poland.

■ Books-Books-Books

Anyone bemoaning the demise of the independent bookstore should come to Greenpoint. There are at least a half dozen fine bookstores—*ksiegarnie*—within ten blocks. All specialize in Polish-language books but also offer books about learning English, living in the United States, and getting American citizenship. Just about the only English-language books I've found there are either for children or about New York or books about Poland for English speakers. I've also found one or two English-language Polish cookbooks. The classic is Maria and Robert Strybel's *Polish Heritage Cookery* (New York: Hippocrene Books, 1997), which I found much cheaper on line. The area also abounds with newsstands that carry dozens of Polish-language titles.

■ Black Arts

Despite its name—given by Dutch settlers who bought this neck of grasslands jutting into the East River from the Lenape Indians—Greenpoint is better known as a producer of the five black arts—printing, pottery, ironwork, petroleum, and gas refining (as well as glass making). Factories once lined its western perimeter and some remain to this day. The ironclad *Monitor*, known for its role in the Civil War battle with the Confederate ship *Virginia* (renamed from the *Merrimack* after its capture), was built in Continental Shipyard at Calyer and West Streets. (There's a monument to the *Monitor* in McGolrick Park.) Even today, manufacturing and housing overlap in this area.

■ Other Arts

A growing art scene is emerging in Greenpoint, spilling over from Williamsburg. I passed a handful of galleries but they were not open during the weekdays when I made my visits. I noticed quite a few AIR (artist-in-residence) signs in loft-type buildings, especially in the north end of Greenpoint. The Greenpoint guide I mentioned (see page 129) says 500 cabinetmakers and artisans use space in the buildings there.

■ Big Screen/Small Screen

Scenes from the films *Sleeper, Serpico,* and *Donnie Brasco* were shot in Greenpoint. And the NBC series *Third Watch* has its principal studio in the area and many scenes are shot here. (Others are shot in Long Island City—I've often noted the 59th Street Bridge and Astoria Park in the background.) And Mae West was born here!

■ Bed and Breakfast

The **Greenpoint YMCA** at 99 Meserole Avenue has a great deal for folks seeking an inexpensive overnight stay in New York City—$37.50 for a double room per person per night, or $375 a week. (Baths are shared.)

■ Grand Old Flag

Strolling along Manhattan Avenue on Wednesday afternoon, I passed an open door at #597, which turned out to be the office of the weekly *Greenpoint Gazette,* co-edited and copublished by Ralph Carrano and Virginia Haines-Bednarek. Carrano cofounded the paper in 1971 with Haines-Bednarek's mother. Now in his seventies, Carrano told me about the 1967 flag competition organized by local folks who decided that if cities and states could have flags, a neighborhood could too. Greenpoint's Betsy Ross turned out to be Anna Kandratino, the daughter of Russian immigrants. Mayor John Lindsay was helicoptered in for the dedication (which coincided with the outbreak of the Six-Day War). Some years later, the original flag caught fire while in storage at the Greenpoint Bank. But you can see what it looked like and read about the contest and dedication at www.greenpointusa.com/gptflag/picfra.html.

So where *does* the name "Greenpernt" come from, anyway? According to the Web site www.greenpointusa.org, Peter J. McGuinness, a local Democratic boss, once described the area as "Greenpernt, the garden spot of the univoice"—and it stuck.

...

Kosher Brooklyn

There used to be a kitchenware store in Crown Heights called Kochleffel—Yiddish for mixing spoon (and also busybody and go-getter)—and that's what I felt like as I noshed my way through five mainly Jewish neighborhoods of Brooklyn in search of the most interesting kosher markets and eateries.

Wandering through Williamsburg—far from the trendy area of artists' lofts and diner-chic—and the Hassidic section of Crown Heights/Eastern Parkway, and later to the Sephardic area of Kings Highway near Ocean Parkway, and then to Borough Park, I saw that the Kochleffel shop was gone. I also checked out Avenue J in Midwood, east of Coney Island Avenue, which I'd read about having evolved into a heavily "modern Orthodox" community.

In my journeys I was curious to see how much "fusion cuisine" had been integrated into kosher cookery, knowing that in my own neighborhood of the Upper West Side in Manhattan, which has a growing modern Orthodox community, there's a kosher Mexican restaurant and a kosher Thai take-out place. I wasn't disappointed. I found kosher focaccia in Borough Park, a glatt kosher sushi/Italian place on Kings Highway, and a restaurant on Avenue J that looked like every neighborhood diner (though slightly upscale) that I'd grown up with in the suburbs.

The Orthodox Jewish neighborhoods of Brooklyn add richness to a borough already teeming with cultural diversity. I hadn't seen some of these areas in ten years, and I was fascinated to see how much they had changed—and also how much they hadn't. That's often the great mystery of New York City!

By the way, a great resource on these communities is a new book called *The Jews of Brooklyn,* edited by Ilana Abramovitch and Sean Galvin (Hanover, New Hampshire: Brandeis University Press, University Press of New Hampshire, 2002).

▪ Getting Oriented

BY SUBWAY

Each neighborhood described below is reached on a different subway line—the M or W for Borough Park, the Q for Midwood, the F for Kings Highway, the J or M for Williamsburg (the M going in the opposite direction from the one you take for Borough Park), and the #3 or #4 for Crown Heights. None is in easy walking distance of another.

But you can easily combine visits to two or even three of these neighborhoods at a time, whether you're driving or using mass transit.

BY BUS

Bus connections are easy to make—and, I find, interesting—so I recommend mass transit. To get a bus map on line, go to www.brooklyn.com and click for a map site.

BY CAR

I've found no major parking lots in any neighborhood, so you'll have to take your chances if you drive. (Weekdays should be easy, Sundays a lot harder.)

■ Suggested Tour Combinations

TOUR 1

Midwood to (or from) Borough Park. The B11 is an east-west bus that connects the two. It runs both directions on Avenue J in Midwood. In Borough Park, it runs east on 49th Street to Midwood and west on 50th Street from Midwood.

TOUR 2

Williamsburg for breakfast or lunch and a visit to Crown Heights (where I've found just one eatery worth visiting). Then go to the Brooklyn Museum and/or the Brooklyn Botanical Gardens, a longish walk (twenty to twenty-five minutes heading west on Eastern Parkway) or three stops on the #3 or #4 train from Kingston Avenue to the Brooklyn Museum/Eastern Parkway stop. The B44 bus connects them on Lee Avenue going south to Eastern Parkway at Nostrand Avenue; walk three long blocks east to Kingston Avenue.

TOUR 3

King's Highway (a Sephardic neighborhood) for lunch and Borough Park for dessert and wandering. Take the F train from Kings Highway four stops to Avenue I and connect to the B11 (due west) marked First Avenue. Get off at 13th Avenue and 50th Street and you'll be in the heart of Borough Park.

TOUR 4

Midwood to Kings Highway (requires two buses). From Midwood, take the
B68 bus south on Coney Island Avenue to Kings Highway and then the B82
bus west on Kings Highway. If you like to walk, get off at Kings Highway;
the Sephardic area is just six blocks west, a nice stroll that crosses lovely
Ocean Parkway.

■ Before Touring Kosher Neighborhoods

1. Don't bother going on a Saturday; the stores will be closed for
   the Jewish Sabbath. Sundays are fun if you want to see the
   crowds—and the streets are often clogged with double strollers.
   For the best shopping, go on a weekday, especially Friday several
   hours before sunset.
2. Stores are closed on Jewish holidays.
3. During the summer some shops may close for part of the time
   and the neighborhoods will be quieter overall. In Williamsburg,
   many families head to vacation colonies upstate. I suggest going
   in spring (except during Passover) and autumn—after the High
   Holidays. Going before a holiday (such as Purim and Passover)
   is fun: you'll see the stores geared up with special items in
   anticipation of the festivities.
4. Dress modestly, especially if you plan to have a sit-down meal,
   out of respect for religious tradition.
5. Vegetarians can do particularly well in these neighborhoods.
   Dairy restaurants offer many vegetarian dishes. And the meat
   restaurants often have side salads and vegetables that can be
   turned into an ample meal.

For more information, check out a wonderful book, *The Neighborhoods of
Brooklyn,* published by the Citizens Committee of New York/Yale University Press in 1998. It profiles dozens of neighborhoods and includes concise
maps and good illustrations. I also like Lis Harris's *Holy Days: The World of
a Hasidic Family,* which was originally serialized in the *New Yorker* and
focuses on Crown Heights.

...

Kosher Brooklyn

Borough Park

"You can find everything—but money—on 13th Avenue," said the cashier at Strauss Bakery as I paid for a kosher onion focaccia bread. She was right: I found a lot to buy on 13th Avenue—and "lost" my money in the process.

In some ways, Borough Park reminds me of Mexico City in miniature, a sprawling metropolis whose boundaries keep expanding. I used to think of its commercial area in terms of 13th Avenue only. Now many shops overlap onto 16th and 18th Avenues and some side streets. But for the essence of commercial Borough Park, stick to 13th Avenue.

I originally knew of this community as primarily Eastern European, so I was fascinated to find one Yemeni market and several shops run by Bukharan Jews, originally from Uzbekistan. (There's a sizable Bukharan Jewish community in Forest Hills.) But most of what you'll see reflects Eastern European traditions with Israeli influences.

Getting There   Take the M or W train to 50th Street, which stops at the intersection of 12th Avenue and New Utrecht Avenue, or to 55th Street, where New Utrecht crosses 13th Avenue. The tour spans 13th Avenue from 36th to 56th Streets.

Bakeries   Among the first things I noticed while revisiting Borough Park were a few makeovers in progress. **Strauss's Bakery** (5115 13th Avenue, 718-851-7728), an area institution for decades, has a lovely new façade and interior and brims with activity. A new feature, says manager Avi King, is its emphasis on service, and there's a lot of counter staff to fill orders from crowds of customers. Specialties include three types of Italian focaccia bread (olive, tomato, and onion; I most recommend the onion), an inspiration of an Italian baker there, in addition to a wonderful selection of challahs, old-fashioned cookies, fabulous cheesecakes, and pastries. The rich chocolate horn is like a *pain au chocolat* with an even more intense chocolate filling. One block north, **Weiss Old Fashioned Bake Shop** (5011 13th Avenue, 718-438-0407) was in the midst of an elegant interior and exterior renovation when I visited, with attractive wood paneling and mirrors added, as well as mouthwatering cake displays seemingly designed as meticulously as the renovation itself. A strawberry cake was iced like a Jackson Pollock canvas—gorgeous to look at, difficult to resist, and delicious to eat. (Weiss has a counterpart—also newly renovated—at 1214 Avenue M in Midwood.) One other bakery stands out: **Home Style Bake House** (4016 13th Avenue, 718-972-6026), a snug, austere place where you fill your own bag with various flavors of miniature rugalach, cookies, and buns. There's

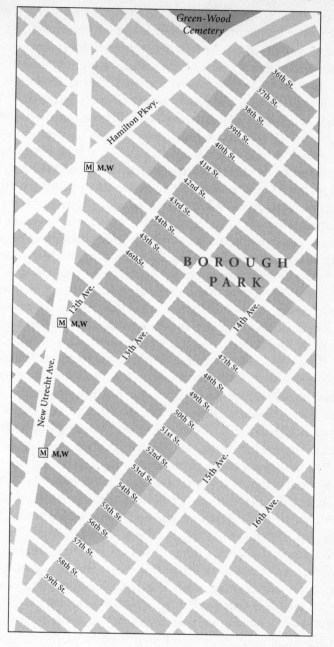

also delicious strudel. A newcomer to Borough Park is **Yefrain Kosher Bakery** (13-11 48th Street, 718-437-2264), which makes the delicious round bread that draws fans to Beautiful Bukhara in Forest Hills. The shop also produces a matzoh-like crisp bread. At 1285 36th Street, **Borough Park Shmura Matzoh** (718-438-2006) produces handmade Passover matzoh.

Restaurants   Most places here are mundane—pizzerias and delis similar to what you'll see in the other kosher neighborhoods and in Manhattan's garment district. For fast food I prefer the offerings on Avenue J in Midwood (see pages 148–151). The best here for meat dishes, but better, in my opinion, for its ambiance and Israeli vegetable salads, is **Chefah** (4810 13th Avenue, 718-972-0133). For dairy I prefer **Rishon Pizza** (5114 13th Avenue), where you can get pizza as well as good Israeli-style *bourekas* (filled pastries). For something completely different, in food and experience, try **Vostok** (5507 13th Avenue, 718-437-2596), a glatt kosher Uzbeki place between 55th and 56th Streets (next door to a Polish grocery). The $5.50 lunch special includes a hearty soup, two kebab sticks or another meat entrée, French fries, and a salad of tomatoes and cucumbers with dill and parsley. My companion had a lovely lamb kebab. For $1 more I had a terrific salmon kebab spiced with pepper and dill. There's music on Saturday nights and Sundays, which was recommended by a table of young artsy customers dressed in black T-shirts and jeans. The miniskirted female patrons and waitresses are a contrast to most of the people you'll see in Borough Park.

Markets   On 39th street, an industrial stretch, check out **K.R.M. Co-op,** (1325 39th Street, 718-436-7701), a sprawling kosher supermarket that reminds me of Uptown Fairway in Harlem. Its shelves bulge with a huge selection of products, including a special Passover section where I found prices far lower than in Manhattan markets. Just prior to Passover it has special late-night hours and is open until 1 A.M. The blandly-named **Kosher Meat Market** (4008 13th Avenue) offers specialty products catering to Bukharan Jews. Outside you'll find stalls of nuts, legumes, and dried fruit, plus loaves of Uzbek bread. Inside are boxes of teas, spices, sauces, cookware—and, yes, kosher meat. The owner at **Zion Market** (4100 13th Avenue, 718-436-1199) told me his is the only Yemeni-Jewish market in New York—except that he owns another Zion at 1439 First Avenue in Manhattan! The aroma of cardamom here is hypnotic. There are lots of products from throughout the Middle East and also home-mixed spices, fresh pita bread, and a wonderful grilled thin soft bread called *lachlooch* for wrapping that's baked in the back of the store, as well as olives, cheese, and produce. I bought a yummy Moroccan carrot salad, frozen spinach, cheese *bourekas*, and a Turkish pudding made with rose syrup, coconut, and peanuts. For fish, check out **Ossie's Fish Market** (1314 50th Street, 718-436-4100), where one of the specialties is a designer gefilte-fish line that includes salmon, radish, jalapeño, almond raisin, and Cajun. A kosher sushi bar was added in 2002. Ossie's is closed on Sundays. Why? "Everyone comes on Thursday or Friday to buy for Shabbat," said the woman at the cash register. "No one buys on Sunday!"

Off 13th Avenue I found **Cheese "D" Lox** (4912 New Utrecht Avenue, 718-436-7833), where I felt I'd stumbled into my childhood—a crowded lox-and-pickles place that embodies an older Borough Park. It's worth a

GRANDMA'S GEFILTE FISH

*Courtesy of Barry Simanowitz of Ossie's Fish Market
in Borough Park, Brooklyn*

1 box Ossie's Classic Original Gefilte Fish
1 carrot, peeled and quartered
1 onion, peeled and quartered
1 stalk celery, quartered
1 carp head
2 tablespoons sugar
Salt and pepper to taste

1. Thaw the gefilte fish overnight in the refrigerator.
2. Bring the remaining ingredients to a boil in 4 quarts of water.
3. Form the fish into balls and place them in the water.
4. Bring to a boil again and then reduce to a simmer and cook for about 1 hour. Remove fish balls with a spoon. Serve either hot or cold.

visit, even if the counter person treats you rudely, as happened to me. Grin and bear it; lots of lox!

Sweets   Sweet tooth? Check out **Ice Cream Center** (4511 13th Avenue, 718-438-0018), a hangout for local teenagers (mostly boys) that has candy, Israeli-style frozen fruit yogurt, ice cream confections, and gifts. **Candy Man** (4702 13th Avenue, 718-438-4392) has been in Borough Park seemingly forever and teems with domestic and imported chocolates and other old-fashioned candies. **Oh! Nuts!**, a candy and nut shop that had been on 50th Street for years, has expanded onto 4923 13th Avenue—it's a beautiful new store. Note the colorful pint-sized shopping carts for little kids. This is dangerous stuff, though—imagine toddlers let loose in a candy store!

Also . . .   **Eichler's Judaica,** a shop that sells books, CDs, and everything else that goes into helping make a Jewish home, has a big branch at 5004 13th Avenue. Take a walk two blocks east on 48th Street to 15th Avenue and you'll see Young Israel Beth El (4802 15th Avenue) and the Bobover Yeshiva (1522 48th Street). Young Israel is Borough Park's oldest synagogue and has a gorgeous interior; Bobover represents the neighborhood's largest Hasidic sect. On Saturdays 48th Street is referred to as Bobover Promenade because it's packed with Bobover families taking a Sabbath stroll.

• • •

Kosher Brooklyn
Williamsburg and Crown Heights

People seeking a glimpse of traditional life firsthand often head to Williamsburg and Crown Heights. Both have substantial Hassidic neighborhoods, although they each represent different sects and traditions. I decided to group them together because they are geographically close enough that you can visit both in one day and because the two apart have few significantly interesting places to eat or buy food.

■ Linking the Neighborhoods

BY BUS

Starting in Williamsburg, if you want to visit both neighborhoods in a day, take the B44 on Lee Avenue, which will become Nostrand Avenue. It's an interesting ride, and you should get off as soon as the bus crosses Eastern Parkway into Crown Heights. Then walk three blocks east on Eastern Parkway or President Street to Kingston Avenue. For the reverse route, walk two blocks west to New York Avenue, where the B44 will head north, eventually turning onto Bedford Avenue and leaving you one block west of Lee. The #3 and #4 trains stop at Nostrand and Kingston Avenues, so if you don't want to walk you can take a one-stop subway ride, but you still have to tackle the stairs. Walking sometimes can be faster.

BY CAR

Driving is very easy: shoot south on Lee Avenue, keep going to Nostrand Avenue, and then turn east (left) on President Street until you reach Kingston Avenue.

Williamsburg

This is is the heart of the Satmar community, which originated in Hungary. A much more inward-looking neighborhood than Crown Heights, it is remarkably self-contained. Once you cross the proverbial Division Street (Division

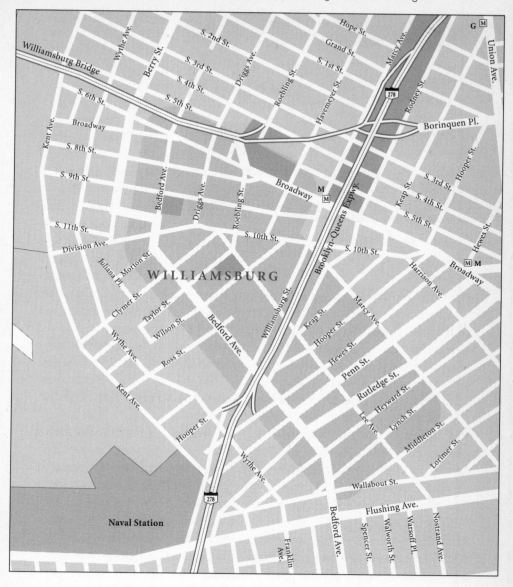

Avenue here, to be accurate), you will cross from a markedly Hispanic area into Satmar Central, although there now is some overlap as the Satmar community, with its very large families, expands past traditional boundaries.

When I visited Williamsburg for this book after more than ten years of not seeing it, I found that little had changed in the neighborhood—on the surface. Many of the stores looked exactly the same. Yet I was surprised to see Game Boys and cell phones marketed alongside wigs and black felt hats.

On the other hand, when you shop for food and look at the brands and how they're marketed, the Satmars clearly are aware of what people like—the

Owner Avram Glauber displaying his wares at Glauber's in Williamsburg.

bakeries now have self-serve coffee machines with cappuccino. An old appetizing store now has slush and a juice bar. And pizza, of course, abounds—but then pizza is a great meal for large families: little work and not a lot of mess.

Getting There   Take the J, M, or Z train to Marcy Avenue, the first stop out of Manhattan. The train becomes elevated over the Williamsburg Bridge, offering sparkling views of the East River and the Brooklyn and Manhattan skylines. At the busy intersection of Broadway and Marcy Avenue, cross south on Broadway and then head west on Broadway (looking toward Manhattan) for two blocks to Roebling Street. Turn left (south) on Roebling Street to Division and Lee Avenues. Lee Avenue is the commercial spine. From Manhattan, take the Williamsburg Bridge and turn left at Roebling Street. The B33 bus runs south on Lee Avenue and north on Bedford Avenue.

Restaurants   For old-fashioned deli sandwiches, try busy **Gottlieb's Restaurant** (352 Roebling Street, 718-384-6612). To my surprise, cole slaw cost extra ($1.75) and the sandwiches, while big, aren't spectacular, and they're almost Manhattan prices ($6 to $9—at least the pickles are free.) You can make a meal of vegetarian side dishes like Chinese vegetables, kugel, and barley. For dairy, I like **Itzu's** (45 Lee Avenue, 718-484-8631), a sunny little place where I used to have breakfast during the bicycle tours I led in the 1980s. **Friedman Luncheorant & Pizza** (193 Lee Avenue, 718-387-0818) has a good vegetarian selection. I tried a tuna cutlet and saw—but didn't try—spaghetti with gefilte-fish balls. The drab interior at **Green & Ackerman's Restaurant & Pizza** (216 Ross Street, 718-384-2540) looks unchanged since I visited in the mid-1980s. But I've had terrific blintzes, latkes, and vegetable salads there. It also has a bakery that sells cakes and rugalach to Zabar's.

Bakeries   **Lee Ave. Bakery** (73 Lee Avenue, 718-387-4736), which was always my favorite for its slathering chocolate pastries and cheesecakes, was beautifully renovated in 2002. Now you can also get gourmet coffees with the cakes. **S. Weiss** (123 Lee Avenue) is another nice bakery that hypes its use of organic flour, including spelt flour, and organic sugar in its breads and cakes for folks with allergies.

Markets   My favorite appetizing place is **Glauber's** (161 Division Avenue, 718-388-3388), a classy shop that opened in 1997. It's packed with candies (lots of imports), condiments, vegetable dips, fish salads, olives, nuts, dried fruit, and elaborate gift baskets. Floor manager Jacob Glauber told me they make forty different salads; about two dozen are offered on any given day. They also sell homemade *etrog* marmalade, from the fruit used for the holiday Sukkot. One gift basket had figurines of a klezmer band, but when I looked closely I realized Glauber's had "adjusted" a set of figurines of black Dixieland musicians by painting on earlocks and yarmulkes. Old-timer **Flaum's Specialty Appetizing** is at 40 Lee Avenue (at Wilson Street, 718-387-7934) and 142 Lee Avenue (Hewes and Penn Streets). Like Glauber's, it has great prepared dishes (try the sesame chicken), old-fashioned candies, wonderful chocolate miniatures, fish, dips, and pickles. The combined smells are enough to transport you to an era that you may not have lived through but can still imagine here. **Landau's Supermarket** (650 Bedford Avenue between Penn and Rutledge Streets) is the area's best: it has been upgraded and expanded recently (it even has electronic doors, a rarity here and a boon for moms with double strollers) and it sells, literally, soup to nuts. They also offer prepared dishes. It is, however, showing some wear and tear, but everything is relative—compared to the other markets in Williamsburg, this is a shopper's dream. The clerks were helpful and even witty. Williamsburg also has a classy new liquor store, **L'Chaim Fine Wines and Liquors** (348 Roebling Street, 718-599-0074), which opened in early 2002. Attractively designed, it has an extensive selection of kosher wines, liqueurs, and other spirits from Israel, Australia, South Africa, and various European countries, as well as North America.

Crown Heights

There are several reasons to visit this section of Crown Heights, but food isn't one of them. There's a lot to see in the neighborhood, however, including the world headquarters of the Lubavitch movement (770 Eastern Parkway), several very good Judaica shops, as well as party goods stores catering to a Purim or Pesach celebration, for example, and two gorgeous blocks of spacious homes—a former Doctor's Row—on President Street between Kingston and New York Avenues.

I'm also intrigued with how the Lubavitch community in Crown Heights melds Hassidic tradition and rebbe worship with hi-tech. A pharmacy there advertises a Web site for kosher vitamins, and you can find local store information on www.crownheightsconsumer.com. A Jewish children's museum is under construction at the strategic intersection of Kingston Avenue and Eastern Parkway and could become a major tourist draw when it's done. But I hope it doesn't draw people away from the wonderful Brooklyn Children's Museum, which is reached from the same subway stop but requires a ten-minute walk.

Getting there   Take the #3 or #4 train to Kingston Avenue. The commercial core is the six-block stretch of Kingston Avenue south of Eastern Parkway to Empire Boulevard. The only place I've found relatively friendly and interesting here is **Isaac's Bakery** (380 Kingston Avenue, 718-467-2047), which combines a coffee bar, traditional bakery, and bright new seating. They also offer salads, soups, and sandwiches. **Kingston Pizza** (359 Kingston Avenue) now also serves cappuccino and espresso. The large **Kahan's Superette** (317 Kingston Avenue) meets local needs, and **Albany Bake Shop** (425 Kingston Avenue) looked okay, but you'll do better in Borough Park. A nice place for ice cream and candies is **NoshWorld** (386 Kingston Avenue). **Apple Drugs** (376 Kingston Avenue), a local pharmacy, has a nice selection of health foods and vegetarian cookbooks with recipes suitable for kosher cooks. Its Web site, www.kosher-health.com, provides useful

information on vitamins and herbal teas. At the party goods store, **Sell-e-bration** (382 Kingston Avenue), I found great Purim bags, ribbons, and stickers. The well-known caterer **Mermelstein** (351 Kingston Avenue) also makes sandwiches, but the place is too dreary for a sit-down meal.

. . .

Kosher Brooklyn
Kings Highway

More than twenty-five-years ago, author Joseph Sutton profiled his community of Syrian Jews in *Magic Carpet: Aleppo-in-Flatbush* (New York: Sarah M. Sutton, 1980). He estimated that some 25,000 Syrian Jews lived here. The community has at least doubled in size based on the presence of large new synagogues and a busy Sephardic community center built here since then; it even merits a hefty volume of the *Sephardic Yellow Pages*. I've noticed changes just in the last decade—more shops, bigger shops, more restaurants—and fancier ones. This tour focuses on several blocks of Kings Highway nestled between Ocean Parkway and McDonald Avenue, with some overlap east of Ocean Parkway.

Getting There   Take the F train to Kings Highway. Exit at the sign saying NE Corner and turn right. If you're driving, take Ocean Parkway south (from Prospect Park) to Kings Highway and turn right. You should be able to find parking in the area.

Markets   I've always been amazed at the number of grocery stores—eight, including one supermarket—packed into this small area, even some next door to others that sell almost exactly the same products. The differences have to with where the owners come from—some from Egypt, others from Syria or Lebanon or Israel. Shoppers are generally drawn to those from the same place they come from. Moti Rabinowitz at Think Sweet Café (see page 147) says most shoppers choose their stores by how they get along with the owners. My favorite is **Setton** (509 Kings Highway), which is the largest and easiest to negotiate (many have narrow, crowded aisles) and has its own bakery. The selection here is terrific—you'll find products from Israel, Syria, Lebanon, and Turkey, plus freshly ground spices and yummy cheeses, dried fruit, nuts, baked goods, and frozen goods such as fava beans and *bourekas* (puff dough pastries). I had great success with frozen cheese *bourekas* and also found some terrific dips. I also enjoyed "mishmish," a sweet concoction made of mashed apricots and pistachios. You can also buy pre-cut dough to make Middle Eastern pastries. Of the other markets, I like **Holon** (529 Kings Highway) and **Chalouh** (567 Kings Highway)—its awning says it has been here since 1920. **Kings Highway**

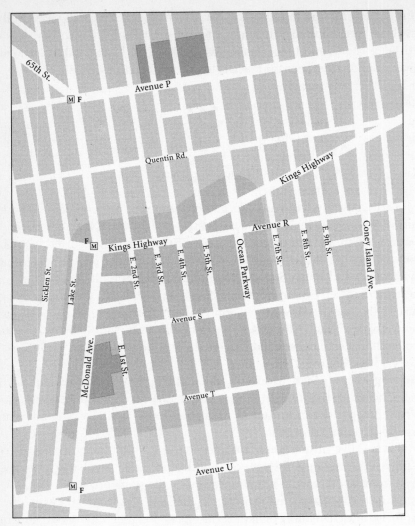

Glatt Kosher Meat & Fish (499 Kings Highway) is the area's main pur-
veyor of meat and fish and sells lots of Israeli products.

Bakeries   There are two stand-alone bakeries here. **Pita Sababa** (540
Kings Highway, 718-382-1100 or 888-CHALLAH) sells packages of mini-
pitas including *zataar* (thyme), sesame, onion, and garlic at just $1.75 for
eight. The other stand-alone bakery is **Mansoura's** (515 Kings Highway,
718-645-7977)—an old-timer—that sells not only baked desserts but also
meat-filled pastries including *bourekas* and *samboosek,* as well as *kibbee,* a
spicy type of meatball. Josiane Mansoura and other family members will
explain what the specials are. (Chocolate-covered pastries are expensive at
$20 a pound because top Belgian chocolate is used.) But just as interesting
to me was the tale she told of her family's business—starting in Lebanon

more than two hundred years ago, they eventually moved to Cairo, where the family established a thriving business, and then relocated to Brooklyn when Egypt was no longer a comfortable place for Jewish families to live and work. They've been on Kings Highway since the 1960s. During Passover they sell matzoh meal *kibbees* and other pastries adapted for the holiday.

Restaurants   When I last led bicycle tours in this area in the 1980s, the restaurants offered either Middle Eastern food in a relatively austere setting or kosher pizza, and none of the establishments were fancy. Now there are three glatt kosher Italian places. One of these, **T for Two Café** (547 Kings Highway, 718-998-0020), also has a sushi bar. I decided to stick with Middle Eastern food, but the menus at **Stella Luna** (557 Kings Highway, 718-376-2999) and **Carmel** (521 Kings Highway, 718-339-0172) looked appealing. I recalled Carmel as a bland Middle Eastern place in the 1980s, but in 2000 its owners changed the decor and menu and they now feature Italian dishes, with pasta entrées at $13 to $15 and meat and seafood dishes ranging from $16 to $24. For Israeli and other Middle Eastern fare, **Jerusalem Steak House** (533 Kings Highway, 718-336-5115) is excellent. When I walked in, the waitress asked in Hebrew if I wanted to sit down. (I don't really speak Hebrew, but I remember the word *lashevet*—to sit—from way back.) I chose a luscious hardy Yemeni soup. **David's Restaurant** (539 Kings Highway, 718-998-8600) also serves Middle Eastern food and, unlike Jerusalem Steak House, serves breakfast including Middle Eastern specialties such as *ful medamas* (fava beans in onions served with tahini or hummus dip). I had a great combination platter here.

Eateries   I had fun visiting **Think Sweet Café** (546 Kings Highway, 718-645-3473), one of the area's two dairy eateries. (The other is **Pizza Dairy Delights** at 549 Kings Highway). Israelis Moti and Debi Rabinowitz have run it for fifteen years. It's homey and friendly—I saw folks drop by just to schmooze with Moti (and buy a Lotto ticket). With just two tables and a counter area where you can nosh a sandwich or nurse coffee with the pastries baked here, Moti dubs his place Home of the *Mafuneket* (Hebrew for "spoiled child") after a rich, high-cholesterol and very popular sandwich he concocted.

Also . . .   It's worth taking a walk along Ocean Parkway between Kings Highway and Avenue U to view some of the local landmarks. The beautiful **Sephardic Community Center** (1901 Kings Highway), which opened in 1982 to serve the community, has been so successful that the organization has acquired adjacent properties and plans to double its size. Some of the synagogues that serve this community are also noteworthy. The largest, **Shaare Zion,** is at 2030 Ocean Parkway between Avenues T and U. To see some beautiful homes as you walk back to Kings Highway, head up East 4th or East 5th Street. The synagogue for Damascus Jews, **Ahi Ezer,** is at 1885 Ocean Parkway. For more information, contact the *Sephardic Yellow Pages* at www.syny.com.

MAFUNEKET SANDWICH

*Courtesy of Moti Rabinowitz of Think Sweet Café
in Kings Highway, Brooklyn*

1 sesame hero roll, sliced lengthwise
Olive cream cheese
Thin cucumber slices
Thin tomato slices
Spicy eggplant salad (available in local groceries)
1 omelet, made from 1 egg
Srug (a condiment made of cilantro, parsley, and olive oil)—
    enough to cover the roll
Salt and pepper to taste

Spread olive cream cheese on both sides of the roll, then layer in the
ingredients in the order listed to make a delicious sandwich.

• • •

Kosher Brooklyn
Avenue J—Midwood

Midwood surprised me. I'd bypassed it in previous visits to Brooklyn,
and I knew Coney Island Avenue as a mostly treeless, unattractive commercial strip. But much of this residential neighborhood near Brooklyn
College consists of lovely homes—some Victorian—with gentle, pretty
lawns. For years it was a solid area of Italian and secular Jewish middle-
class families, but in the last fifteen years or so it has drawn a growing
new Orthodox Jewish community—new because many families *are* new
to the area, and new because a percentage are newly observant families. It
has also drawn new immigrants from Russia and Israel. I was interested
to see miniskirted Barbie dolls and other "secular" toys in stores catering
mostly to Orthodox families.

The densest cluster of kosher shops is on Avenue J between Coney

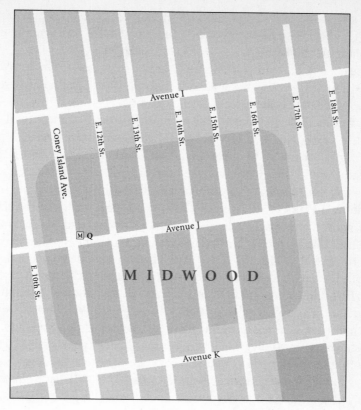

Island Avenue and East 16th Street and on Coney Island Avenue between Avenues J and M. These shops are punctuated with Pakistani stores that accommodate a growing Pakistani community.

Getting There   Take the Q train to Avenue J. The tour covers the five blocks between the station entrance, just west of 16th Street, and Coney Island Avenue, equivalent to 11th Street.

Markets   This area has several excellent gourmet-style markets. I recommend two. **Gourmet on J** (1412 Avenue J, 718-338-9181) was opened two years ago by Zabar's alumni Harvey and Arthur Pearlman. There's a large selection of, well, everything (except dairy): soups (including fruit soups), salads, pasta, poultry, and meat entrées, and lots of fruit and vegetable sides (such as soufflés). Much is available for take-out; some must be ordered. The **Kosher Spot** (1316 Avenue J, 718-677-4288) promotes its "kugelmania"—main dish (vegetable) and dessert (fruit) puddings. I tried the tri-color kugel layered with carrots, spinach, and broccoli. The Kosher Spot also has lots of Israeli dips and salads. **Golan Fruits** (1348 Coney Island Avenue) has a great selection of Israeli imports, produce, dried fruit, nuts, and cheeses, including a lush, creamy Israeli feta. A popular candy store is **Oh! Nuts!** (1503 Avenue J, 718-951-6039 and 888-OH-GIFT-1), which also has a new, fancy branch at 4923 13th Avenue in Borough Park and a Web site.

Bakeries   The bakeries on Avenue J aren't impressive. Go to **Weiss** at 1214 Avenue M. (It also has a sister bakery in Borough Park, where there are a number of good bakeries to choose from.)

Restaurants   Eateries here are informal, with kosher Chinese food, Israeli specialties, pizza, and deli food. I had an excellent falafel sandwich packed with veggies for under $3 at **Natanya Fast Food** (1506 Avenue J, 718-258-5160) and would stick with the Israeli specialties here. (The upstairs area is designated for boys only. Yeshiva of Flatbush is down the street.) **Jerusalem II Pizza** (1312 Avenue J, 718-338-2105) offers a big selection—pizzas, stuffed pretzels, Israeli salads and dips, and a salad bar that includes gefilte fish. I had a pretzel stuffed with spinach and cheese. **Garden of Eat-in** (1416 Avenue J, 718-252-5289) looks like an upscale Greek-style diner, but with kosher food. I had a great salmon burger. The menu also has a tantalizing salmon stuffed with spinach and other good-sounding fish and pasta dishes. The owner of Gourmet on J (see page 149), Harvey Pearlman, is its chief chef. His *linguine alla Harvey* includes ricotta, pine nuts, olives, Spanish tomatoes, and garlic. Prices are reasonable (pastas are $10 to $14, fish entrées are $14 to $18) and you also can get breakfast here. **Essex on Coney** (1359 Coney Island Avenue, 718-253-1002) is a large deli-restaurant that serves oversized sandwiches (you can get half-sizes, which still are big) and Chinese food. The ambiance is fun—the place is filled with vintage signs and baseball memorabilia. **Olympic Pita** (1419 Coney Island Avenue, 718-258-6222) has wonderful Israeli food, and you can watch the pita being made while you wait—it's sensational! (By the way, Jerusalem Steak House [see page 147] on Kings Highway and Isaac's Bakery [see page 144] in Crown Heights have branches on Avenue J.)

Also . . .   Check out **Eichler's Book Store** (1401 Coney Island Avenue). Eichler's has branches in Manhattan and Borough Park (and a Web site, www.eichlers.com) but this is the flagship store—Barnes & Noble, Pier 1, Blockbuster, and Pottery Barn rolled into one—with books, yarmulkes, toys, videos, fancy Passover seder plates, and Megillah holders and house-wares. I was intrigued to find car mezuzahs with prayers for travelers, but a local fellow told me he didn't use one "and they're not obligatory." **Harnik's Happy House** (1403 Avenue J, 718-951-9805) is a throwback. Opened as a toy store in 1947, it later added cards and now also sells books. It's a rarity these days, a true neighborhood bookstore, now run by the second generation of Harniks. Its owners are secular Jews and the store has a multicultural selection, but its approach is Brooklyn to the core: heavy on family and very personal. Even its Web site (www.harnikbk.com) seems to talk to you (and even talk back). "We've lasted because we've changed with the times," says employee Rose Marquez, who grew up in the area and credits owner Noreen Harnik with pushing her to do well. She has.

...

Sunset Park

Bridging Brooklyn

Early in my research on Sunset Park, I visited a small Chinese bakery on Eighth Avenue near 41st Street. The woman at the counter was, well, clearly not Chinese, and I just had to find out not only who she was but what she was doing here. At seventy-eight, and a grandmother several times over, Helen Zingone was working five days a week at a branch of the Savoy Bakery, serving and schmoozing with Chinese customers. She needed to keep busy, she told me, and she had a long, warm friendship with the bakery's owner. A Sunset Park resident for most of her life, Helen has watched the neighborhood change. But rather than leave (as many friends did) because the languages, foods, and customs of the neighborhood newcomers were "uncomfortable," she adapted to the changes. Helen has retired since I met her, but I admire her spunk and unusual willingness to build a bridge to another culture. You'll find all sorts of bridging in this remarkable community, and that's one of the reasons why I have always found Sunset Park especially intriguing.

When I profiled Sunset Park for *NoshNews*—it was just my second issue—I wanted to show not just diversity but contrast. Like Sunnyside, Queens, Sunset Park is enormously diverse. But unlike Sunnyside, the ethnic groups in Sunset Park have carved out more distinctive neighborhoods. Whether it's geography or economics or real estate, or all of the above, there's far less of the blending than I found in Sunnyside, where you could turn a corner from a Romanian restaurant, find a twenty-four-hour Korean produce market, and then, a block or two down, pass a Mexican bakery (and then, next door, a Turkish grocery).

Sunset Park has two dominant flavors: on Fourth and Fifth Avenues, it's primarily Mexican, Ecuadorian, Dominican, and otherwise Latin American. Along Eighth Avenue, particularly between 50th and 62nd Streets, it's overwhelmingly Chinese, although some Scandinavian holdovers remain from an earlier era (but barely). The area immediately north offers an eclectic mix of Polish, halal, Mexican, and some Chinese places. This area is clearly in the throes of change—though it's hard to predict in what direction.

You'll love Sunset Park itself. It's one of the city's real jewels. Once you've been there, you'll wonder what took you so long. Its views of the New York harbor are unparalleled—and free.

And by the way, you'll find great food bargains here, like a heaping cup of espresso for just 65 cents—and some of the city's best dim sum and Mexican markets. So, eat—and save!

▪ History

In the seventeenth century Dutch settlers bought the area from the Canarsee Indians; it remained mostly farmland. The Revolutionary War's Battle of Long Island took place just north of the park. Irish immigrants fleeing the potato famine began arriving in the mid-nineteenth century, taking jobs on the waterfront and with emerging industries. They were followed by newcomers from Scandinavia and Poland and then from Italy and Greece. The park itself was designated and named in 1891. The source of the name is obvious: the park provides a spectacular vista of New York harbor and brilliant sunsets. Thanks to the "anti-people" planning of Robert Moses, the 1941 construction of the Gowanus Expressway divided and destroyed industrial and residential sections of Sunset Park, which also disrupted the area's integrity and led to decades of decline. The next wave of settlers tended to be poorer families from Puerto Rico and elsewhere seeking cheap housing. For years, there was little development.

A turnaround began in the 1980s, spurred by new Chinese settlement from mainland China, Hong Kong, and Taiwan along Eighth Avenue and the rapid establishment of businesses and manufacturing (including sweatshops that are the topic of ongoing controversy; a worker advocacy group on Seventh Avenue near 60th Street serves as a watchdog). Sunset Park's many single-family homes and access to rapid transport are key attractions. Business development is thriving. Fifth Avenue has become the hub of new Mexican businesses and the area now has its own Business Improvement District. Nowadays there appears to be a growing Arabic-speaking Muslim community—there are three mosques on Eighth Avenue (two are storefront mosques in the 40th Street area; the other is a formal mosque established by Turkish Muslims).

▪ Getting Oriented

For this chapter, Sunset Park's boundaries are 39th Street to the north (at Green-Wood Cemetery), Fourth Avenue to the west, 62nd Street to the south, and Eighth Avenue to the east. The official western boundary extends to New York Harbor, but the area west of Fourth Avenue is heavily industrial.

BY SUBWAY

The M, N, R, and W trains go to Sunset Park. To connect from Grand Central Station take the #4 or #5 train to Atlantic Avenue, then transfer to the M, N, R, or W, where the stop is called Pacific Street. From Penn Station, the #2 and #3 trains also go to Atlantic Avenue, where you can make the same transfer.

BY BUS

Buses can save you time if you plan to visit the area in one day. Going north–south are the B63 (Fifth Avenue) and B70 (Eighth Avenue); going east-west are the B33 (39th Street), B11 (49th Street due west, 50th Street due east), and B9 (60th Street).

BY CAR

The best access for drivers is via the Gowanus Expressway. Exit at 39th Street for Fifth Avenue and at Sixth Avenue/65th Street for Eighth Avenue. Parking in the immediate area, especially on weekends, is scarce. There's a municipal parking lot along Third Avenue between 30th and 42nd Streets beneath the Gowanus Expressway. Car services travel the area frequently.

Sunset Park itself sits between Fifth and Seventh Avenues, from 41st to 44th Streets. The best access is from north entrances at Sixth or Seventh Avenue. Check out the views—Sunset Park boasts the second-highest elevation in New York City. (Only Green–Wood Cemetery has a more elevated view.)

BY TRAIN

Long Island Rail Road travelers on the Hempstead line can exit at Atlantic Avenue to make the connection.

▪ Walking Tour

Renee and Tony Giordano, long-time Sunset Park residents, used to lead walking tours and generously shared their maps and history with me. Renee notes that the area embodies the largest national historic district in the northeast, as listed in the federal register maintained by the Department of the Interior.

Wandering through its side streets, you'll be impressed by the variety and quality of much of Sunset Park's residential architecture. Some clusters of houses, and in some cases complete blocks, are almost fully restored to the way they looked at the turn of the last century, when most were constructed, and a few are positively elegant. Look in particular at 54th to 59th

Streets between Fourth and Fifth Avenues. (Fifty-fifth is probably the best, with lovely greenery and the area's only freestanding mansion at its southeast corner on Fourth Avenue; it now houses offices). Also check out such exceptional blocks as 44th, 47th (my favorite), and 59th Streets between Fifth and Sixth Avenues. Many houses can compete with the best of Park Slope. The huge **Basilica of Our Lady of Perpetual Help Church,** at 59th Street and Fifth Avenue, opened in 1909; 6,000 people attended its first mass.

Absolutely don't miss **John Zammit's house** at 653 58th Street. Zammit has turned the tiny front lawn into a mini-shrine for the various major holidays during the year, creating amazing collages using a combination of handmade, store-bought, and found objects, neighborhood photographs, and hand-printed signs (many on paper plates). Zammit, who has lived here since 1955 with his mother (who is in her nineties), says he began his project after surviving a cancer that was supposed to be fatal.

PARKS AND GREEN SPACE

There's no question that if you're going to eat outside, Sunset Park is the place. There are lots of benches and tables and ample grassy areas for a picnic. For families with kids, a huge, beautiful playground was recently completed. A pool run by the City of New York operates during the summer.

● ● ●

Fourth and Fifth Avenues

South of the Border

The focus of this tour is the dynamic twenty-three block stretch of Fifth Avenue between 39th and 62nd Streets. The ambiance is low-cost and colorful: 99-cent stores, music, and a vigorous sidewalk economy of tchotchkes and *churros* (sugar-coated fried crullers popular in Mexico). You might as well be south of the border!

Getting There   The R and N trains run along Fourth Avenue; the R stops at 45th, 53rd, and 59th Streets; the N, an express, goes to 59th Street. Go one block east (uphill) to Fifth Avenue.

▪ Tips for Touring

Many shops target customers of the same background as the owners and are not tourist-friendly (although a second generation of more modern markets and restaurants is now emerging). So even if a menu is bilingual, you may find that the staff doesn't understand or speak English. **Garibaldi Restaurant** (5715 Fifth Avenue, 718-567-0535) is a good example. It has a bilingual menu (and the most extensive among the Mexican places in the area) but I had an awkward time communicating with the waitress. I had a delicious (and huge) house quesadilla. (Among its ingredients was *nopalito*, or cactus.) It helps to speak Spanish, and mine is rusty. The restaurant also has a garden, but it looks less than impressive, although I'm sure that when it's packed with people having fun it's full of atmosphere. (I visited during a quiet afternoon.)

Markets   There are quite a few in the area, but there are two I especially like. Stepping into **Quick Deli Grocery** (4228 Fifth Avenue, 718-851-7875), I feel like I'm in Mexico. This place offers both fresh and packaged goods, including a huge selection of cooking peppers and spices and some cookware. My very favorite Mexican grocery in Sunset Park is not on Fifth Avenue but on Seventh: **Guadelupita Grocery** (4724 Seventh Avenue at 47th Street) is packed with Mexican cookware and gifts as well as a huge selection of food products. Take the N train to Eighth Avenue and the B70 bus north (as street numbers *descend*) to 48th Street, then walk one block west to Seventh Avenue. You can also get there from the R train at 45th Street and Fourth Avenue: walk two blocks *south* to 47th Street and three long blocks east to Seventh Avenue.

Restaurants/Fast Food   Just about every block in this area has a couple of eateries, ranging from bare-walled taquerias with no tables to fancier places that serve full meals. I've written up a few that show the variety of eateries in this area. **Restaurante Salvadoreno Usulateco** (4017 Fifth Avenue, 718-436-8025) is the only Salvadoran restaurant in the immediate area, and modest compared to others I've tried in Washington Heights, Queens, and down Fifth Avenue at 20th Street (see pages 176–179). But it's big (for the neighborhood), with friendly service, and I had a very good tostada platter and great *pupusas* on separate visits. **El Tesoro Ecuatoriano** (4015 Fifth Avenue, 718-972-3756) and **Castillo Ecuatoriano** (4020 Fifth Avenue, 718-437-7676) almost make this part of Sunset Park a "Little Ecuador." Specialties at both include *humitas* (fresh corn wrapped with cheese), a grilled seafood platter, shrimp in garlic sauce, and Ecuadorian crab salad. **Super Pollo Latino Restaurant** (4102 Fifth Avenue, 718-871-5700) is a Peruvian chicken place that I used to bypass on previous visits to Sunset Park. It looked dreary outside and uninviting inside. At my last visit it had been totally redecorated and the owner rented an adjacent space to create a dining room. Now it's a full-fledged Peruvian restaurant, and while the place remains known for its chicken, you also can get other Peruvian specialties including steak, fried rice with chicken, beef, or shrimp, and my personal favorite—*aji de gallina*, a shredded chicken stew in a creamy cheese sauce. Platters are $7 to $10. When I visit **La Flor de Piaxtla** (4202 Fifth Avenue, 718-437-7356), I feel as though I'm in a small, friendly Mexican town. There's good music, and long tables where people chatter over tacos and *antojitos* (snacks) and Jarrito's Mexican soda. The menu is simple—this is just a snack stop—but you can also buy food, magazines, and souvenirs here. **Tacos Matamoros** (4505 Fifth Avenue, 718-871-7627) is one of my favorite places to go if I'm with friends and we want a quick Mexican meal in Sunset Park. Here, you'll wait to extra-loud music while a big, delicious platter of enchiladas, refried beans, and rice is prepared. The fanciest restaurant on Fifth Avenue is **George's** (5701 Fifth Avenue, 718-439-1403), which you can't miss—it's in the salmon-pink building with the green trim. The fare is Greek-American diner-plus, reliable and unexotic, so it's the perfect place if you enjoy wandering but don't feel like experimenting with too many new tastes. **El Agulla Mexican Restaurant** (473 59th Street, 718-567-9580) opened in 2000. When I first visited it was still quite new, but the cooking was on the button: the big platter of enchiladas in mole sauce was delicious. There's a substantial seafood menu and a traditional Mexican breakfast menu. *Tamales* and rotisserie chicken are also available. **Starway Peruvian Chicken and Chinese Food** (6007 Fifth Avenue, 718-567-2873) serves mostly Chinese dishes but also makes the Peruvian chicken that's become popular in Jackson Heights.

Bakeries   Among many here, I have four favorites. **La Flor** (4021 Fifth Avenue, 718-683-1254) is a cute Mexican place offering Mexican breads and pastries as well as *antojitos* (appetizers) and a counter where you can sit and have coffee. **La Gran Via Bakery** (4516 Fifth Avenue, 718-853-8021) is a terrific Dominican bakery and dessert emporium; they serve ice cream sundaes and shakes too. I stick with the cakes, including a yummy cappuccino-soaked angel food cake, which I chase with a single espresso that's just 65 cents. I thought for that amount I'd get two gulp-fuls, like what you find in Italy. But, no, you get a full, strong cup. **Más Que Pan**—"More Than Bread"—(5401 Fifth Avenue, 718-492-0479) has an attractive setting featuring hanging baskets and *piñatas* and several tables where you can nurse a cup of espresso (75 cents) or cappuccino ($1.25). Though Dominican-owned, with Dominican specialties, you also can get Mexican and Italian breads, cookies, pastries, and custom cakes. I recommend the coconut kisses, strawberry mousse tarts, and jelly-filled chocolate cookies with vanilla icing and chocolate chips. The Generoso family has run **Generoso's Bakery** (5812 Fifth Avenue, 718-492-0895) for only about ten years but a bakery has been in this spot for about seventy. They specialize in brick-oven bread and Italian cookies, pastries, and fancy cakes. I love their

Freshly baked bread at Generoso's Bakery in Sunset Park.

pignoli cookies, which melt in your mouth (see page 159). There are several tables so you can savor the cookies (and the aromas) over espresso and cappuccino.

And don't miss **La Michoacana Paleteria** (4118 Fifth Avenue, 718-431-9312), which sells more than forty flavors of homemade ices, including pistachio, tamarind, mango, citrus flavors, nancho (made from a Mexican fruit known in English as nance), almond, and many others. Several of these flavors also come flavored with hot chile! You can also get enchiladas, burritos, and other "quick" dishes.

Also . . .   Besides food, you'll find many music stores and a few crafts and notions shops. Home-sewing is common for weddings and traditional "Sweet 15" parties. **Zapateria Mexico** (4505 Fifth Avenue) sells Mexican clothing, shoes, and leather handicrafts including sandals, hats, and belts. **Irma's Craft Store** (503 46th Street) specializes in sewing notions. **Vamos pa' Tabasco** (6210 Fifth Avenue) sells all sorts of inexpensive souvenirs, posters, ceramic crafts, and handmade wood picture frames.

. . .

Eighth Avenue

(39th to 50th Streets)

Multicultural Melange

Although you'll find many more Polish markets in Greenpoint, a bigger selection of Middle Eastern food in Sunnyside or on Atlantic Avenue in Brooklyn, and greater variety of Latin American food in Jackson Heights— or just a few blocks away on Fifth Avenue—this stretch of Eighth Avenue offers a fascinating and oddly charming mix of shops. I recommend that you include it in your tour to get a sense both of how neighborhoods change and of the wholeness of Sunset Park.

PIGNOLI COOKIES

Courtesy of Generoso's Bakery in Sunset Park, Brooklyn

Yield: 6 dozen cookies

3 pounds almond paste*
2 pounds granulated white sugar
Pinch vanilla powder or almond extract
1 cup egg whites, unbeaten
2 cups Pignoli nuts (3 to 4 per cookie)

1. Preheat the oven to 375 degrees F.
2. Beat the almond paste with the sugar with an electric beater for about 2 minutes.
3. Stir in the vanilla powder or almond extract.
4. Add the unbeaten egg whites, little by little, sparingly. Hand mix for about 2 minutes.
5. Squeeze the dough through a pastry bag onto a greased baking pan and top with the nuts. Each cookie should be about 1" round. Bake for 15 minutes or until golden brown.

*Generoso's uses American almond-macaroon paste, which Nick Generoso says is expensive, but the best.)

Combine this visit with a stroll to Sunset Park itself; Saturdays are best. One memorable afternoon ten years ago I observed clusters of observant Jewish families from nearby Boro Park taking a sabbath stroll, a group of Puerto Ricans holding a fundraising rally to help victims of Hurricane Andrew, and Mexican families picnicking and playing soccer. While vendors of Mexican fast food were doing a brisk business, people of different backgrounds were enjoying the special space that Sunset Park occupies.

Getting There   Take the M or W train to the Ninth Avenue stop (near 39th Street). Thirty-ninth Street itself is industrial and dull, so walk to 40th Street and turn right toward Eighth Avenue or go one block further to look at the cluster of cute homes at 4016-4022 Ninth Avenue.

Mexican/Latin American Food   You'll find a handful of Mexican, Dominican, and Ecuadorian restaurants and one Mexican bakery here. Since I focused on Latin American food in the Fifth Avenue section (see pages 155–158), I didn't try the restaurants here. But I love the decor at

Lupita's (4414 Eighth Avenue, 718-871-5244), which has a beautiful miniature Mexican hacienda in the window and jolly murals. I couldn't resist the aromas emanating from **Santa Anita Bakery** (4506 Eighth Avenue). Typical *pan Mexicano* (sweet Mexican rolls with a sugar coating) and big cookies that would cost up to $2 in Manhattan are just 50 cents here, and I must say that the Mexican breads are especially delicious when they're fresh out of the oven. You can sit and eat—they also serve tacos and tortas—but, sorry, no espresso! **La Placita** (4219 Eighth Avenue) is a vast supermarket, butchery, and fish store selling fresh, frozen, and packaged products from all over South America.

Polish Markets/Restaurants   There's a small Polish enclave here with two Polish markets, one restaurant, and several Polish-owned shops. **Teresa's Restaurant** (4502 Eighth Avenue, 718-438-2845) offers low-cost, hearty soups, heavy meat entrées (veal, beef, and pork), and platters of pierogi stuffed with meat, potato, cheese, or mushrooms. The soups, most between $1 and $3, include three different types of borscht, various vegetable and bean combinations, and sauerkraut soup, and they're big enough to be meals. I had an excellent Ukrainian borscht and a platter of cheese pierogi and my companion had a rich bean soup, which, despite its name, was packed with vegetables. Both markets, **S&M Polish Deli**— "S&M" for owners Stanislawa Skrzatek and Mariusz Kisielewicz—(4703 Eight Avenue) and **Podlasie Market** (4722 Eighth Avenue) offer preserves, syrups, fish, sausages, frozen pierogi, cheeses, yogurt drinks, bread (often made in nearby Greenpoint, New York City's largest Polish community), pastries, and chocolates. I'm fond of Hortex vegetable and fruit juice including combinations such as apple and rose; apple and mint; and celery, carrot, and pineapple.

Halal Markets   A storefront mosque at 4315 Eighth Avenue seems to anchor the halal stores in the immediate vicinity. You'll find fresh and packaged goods similar to those in the Middle Eastern shops of Atlantic Avenue here, but it might be trickier to get explanations from owners who don't speak English and aren't used to tourists. I did get a friendly welcome from the owner of **SK Grocery** (4307 Eighth Avenue), which carries products from India, Bangladesh, and Pakistan. **Issawi** (4824 Eighth Avenue) specializes in Middle Eastern food and also sells cookware, Arabic-language periodicals, and some gifts.

Chinese Food/Restaurants   In the early 1980s Winnie Chu was an aspiring entrepreneur and Helen Zingone worked for the Council of Neighborhood Organizations as an area manager. Back then, Helen helped Winnie get a loan to open her first branch of the **Savoy Bakery** at Eighth Avenue and 59th Street. After she semi-retired, Helen recommended that Winnie look further north on Eighth, where commercial development was plodding along, but still plodding nonetheless. She helped Winnie open a branch at 4019 Eight Avenue, joining a growing number of Chinese-owned service stores (such as security gates, metal recycling, and car services), fast-food shops, and factories, as well as Central American, Polish, and halal markets. **New Seafood Restaurant** (4418 Eighth Avenue, 718-686-8888) is the fanciest eatery north of 50th Street. Its menu is listed in Spanish as well as English and Chinese. I much appreciated the friendly help I got at **Naikei Trading Co.** (4817 Eighth Avenue), a gift and tea shop where I bought an adorable blue and white teapot shaped like a duck, with a duckling forming the lid, for $6. Watch this area grow.

This neighborhood has numerous reminders of the once-dominant Scandinavian presence. Forty-third Street between Eighth and Ninth Avenues was once known as Finntown because so many people from Finland had settled there. In 1916 they founded New York City's first housing co-operatives at 816 and 826 Forty-third Street. Their Finnish names adorn the entryways. On the north side of 57th Street just east of Seventh Avenue a pentecostal church with a Spanish-speaking congregation displays a 1931 stone marking the "First Norwegian Church." At one time the Norwegian presence was so great that Eighth Avenue was known as Lapskaus (Beef Stew) Boulevard.

* * *

Eighth Avenue

(50th to 61st Streets)

"Bat Dai Do"—Brooklyn's Chinatown

Sunset Park is often described as New York City's third Chinatown, after the much larger ones in Manhattan and Flushing. For those who know the other two, the twelve blocks of Eighth Avenue where most of the Chinese shops and restaurants are located (50th to 61st Streets) may seem almost puny. But for folks who know it, it is big indeed: Its nickname, "Bat Dai Do," translates from Cantonese into "Big Eight Street."

And a walk through this neighborhood reveals a greater depth than you might expect at first glance, as well as a fascinating overlay of many cultures within the larger community. Within this area you will see a remarkable number of markets, restaurants, bakeries, service stores, banks, hair and nail salons, and other service establishments. You don't need to go further to have a wonderful experience!

And the area is expanding. The northern stretch of Sunset Park's Chinatown—Eighth Avenue between 39th and 49th Streets—has a few Chinese food markets and restaurants sprinkled among Chinese-owned stores that sell building supplies and services, but each time I come back there are more. Notably, the popular Gia Lam Vietnamese restaurant relocated one of its branches to this section of Eighth Avenue (see pages 163–164). The Chinese places are newcomers among longer-standing halal (Muslim) markets, two Polish markets, one Polish restaurant, and several Latino places (Mexican and Dominican eateries and markets and an excellent Mexican bakery).

Sunset Park's Chinatown has been officially recognized for only the past twenty years. Even though there had been some earlier Chinese settlement in the area, historians at the Museum of Chinese in the Americas mark its Chinatown designation with the opening of a Chinese grocery in the area. In the ensuing years, the Chinese population of Brooklyn, concentrated in Sunset Park but expanding in areas such as Bay Ridge, Bensonhurst, and Homecrest, has grown by an astounding 254%!*

Getting There   The closest subway stop is the N train at Eighth Avenue, which lets you out at 62nd Street.

Markets   Most markets here—and there are dozens—sell similar products, although some may specialize in meats or seafood, others in dry goods, and still others in fresh produce. My sense is that you need to find the shop in which you feel most comfortable—in size, offerings, and helpfulness of staff—so browse around. You may, if you wish, do all your shopping at the enormous **Hong Kong Dynasty Supermarket** (6013-6023 Eighth Avenue), which has its own parking lot. But this store can be daunting and sometimes too crowded to be pleasant. My personal favorite is **Lien Hung** supermarket (5705 Eighth Avenue, 718-435-3388). It's modern, clean, easy to negotiate, and has a great selection. A big plus is that some seafood and produce items are labeled in English as well as Chinese. Some of the products you'll find include Vietnamese coffee, sets of birds' nests that can be drunk as herbal treatments, and Malaysian ices in durian and taro flavors. I've never tasted durian melon, but a Chinese friend says that the inside is rather, uh, mucousy and it's an acquired taste (that she has not yet acquired). You'll see lots of durian around—it's the squishy-looking, thorny, oblong fruit wrapped in a net. They also sell frozen Chinese food, ingredients for making dim sum, and cooking utensils.

Two excellent seafood markets (among many here) are across the street from one another: **Fu Wang** (5724 Eighth Avenue) and **Sea Town** (5802 Eighth Avenue). Using my personal "shrimp meter" (comparing shrimp prices here with what I pay close to home), I've found prices almost

*Newsletter, Museum of Chinese in the Americas, Spring 1999.

half of what I pay in Manhattan (except in the seafood stores of China-town). Despite difficulty communicating, I found the staff helpful and the seafood incredibly fresh.

Taste Good Soya Food (5103 Eighth Avenue, 718-633-3913) manufac-tures and distributes soy products and they sell both retail and wholesale. A package of five fresh tofu squares is $1. You also can get fresh soy milk to take out or drink there.

Two halal shops sit between 59th and 60th Streets, catering to Muslims (mostly Turkish) who worship at the Fatih-Canii Mosque on that block. Go to the larger one, **Birlik** (5919 Eighth Avenue, 718-436-2785). Birlik's produce section is excellent and *very* reasonable; I found a canary melon for $1 (I'd pay at least $3.50 in Manhattan). There also are some great Turkish breads plus an odd hybrid bread that is described as Italian-Jewish-Turkish. It's also worth taking a look at the mosque. I have found the people there to be very friendly, and you can go inside if a service isn't under way. There's a lovely gift shop and also a historic Koran on display.

Restaurants Jade Plaza Restaurant (6022 Eighth Avenue, 718-492-6888) serves dim sum seven days a week from 8 A.M. to 4 P.M. There are dozens of dishes and the offerings change daily. (There's no listing.) Ser-vice is brusque and every time I've been there the place has been packed—and I've always been given a fork, even though I don't need one. At one visit a waitress recommended scallops with a light cheese topping. "White people like this," she told my Chinese-American companion. Cheese is rare in Chinese cuisine—this dish represents a type of fusion cooking. You'll do best here in a group of at least three people.

Not knowing how to choose the best of so many Chinese restaurants, I asked folks who live in or near Sunset Park for recommendations. Many cited **Ocean Palace** (5423 Eighth Avenue, 718-871-8080) for its seafood and the nicest welcome for newcomers. Its menu struck me as somewhat conventional, so I tried **New Ocean Empire** (5418-22 Eighth Avenue, 718-851-8008) across the street. I tried shrimp with walnuts and broccoli in special sauce. (Diners have a choice of American or Chinese broccoli.) The "special sauce" was mayonnaise, which I later started to see at dim sum places in Flushing and Manhattan's Chinatown. Most of the restaurants in this area are open from 7:30 A.M. to 2 A.M.

Gia Lam Vietnamese Restaurant opened at 54th Street in Sunset Park in 1998 and within a year had opened a second branch at 5608 Eighth Avenue (718-567-0800). The original one has since relocated to Eighth Avenue between 47th and 48th Streets (718-633-2272) and it was pretty busy when I was there, even though the surrounding area is still quiet. The menu is fun to read—and the food is good. More exotic specialties include pigeon, frogs' legs, and eel. I went for a more conventional—and deli-cious—crab and melon soup, vegetarian spring rolls, and a so-called tri-color drink—an iced beverage of sweet condensed milk with red and yellow beans and green jelly. Folks with adventurous palates will have fun here without spending a lot. The area's two Malaysian restaurants are **Nyonya** (5323 Eighth Avenue, 718-633-0808 or 718-972-2943), a large, bustling place which has a larger Manhattan counterpart at 194 Grand Street, and **Sun Ky** (5918 8th Avenue, 718-439-4502), which is smaller, more crowded, and clearly more appealing to non-tourists. I love the varieties and savory challenges of Malaysian food, so I've tried a number of dishes. If you can have only one, try the traditional *nasi lemak*—coconut rice with curried chicken (and lots of other ingredients, including vegetables, peanuts, and tiny fish). The range of tastes and textures fascinates me—sweet, spicy, fruity, cold, hot, smooth, crunchy. I also ordered some crispy Malaysian honey sweets with a peanut flavor for dessert. I'm still learning about Malaysian food, and this was a good place to start. The owner was helpful and good-humored while explaining things to me.

Ying Tan Restaurant (4924 8th Avenue, 718-633-5333) was brand-new when I visited in 1999. It replaced a fast-food falafel place, perfectly symbolizing Sunset Park's ongoing transition to a full-fledged Chinatown. Ying Tan has a huge menu including dishes unfamiliar to non-Chinese palates such as duck blood, frog "any style," and intestines "any style." At lunch you can order a mini-casserole made up of your choice of three dishes (already prepared—they're in the front window) over rice. I chose a whole croaker (very bony), eggs with scallions, and tofu. This huge dish, prepared for take-out, was just $3. **Fung Sing** (5605 Eighth Avenue, 718-854-3996) is the main noodle shop here, with a fast-food version (open from 8 A.M. to 11 P.M.) and a full-fledged restaurant next door (open 11 A.M. to 4 A.M.).

Bakeries, Snackeries, and Sweets   Bakeries abound along Eighth Avenue. Many have tables, and their selection is similar—Western style sponge-like cakes with a light icing of various flavors, jelly fillings, and some fruit, as well as more-typical Chinese pastries and buns such as sticky sesame bean paste and coconut buns, and some sandwiches as well. **Savoy** (5223 Eighth Avenue and 5922 Eighth Avenue (see page 160) is one of the oldest of the bakeries. Check out the yogurt cheesecake. On the slightly more upscale side, a couple of new tea houses and snackeries have arrived in Sunset Park, catering to a younger crowd. Typical is **Kakala** (5302 Eighth Avenue, 718-437-6336), which advertises itself as the "New Generation on Eighth Avenue." Here, in a more hi-tech setting, you can choose from ham sandwiches, peanut butter and jelly on toast, spaghetti, "luncheonmeat" omelets, and hot-dog appetizers, along with green curry soup, Hong Kong fin soup, fried squid, chicken wings, and other more identifiably Chinese dishes, plus a huge selection of flavored milk, Taiwanese ices, jelly drinks, pearl teas, and pudding drinks. One of the owners told me that this is the new wave of eatery coming out of Hong Kong. Some years back a branch of the St. Alps Tea House chain opened in Sunset Park but it's now known as **Tea & Tea** (5801 Eighth Avenue, 718-437-6622). It sells the popular pearl teas for $2.50 to $3.50. These come in forty flavors including fruit and nut flavors and others like chocolate and peppermint. You also can get dumplings, noodle or rice dishes, and snacks (toast, jellies and buns) here.

An Dong (5424 Eighth Avenue, 718-972-2263) is a Vietnamese snack bar that opened in 1999. You can get delicious fruit shakes here (including a durian version, which the owners said is popular, but smells); Vietnamese sandwiches of pork wrapped in banana leaves; and various gelatin, sesame, and other types of desserts. Their popular Vietnamese coffee is $1.50. On another visit, I tried a Thai bottled drink called Basil Seed Drink with Honey that actually tasted like banana (as the owner told me it would). The seeds were gelatinous and it was, to say the least, interesting. I've since noticed this beverage in bottled and canned versions in Southeast Asian stores throughout Brooklyn, Queens, the Bronx, and Manhattan's Chinatown.

Sundaes & Cones (5622 8th Avenue, 718-439-9398) is an ice cream parlor that Royce Chan, originally from Hong Kong, has owned since 1994, and it's a fun place. He's been gradually adding more Chinese flavors including lichee, the most popular, as well as sesame (in a weird slate-gray color), ginger, taro, green tea, and red bean, along with a long list of more traditional flavors. He'll make shakes out of anything. He does sell durian ice cream and one of the folks on my Sunset Park NoshWalk decided to try it. I noticed a Chinese woman grin as Alan made his selection. Royce was there that day and he scooped the cone for Alan with a dubious look on his face. Sure enough, the ice cream, to our western palates, was inedible. I took a taste, too. Imagine cold, old, cooked onions—that's what it tasted like to me!

▪ Other Points of Interest

Ten Ren Tea and Ginseng Company (5817 Eighth Avenue), headquartered in Taiwan, has a better-known branch in Manhattan's Chinatown (75 Mott Street), another in Flushing (135-18 Roosevelt Avenue), and others in major U.S. cities. Everything you want to know about tea can be found here and in addition to choosing from elaborate and rather pricey tea sets you can get tea shakes—iced or hot green tea or black tea—in a number of flavors. The more exotic drinks include star fruit, kumquat, lemon, and plum. Flavored milk shakes come in papaya, taro, red bean, almond, and chocolate. Cold shakes are $2.00 and hot shakes are $2.50. For 50 cents more you can get tapioca with your shake, which is supposed to be good for the skin, and also extends the life of your shake by making it edible.

▪ Also . . .

World Journal Book Shop (6007 Eighth Avenue, 718-871-5000) has a huge branch in Manhattan's Chinatown (379 Broadway), in Flushing, and in many other locations. It doesn't sell food—but it's still a must-see. Some nice inexpensive items include Chinese stickers, bookmarks, holiday decorations, and, of course, books and tapes. They carry two good cookbooks in English illustrated with photographs: *Wei-Chaun's Chinese Cuisine,* edited by Chengh-huei Yeh and Su-Huei Huang (Boston: Cheng & Sui Co., 1982), and *Chinese Cooking with Herbs.*

Signe's Imports (5906 Eighth Avenue) is an area oddity, one of two remainders of Little Scandinavia (the other is Halvorsen's Funeral Home). They sell Norwegian audiotapes, sweaters, jams, and knickknacks. You can often find the owners sitting outside. The interior is musty and chaotic and the goods are eclectic and authentic. I was looking for a child's sweater, but they were out of stock. Then I considered buying a pair of palm-sized dolls, but they seemed pricey at $41—perhaps good for a collector. It's worth a visit if only for a whiff of Eighth Avenue's past. I fear it may not be around much longer. (NOTE: By publication date, Signe's may be closed.)

Seventh Avenue in Sunset Park has a few shops, mostly little service businesses. But a handful of places are worth trying out. **Blackjack** (5424 Seventh Avenue, 718-435-2138), the area's first Japanese restaurant, opened in 1999 and was followed more recently by **Kyu Syu**, one block away at 5316 7th Avenue.

Brooklyn Side Trip

Atlantic Avenue

Atlantic Avenue in Brooklyn, like Arthur Avenue in the Bronx and Manhattan's Ninth Avenue, is one of those street names that connotes a great place to eat and buy food. Even though Atlantic Avenue itself stretches throughout the borough and into Queens, ethnic food fans know it as a two-block stretch of Middle Eastern (and some other) markets and restaurants that links Brooklyn Heights with the neighborhoods of Boerum Hill and Cobble Hill. A few Yemeni businesses and at least one Middle Eastern restaurant also can be found around the corner on Court Street. For the purposes of this tour, I'm profiling only the Middle Eastern places, which have a long and important history in this area.

The Middle Eastern presence on Atlantic Avenue dates back to the turn of the twentieth century. Syrian-Lebanese markets used to flourish in lower Manhattan, but when the area they occupied was razed for development the owners migrated to Brooklyn and settled along Atlantic Avenue. (In those days, the two areas were linked by the Fulton Ferry; the Brooklyn landing place was at the foot of Atlantic Avenue.)

Some of the families, including the Sahadis and Malkos, set up businesses that still operate today. Most are led now by the second- and third- and sometimes fourth-generation members of the founding families. The Yemeni businesses are relatively new and include several service companies around the corner on Court Street. But the overall number of these stores is declining—or the nature of them changing—as larger and more contemporary Muslim and Christian Middle Eastern and North African neighborhoods develop along Steinway Street in Astoria, Queens, and on Fifth Avenue in Bay Ridge, Brooklyn. Their Jewish counterparts are concentrated on Kings Highway in Brooklyn between Ocean Parkway and McDonald Avenue and, to a lesser extent, in areas of Forest Hills and Rego Park.

Getting There   The closest subway stop is Borough Hall, where several subway lines including the #2, #3, #4, #5, A, C, N, and R lines converge. There are quite a few exits along Court Street. A good guidepost is the clock atop Brooklyn's Borough Hall itself. It should be to your left as you walk south on Court Street about five blocks toward Atlantic Avenue from the main intersection of Court and Remsen Streets. Your focus will be the two blocks of Atlantic Avenue bordered by Court Street on the east and Henry Street on the west.

Markets   Without a doubt, the king of markets here is **Sahadi's** (187 Atlantic Avenue, 718-624-4550), an extraordinary place that has been in this area since 1948 (but in New York City since 1898) and now looks more like Zabar's—but with an emphasis on Mediterranean food. There are two entrances; the left-hand side brings you to an area packed with coffees, nuts, and spices (some coffee beans are below usual market price—$3.75 for a pound of espresso beans, for example) and the right-hand door will take you into the more international area of the store. But the two merge at the center, and as you explore and turn corners you will realize that Sahadi's stocks marvelous prepared and packaged foods from around the world. I find it similar in some ways to Kalustyan's in Manhattan, but with more floor space to wander through. It's a family affair headed by Charles Sahadi, who has kept the store closed on Sundays so he can spend time with his family despite the potential business he could do on that day. You have to love a guy like that—and the store. **Oriental Pastry & Grocery Co**. (172 Atlantic Avenue, 718-875-7687) has long been a personal favorite. It has changed little in the twenty years I've shopped there and, as its name implies, its inventory focuses on baked goods and other products from the Middle East. I love their fresh *zataar* bread, fabulous *kanaifi* (a cheese-filled, honey-topped pastry), and halvah. There are all sorts of canned and fresh goods plus cookware and books on Middle Eastern cookery. It's neither too big nor too small, and that's one of the key attractions for me—it remains comfortingly predictable, authentic, and very personal. Some of the markets in this area also sell Egyptian water pipes, musical instruments, and carved-wood board games.

Bakeries   **Damascus Bread & Pastry** (195 Atlantic Avenue, 718-625-7070) predates Sahadi's on Atlantic Avenue, having arrived in 1936. Much of the pita bread sold in stores around Manhattan is baked by Damascus. You'll find all sorts of pitas, but you'll also see a wonderful range of Middle Eastern pastries—various types of baklava, birds' nests, almond-date cookies, and other delicacies ideal to savor with a cup of mint tea.

Restaurants   There are several excellent Moroccan and Lebanese restaurants remaining on Atlantic Avenue, and most are informal and very reasonably priced. They serve many of the same dips, salads, kebabs, and grilled entrées and they have lots of vegetarian options. Both **Waterfalls Cafe** (144 Atlantic Avenue, 718-488-8886) and **Café Restaurant Caravan** (193 Atlantic Avenue, 718-488-7111) have magazines and newspapers for customers to read as they enjoy their meals—clearly these places really serve their community and don't rush customers out! Waterfalls serves more basic combinations made with *tabboulleh* (bulgar or cracked wheat salad) and falafel, while Caravan offers a more substantial menu that includes *tagines* and couscous. One dish that particularly appealed to me was a sweet vegetable *tagine* with mixed vegetables sautéed with onions, raisins, cinnamon, and prunes. **Moroccan Star** (148 Atlantic Avenue, 718-643-3042) relocated to its current address after many years elsewhere on the block. Among its appetizers are chicken and seafood crepes—not something I often see on a Middle Eastern menu! (They're $3.50 and $3.95 respectively.) I've known **Tripoli** (156 Atlantic Avenue, 718-596-5800) for years, including when the owner, Mohammed Salem, also operated Tripoli Café on the north side of the street, where he sold homemade ice cream and other desserts. I still remember the creamy canteloupe ice cream that I have yet to see sold elsewhere. It closed in the mid-1980s. Tripoli restaurant itself always has been somewhat fancier than the other local restaurants, with a handsome bar and two floors—the Salem family operated the lower floor for years as an upscale seafood restaurant. Entrées are a bit costlier here than the other places. You'll find many vegetarian dishes as well as specialties such as fish fillet cooked in a sauce with chopped almonds and walnuts and fresh okra cooked with lamb chunks in tomato sauce and pomegranate nectar. They use all sorts of interesting combinations of nuts and flavors here. At this writing, the Salems were renovating the lower floor, preparing to introduce a "live" food restaurant (with a menu of raw-food cuisine), and were converting the liquor bar into a fresh juice bar. In addition to their menu, the Salems also sell Tripoli-brand cold-pressed olive oil made in Lebanon. All the restaurants around here also sell Middle Eastern dips and various appetizers to go.

There are two Yemeni restaurants on Atlantic Avenue. Although I've never seen a female Yemeni customer, women are indeed welcome. The settings tend to be simple (although there are beautiful photographs of Yemen), the service is friendly, and the prices for their dishes—including lamb specialties, delicious soups, stews, and stuffed pastry—are very reasonable. The fabulous grilled breads, similar to Indian *nan*, that come with meals are a hallmark and (almost) a meal in themselves. The most expensive dishes are about $12, but they average $7 or $8. **Yemen Café & Restaurant** (176 Atlantic Avenue, 718-834-9533) and **Green Province** (172 Atlantic Avenue, 718-722-7246) are examples. Around the corner from Atlantic Avenue, **Unity Restaurant** (145 Court Street, 718-624-9325) has a menu of recognizable Middle Eastern dishes—hummus, *foul* (a delicious dish of fava beans with tomatoes and onions in olive oil), as well as Yemeni specials including *salta* (potatoes and celery cooked with fenugreek) and *gelaba*—lamb sautéed with tomatoes and onions.

I noticed that the store window at **Malko Karkanni Brothers, Inc. Market** (718-834-0845) had several products made in Israel—the Hebrew on the cans stood out. And at **Rashid Music Sales**, a store that was on Atlantic Avenue for years but is now located at 155 Court Street at Pacific Street, I also noticed some Israeli music CDs in the window (mostly related to Israel's Arabic-speaking communities). **The Yemen Café & Restaurant** had a big American flag in its window. These stores—and this whole neighborhood—suffered financially after the events of 9/11/01, so I think these gestures shouldn't be overlooked. The markets and restaurants on Atlantic Avenue have been part of the fabric of New York City's culture for decades and have brought much richness to those of us who savor the opportunity to get to know the world better within the boundaries of our hometown.

Brooklyn Side Trip

Bensonhurst

When I first visited Bensonhurst, I felt let down. It wasn't that I expected to see young John Travolta look-alikes on every corner, but I suppose I anticipated a larger Italian presence, particularly along the renowned shopping boulevard of 18th Avenue. Maybe a boccie court or two, a troubador, and perhaps a cheese shop at every corner. Compared to the thick energy of the Italian markets in Belmont in the Bronx, this area seemed to be a shadow of its reputation. But between about 64th and 86th Streets, I found some truly outstanding places. There are still plenty of social clubs and soccer teams and several cute little cafés (where most of the customers are men).

Yet, here's the paradox: whereas relatively few Italians actually live in Belmont any longer, Bensonhurst retains a far greater community of Italians, spread throughout the area and into the neighboring communities of Bath Beach and Gravesend. But as a middle-aged cashier at 69th Street Fruits & Vegetables, a bustling produce market, lamented, most of the young Italians have moved away. She told me that Piccolo Mondello Pescheria, the fish store around the corner, is owned by Koreans. And the proprietor of Aiello Brothers Cheese observed that he had moved his family to a New Jersey suburb so his children could have their own yard and attend better schools. I met his kids on "Take Your Daughter to Work Day."

Bensonhurst is changing. Visit the large playground at 77th Street and Bay Parkway and you will find yourself in a toddler United Nations. I heard little English, but lots of Spanish, South Asian languages, Chinese, and Russian and other Slavic languages. On 18th Avenue you will see several Russian markets, an Uzbek restaurant, a Vietnamese restaurant, and a new Chinese restaurant next to a Chinese market, to name a few.

Getting There   There are two ways: one is to take the N train to 18th Avenue. It exits at 18th Avenue mid-block between 63rd and 64th Streets. Turn right (there's just one exit) and start walking south (as the numbers *ascend*). The stores are located between 68th and 86th Streets, with several stretches where there won't be any stores. At 86th Street, you'll also come to the W train. The disadvantage of the W line in Brooklyn is that it takes forever to get to this station, so I recommend taking the N.

Markets   Two markets that you'll see as you begin your journey are **Piccolo Mondello Pescheria** (6823 18th Avenue at 69th Street), which, as I mentioned above, is now Korean-owned but sells all the seafood you would need for Italian (and other) cuisine. The vegetable stand around the corner is amazing—it fills much of the block and its prices are very reasonable. **Queen Ann Pasta & Ravioli** (7205 18th Avenue) has a huge selection of homemade and imported pastas, with more shapes than you knew existed. You can scoop what you want out of big bins. The store (which is a major manufacturer and wholesaler) also sells cheeses, meats, and sauces. Some of the more unusual combinations I found were ravioli made with asparagus and smoked mozzarella, artichokes with roast peppers, and squid. **Aiello Brothers Cheese** (7609 18th Avenue) mostly wholesales its products, so there's not much to see when you get there. But you can buy the fresh mozzarella and ricotta that's made on the premises. The standout in Bensonhurst is **Frank & Sal** (8008-10 18th Avenue), which is large and beautiful and has everything you could want for Italian cooking including a substantial selection of produce in front of the store. Although I often prefer to shop in smaller stores, the shopping environment here is fun and open, with old-fashioned cash registers (and cashiers of all ages) and counter staff who are helpful and expert. The quality is tops. **Sea Breeze Fish** (8500 18th Avenue, 718-259-9693) has a counterpart at Ninth Avenue in Manhattan and is the place to go if you're making a seafood dinner and have gotten the other ingredients at Frank & Sal.

Bakeries and Desserts   Bensonhurst has some *wonderful* bakeries, but I have to confess to two favorites. **Villabate Bakery** (7117 18th Avenue) has not only incredible cakes and cannolis but also gelati in more flavors than I've seen elsewhere—fragola, tiramisù, cassata, torrone, and more—and they serve year-round. Toward the end of 18th Avenue at 86th Street is **West End Bakery** (in Brooklyn sixty-five years). Its raspberry mousse cake ($18) and pretzel cake ($10) are just two of the amazing, fattening concoctions you can buy here.

Eateries   Surprisingly, Bensonhurst does not have a lot of good Italian restaurants. **Gino's Focacceria** (7118 18th Avenue) is my recommendation. It's an easygoing place with great prepared food—roasted vegetables, chicken dishes, and some pastas and salads—and a welcoming atmosphere. **Pizza Stop** at 8204 18th Street touts the fact that it's an independent, family-owned place. Their garlic knots are great and among their specialties is a "grandmother's slice" with marinara sauce.

Also . . . On 18th Avenue between 83rd and 84th Streets, by the way, you'll pass the landmark **New Utrecht Reform Church,** built in 1828.

Brooklyn Side Trip

Caribbean Crown Heights and Flatbush

If you ever had a doubt that Brooklyn is just about the best place in the United States to get Caribbean food, make sure you're on Eastern Parkway on Labor Day. That's when the annual Carnaval takes place after many months of rehearsals and putting together elaborate costumes. Often described as the largest parade in the United States, it attracts many thousands of fans when the weather's good—and when it's bad, too. After all, Carnaval happens just once a year, and if you're going to spend months getting ready you're not going to turn your back on it for a little downpour!

One source maintains that four million people participated in the parade in 2001, a claim that's somewhat dubious because that's more people than live in all of Brooklyn! All the same, Carnaval, which began in Harlem in the 1930s and moved to Brooklyn in the 1960s, is probably the single event where you can best get a sense of the size and diversity of West Indians in New York City.

In addition to the music and general celebrating, there's always tons of food for sale—oxtail soup, jerk chicken, spicy patties, and *roti*—and spicy ginger beer, smooth sorrel, or a vanilla-tasting Irish moss beverage to chase your food.

When Carnaval is over you can explore dozens of restaurants and shops north and south of Eastern Parkway selling food from Trinidad, Jamaica, Barbados, Haiti, the Antilles, the Dominican Republic, and all over the Caribbean. Guyana is also well represented.

New York City's West Indian community is spread out over large swaths of Brooklyn including not just Crown Heights and Flatbush but also Bedford-Stuyvesant, East New York, and Canarsie. The north Bronx also has a considerable West Indian presence, particularly along White Plains Road, as do areas of Queens, especially Richmond Hill (see pages 86–91), Jamaica, and other neighborhoods of eastern Queens. I've chosen to focus this tour on a section of Flatbush because you can find many good places in this area within easy traveling distance. They by no means represent all of Caribbean Brooklyn, but they do give you an excellent idea of what's available.

Two nice things about eating in these neighborhoods is that most dishes are precooked and ready to serve and you can have a substantial meal for under $10—and often for much less. *Roti* (meat or vegetarian combinations served in a thin pancake) makes a particularly nice meal. Wraps were already popular in Island cuisine before other places latched onto them! So you can come in, order, and be served almost immediately—provided there's no line. (I used to love eating at Gloria's In & Out at 991 Nostrand Avenue just north of Empire Boulevard, but I often had to wait until the many customers before me, clamoring for the delicious *roti*, had been served.) There are many good vegetarian options, including several vegan places listed below. And for lovers of hot, spicy food, this is the neighborhood!

Getting There   The key commercial avenues for this tour are Flatbush and Nostrand Avenues, which run north-south through much of the borough, and Church Avenue, a busy east-west roadway. The #2 and #5 trains follow Nostrand Avenue south of Eastern Parkway, with key stops at Sterling Avenue (one block south of Empire Boulevard) and Church Avenue. You can also take the Q train to Church Avenue near 16th Street (about five blocks west of Flatbush Avenue). To follow this tour, I recommend that you take the #2 or #5 train to Church Avenue and conclude at Church Avenue near the Q train, so you won't have to backtrack; the Q links up with many trains in Manhattan. The tour starts at Nostrand Avenue and Church Avenue.

If you're more curious still, Little Guyana in Richmond Hill (see pages

86–91) is packed with Caribbean eateries, mainly representing the foods of Guyana and Trinidad. And if you're absolutely compulsive, the area of White Plains Road in the Bronx north of Gun Hill Road (where the #2 and #5 trains run) is lined with West Indian and Guyanese eateries as well as African shops. (I've explored this stretch, and nothing stands out in the way some markets and eateries impress me in Brooklyn, so I didn't cover it in this book.)

I had a wonderful Jamaican jerk chicken and mustard greens at **Soldiers Restaurant** (1425 Nostrand Avenue, 718-826-0992) for just $3.50, and the spice was hotter than anything I'd tasted in ages (and I eat a lot of spicy food). It's an utterly unfancy place, and although the canopy was brand-new, the interior walls still had drawings from the days when a Blimpie evidently occupied this space. Lunches and suppers (oxtail, chickpea or split peas stews, curry goat or chicken, and jerk chicken, for example) come with sides of banana, yam, dumpling, or rice plus cabbage or greens. Featured here, as in most Jamaican places, are the traditional meals of *ackee* (a Jamaican fruit with West African origins with the consistency of avocado), codfish, and callaloo, a spinach-like green. Across the street is **Hammond's Finger Lickin' Bakery** (1436 Nostrand Avenue), which has a full line of cocobread, banana, pineapple, and raisin cakes, bread puddings, patties, and hardo bread (also spelled hardough) plus beverages including ginger beer (which is non-alcoholic), sorrel, and Irish moss. They serve take-out only.

Two good food markets in the immediate area are Korean-owned: **Seung Won** (1424 Nostrand Avenue at Martense Street), with shelves packed with jerk and other hot sauces, packets of sweet mango, spicy plum and tamarind and other Trinidadian snacks, bins of pig snouts and pig tails, and various herbs and flavorings, and **Master Food** (3008 Church Avenue, just east of Nostrand Avenue), a supermarket that has a huge inventory for Caribbean customers.

If you walk one block north, between Martense and Linden Streets you'll come to **Marché Laurent** (1409 Nostrand Avenue, 718-941-4515), a Haitian market that in good weather has a table outside the store filled with colorful carvings and household items; it brightens up an otherwise quite dull block. Inside the market there are packaged and bottled goods— spices, sauces, and other flavorings for Haitian cooking; Haitian sodas (the Lacaye brand, which years ago used to use recycled Heineken bottles); big bags of rice; and various types of flour. There is also cookware, music CDs, and some decorative items, as well as items used in religious observance. Places like this often serve multiple purposes such as helping folks to send money and parcels back home. Just next door, at 1411 Nostrand Avenue, is **Boulangerie St. Claire,** a small, plain bakery that sells Haitian breads.

Back on Church Avenue, walk west to Rogers Avenue. At the corner is the excellent **Nio's Trinidad Roti Shop & West Indian Bakery** (2702 Church Avenue, 718-287-9848), which has a range of chicken, vegetarian, and other entrées to make *roti* plus a full line of baked goods. The prices are amazingly cheap—a potato and channa (chickpea) *roti* is just $4; chicken *roti* is $4.50 and the fanciest seafood version is $7. The fillings all include delicious curried vegetables as well. Nio's is an attractive sit-down place with an interesting exterior: the walls of this corner eatery are covered with murals depicting Caribbean and African-American leaders including Marcus Garvey, Malcolm X, and Martin Luther King, Jr. Their business card lists branches in Bay Town, Texas; Mount Vernon, New York; and a mobile truck in Manhattan at Front Street between Wall Street and Pine Street.

North of Church Avenue at Rogers Avenue is **Sandee's Restaurant** (801 Rogers Avenue, 718-826-2456), a very small, somewhat typical Jamaican place that's quite charming. It has three tables and you can see (and smell) the food cooking as you stand at the counter to order. You can get an inexpensive breakfast here of banana or plantain porridge or a meal of oxtail stew or jerk chicken, depending on what the chef has prepared that day. South of Church Avenue is a medium-sized Haitian place called **C'est l'Eternel qui est Dieu Restaurant** (**It's the Eternal God Restaurant**, 830 Rogers Avenue, 718-469-3548). Quiet during the day, it offers typical Haitian goat, beef, and chicken stews with rice, often served with a very spicy sauce. Meals average $6 to $8.

On Church Avenue between Bedford and Flatbush Avenues are several Caribbean vegetarian places, including two that are large and quite nice: **Four Seasons Restaurant** juice bar and bakery (2281 Church Avenue, 718-693-7996) and **Veggie Castle** (2242 Church Avenue, 718-703-1275), which highlights its vegan cuisine including non-dairy pastries (carrot, pineapple, and banana breads, and muffins and pies), a natural juice bar, and breakfasts that include scrambled tofu, veggie strips, and plantain dishes plus complete lunches and dinners. It's the nicest-looking place I've seen in the neighborhood also has a health food market—and a parking lot. The owners are Guyanese but the substantial menu is pan-Caribbean.

Your last stop before the Q train is **Sybil's West Indian Bakery and Restaurant** (2210 Church Avenue, 718-469-9049), the largest of the three Sybil's outlets in New York City—the other two are in Richmond Hill (see page 90) and Jamaica, Queens (see pages 89–??)—and one of the oldest Guyanese eateries in New York. Typical West Indian entrées of beef, chicken, and goat curries as well as codfish cakes star on the menu here, but, as elsewhere, you can also do very well if you want to create a vegetarian meal. You also can just come for dessert, choosing from a wide range of pies and cakes.

For more information on West Indian food, here are a couple of good Web sites with addresses, listings, and information: www.eatjamaican.com and www.rotishops.com/usrotishops.html. For background on Carnaval, the excellent Web site www.wiadca.com provides history and other details on this Labor Day parade.

Brooklyn Side Trip

Coney Island

How can Coney Island be merely a side trip when it's so rich in history? There's a simple answer: try to have a good meal there. Pizza and fast "beach" food (French fries, clams, sausages, and smoothies) are, for now, the local staples, with a couple of nice Italian restaurants as the main exceptions—places that have managed to survive as Coney Island's reputation declined from the 1970s through the 1990s. Since the 1990s, Coney Island has begun to bounce back. The Boardwalk has been beautifully rebuilt; a new sports arena at West 15th Street and Surf Avenue to house the Brooklyn Cyclones, a New York Mets farm team, was inaugurated in 2000; and a number of the famous amusements have been renovated and updated. They may lack the magic of the pre-computer-games glory days, but they're bringing people back. And the Mermaid Parade, which began in 1983, linking Coney Island's old bawdiness with today's *outre* art scene, is now an annual institution held on the third Saturday in June. Its sponsor, Coney Island USA, runs the area's only non-profit sideshow (see www. coneyislandusa.com for details).

However you get there, don't miss the elevated train ride between West 8th Street and Stillwell Avenue (which you can take on the Q and F trains; reconstruction of these stops was underway as I was writing this book but will, I hope, be done when you read this!). Even if you drive in, this one-stop experience is special. Its magical view of the Cyclone, Wonder Wheel, and other landmark rides, especially at night when they're illuminated with the Atlantic Ocean in the distance, is for me a remarkable experience. Too bad the Stillwell Avenue station is so shabby—a metaphor, perhaps, for the current state of the neighborhood.

Getting There   Coney Island is located immediately west of Brighton Beach and can be reached from Brighton Beach by walking ten to fifteen minutes along the Boardwalk. The F, N, Q, and W trains all end at the Coney Island/Stillwell Avenue stop, but you can also take the Q or F to West 8th Street, where the **New York Aquarium** is located (call 718-265-FISH for information or see www.nyaquarium.com). The amusement rides and food stands are between West 8th Street and Stillwell Avenue, equivalent to West

14th Street. The street parallel to the Boardwalk, where major eateries are located, is Surf Avenue.

As you wander, you'll see endless streams of fast-food joints to complement the rides. The great **Nathan's** is still around, with a small outlet on the Boardwalk and its famous flagship at Stillwell Avenue and Surf Avenue. Otherwise, you'll see the same stuff at every boardwalk stand—fried clams, French fries, slush drinks, soggy hamburgers, mediocre hot dogs, and sausages. The only interesting places I've found are **Williams Candies** (1318 Surf Avenue), which sells jelly and caramel apples, cotton candy, candy buttons, rock candy, and other childhood relics, and **Ralph's Italian Ices,** a Boardwalk stand at West 12th Street that has about two dozen flavors. (Places like this are fairly common, actually.) Old-timer **Gargiulio's Restaurant** (2911 West 15th Street) is still there, but the sight of this Italian "villa" in the middle of a dilapidated neighborhood is rather startling. It's the size of a catering hall and is most appropriate for a group of people. **Totonno's Coal Brick Oven Pizzeria** (1524 Neptune Avenue, 718-372-8606) sells whole pies only and has been around since 1924. Knowing how fans make pilgrimages for their pies, I had to check it out, and it was worth it! It's located on a seedy stretch of auto-repair business, but people still make their way there, from noon until the pies run out, but no later than 7 P.M. (Just don't go on Monday or Tuesday, when it's closed.) Tortonno's also has a branch at 1544 Second Avenue in Manhattan, near 81st Street, which is open seven days but, like its parent, serves whole pies only.

Brooklyn Side Trip

Greenwood Heights

Thanks to creative real-estate brokers, the Brooklyn neighborhood sandwiched between Sunset Park and Park Slope (not profiled in this book) has a name of its own: Greenwood Heights, although some folks call it Lower Park Slope or Park Slope North, which I think is a stretch. It's an odd area located between Fourth and Fifth Avenues from about Prospect Avenue (16th Street) to 36th Street, just west of Green-Wood Cemetery, with a motley collection of homes and businesses. Some blocks are quite attractive while others look rather plain.

There are still some interesting eating and shopping opportunities here and, of course, you can visit Green-Wood Cemetery while you're at it. This area is filled with churches of all types. The anchor church seems to be **Our Lady of Czestechowa,** founded in 1904, located on 24th Street between Third and Fourth Avenues. The area also has a number of Polish delis and shops. I've also seen a Greek Orthodox church, a Ukrainian Orthodox church, and various Pentecostal churches. The Muslim community also has roots here: at 675 Fourth Avenue between 20th and 21st Streets is the large Islamic **Al-Noor** school and community center.

Getting There   The M and R trains stop at 25th Street (for the cemetery) Prospect Avenue (equivalent to 16th Street) if you want to shop or eat first. If you've been touring Sunset Park, you can catch the B63 bus on Fifth Avenue to reach this area.

Restaurants   Honduras Maya (587 Fifth Avenue, 718-965-8028) is one block north of what's defined as Greenwood Heights, but since it's the only Honduran restaurant I've found in New York City, I've included it in this tour. The menu includes tacos, Salvadoran-style *pupusas*, a dish called *pincho* (a type of kebab), and a "plato típico Hondureño" made of rice, beans, cheese, cream, avocado, and sweet plantains, as well as entrées similar to those in Salvadoran, Mexican, and Guatemalan restaurants.

Milan's Restaurant (710 Fifth Avenue at 23rd Street, 718-788-7384), a Slovakian restaurant that opened in 1997, offers inexpensive Eastern European dishes, with meat entrées ranging from around $3 to no more than $7, combinations of borscht, and pierogi. The specialty there is *halusky* with sheep's cheese or sauerkraut, plus dishes you'll find in other Eastern European restaurants. I had to have *halusky* just because I wanted to say that I'd had it, but it's just a potato and flour dumpling (like gnocchi or *spaetzele*), and not very interesting. Go for dishes with vegetables so you can leave feeling as though you've ingested more than just starch and fat. The desserts include delicious fruit blintzes, strawberry rolls, mocha cake, and puddings.

I love Salvadoran food, so I was delighted to discover **Continental Restaurant** (672 Fifth Avenue at 20th Street, 718-832-1327). I particularly love the *apertivos típicos* (appetizers) such as *pupusas* (see page 178) and tamales, as well breakfast combinations of refried beans with yellow plantains topped with cheese or cream. Do check out the entrées—I had a terrific shrimp kebab. **Lizette** (688 Fifth Avenue) is a Mexican bakery that also serves fabulous omelet platters with heaping sides of potatoes and salads for just $3.00. The baked goods are great, too.

Markets   For the area, **Eagle Provisions** (628 Fifth Avenue at 18th Street, 718-499-0026) is huge, specializing in Polish and other Eastern European products but also with a large general selection. There's an unusual selection of beer, some from Albania and Kenya. It's open every day from 6 A.M. to 7 P.M. But I prefer **Galicja Delicatessen** (694 Fifth Avenue, near 23rd Street, 718-768-6545), a much smaller shop, which sells Eastern European goods (including Czech and Polish beer) exclusively. The presentation, colors, and aromas are perfect. It's closer to Green-Wood. There are also some Polish shops on Fourth Avenue around the corner from the church.

A local point of interest as you wander north on Fifth Avenue is **Grand**

Prospect Hall, a Victorian catering hall at Prospect Avenue (equivalent to 16th Street, 718-788-0777). The decor is neo-rococo, decorated with vast chandeliers and elaborate paintings. You'll feel as though you've stepped back a century—and, in a sense, you have: the hall opened in 1892. It represents a number of Brooklyn milestones: it was once Brooklyn's tallest building and the first to have electricity, its French birdcage elevators were the first passenger elevators in Brooklyn, and such notables as William Jennings Bryan and Lena Horne appeared on its stages.

■ Green-Wood Cemetery

Green-Wood Cemetery is the major historic site near Sunset Park and a superb place to explore history through the lives (and deaths) of New Yorkers who've "been there, done that," including a few who did things they shouldn't have. Well-known "residents" include Leonard Bernstein, women's

PUPUSAS

Courtesy of Continental Restaurant in Greenwood Heights, Brooklyn

Serves 4

> 1 cup mais de harina*
> ½ cup water
> ½ cup shredded mozzarella cheese, for the filling (may also use refried beans or diced chicken or pork)
> Cabbage slaw for topping (a mixture of shredded cabbage and shredded carrots tossed with vinegar and oregano)

1. Throughly mix the mais de harina with the water.
2. Take ¼ of the mixture and form it into 2 balls, one slightly larger than the other. Flatten them into patties.
3. Add the cheese or other filling to the center of the larger patty.
4. Place the smaller patty on top.
5. Grill (do not fry!) on both sides until the patties turn light brown. Remove and let cool. Serve topped with shredded cabbage slaw.

*Corn flour used in Latin American cooking found in specialty markets.

activist Margaret Sanger, and Townsend Harris, who helped found the City College of New York. More notorious folks include Lola Montez, mistress to Franz Liszt; Alexandre Dumas; King Ludwig I of Bavaria; and Boss Tweed, the Tammany Hall political fixer. A great resource is *Permanent New Yorkers: A Biographical Guide to the Cemeteries of New York* by Judi Culbertson and Tom Randall (New York: Chelsea Green Publishing Co., 1987).

Green-Wood was incorporated in 1838 as the first public burial ground in the city of Brooklyn and was designed principally by by engineer David Bates Douglass. Seen as a prototype for Central Park, it became a weekend destination for families seeking escape from the city. Besides being in an exquisite natural setting (there's a lake, and you'll see geese on a good day), a portion of it sits on the highest elevation in New York City, where you'll see sweeping harbor views. You can make a one-day excursion out of a visit or, if you're ambitious, snack in one of the places listed above, do the tour, cool out in Sunset Park (get some ices nearby), and then, if it's a long summer day, have a Mexican or Ecuadorian supper on Fifth Avenue or a Chinese, Vietnamese, or Malaysian meal on Eighth.

GETTING THERE

From the 25th Street subway stop, walk east up the hill on 25th Street to Fifth Avenue, to the main entrance. Follow the roadway to the main gate. The cemetery office will give you a map. Green-Wood is open seven days a week from 8 A.M. to 4 P.M. year-round. No, visiting hours aren't longer during the summer. And no, you may not take pictures, ride a bicycle, have a picnic, or jog there. And they'll enforce these rules.

Brooklyn Side Trip

Sheepshead Bay

Sheepshead Bay is best known for its restaurants and for the bay itself, where fishing boats are moored along nine concrete piers facing Emmons Avenue. (The piers were built in 1936 for $180,000—imagine trying to do something like that today!) For decades, the Lundy family dominated Sheepshead Bay with their gigantic seafood restaurant at 1901-1929 Emmons Avenue that in its heyday served more than 5,000 meals. Today, **Lundy's**, which was closed from 1979 to 1996, occupies just part of the building (it now seats only 500); the rest of the building houses a Turkish café, small shops, and offices. The area is multi-ethnic, with Chinese, Turkish, Thai, Uzbek, and Japanese places alongside the older Italian and Irish clam bars. New places reach out to Russian customers, including Baku

Palace (a nightclub) on Ocean Avenue and an Armenian café with a menu in English and Russian, not Armenian. (For clothes hounds there's a large new branch of the Loehmann's clothing chain.)

Sheepshead Bay can be packed on weekends. If you can, go during the week when it's much quieter. If you hang around long enough in the afternoon you'll hear the shouts of fishing captains as their boats come in from a day at sea. You can buy fresh fish on the spot from a daily haul of blues, fluke, cod, and other local fish—and they'll clean it while you wait. Many boats offer half-day fishing trips, which leave early morning and return mid-afternoon. These cost about $35. On weekends there are cruises to the Statue of Liberty and elsewhere.

Getting There   Take the Q train to Sheepshead Bay station. Turn west two blocks to Sheepshead Bay Road (left if you exit the north end at Voorhies Avenue, right if you exit the south end, which is Sheepshead Bay Road, which then curves around) and walk about five minutes to Emmons Avenue (which is an extension of Neptune Avenue, if you've been to Brighton Beach.) Note that you will be crossing at an intersection with busy Shore Parkway. Do not jaywalk!

From Brighton Beach it's a fifteen-minute walk. Head north on Brighton 12th Street to Cass Avenue, turn right, and you'll see the bay from the south side (Shore Boulevard). Walk west on Shore Parkway to the Ocean Avenue Bridge, a wooden footbridge that crosses the bay. It will take you to Emmons Avenue at 19th Street.

If you're driving, take exits 8 or 9A on Shore Parkway to Emmons Avenue.

Restaurants   Although Sheepshead Bay is packed with eateries, especially on Emmons Avenue, I've chosen to profile just a handful that stand out. **Garden Bay Café** (1788 Sheepshead Bay Road, 718-648-2225) is an Armenian place with a menu in English and Russian, not Armenian. The food is very good and very inexpensive. Cold appetizers and salads range from $2 to $5, except for puff pastry with cheese, which will set you back just $1 per piece. Kebab entrées are $4 (chicken kebab) to $8.50 (lamb kebab). I tried the delicious *xashlama* (lamb in sauce) with a "Salad Ani," a thick, spicy dip of yogurt, walnuts, and garlic which was delicious, served with *lavash* bread, a soft, thin, flat bread used to make wraps. (I also like to heat *lavash* in the microwave.) Facing the bay is the impressive **Istanbul** (1715 Emmons Avenue, 718-368-3587), with a menu featuring a large selection of cold and hot appetizers, seafood entrées, and, of course, kebabs. Unusual among area restaurants, it offers four vegetarian entrées, including one kebab and three *pides* (filled dough). The *menemen pide*, for $8.50, has pieces of tomato, green pepper, onion, and parsley topped with fried egg. I tried the **Bay Shish Kebab Turkish-Uzbek Restaurant** (2255 Emmons Avenue, 718-769-5396), which features familiar Mediterranean dips and salads including hummus, tahini, and tabboulleh, as well as Turkish specialties including *soslu patican* (small pieces of eggplant in a spicy sauce of tomatoes, green peppers, onion, garlic, and parsley) and *sigura borek* (phyllo dough stuffed with feta cheese). Appetizers are $3.50 to $5; kebab entrées range from $10 to $16.75 for a mixed grill. A young Russian woman told me the newer Turkish place, **Liman** (2710 Emmons Avenue, 718-769-3232), has become the big hangout for her friends. It specializes in—surprise!—seafood. The hot appetizers are terrific, especially *balik koftesi* (fried fish patties), made with chunks of striped bass with *kasseri* cheese ($7), and *midye dolma,* a cold appetizer of mussels stuffed with pine nuts, rice, and currants ($6).

Markets   Sheepshead Bay has an excellent gourmet market and a superb produce store facing one another one block from the Sheepshead Bay subway station. **Sheepshead Bay Gourmet** is at 1518 Avenue Z; **Sheepshead Bay Fruits & Vegetables** is located at 2601 East 16th Street. The gourmet market has an excellent selection of Russian-style appetizers as well as lots of quality seafood and cheese plus tempting desserts—chocolates and all sorts of cakes and pastries. (Take me out of there!) The produce market features some rather esoteric products including apriums (apricot-plum hybrids) and kiwalos (horned melons)—which are not attractive, to put it mildly. (And these little things are expensive. Give me a good cantaloupe instead!)

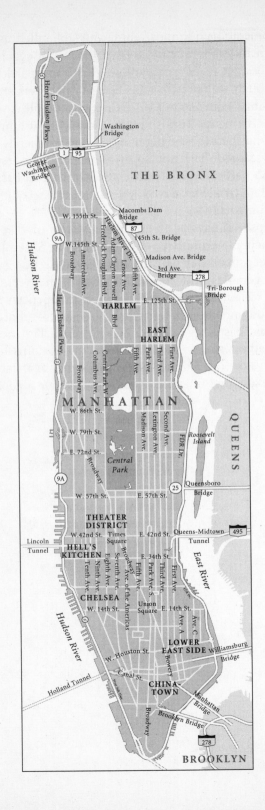

Manhattan

■

CHINATOWN

EAST HARLEM

HARLEM (WITH A SIDE TRIP TO WEST HARLEM)

LOWER EAST SIDE

NINTH AVENUE

SIDE TRIPS

- *Curry Hill*

- *Little Seoul*

- *Tastes of Persia*

- *Washington Heights and Hudson Heights*

- *Yorkville*

•••

Manhattan Notes

Of all the boroughs, I eventually concluded—to my own surprise—that the one most in flux is Manhattan, where some neighborhoods seem to change just as you think you "get" them. The Lower East Side is no longer just pastrami and pickles; Chinatown is spreading throughout Soho and becoming more pan-Asian (and, in some respects, more American); Manhattan's Little Italy has become little more than one street of restaurants and a bare handful of shops; and Harlem is undergoing such a vast transformation that some areas will be barely recognizable in a few years.

Yet Manhattan is still how many people define New York, and the challenge in writing about the neighborhoods is to figure out how to profile them with enough flexibility to accommodate change. I decided not to even attempt to write about the East Village and other areas where turnover is very rapid and the neighborhood ethos is difficult to grasp.

So what's left? A lot, really . . .

I was happy to find that Ninth Avenue still has some of its old-timers hanging on. (They are able to survive because the shop owners also own the buildings they occupy.) A new weekend flea market has helped spark new life in the area.

I tackled as much of Harlem as I could, hoping to launch readers on exciting neighborhood walking and tasting tours. In East Harlem I discovered the re-emergence of an arts community throughout the area—and many new eateries.

I explored the neighborhood of Washington Heights, which I've also enjoyed on my own but never knew quite how to encapsulate for anyone who isn't quite as compulsive as I am about covering every nook, cranny, and eatery in a neighborhood.

The Lower East Side was full of revelations—like a slab of clay being molded into a sculpture, this neighborhood is reshaping and reinventing itself in creative new ways. It's still the same clay, though, and much of the old Lower East Side still survives despite waves of change.

What I've tried to do is show a Manhattan beyond the usual tourist perspective. And yet, whenever we visit the neighborhoods we don't live in, we're all tourists, aren't we?

•••

Chinatown

Manhattan's Chinatown dates back about 150 years when a tiny core community of men settled around Mott and Pell Streets. The oldest stores still stand there, including the 32 Mott Street General Store, in its current spot since 1899. These days this area is the heart of what is now a Greater Chinatown whose boundaries have expanded, particularly in the last two decades, with a surge of newcomers from Fujian Province, complementing large Taiwanese and Cantonese communities. With over 100,000 residents, Manhattan's Chinatown is the largest in the United States. And New York City's two other Chinatowns—Flushing, Queens

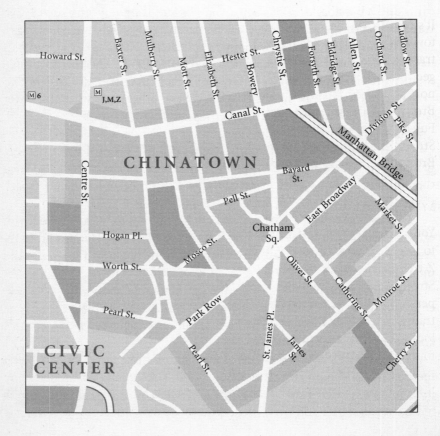

(see pages 29–33), and Sunset Park, Brooklyn (see pages 161–166), are also booming.

Chinatown tourism is now on a rebound from the economic devastation wrought by the awful events of 9/11, and on an average day the area is packed with workers in the community's hundreds of shops and factories, schoolchildren, and tourists. Now, as before, stores cater both to local Asian clientele (a number of groceries specialize in Thai, Indonesian, Vietnamese, and Malaysian products in addition to Chinese) and to visitors from around the world. Taiwanese, Hong Kong, and Chinese banks have a strong presence in this bustling economy and Chinatown itself now stretches into much of the Lower East Side, Soho, and the area called NoLiTa (North of Little Italy). It is rather ironic, then, to discover that the elaborate Chinese structure on the northwest corner of Canal and Centre Streets, which was built in 1983 as the headquarters for the Golden Pacific National Bank, now houses a Starbucks coffee house and the offices of an American investment firm!

■ Getting Oriented

It's certainly possible to devote a long, comprehensive chapter to Chinatown. But I have decided to limit my restaurant reviews to places that illustrate the variety of food you can have, and to divide coverage into three geographic sections: "Old Chinatown," south of Canal Street; Chinatown north of Canal Street, bounded on the east by the Bowery and the west by Broadway; and the fast-growing area east of the Bowery—the heart of Fujianese Chinatown—which includes Grand, Canal, and Division Streets, as well as East Broadway; I've chosen to focus on blocks of East Broadway that sum up the essence of this area.

BY SUBWAY

You can take the #6, J, M, N, Q, R, W, or Z train to Canal Street, or the F train to East Broadway (to start your tour in the Fujianese section). The J, M, and Z trains also stop at the Bowery. A shuttle train (S) currently links West 4th Street to the busy Grand Street station (Grand and Chrystie Streets) during a period of construction. When this station resumes full service, the B and D trains may resume travel here (if old routes are reinstated). It's an important location for Chinatown, so double-check station availability as you plan your tour. From Manhattan's West Side (including the Port Authority bus terminal and Penn Station), you can also take the A, C, E, #1, or #9 trains to Canal Street. These stops are several blocks west of Chinatown, but if you dislike changing trains you'll quickly reach Chinatown by walking east.

BY BUS

Several buses run along the north–south arteries leading to Chinatown. Call 718-330-1234 for twenty-four-hour mass transit information.

BY CAR

Parking is scarce here and I don't recommend driving to Chinatown unless you absolutely must. There is one municipal lot nearby, on Leonard Street, south of Canal Street between Lafayette and Centre Streets—weekends only—and there's a large municipal garage on Essex Street between Rivington and Delancey Streets, which is about ten to fifteen minutes from the hub of Chinatown.

. . .

Chinatown

South of Canal Street

This area is the heart of Manhattan's Chinatown—where it began and where tourists still flock.

Getting There   The #6, J, M, N, Q, R, W, and Z trains stop at Canal Street. There are exits on Broadway, Lafayette Street, and Centre Street.

Markets   Mulberry Street has many of this area's best markets, including the new **Mulberry Meat Market** (89 Mulberry Street), a pretty, brightly lit place that features pre-cut meat, spiced and ready for a stir-fry, and some dishes to go that are just $2. Next door, **Tongin** (91 Mulberry Street) sells packaged and frozen products from Japan as well as sushi. Shelves of Indonesian, Malaysian, and Filipino soups, spices, cake mixes, and cooking ingredients, as well as produce, are available at **Asia Market** (71½ Mulberry Street). I enjoy wandering through the store and imagining buying the mixes and whipping up the concoctions myself, especially some of the delicious-sounding Indonesian desserts. This block also has **Golden Gate Buddhist Supplies** (85 Mulberry Street) and **BLT Martial Arts Market** (77 Mulberry Street). Across the street, **Thuân Nguyên** market (84 Mulberry Street) specializes in products from Vietnam.

For Thai food, you'll find ingredients and packaged goods at the crowded **Bangkok Center Grocery** (104 Mosco Street, 212-349-1979). At 200 Canal Street, **Kam Man** remains one of Chinatown's best-known markets, not just for its fresh and packaged foods but for its rich inventory of Chinese and Japanese dishes and cooking utensils; some of the Japanese ceramics are stunning—and so are the prices. **KD Food** (234 Canal Street at Centre Street) specializes in soy products including soy milk and tofu skins and also sells fried tofu from a stand at the strategic southeast corner of Centre Street. Two popular seafood markets, **M&F Fish & Meat** and **Hoa Choy** (214 and 218 Canal Street at Baxter Street), compete vigorously for customers and offer real freshness and variety. M&F has a small restaurant in the back; Hoa Choy has about sixteen different sizes and cuts of shrimp and prawns. Knowledgeable shoppers from many backgrounds come here for both the quality and great prices. You also will find many street vendors peddling fresh produce.

Bakeries, Teahouses, and Snackeries   Bakeries and teahouses are proliferating not only throughout Chinatown but also in areas of midtown Manhattan such as the Garment District. Many have branches in Flushing, Sunset Park, and other neighborhoods with a critical mass of Chinese residents. There are good reasons for their popularity. First of all, they're fast and cheap. Second, they can serve as an alternative to a restaurant if you're hungry and want a quick meal—many sell dim sum buns filled with pork, beef, or chicken, as well as hot dogs in croissants, and some also serve inexpensive hot dishes ($2 to $3). As for the baked goods, they're very low-price too—most buns and cake slices run 60 cents to 80 cents, while some of the more fanciful and fun pastries (such as chocolate-covered mice and fruit tarts) are around $1. A favorite of mine is **Tai Pan** (194 Canal Street, 212-732-2222), which has some of the most artfully designed cakes I've seen. I buy a Chinese birthday cake for my daughter every year, so I know how reasonable the prices are—they range from about $7 for smaller cakes to $12 and up for much larger ones. Nice features of these cakes are that they have a lot of fruit on top, the filling layers sometimes contain pieces of fruit, and the consistency of the cakes themselves is quite light. Most bakeries these days also offer a choice of dozens of colorful juices and teas, often in combinations, and with optional beads of black tapioca known as bubble tea. **Aji Ichiban,** a Hong Kong–based company, calls itself a "munchies paradise" and sells Japanese-style snacks made of dried olives, plums, ginger, prunes, dried lemons, shrimp, and other ingredients, which all taste delicious because most contain sugar (although some are made with saccharine). It's fun to visit—you're allowed to take tastes of most of the snacks—and they also have vats of chocolates and other sweets, which are great for kids and adults with a sweet tooth. There now are five scattered around Chinatown.

A fresh crab at a Chinatown fish market.

Of these, only the one at 153A Centre Street, south of Canal Street, has seating, and here you can also order hot snacks, bubble teas, and fruit juices in addition to the usual offerings. The setting is very cute and the seating features clear plastic chairs of pastel colors.

Restaurants   I've sought out restaurants that offer something unusual. Starting basic, I recommend **Central Buffet** (195 Centre Street, 212-226-2905) north of Canal Street, the largest of the "four dishes + rice" fast-food eateries that have sprouted in New York's Chinatowns. Cafeteria-style in format, you pay $4 for your choice of five dishes including rice, or you can skip the rice and get five dishes from the buffet. Servers generally dole out nice portions and there are dozens of choices. The owners have two other restaurants—**Buffet Lin** at 15 Division Street and **Café Lin** at 106 Delancey Street, which replaced a Wendy's. The one at Centre Street north of Canal Street is the largest and everything has English labels, so be prepared for pig's heart, pig's feet, pig's ears, and pig's tongue in gravy, not to mention many other pork variations (you may wish you didn't know). Fortunately, there are many vegetarian dishes as well—wonderful sautéed Chinese greens as well as tofu and sprout combinations, sautéed noodles, peanuts in seaweed, stir-fried eggs, and scallion pancakes. Best of all, my picky-eater daughter really liked this place so, clearly, anyone can do all right here. **Singapore Café** (69 Mott Street, 212-964-0003) is a newish Malaysian place with a lovely setting and a great variety of flavors. My choice was a spicy chicken dish and *chendol*, a delicious iced dessert/drink of condensed milk and coconut over shaved ice with red bean and green jelly, recommended by the waitress as a good taste contrast. She also warned me that my entrée was very bony and suggested I consider something else. She was right. (There are least a dozen Malaysian places in Chinatown.) **Ping's** (22 Mott Street, 212-602-9988) specializes in seafood and has some unusual specials. I chose prawns in cream sauce with fried milk, which is a Cantonese concoction in which sweetened condensed milk is first steamed and then the curd is deep fried. The pictures in the menu featured American broccoli; when I requested Chinese broccoli or another Chinese green, I got it—for a $2 surcharge. **Peking Duck House** (28 Mott Street, 212-227-1810) is an attractive establishment with a simple, gracious decor and a setting that lends itself to thoughtful eating. I rather liked listening to Bach's "Art of the Fugue" while I dipped moist pieces of duck skin into a sweet soy paste. The finished product involves placing duck, with some soy paste and slices of scallion, into a pancake. The menu specified that a $34 order of take-out Peking Duck was for one but it was packaged for two (two sets of chopsticks, two towelettes) and there was enough for three. **Vegetarian Dim Sum House** (24 Pell Street, 212-577-7176) is the uncreative name that tells you precisely what this small, nice-looking restaurant has to offer. There are no waiters walking down aisles, so you simply order from a menu of dim sum and entrées. **Vegetarian Paradise** (33 Mott Street, 212-406-6988) offers a creative menu with many choices. The soy chicken dishes are quite good and few entrées are more than $10. Don't bother making reservations at the dim sum palace **Jing Fong** (20 Elizabeth Street, 212-964-5256). Wait your turn as a hostess with a megaphone takes your name, gives you a number, and shoos you to the side to make room for the next group. Then prepare for the din of the crowds as you ascend an escalator into a huge space, but you will have more selections here than almost anywhere else—and take what you want when you see it, because you may not see it again. A friend from Beijing nearly crowed with delight as she ordered favorite dishes from home. I'd offered to treat her and she gleefully wolfed down one dish after the other—eel, blood, chicken feet—which neither a friend nor I would touch—and concluding with clams, which we all enjoyed. She somehow never got full. Here I noticed platters with jars of mayonnaise and Worcestershire sauce, which I first started seeing in Chinese restaurants several years ago. "What's going on?" I asked an English-speaking Chinese customer. "Chinese are getting bored with the same old dishes, so the restaurants are offering new tastes," he told me. You'll see more examples of such East-West fusion in the new wave of Hong Kong snackeries, which feature peanut butter on toast and ham sandwiches side by side with Chinese tea drinks.

. . .

Chinatown

North of Canal Street

This area is less touristy, with no souvenir shops aimed at attracting impulse buyers. There is, however, a branch of **Pearl River Department Store** at 194 Grand Street west of Mott Street, a popular emporium for Chinese and tourists alike seeking clothing and decorative items. Otherwise, this section of Chinatown is packed with markets, bakeries, and many service stores. (This area of Chinatown also has a Holiday Inn at 138 Lafayette Street north of Canal Street. It has bathrooms available to the public.)

Getting There   Follow the same mass transit directions for the area south of Canal Street (see page 188), but turn north instead.

Markets   I highly recommend a stroll along Mott Street between Grand and Hester Streets, starting at Grand Street (across from Di Palo's Market—see pages 253–254), where perhaps twenty produce, fish, meat, and herb markets pack the narrow sidewalks—you'd think you were really in China!

Toward the south end you'll come to 122 Mott Street, one entrance to **Deluxe Market,** a remarkable and fun place that crowds a bakery, food court, butchery, and frozen food grocery within a relatively narrow space that runs through to the main entrance at 79 Elizabeth Street (the Mott Street entrance is marked only in Chinese). You'll find great bargains here plus a "four dishes + rice" fast-food counter ($2.75). If, like me, you want just one dish (I'm partial to sautéed greens), you can get a large portion for $2. I love the energy of this place. Across from it is **Dynasty** (68 Elizabeth Street), a large supermarket which is almost always crowded. **Elizabeth Street Liquors** (86 Elizabeth Street, 646-613-9288) is the nicest and probably the newest of several liquor stores I've visited in Chinatown. I know nothing about China's wine industry but, as a Chinese woman told me, Chinese wines tend to be "rugged and strong"—and not very good. (A typical table wine costs $3 to $4.) I was intrigued by a Shantung rosé (more, I admit, for the bottle, shaped like a pagoda), a ginseng liqueur, and a lichee wine (which I bought for $8.99). Ginseng liqueur (which I haven't tried) was tempting and I'd love to hear from a reader who has tried it! There are two vegetarian markets in this area: the three-year-old **Vegecyber** (213 Centre Street), an attractive and large place that has much more than Chinese vegetarian food, and **May Wah Healthy Vegetarian Food** (213 Hester Street), which specializes in frozen and dried products for Chinese cuisine.

Snackeries   This area of Chinatown has a number of bakeries, a branch of **Aji Ichiban** (167 Hester Street), and a funky grocery/juice bar with seating called **Okashi Land** (163 Hester Street). It specializes in Japanese products but is also Hong Kong–owned.

Restaurants   Just one stands out to me: **Bingo** (104 Mott Street, 212-941-6729), which offers a seafood buffet—you choose from plates of cut seafood, beef, poultry, and vegetables and then cook it at the table. The price is relatively high: $16.95 per person for lunch and $20.95 for dinner.

■ ■ ■

East Broadway

Entering this neighborhood from "Old Chinatown," South of Canal Street will give you the impression of having just crossed a continental divide. Gone are the stalls selling NYPD T-shirts and postcards. The throngs of tourists have been replaced by dense crowds of local folks. As you wend your way east, you'll experience a different Chinatown that tends to be more inward-looking and concentrated. In some stores, the only concession to English may be a sign which, a Chinese friend explained, has nothing to do with the establishment's Chinese name. Pointing to a shop called "Happy Seafood," she said that the Chinese name referred to a village in Fujian Province.

Getting There   Take the F train to East Broadway; exit at the north end (the last car if you board in Queens or Manhattan, the first if you board in Brooklyn). Walk west on East Broadway (stay on south side of the street). You'll know you're going in the right direction if you see the ornate towers and gold statuette on top of the municipal building in the distance. On foot, from "Old Chinatown," follow Mott Street south, as it curves, to its end at Chatham Square. Cross to the statue of Lin Ze Xu, the "Pioneer in the War Against Drugs." It leads directly to East Broadway.

The tour begins at Pike Street. **Hong Kong Supermarket** (109 East Broadway at Pike Street) is one branch of the Hong Kong supermarket chain that also has locations in Sunset Park (see page 162), Flushing (see pages 29–30), and Elmhurst (see page 79). It's a vast place, packed with inventory from all over East and Southeast Asia. In one bin I found alligator meat, turtle, and frogs' legs; in another section shampoos and soaps from Taiwan, Thailand, and Japan.

New Ling Hong Market (51 East Broadway) is one of the area's better produce markets. After eating stir-fried chives and celery with walnuts at **Dim Sum Go Go** (see page 194), I bought the ingredients here to make it myself.

Chinatown has its own Dumbo, the Manhattan counterpart to Brooklyn's "Down Under the Manhattan Bridge Overpass," including a clutter of outdoor stands offering sticky rice, buns, and fruit, along with shoe repair. The markets inside 88 East Broadway, an older complex, include herb shops, clothing stores, beauty parlors, watch repair shops, and, in the center via a pair of escalators, **Triple 8 Palace** (212-941-8886), a bright and boisterous dim sum palace full of families with young kids. Just opposite 88, new markets, including a pharmacy, a large supermarket, and a music shop, were being built at 75 East Broadway in the summer of 2002. One restaurant, **Ming Dynasty** (75 East Broadway, 212-732-8886), features Hong Kong dim sum and Fujianese and Szechuan dishes, but the dim sum, which I tried with a Chinese friend, was mediocre and there were far fewer choices than you can get at a more reliable place such as Jing Fong (see page 191). (I was more intrigued by the buns, sticky rice, and other snacks, two for $1, sold by a street vendor, who eventually moved into one of the new shops in the complex.) You'll get a terrific meal in a lovely setting at old-timer **Canton** (45 Division Street, 212-226-4441; closed Monday and Tuesday). When I asked for a take-out menu, the manager, Eileen Leong, said, "No take-out here!" And when I explained what I do, she said, "We don't *nosh* here!" What you *do* do is eat extremely well in a quiet and lovely setting that is a stark contrast to the many crowded and loud places in this area. "Chinese like noise," my Chinese companion had said when we visited Ming Dynasty, but if you don't, Canton is for you. You'll pay quite a bit more for the calm, but it's worth it. We tried a "lettuce taco" appetizer (that's how Eileen described it), which includes crisp steamed lettuce leaves filled with a mixture of chopped water chestnuts and other vegetables and we shared a delicious entrée of chicken in ginger sauce and a side order of Chinese broccoli. It was perfect for two. The bill (without beverages) was just over $50, so it's not a budget lunch.

For a quality budget meal, check out **Dim Sum Go Go** (5 East Broadway, 212-732-0797), co-owned by chef and food writer Colette Rossant. As the name implies, the cuisine takes a playful approach to dim sum, experimenting with colors (using beet juice to create purplish dumplings) and combinations. And the dishes *look* attractive. Entrées such as the stir-fry I described earlier are very reasonable (mine was $9.95) and you'll see some unusual dishes such as bamboo heart soup with shredded pork, potato basket with spicy vegetables, and Go Go hamburgers in steamed buns (four for $8.95)—the ultimate in fusion cuisine! **Golden Unicorn** (18 East Broadway, 212-941-9811) occupies two floors of an office building. (I passed it by the first time, as you can't see the restaurant from the street.) It's beautiful, big, and noisy, and has great dim sum.

This neighborhood has two fine, large bookstores that offer cookbooks in English, stationery, music CDs, and interesting decorative items. **Oriental Books & Stationery** is at 29 East Broadway and **Eastern Books** is located at 15 Pike Street in a former synagogue that also houses a Buddhist temple. It's across the street from Hong Kong Supermarket (see page 193).

. . .

More About Chinatown

Green Space   There isn't much of it in Chinatown, but I always make time to visit **Columbus Park,** which faces Mulberry and Bayard Streets (see map on page 186). During the weekends its north section often is packed with people practicing tai chi, playing cards or music, or telling fortunes. In warm weather you're likely to see a group of people—often older men—playing old Chinese instruments. The streets throughout much of the area vibrate with activity and are filled with freelance shoe repairmen, fortune-tellers, artists who write place names using whimsical designs for each letter, and weavers who fashion miniature creatures out of dried palm leaves.
Local Culture   Take time to visit the **Museum of Chinese in the Americas** (70 Mulberry Street at Bayard Street, 212-619-4785, www.moca-nyc.org),

a wonderful resource for Chinese-American history. Across the street from Columbus Park, it houses a permanent exhibit on Chinese immigration to the United States and includes artifacts from some of the first settlers in New York's Chinatown. The museum sponsors occasional readings as well as neighborhood tours. In warm weather, artisans and artists often surround the building, doing calligraphy and selling jewelry and Chinese crafts such as paper cutouts and "chops"—stone stamps with Chinese characters. The chops are made of a soft stone—probably soapstone—and a chop can be made for you on-site if you know what you want.

■ Tickets to Ride

A frenetic industry of buses linking New York City to Boston, Philadelphia, and Washington, D.C., operates around Chinatown, with perhaps the most activity around the Dumbo area of the Manhattan Bridge Mall, where many of the buses leave. There, at least three companies compete for passengers, offering deals like $15 to $20 for a round-trip ticket (higher on weekends and at prime travel times). One day I could have traveled to Boston for $10, so I asked the young man distributing flyers what was going on. "Fare war!" he said brusquely. No, this is not a ploy to grab business from Greyhound—it began as a service for the many Fujianese who live and work in the northeast, often in restaurants, and regularly visit New York City to see relatives and to shop. News of these services has spread and many customers are non-Chinese folks looking for bargain travel.

■ Bulgaria in Chinatown

For years I'd wondered what was behind the dark green canopy of **Mehanata Bulgarian** (416 Broadway at Canal Street, 212-625-0981; Tuesday through Saturday, 6 P.M. until very late). This book gave me an excuse to visit New York's only Bulgarian restaurant! As you walk upstairs you'll follow the nasal minor chords of (recorded) Bulgarian music to a friendly but smoky space with a bar, dance floor, a few tables, and a modest menu that features sausages and kebabs. I had a roast eggplant salad ($4) and a baked feta dish ($7). Entrées are $9 to $15. DJs start spinning world music at 11 P.M., and there's occasional live music.

■ Expanding Boundaries

For many people who know Chinatown, a long-popular destination was the **Pearl River Department Store** at the northeast corner of Canal Street and

Broadway. Its two large floors were packed with Chinese clothing, cookware, paper goods, toys, gifts, musical instruments, a pharmacy, a small grocery, musical CDs, Chinese videos and DVDs, basketware, ceramics and . . . what have I left out? It's there, too! Pearl River has since relocated to 477 Broadway near Broome Street. As Chinatown's borders expand northward and eastward (but not so much further south or west) and as throngs of shoppers visit this new place, the new Pearl River will surely reflect a much larger Chinatown. (Pearl River has a smaller emporium at 194 Grand Street just west of Mott Street—see page 191—near Di Palo's Fine Foods.)

. . .

East Harlem

Siempre—Spanish for always—is a hopeful name for an East Harlem community newspaper, one that had published just two issues back in 2000 when I was working on my issue of *NoshNews* about East Harlem. I first saw it when Jorge Ayala, a local restaurateur, showed me a long feature article about his place, La Fonda Boricua (see page 205). I seek out newspapers like *Siempre* when I visit new neighborhoods because they often provide good leads on local culture. I was interested in the timing of this new publication, which coincided with a transformation still under way in East Harlem.

Take Ayala. Raised in Puerto Rico, he's a psychologist with a Harvard master's degree (and a doctorate in progress) who has taught at Hunter College, lives in East Harlem, and has chosen, for now, to focus on his busy and exciting eatery. Elsewhere, I found many other signs of the new in East Harlem: Pablo Gutierrez's taquería, which could have been lifted from a barrio in his native Puebla, Mexico; Moutapha Niang's West African market called Touba (see page 200), named for the city in Senegal that he comes from; artist James De La Vega's storefront studio; a French patisserie; a Salsa Museum (named for the music, not the sauce!), and so on. Hints of gentrification—an ominous trend to some here, and a hopeful one to others—were in the air. But I also found abiding signs of continuity such as a *botanica* that has sold religious items for thirty years and a meat market that has served residents for more than fifty.

New technology was also my guide. The Web site www.east-harlem.com, created by neighborhood devotee José B. Rivera, was invaluable. Imagine this: seeking more opportunities, Rivera relocated his family to Florida from East Harlem, where they had a house, a car, and the material trap-

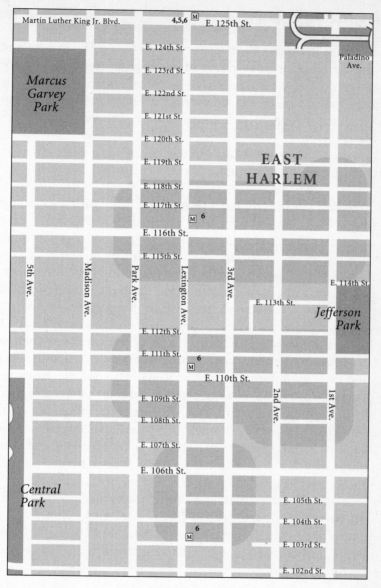

pings of success they thought they wanted. But they missed the freedom
and rhythms of East Harlem—in short, their roots—and moved back. The
Web site is Rivera's labor of love; he also has a day job.

There is a rhythm to East Harlem (also known as El Barrio, The
Neighborhood) that keeps bringing me—as well as folks like Jorge Ayala
and José Rivera—back. Their experiences prove that you *can* go home
again.

▪ Tips for Touring

East Harlem is underrated as a neighborhood to explore. I've enjoyed my ramblings here, but be aware that some blocks are decrepit and disappointing—poverty remains a real problem—while others are delightful. For me, one of the joys of the area is the element of surprise: finding a beautiful mural, building, or garden, or an unusual shop. The area is experiencing a palpable upsurge.

You can certainly walk East Harlem in one day, especially if you're ambitious! For the best experience, I'd plan two visits:

- One day on and around **116th Street** from Park to Pleasant Avenues. A detour to the huge Pathmark supermarket on the south side of 125th Street between Lexington and Third Avenues is worth the time; the store has an enormous inventory of produce and packaged goods from the Caribbean and Latin America at good prices. It's worth seeing the transformation under way in the immediate vicinity: vacant buildings on the north side are being re-developed and new construction is taking place across the street. Check out a De La Vega mural a variation of Picasso's *Guernica,* at the southwest corner of 124th Street and Lexington Avenue. At 121st Street between Lexington and Third Avenues is a renovated century-old courthouse (now used by the Sanitation Department) with a unique and lovely exterior. What's left of La Marqueta (see pages 208–209), El Barrio's famous indoor market, operates in arcades underneath the Metro-North elevated tracks on Park Avenue between 114th and 115th Streets.
- One day exploring **106th and 110th Streets.** Begin with Museo del Barrio or Museum of the City of New York followed by a tour of De La Vega's murals in the quadrant of 101st and 105th Streets between Lexington and Third Avenues. (Lexington Avenue from 102nd to 103rd Street is a very steep, downhill block.) Note a beautiful mural—not by De La Vega—on the southeast corner of 104th Street and Lexington Avenue, occupying most of the wall of the building!

Parks and Green Space   The best are the gorgeous **Conservatory Garden and Harlem Meer** in **Central Park. Thomas Jefferson Park** at First Avenue and 114th Street has lots of green space but is less appealing. East Harlem has many community gardens, but they tend to be more like social clubs for people from the same communities in Puerto Rico.

■ Getting Oriented

For this book, I've defined East Harlem as the area spanning Fifth Avenue and the East River from 102nd Street to 125th Street. (Harlem covers a larger expanse but there's little food-wise beyond these boundaries.) The main east–west boulevards are 106th and 116th Streets.

BY SUBWAY

Transportation to East Harlem is excellent. The #4, #5, and #6 trains run along Lexington Avenue, with local stops on 103rd, 110th, and 116th Streets (#6 train only) and an express stop at 125th Street (all trains).

BY BUS

Buses run north on First, Third, and Madison Avenues (only the M1 runs all the way up Madison; others turn west on 110th Street) and south along Second, Lexington, and Fifth Avenues. Almost all crosstown buses on West 125th Street connect East Harlem to the West Side, but check maps posted at most bus stops or ask the driver because some buses turn south on Lexington Avenue and others turn north toward the Bronx at Third Avenue. The M96 bus runs straight along 96th Street all the way; the M106 runs on 96th Street on the West Side, then heads north on Madison Avenue and east on 106th Street toward the East River. The M116 crosses the West Side at 106th Street, turns north on Manhattan Avenue, and becomes a crosstown bus at 116th Street.

BY CAR

Many car services operate in East Harlem but they don't have meters, so ask for the fare in advance. There's no municipal parking lot in East Harlem but there are several lots along Madison Avenue from 102nd Street to 106th Street or so, aimed at visitors to Mount Sinai Hospital.

BY TRAIN

Metro-North trains stop at 125th Street and Park Avenue.

...

116th Street

Park Avenue to Pleasant Avenue

Getting There   Take the #6 train to Lexington Avenue and 116th Street or take a combination of buses. Begin by heading one block west to Park Avenue to La Marqueta (see pages 208–209), which runs from 114th to 115th Streets. Then walk east along the south side of 116th Street and walk back west along the north side.

Park Avenue to Lexington Avenue

Start at Park Avenue and 115th Street and visit La Marqueta (see pages 208–209). Today's Marqueta isn't even a shadow of its former self, but on a good day you will see an interesting stall of West African products run by a friendly woman from Ghana. On warm-weather Saturdays you'll also see a small greenmarket. I personally suspect La Marqueta will become something different in a few years. Also check out **Otto Chicas Rendon Botanica** (60 East 116th Street, near Park Avenue), which sells candles, herbs, incense, statuettes, beads, and books related to *santeria,* a religion based on Christian, African, and Caribbean beliefs.

Foodwise this stretch has been almost moribund for quite a while, but it is beginning to revive with the arrival of West African shops and new housing construction west of Park Avenue. The best new place—the sleek and bright **El Criollito** (100 East 117th Street, 212-828-7497) would seem out of the way until you see all the activity around it. There are blocks of new homes filling in land that was vacant for years, and the newcomers needed a great place to eat out. Now they have it: newly opened in the fall of 2002, El Criollito offers a terrific Dominican menu with about eight daily specials including fish in coconut milk, pork ribs in eggplant, stewed chicken, and all sorts of other seafood, poultry, and steak dishes that cost no more than $5.75. On the main menu you'll find a few seafood and fillet mignon entrées for over $20, but these are the exceptions. Most are $8 to $12.

West African markets in west Harlem and, increasingly, in sections of East Harlem, almost never sell food only. While **Touba West African Market** (102 East 116th Street) is filled with the ingredients that go into West African cuisine, it also offers drums and drum covers made from West African fabrics; cookware; audiotapes; and other objects from the owner's home in Senegal. (You'll see the "Touba" name in many Senegalese markets; it refers to a city in Senegal that has a famous mosque.)

Lexington Avenue to Third Avenue

The food here is typical of the "old" Barrio's Puerto Rican roots. If I didn't mention it, you'd surely miss **Lexington Restaurant Comidas Criollas** (1869 Lexington Avenue, 212-534-4732) near the uptown subway entrance. Its crowded counter seats six but others invariably crowd in. With hearty soups and teeming stews (about six dishes daily, with mainstays such as beef stew and chicken with rice)—none more than $4.25—this is one of the best bargains in town. (So are the huge breakfasts for $2.50 to $3.) **El Barrio Steak House** (158 East 116th Street, 212-987-1442) throbs with jukebox salsa and offers a menu of Caribbean specialties—oxtail stew, pork, stuffed plantains—more variety *and* more space than at Lexington. You don't need a phone number for **Cuchifritos 116** (150 East 116th Street), a homey, popular place for Puerto Rican fried specialties. The menu is on the wall but mostly you just ask for what you see, and most dishes go for $2 to $4. I particularly like the sweet beverages you can get here—coconut, papaya, pineapple, and other tropical fruit drinks (with *lots* of sugar added—beware). My favorite is *ajonjoli,* a sesame drink, which is incredibly refreshing on a hot day. You can get about four sizes of these—the smallest is just 50 cents. Further east, check out **Capri Bakery** (186 East 116th Street, 212-410-1876), which specializes in Puerto Rican cakes and pastries—flan, rice and bread puddings, pastries filled with guava, pineapple, or coconut, and *dulce de leche.* (Enjoy the ornate cakes in the window—one celebrates the World Wrestling Federation.) On the north side of the block are two great music stores: **Casa Latina** (151 East 116th Street), where I saw LPs of classic salsa along with drums, guitars, and mementos of Puerto Rico, and **Fernandez Records** (167 East 116th Street) which markets Latin rock and hip-hop. If you have time, go nine blocks north to 125th Street, where a huge **Pathmark** supermarket covers the entire south side between Lexington and Third Avenues. No wonder smaller markets may be suffering—and La Marqueta seems irrelevant. Pathmark's large selection of produce and packaged goods from the Caribbean, Mexico, and the rest of Latin America is well-priced—and there's parking. Three blocks north of 116th Street, and a quick turn east, you'll eat well at **El Rincón Boricua** (153 East 119th Street, 212-534-9400), a popular destination for fresh pork, chicken, and fish specialties, which are prepared early in the day and sold out by the time the shop closes at 6 P.M. There's a tiny counter and one table (plus another on the sidewalk in good weather). Prices are dirt cheap, too. I came in and asked for some samples of the main dishes, expecting to pay $6 or $7. My delicious take-out platter of fish, chicken, and pork pieces plus a strip of sweet plantain was just $3. (How is this possible?)

Third Avenue to Second Avenue

This stretch represents East Harlem's "Little Mexico" (sometimes also referred to as "Little Puebla"). But before you continue on 116th Street, check out **Lee's Fruit Market** (2116 Third Avenue, south of 116th Street), which sells many hard-to-find ingredients for Central American and West Indian cuisine including *hobo, mispero,* and various greens, nuts, and fruits. Across the street is **Little Mexico** (2117 Third Avenue), a Mexican butcher and produce shop. Cross 116th Street heading north and you'll find the bustling **Don Paco Lopez Panadería** (2129 Third Avenue, 212-876-0700). It's one of three Lopez-family bakeries; the flagship is on 4703 Fourth Avenue in Sunset Park; the other is in Staten Island. Take a tray and fill it with cakes from the display case. Everything is fresh—Miguel and Armando Lopez do the baking right here, and on a quieter day you might even be allowed to see them at work. Also, be sure to visit the Salsa Museum next door (see page 208).

Sometimes this corner has street vendors selling fresh *tamales* and *atole,* a hot Mexican beverage made with cornstarch and flavorings, often vanilla and strawberry. It's a bit like drinking oatmeal, and that's the intention—to warm up your insides on a cold day. The vendors are unobtrusive—you'll recognize them from their food storage containers but you won't see signs. Usually the *tamales* and a cup of *atole* are $1 each.

Now head east on 116th Street. Before you reach "Mexico Central" on this block, one of the first shops you'll see is **Al-Rehab Halal Meat & Grocery** (206 East 116th Street, 212-831-0228), a relative newcomer. Egyptian-owned, it includes a small prayer area in the back while the front is stocked with beverages and packaged goods from Egypt and elsewhere in North Africa and the Middle East. It also has a meat counter selling halal meat, which is slaughtered according to Muslim requirements. If the name is different when you visit, don't be alarmed; the owner was considering adding Mexican products when we last met.

As you head east, you'll see numerous Mexican businesses—a clothing store, a barbershop, and a record shop. For food, check out **Mi Pueblo Grocery** (238 East 116th Street, next door to Mi Pueblo Records), and you'll do a double take: Am I still in New York City, or have I magically migrated to Mexico? Just outside the entrance are shelves of loose chiles—poblanos, anchos, and other types. I don't think I've ever seen so many in one place. I had an excellent meal at **La Hacienda** (239 East 116th Street, 212-987-1617), a large, relatively fancy place (nice decor, tables with tablecloths, and a refined setting) with specialties from Puebla and Veracruz and friendly service. My companion had an $8 lunch special that included a hearty chicken vegetable soup, chicken in red sauce, and dessert. I had fantastic pumpkin flower quesadillas (with a crunchy wrapping rather than the soft tortilla used in Tex-Mex cooking) for $8.50. La Hacienda also serves breakfast, huge "sport sandwiches" at $5 to $6 (with names such as Valenzuela, Tyson, and Maradona), and more sophisticated meat and seafood entrées, priced up to $16 for a large mixed seafood special. For fast (and delicious) Mexican food, **TacoMix** (234 East 116th Street) serves truly extraordinary tacos, and you'll pay just $2 for a fresh one with beef, pork, chicken, or vegetables, and you'll have a hard time finishing just one—that's how thick they are! I met a man who travels here from Brooklyn when he needs a taco fix. It's a narrow stand-up place, but people love it. (I certainly do!)

Sandwiched among the Mexican shops is **African Art Grocery** (228 East 116th Street), which sells African food, audio and video tapes, clothing and textiles, jewelry, and other products to a growing community of West Africans. (The business card also lists an address in Dakar, Senegal.)

Second Avenue to First Avenue

Wherever there's a critical mass of Puerto Ricans—areas of the Bronx, the Lower East Side, the West Side, East Harlem, and Brooklyn—you'll see *cuchifritos*, a variety of foods fried in olive oil: pork, pigs' ears, pigs' tails, other meats and fish; vegetables, which are boiled and then served in oil; and *pasteles* (patties) with various fillings including beef, chicken, and potatoes. Just think of them as Puerto Rican soul food, as José Rivera described them to me. Places selling *cuchifritos* dot 116th Street but my favorite, **Lechonera Sandy**, is on this stretch of East Harlem—at 2261 Second Avenue on the northwest corner of 116th Street (212-348-8654). Of the *cuchifritos* places I've seen, it has the nicest setting, the best menu and variety, and a staff that—with sly grins—explains the different foods to me. *Cuchifritos* cost 50 cents to $2 per piece. Oh yes, and they have delicious *café con leche*—espresso with milk—for just 85 cents.

Heading north of Lechonera Sandy, check out **Lindo Mexican Grocery** (2265 Second Avenue), which was the first Mexican grocery in East Harlem when it opened in 1990 and is loaded with food, utensils, and souvenirs. Next door, **Mi Lindo Bakery** (2267 Second Avenue) is plain-looking, but the goods are not—their tacos, breads, and pastries are fresh and delicious. I was happily surprised to find that **Morrone's** Italian bakery (324 East 116th Street, 212-722-2972) was still around after some fifty years in East Harlem. No hours are posted, so call first or take your chances, but get there early. They sell traditional Italian breads and cookies baked in a coal oven. On the southwest corner of First Avenue there used to stand Andy's Colonial Tavern, a tired bar with an Italian menu. I had a forgettable pasta meal there and never wrote it up. In 2002 it was replaced by **Orbit East**

Harlem (2257 First Avenue, 212-348-7818), whose owners operate a place in Soho. Coming to Italian East Harlem was a shrewd move, as this area is poised (maybe) to become the next "in" place for artists. (I've dubbed it the Upper East Village because this neighborhood is now attracting young artists and arty types in search of relatively cheap space, while the "old guard" seeks to maintain and even expand its hold in the area.) During one neighborhood visit I met an older fellow named George de Martino, who calls himself the "Mayor of East Harlem." He grew up here and, in retirement, is watching the place bounce back. Orbit, with comedy and jazz nights and a noisy bar, may not be up his alley, but it's an improvement over the decrepit storefronts that used to mark this neighborhood. The menu is Soho-meets-East Harlem, with lots of seafood appetizers and seafood and steak main dishes (the most expensive is filet mignon, at $17), pasta ($10 to $13), and wraps ($6 to $10) plus $3 side dishes that include yellow rice and polenta. A lunch special of *chicharron de pollo* (fried chicken pieces marinated in Bacardi rum and garlic) is just $8. At 2287 First Avenue between 117th and 118th Streets is the famous **Patsy's Pizzeria** (212-534-9783), here since 1933. I'd last eaten there fifteen years ago and had forgotten their superb, crisp crust baked in a coal-brick oven. No doughy globs here! On one of my NoshWalks an executive chef from out of town had a slice and loved it so much that she went back for another.

First Avenue to Pleasant Avenue

A large new branch of the **Caridad** restaurant dynasty (455A East 116th Street, 917-492-8601) is a welcome arrival to this quiet block. Serving Caribbean specialties, it's well situated for a new development that—if it goes through—will bring Home Depot, Costco, and lots more traffic (one reason many locals dislike the idea). Nearby is **Rao's Italian Restaurant** (455 East 114th Street, 212-722-6709), run by Rao family members since 1896. A holdover of a once-thriving Italian community, it's located on the ground floor of an old house at 114th Street and Pleasant Avenue. It's now a celebrity hangout and has a Web site, www.raos.com (which has lots of recipes), and name-brand sauces and pasta that you can find in gourmet markets. When I called for a reservation during the process of researching this book (I didn't explain what I was doing), they said the next opening was seven months later. Most people end up traveling to Rao's by taxi or car service, and it's open just for dinner. I've since read that the property housing Rao's will be renovated, with new apartments added on top, which isn't a surprise, considering the increasing desirability of this area and its potential for development. The waterfront also is being revived here, with the addition of new bicycle and pedestrian paths. On East 115th Street between First and Pleasant Avenues is **Mt. Carmel Church**, once the heart of East Harlem's Italian-Catholic community. These days it serves mainly Spanish-speaking members. Next door, a former parochial school has been renovated into its new incarnation as the National Museum of Catholic Art and History (see page 210).

...

106th and 110th Streets and Environs

There are several approaches to this tour, but I recommend that you start or end with a visit to the Museo del Barrio (see page 210). In warm weather, add a stroll in the Conservatory Garden in Central Park, across the street. Also check out the neighborhood murals of James De La Vega (see page 211).

Getting There The hub of this area is 106th Street and Lexington Avenue, but if you begin with a visit to El Museo del Barrio you can get there from downtown Manhattan by taking any bus up Madison Avenue to 104th Street and walking one block west to Fifth Avenue or from further uptown on buses that head down Fifth Avenue. The #6 train stops at 103rd Street and 110th Street and Lexington Avenue. I prefer the 110th Street stop, which has wonderful mosaic renderings of East Harlem on each platform—check them out!

106th Street

Around 1996 Jorge Ayala, a former professor in social psychology at Hunter, opened **La Fonda Boricua** (169 East 106th Street, 212-410-7292), a lively local hangout with a counter, a handful of tables, and no menus, but with high energy and walls covered with artwork to create what Ayala calls a "spontaneous gallery." (It actually replaced a simpler eatery that one couple had operated for about thirty years.) Several months later, per Ayala's plans, La Fonda re-opened with twice the space, taking over a vacant market next door. It has a snazzy decor of exposed brick, handsome wooden tables and benches, and the same wonderful cuisine-with-no-menu, but friendly, lively staff. You can count on daily dishes such as roast pork, beef stew, rice, and two types of beans each day, and specials such as baked chicken, goat or oxtail; codfish, octopus, or shrimp salad; and *ceviche* fish entrées (marinated in lime) or *escabeche* fish, fried first and then marinated. Most dishes are prepared early in the day, so service is fast—unless the place is packed, and then you just have to wait. Dishes range from $6 to about $11. "Could this become East Harlem's Sylvia's?" I asked Ayala (Sylvia's started as a tiny luncheonette). He smiled—a nice comparison. **El Caribeño** (1675 Lexington Avenue at 105th Street, 212-831-3906) offers a traditional Caribbean menu in a pleasant but worn-down setting. While some seafood specialties cost on the high side for the neighborhood—lobster and a few other entrées are $25—others are quite reasonable: shrimp with garlic or spicy creole sauce is just $12.75 and octopus stew is $13.75. For bargains, go at lunchtime—a roasted half chicken platter is just $4. Wine is also served here. **El Paso Taquería** (1642 Lexington Avenue, 212-831-9831), a newish, bright place at 104th Street, is small, clean, and cheerful, with contemporary Mexican (and some English-language) music in the background and a thoroughly authentic menu. They offer a dozen different tacos, most filled with different types of sausage, pork, or beef; four different types of *flautas* (fried tortillas with fillings of cheese, beef, potato, or chicken); *chilaquiles* (fried tortillas sautéed in green or red sauce); enchiladas with three fillings and mole, red, or green sauce; a good selection of traditional meat entrées; and hearty soups on the weekends (goat consomme, *pozole*—pork soup— and shrimp soup are available weekends only). It's *always* busy and would make a good lunch stop before or after a visit to Museo del Barrio.

110th Street (Park To First Avenues)

Although the 110th Street subway stop is busy—there's a police precinct, a public library, and a big post office nearby—110th Street itself is narrow and feels almost like a small village. There's an interesting cluster of shops here. Always busy (retail only!), **Casablanca Meat Market** (127 East 110th Street), founded in 1949, is East Harlem's largest butcher and sells sandwiches as well as meat. A few Mexican markets and one restaurant round out the immediate area. On the same block as Casablanca are two Mexican markets, **Malinche Gifts & Records** and **La Margarita,** which share the same address, 135 East 110th Street. La Margarita is a wonderful place for Mexican produce and cooking ingredients such as spices and peppers. Malinche is a cozy Mexican grocery and *antojitos* (snack) bar; they also make fresh juices and coffee and sell clay cookware, baskets, and some Mexican crafts. There are a couple of tables where you can sit and sip a beverage and eat homemade *tamales* or fresh Mexican bread. These shops will give you the impression that you've just crossed the border! Around the corner, **St. Francis de Asis** restaurant (1779 Lexington Avenue) is a small, homey Mexican restaurant. Among these three places you can satisfy your need to buy or eat Mexican food! In this neighborhood, don't miss **El Congo Real,** a thirty-year-old *botanica* at 1787 Lexington Avenue between 110th and 111th Streets.

I recommend that you now walk east on 111th Street toward Third Avenue. En route, on the southeast corner at 111th Street, you'll see another James De La Vega version of Picasso's *Guernica.* (In the spring of 2002 a neighborhood vandal covered the faces of many De La Vega murals with black paint; De La Vega later replaced them with happy faces, but I don't think his *Guernica* was affected. A mural elsewhere, depicting the Last Supper, was affected though, so now all in attendance have happy faces, except Christ, who has a sad face.)

The first place you'll see is **Maine Lobster** (2018 Third Avenue, 646-672-1808), a newcomer to the area. It's located at an intersection known as Machito Corner, named for the great Afro-Cuban jazz musician (born Frank Grillo) who moved to New York City in 1937 and led his own ensemble, the Afro-Cubans, for more than forty years. (Tito Puente was one of his protégés.) Newly renovated, it's a bright, open place that welcomes families and has a children's menu, with dishes—mostly hamburgers and chicken—ranging from $3.50 to $4.95. This new restaurant, with exposed brick, a bright new wood floor, and handsome decor, is an important step up—and offers healthy competition for quality and ambiance to La Fonda Boricua on East 106th Street (see pages 205–206). (East Harlem needs several more terrific Caribbean eateries!) The ample menu specializes in seafood and steak, with a sirloin steak lunch special at $5.95. There's Latin jazz several nights a week.

For a more homey steak meal head one block south to **Pee Dee Steak** (2006 Third Avenue at 110th Street, 212-996-3300), which offers a hearty menu of steaks, burgers, shrimp, ribs, crab, and other Southern-style dishes. It's one of the nicer (and larger) places in East Harlem.

Now walk east again to Second Avenue. At 109th Street you'll come to **Halal Kitchen Chinese Restaurant** (2127 Second Avenue), one of the few halal Chinese places in Manhattan. But other than using halal meat (prepared according to Muslim religious guidelines; and no pork served here) and selling Islamic publications, it's a typical dreary-looking take-out place. For a traditional Mexican taco, check out **Tecali Tacos** (2126 Second Avenue), which Pablo Gutierrez opened in August 1999. It was an informal stand-up fast-food place when I first visited but it was in the throes of renovation: Gutierrez had recently removed the counter and installed a new stove as he was preparing to open a sit-down restaurant. He explained how he juggled running a restaurant with working in the Flower District, trying to realize his piece of the American dream. Further east still is **Pupuseria San Miguel** (347 East 109th Street, 212-860-1990), a Salvadoran eatery. I love Salvadoran food and the menu offers more types of *pupusas* (cornmeal patties) than I've seen elsewhere, including fillings of pork rind and beans

(I'm used to seeing cheese and chicken). The menu features a larger selection of *platos authenticos,* traditional Salvadoran dishes, that I've not seen elsewhere, including several types of corn porridge (*chilate*) with fruit. Just next door is **Piatto d'Oro** (349 East 109th Street, 212-828-2929), a newcomer to East Harlem in 2002. The owners relocated from lower Manhattan when rents got too high and now run a lovely small Italian eatery—they describe it as *"cucina con amore"* ("cuisine with love")—serving pastas, poultry, veal, soups, and desserts at East Harlem prices: expect to pay only $10 to $15 for entrees (and less for pasta). It's open daily from 11 A.M. to 11 P.M. Finally, don't miss **La Tropezienne** (2131-2133 First Avenue, 212-860-5324), a French bakery with fresh baguettes, croissants, and fabulous pastries. There are tables so you can enjoy coffee and a sandwich or pastry *en place.* Unfortunately, there's no espresso or *café au lait.*

■ Elsewhere in East Harlem . . .

Two of the nicer spaces in East Harlem are **Taller Boricua,** contained in two stories of the **Julia de Burgos Cultural Center** at 1680 Lexington Avenue, between 105th and 106th Streets (212-831-4333), and the **International Salsa Museum** at 2127 Third Avenue, just north of 116th Street (212-289-1368, www.nuevamerica.com).

The Taller opened in 1992 after a long battle with New York City officials, who wanted to turn the long-vacant five-story space into a homeless shelter. Because of its location near many schools, residents fought fiercely to claim the building for more neighborhood-friendly uses. In addition to the cultural center, which includes an exhibition space, an auditorium, offices for local cultural organizations, and classrooms (including a workshop on computer graphics), a magnet high school occupies two of the stories.

The **Salsa Museum** was created by salsa fan Efrain Suarez. Inside, you'll find a quasi-altar to salsa: LPs, posters, programs, photographs of the great salsa musicians and singers, instruments, statues, and photo albums. Classic salsa recordings are playing constantly in the background. You'll find T-shirts honoring the great salseros, particularly Tito Puente, and there are CDs, audiocassettes, and LPs for sale. Admission is by donation.

In its heyday several decades ago, **La Marqueta** was *the* place to buy fresh produce, spices, seafood, and meat, and even dried goods, toys, and upholstery. It should be on the itinerary of anyone touring the area. "There wasn't any place else," recalls Fernando Salicrup, executive director of the Taller Boricua. It's a sprawling indoor complex located under the elevated Metro-North train tracks along Park Avenue from 111th to 116th Streets that was established during the LaGuardia era to give the area's pushcart peddlers, then mostly Jewish, sanitary indoor space. Puerto Rican migration to East Harlem began in the 1940s and the area gradually became mostly Latino. La Marqueta remained dynamic through the 1980s and I included it on my itinerary when I led bicycle tours through East Harlem.

Where did the customers go? On a visit while I researched this book I found it almost deserted. The market area stretched only from 114th to 115th Streets; I have no idea how the remaining space is used, if at all. Granted, this was a weekday afternoon, but it's not as though the neighborhood itself was quiet. And new renovations, new floors, bright lighting, and upgraded stalls couldn't compensate for the sense that the place had, perhaps, reached a dead end.

I chatted about this with a maintenance staffer. "This is what they call re-no-va-tion," she said with a sigh. "The government came in, drove out the old stall-owners, and look what's left!" I said that maybe a coffee shop would help, as there's no place for a tired shopper to sit down. "Good idea," she said, and promised to relay it to her boss.

But an article in the local newspaper Siempre suggests other reasons for the decline of La Marqueta: a more mobile younger generation that eats out and likes more diverse cuisine, including fast food. Also, there were no supermarkets in the old days, and now there are many in El Barrio. Pathmark may be the biggest, but I've seen others that also have excellent selections of Caribbean products.

So what's next? If Fernando Salicrup has his way, La Marqueta will become a cultural center. He already has commissioned drawings for a redesign which would include art studios, exhibition galleries, and performance venues that would make this unusual space a community magnet once more.

■ For More Information . . .

I'm increasingly finding Web sites that offer excellent background and insight on East Harlem. Jose Rivera's www.east-harlem.com provides a terrific introduction and the guest book is full of great anecdotes.

Another site, www.nyboricua.com, doubles your pleasure with music playing in the background (salsa and Carlos Santana) and lists poetry readings, art exhibits, and other cultural activities. Did you know that every September East Harlem celebrates an annual chalk festival, at which local children (and some adults) contribute chalk art? The Web site has great photographs of the event.

Two of the "New Yorkiest" museums in the city are next door to one another and an easy walk from the restaurants around 106th Street. **El Museo del Barrio** (1230 Fifth Avenue at 104th Street, 212-831-7272; www.elmuseo.org) is a must-see if you want to get a rounded sense of East Harlem. Organized more than thirty years ago by Puerto Rican educators, artists, and activists in the neighborhood, it offers exhibits and special programs on local and Latin American art and culture and has a terrific (and pricey) book and gift shop selling folk art, toys, textiles, and jewelry from all over the Caribbean and Latin America. They also have a rich selection of art books, children's literature, and posters. (Their Web site is great, too.) The location has another superb asset: it's across the street from both the gorgeous Conservatory Garden in Central Park and the lovely Harlem Meer. Their hours are Wednesday through Sunday, 11 A.M. to 5 P.M. (8 P.M. Thursday nights). Suggested admission is $5 for adults (free for children 12 and under). There's no snack shop, so plan your visit around a meal in a nearby eatery or bring take-out to munch on in the park.

The Museum of the City of New York (1220 Fifth Avenue, 212-534-1672; www.mcny.org), next door to El Museo del Barrio, also has a terrific gift store, great displays of artifacts of New York history, and free programs. I love the antique toys and dollhouses; my daughter loves the firefighting memorabilia. Their hours are Wednesday through Saturday, 10 A.M. to 5 P.M., and Sundays noon to 5 P.M. Suggested admission is $12 for families, $7 for adults, and $4 for seniors, students, and children.

Also, **the National Museum of Catholic Art and History,** the first of its kind in the United States, has been under construction at 445-447 East 115th Street (between First and Pleasant Avenues) at the site of a former school next to Mt. Carmel Church. The museum will display paintings, an array of religious relics, and a permanent exhibit on the history of Catholicism in the New World and will feature a café, gift shop, and theater. For information, call 212-828-9700.

■ And Still More . . .

BOOKS

The classic *Down These Mean Streets,* Piri Thomas's account of growing up in East Harlem, was first published in 1967 and was reissued several years ago by Vintage Books. A more contemporary version of East Harlem can be found in Ernesto Quinonez's *Bodega Dreams,* a novel published in 2002, also by Vintage.

▪ Local Boy Makes Good

"I'm the most exciting thing here," says James De La Vega, who stopped himself so that he wouldn't seem *too* self-aggrandizing—but then added, "Well . . . but I really am." And he may be right. At thirty-something, this East Harlem multimedia artist, who admits to being influenced by Keith Haring and Jean-Michel Basquiat, has created a signature work—literally— by leaving chalked quotations and artwork, which he signs, on sidewalks in neighborhoods around Manhattan and the Bronx. He's also involved in the community, and hosts an annual Halloween party at his storefront gallery at 1651 Lexington Avenue at 104th Street, next to a community garden. (You can't miss his place: the awning is covered with "De La Vega.") His murals are all over East Harlem, with a critical mass between 101st and 105th Streets and Lexington and Third Avenues. He avoids buying advertising since he does it all himself and he doesn't have a Web site (although other Web sites feature his art). Ever entrepreneurial, in addition to his artwork he sells T-shirts, mugs, postcards, and coloring books bearing the De Le Vega logo—usually a quote such as "Become Your Dream." He even sells mirrors with quotes painted on them, so as you look at yourself, you stare into the truth. He'll do portraits on commission, including one-day specials. For more information, contact James De La Vega at 212-876-8649.

▪ The Return of the Giglio

You may be aware of an annual celebration in the Italian-American community of Williamsburg, Brooklyn (not covered in this book, alas), called the Dance of the Giglio. It honors St. Paolino di Nola and is famous for the five-story, two-ton tower with images of the saint and other Catholic icons that's carried on a platform by about 125 men. The platform also contains a brass band—usually about twelve pieces—playing ritual Italian melodies. It turns out that the Dance of the Giglio began in New York City at around the turn of the last century—in East Harlem! Members of East Harlem's Italian community began moving to the suburbs in the 1950s, and feast attendance gradually dwindled until a final dance was held in 1971. But the Long Island Giglio Society revived it in 2000, with former East Harlemites in the lead, and you can usually see it the second weekend in July on East 115th Street in front of Our Lady of Mount Carmel Church. For more information, see www.ligigliosociety.org.

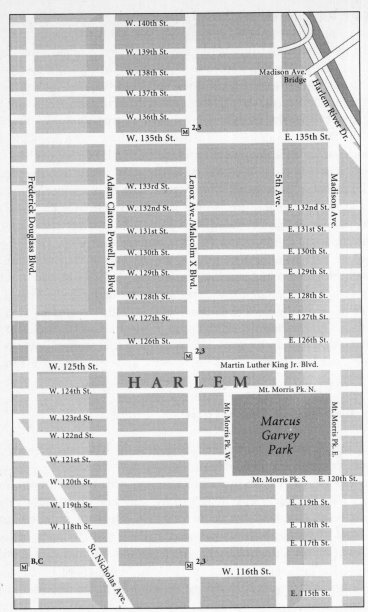

· · ·

Harlem

It is almost too easy these days to use the word "renaissance" to describe
Harlem. But anyone who has visited this world-famous neighborhood in
recent years surely has witnessed a transformation that would have seemed

inconceivable in the 1980s or even the early 1990s. Throughout this vast area old and battered housing has been reclaimed and much of it has been magnificently renovated. Blocks of vacant land have been developed, often with three-story homes designed to fit in with the landmark brownstone architecture from the early twentieth century. The boulevards—particularly Lenox Avenue (now known as Malcolm X Boulevard)—are reclaiming the grandeur of their early years. The famous 125th Street, which had been punctuated with potholes, has been repaved. With so much activity on the long blocks of 125th Street, planners have wisely installed traffic lights and pedestrian crossings mid-block in some locations. Much new construction was under way as I was working on this book, and a new shopping center on the northwest corner of Lenox Avenue and 125th Street opened in mid-2002. It's possible that the last undeveloped stretch of 125th Street, between Fifth and Lexington Avenues, will be fully developed by the time this book is published. (Nubian Books, a large store with existing branches in Jamaica, Queens, and downtown Brooklyn, was due to open on 125th Street and Fifth Avenue in mid-2003; its presence will no doubt have a significant impact on the area since the store plays an important part in the community and sells high-quality books and gifts.)

A major influence on Harlem's rebirth has been the arrival of Africans into the community, mostly from West Africa—the English-speaking countries of Ghana, Gambia, Nigeria, and others, as well as francophone nations such as Senegal, Mali, Guinea, Cameroon, and the Ivory Coast. Explore Harlem and you'll see groceries, restaurants, beauty salons and barber shops, video stores, clothing boutiques, art galleries, and other establishments selling goods and services that cater not only to the people from these countries but to people interested in African culture in general—whether they live in Harlem or just are visiting. At first most these shops were concentrated in the area around West 116th Street stretching from Lenox Avenue to Frederick Douglass Boulevard. These enterprises now can be found in much of northern Harlem and have been spreading into East Harlem as well. It's a magnificent example of how immigration into New York City is adding yet another cultural fillip to our world. I love it!

The Harlem tour is divided into four sections:

- Central Harlem: 116th Street—Fifth Avenue to Frederick Douglass Boulevard (and nearby)
- Central Harlem: 125th Street—Madison Avenue to Frederick Douglass Boulevard (and nearby)
- Harlem's Renaissance Area: 135th Street between Lenox Avenue and Frederick Douglass Boulevard, and nearby
- A side trip to Convent Heights and Sugar Hill (West Harlem from 125th Street to 145th Street)

...

Central Harlem

116th Street, Fifth Avenue to Frederick Douglass Boulevard

Between Adam Clayton Powell Boulevard and Frederick Douglass Boulevard, 116th Street has been in the throes of redevelopment and is now lined with at least a dozen stores and eateries catering to West African customers. **Getting There**   The #2 and #3 subways are the best situated, stopping at 116th Street and Lenox Avenue/Malcolm X Boulevard. The B and C trains stop west of the area at 116th Street and St. Nicholas Avenue and the #6 train stops at 116th Street and Lexington Avenue. You can walk west from there—not too far—or take the M116 bus a few blocks to Lenox Avenue.

Restaurants   After eight years as chief of staff to the Reverend Al Sharpton, Carl S. Redding wanted something of his own, and so in May 1999, after several years of planning, he opened **Amy Ruth's** at 113 West 116th Street (212-280-8779). Within two weeks of its opening (well before the *New York Times* got there), I took nine friends from overseas to a Sunday lunch. (We made reservations, which turned out to be necessary. The place was crowded even then.) We tried almost everything on the menu—ribs, pork, smothered and fried chicken, salmon croquettes, grits, smothered potatoes, and eggs. Waffles are a specialty, and you can get them as a main dish or as an accompaniment to a chicken or meat dish. Redding, who named the restaurant after his grandmother, has a winner here. The setting is lovely, with art exhibits that change bimonthly and gospel music in the background (there are six major churches in walking distance). The service is friendly and accommodating and the price was right—we left with a bill of just $100 including a generous tip—and feeling full and happy.

Carl S. Redding outside his Harlem restaurant, Amy Ruth's.

A second-floor party room seats 125. Alcohol is not served. Across the street, **Aahirah's Palace** (108 West 116th Street, 212-663-5300) is anything but; it's a pleasant, informal restaurant but palatial neither in size, decor, nor price. It's a lower-cost alternative to Amy Ruth's. Come for their good and reasonably priced Southern-style cuisine. Their shrimp bisque is a terrific starter, which I followed with salmon cakes. Vegetarians can get a platter of four vegetables from a choice of ten. Or try a breakfast of special whole wheat pancakes or French toast with a choice of toppings, served twenty-four hours a day.

As you wander west, you'll pass restaurants offering the cuisine of Senegal, Guinea and Mali. Simply decorated, these are mostly gathering places for folks from those countries and don't reach out to outsiders. The Senegalese place **Le Baobab** (120 West 116th Street, 212-864-4700) has attractive batik tablecloths, African artwork, and a great-looking menu— and is loud. If you don't mind the noise, you'll love the lamb, chicken, or seafood here—grilled and in brochette. You can also get Moroccan coucous. Main dishes are no more than $10 and servings are big! I love the *mafé*—a lamb stew with a peanut butter base ($7). You can eat more quietly—and in a less cluttered setting—at **Keur Sokhna** (225 West 116th Street, 212-864-0081), which opened in 2000 and already has a reputation among some local Senegalese storeowners as the best place to eat. For one thing, prices are cheap (lunch entrées are all $7; dinners are $7 to $10) and servings are enormous. The pricier dishes are grilled fish, shrimp kebabs (delicious!), and a special called *michio* (stuffed leg of lamb). Salad and couscous or sweet banana are served with most entrées. I always go for homemade ginger beer in places like this—it tends to be extra spicy, which I love. (It's $2 at Lo Baobab and $3 here.) A yummy Senegalese breakfast cereal or dessert is *thiakry*, made with a fine-grained brown couscous you'll find in local markets; the other ingredients are sour cream, vanilla flavoring, and fruit. If you don't have time for a sit-down meal, **Lowe's Caribbean Restaurant & Bakery** (164 West 116th Street, 212-864-6684) has a bustling take-out business. Specialties include breakfasts of ackee and codfish, callaloo, and slat fish served with bananas, dumplings, or yams, or hearty lunches (including $4 daily specials) or dinner entrées of curried poultry, meat, and fish, with two generous side orders. I tasted the curry shrimp and had rice and peas and collard greens with them. A loaf of bread, called spice buns even though it's a loaf, is delicious and very filling.

You may want to visit the **First Corinthian Baptist Church** at 1910 Adam Clayton Powell Boulevard. This is a new use for a once-majestic movie palace and much of the original interior is intact, though a bit tattered. I once visited a Sunday-morning service—the setting was regal indeed, and appropriate for the church choir. At 1905 Adam Clayton Powell Boulevard, a few storefronts south of the church, is the **PCOG Gallery,** which showcases the work of local and international artists, mainly African-American and African. Opened in 2001 by Paula Coleman and Ousmane Gueye (replacing a Senegalese restaurant), this remarkable space was one of the first of the new wave of art galleries to take root in Harlem on its way back up, up, and up.

Markets   This area has several African markets, selling dry goods in addition to food, and the numbers are growing. Quite a few markets now carry the packaged and fresh products used in Muslim African cuisine. In the immediate area is **Sunugaal Halaal Meats & Poultry** (119 West 116th Street, 212-222-0059). In addition to selling meats (their slaughter is similar to kosher slaughter), the market also carries grains commonly used in West African cooking including a type of couscous I'd never seen before—a super-fine brownish grain that's used, among other dishes, to prepare *thiakry,* the dessert described above. The store is very small and crowded but the people I've met there have always been friendly. Speaking French helps! Across the street I had an interesting experience visiting **Falilou Mbacke** (126 West 116th Street, 212-316-1783). At this shop you'll see a grocery store, a hair-braiding operation, a barbershop, a video store, and a photo developing counter. The lease-holder—the owner of the hair-braiding operation—sublets space within the store to other entrepreneurs, thus giving them a place to do business while keeping up with rentals. I've seen this type of market model in other immigrant neighborhoods (New York City's Chinatowns are examples) and it projects a village feel to the store. People walk in and out to chat—it's all very social and fun. Around the corner and heading north one block you'll come to **Africa 2000** (1943 Adam Clayton Powell Boulevard), owned by folks from the Ivory Coast. This is the nicest of the West African stores I've seen, but the manager explained that the owner had set out deliberately to "occidentize" the store, meaning to make it more user-friendly to Western shoppers. Thus, rather than big bins of products crowding the store space, much of the central floor is wide open. A relative old-timer is **Abyssinia Ethiopian Grocery** (221 West 116th Street, 212-663-0553), which Tadesse Makonnen opened in 1996. It's the only Ethiopian grocery I know of in New York City. It's chock full of the spices, grains, and legumes popular in Ethiopian cuisine, as well as cards, textiles, baskets, music cassettes, and other gifts. Missing, however, is a cookbook. But never fear: **Kitchen Arts & Letters** bookstore on the Upper East Side (see page 307) carries two Ethiopian cookbooks. **Sea & Sea** (60-62 West 116th Street, 212-828-0851) is an enormous fish market that sells fresh, salted, and fried fish including inexpensive take-out combinations of whiting, scallops, shrimp, crab sticks, and others. They also have a huge steam oven to prepare steamed seafood specialties. With chips or plantains on the side, most platters are $3 to $6. Along with the fish, you can also buy Jamaican hot sauces, hot peppers, and other products that target African and Caribbean cooks. (Sea & Sea also has branches at 310 St. Nicholas Avenue at 125th Street and on Adam Clayton Powell Boulevard at 140th Street.)

Around the Area or "The New Harlem"

The key mosque in this area of Harlem, Malcom Shabazz Mosque, sits on the southwest corner of 116th Street and Lenox Avenue. It's impossible to underestimate the impact of the mosque here. It has generated hundreds of jobs through the businesses it sponsors and has created; it supports the African Traders Market; and it has developed new housing. (Check out a lovely block of homes on West 117th Street between Lenox Avenue and Adam Clayton Powell Boulevard and you'll see a plaque noting that the homes were developed by the Malcolm Shabazz Economic Development Corporation.) Buyers get two rental units when they purchase the homes, thus generating income for their mortages. Many smaller storefront mosques and Muslim stores dot Harlem as the African community there expands.

▪ Malcolm Shabazz Harlem Market

On a typical weekend in the 1980s you could barely walk along Lenox Avenue around 125th Street because it was crammed with African street vendors peddling clothing, jewelry, gifts, and African artifacts. Local shop owners complained that the vendors were taking business from them and, worse, paying no rent or taxes while the shop owners paid both. Meanwhile, the vendors were working in crowded, unsanitary conditions. In the early 1990s the city relocated them to a parking lot at 116th Street and Lenox Avenue that was converted into a market. The process was somewhat controversial. Local Muslim leadership played an advocacy role for the vendors, most of whom come from francophone Africa (Senegal, Mali, and the Ivory Coast) and are Muslim themselves.

At the time I thought the move would be the kiss of death for the vendors, so far away from the commercial activity of 125th Street. Was I wrong! Tour buses to Harlem now make the market a destination and many African entrepreneurs have opened stores in the area. As you'll see, most storefronts are now occupied and the area is booming. Malcolm Shabazz Harlem Market now resides at a permanent site mid-block on the southern side of 116th Street between Fifth and Lenox Avenues, having opened in May 1999. The former parking lot is now apartments and stores.

Nearly 100 vendors now sell wares that range from T-shirts and caps to beautiful clothing and gift items. Most merchants are West African and bargaining is part of their culture, so be prepared. Market managers are intent on maintaining diversity—and on encouraging more successful vendors to seek permanent shops elsewhere so that newcomers can kick-start their businesses here. In the past I've seen vendors from the Dominican Republic, Haiti, and Ecuador, but the vast majority these days are West African and Afro-Caribbean. There's a snack area in the market with tables and chairs so you can sit and nosh. Soda machines and fresh fruit are sold on-site, and I wouldn't be surprised to see more food vendors here in the future.

■ ■ ■

Central Harlem

125th Street, Madison Avenue to Frederick Douglass Boulevard

■ Getting Oriented

The Harlem Renaissance of the 1920s signaled a flowering of an intellectual and arts community here. Now a remarkable new commercial and residential renaissance is under way. The presence of African immigrants adds a fascinating new dimension to the area, complemented by extensive architectural restoration. Your tour will feature great eating in a neighborhood in transformation.

BY SUBWAY

You can take the A (and also the D) train to 125th Street (nonstop from Columbus Circle) to the St. Nicholas Avenue stop, as do the B and C trains (see map). The #2 and #3 trains go to 125th Street at Lenox Avenue (also known as Malcolm X Boulevard). From the East Side, the #4 and #5 trains go to 125th Street and Lexington Avenue. Walk west or take a crosstown bus (there are several).

BY BUS

There are many! Along Madison Avenue, the M1 goes straight north and the M2 turns west at 110th Street and then runs north on Lenox Avenue. Both run south on Fifth Avenue. (The M3 runs north on Madison Avenue but at 110th Street heads too far west for this tour, so don't take it.) From the West Side, the M7 starts on Avenue of the Americas, runs north on

Amsterdam Avenue, and then edges into Harlem, ultimately turning east onto 116th Street from Manhattan Avenue and then north on Lenox Avenue (Malcolm X Boulevard). The M10 runs straight up Central Park West and Frederick Douglass Boulevard. Many buses run east-west on 125th Street.

BY CAR

Exit at 125th Street from the West Side Highway or the Triborough Bridge. There's a municipal parking lot on 126th Street between Lenox Avenue and Adam Clayton Powell Boulevard (126th Street is one-way going *west*, so you can access it from Lenox Avenue). Bicyclists may also use the 126th Street lot. Use buses and your feet to get around the area. Car services abound.

BY TRAIN

Metro-North trains all stop at 125th Street and Park Avenue, a short walk to the sites on this tour.

One word that sums up 125th Street is *energy*: people, traffic, business, building—the energy of change. Starbucks now occupies a busy corner at Lenox Avenue. A Slice of Harlem, a gourmet pizza place, and Bayou, a popular Cajun place, share a strategic location at 308 Lenox Avenue (see page 220). At Frederick Douglass Boulevard (equivalent to Eighth Avenue) a new entertainment and retail complex has brought Disney and Old Navy to Harlem. A new mall with a CVS, Marshalls, and other national chain stores opened on 125th Street and Lenox Avenue in 2002, transforming the immediate area (and, to some critics, bringing with it a disappointing homogeneity, while some folks I know who live in Harlem are delighted to have such amenities close to home). These places have not (yet) succeeded in knocking out the dozens of small entrepreneurs who energize Harlem. Check the sidewalk signs advertising tailors and hair-braiders on the second and third floors of buildings. This is similar to what you might see in Dakar, Abidjan, or Johannesburg (where I lived in the early 1990s).

Annette Manbodh outside Flavored with One Love in Harlem.

▪ The New Wave

Within central Harlem several new places have opened since 2000, signaling a new generation of exciting eateries. Among the first was **Bayou** (308 Lenox Avenue, 212-426-3800). Located on the east side of Lenox Avenue just north of 125th Street (where Harlem's first Starbucks is located), it offers Cajun cuisine and became a popular gathering place for local and visiting politicans. Bill Clinton had a meal here shortly after moving into offices at 55 West 125th Street, around the corner. The menu has everything from your basic fried shrimp po'boy sandwich to shrimp creole and jambalaya. Bayou occupies the second floor of the building; on the ground floor is **A Slice of Harlem** (212-426-7400), a pizzeria that uses a brick oven and serves gourmet pizzas with toppings such as chicken Parmesan, asparagus, sun-dried tomatoes, hard-boiled eggs, eggplant, and broccoli rabe. Some of Bayou's dishes can be bought at the pizzeria to take out, and I did that one day, ordering with a yummy okra gumbo soup.

A newer-comer, established in 2001, is **Native** (101 West 118th Street at Lenox Avenue, 212-665-2525). Opened by the proprietors of Bleu Evolution, a popular eatery in the Hudson Heights area of upper Manhattan (see pages 262–263), its menu includes Cajun and new American cooking. Across the street and one block to the north is the Italian-style bakery **Settepani** (196 Lenox Avenue between 119th and 120th Streets, 917-492-4806), which offers sandwiches, pastries, gelato, and all sorts of beverages—in a gorgeous setting. The owners are an Ethiopian-Italian couple who have struck gold with their location and design—and delicious food. Located within the Mount Morris Historical District, it's the first bakery of such caliber to come to Harlem. It's often packed.

Restaurants   In addition to Bayou and A Slice of Harlem, I've found several good eateries and markets here. Some of these are *very* informal—be prepared!

Starting on the southeast corner of Madison Avenue, you'll find **A Taste of Seafood with a Touch of Soul** (50 East 125th Street, 212-831-5584; closed Sunday and Monday). You should come here if you adore fried fish, but be prepared to wait on line in a hot, standing-room-only space for your meal. The reward is a quickly-filled platter—mostly for take-out—of fried fish, huge yummy French fries, and assorted side dishes. (People who choose to eat at the counter have to tolerate sweaty standees and no ambiance.) The fish combo, collard greens, and banana pudding were tasty, but I thought it might be nicer to find a calmer place for a sit-down meal. I found it almost next door, at a Guyanese place called **Flavored with One Love** (1941 Madison Avenue between 124th and 125th Streets, 212-426-4446), run by Annette Manbodh with her sister and her mother, Elvy Simon, who was in the kitchen the day I visited. Their terrific dishes include huge *roti* platters, curries, and stews, mostly of chicken, oxtail, goat, or vegetarian combinations. There are ten vegetable side orders on the menu. Food is ready to go, whether you choose to eat in (a pleasant, quiet setting) or take it out, and you'll get away with a full meal for under $10. (NOTE: Flavored with One Love is closed temporarily due to a fire in the building.) A few doors down you'll find **Sisters Cuisine** (1931 Madison Avenue, entrance on 124th Street, 212-410-3000), with a Guyanese menu almost the same as Flavored with One Love, but with fewer seats. I've heard that the same families own both places, so you can expect good eating.

At 51 East 125th Street is **Manna's II** (212-360-4975), which combines a market and soul-food salad bar. Open seven days, it has a wide selection of soul food and Caribbean specialties including jerk chicken, plantains, collards, and banana pudding, as well as more conventional salad bar fixings. Even the pickiest eater can have an enjoyable meal here. **Rencher's Crab Inn** (15 West 125th Street) has a lovely, bright, casual setting with ceiling fans and blond wood paneling and posters of various types of shellfish, which can help explain what you're eating—or help you to choose. (Check their Web site, www.crabinn.com.) The menu offers tasty, inexpensive combinations.

Bakeries and Sweets If you have a hankering for ice cream while in the area, the place to go is **A Taste of Sweetness** (1934 Madison Avenue at 124th Street, 212-427-6701). Their specialties include tropical flavors such as groundnut, soursop, and Irish moss. My favorite is carrot cake ice cream, made with chunks of carrot cake, but it's often not in stock. Be persistent! You can also buy nuts and beverages here. **Wimp's Southern Style Bakery** (29 West 125th Street, 212-410-2296) is a neighborhood old-timer specializing in fruit cobblers, custard, sweet potato pie, and other traditional baked goods. You can get slices in addition to whole cakes and pies. It's just a few storefronts from the Harlem office of former President Bill Clinton at 55 West 125th Street—it's said to be one of his favorite places to buy cake. Across the street, **Uptown Juice Bar & Market** (54 West 125th Street, 212-987-1188) is an attractive and often crowded sit-down place for dairy-free, vegetarian, organic foods, including baked goods and all sorts of juices. During the summer the owner sometimes operates a juice bar two doors west of the restaurant, which sells fresh sugar cane and coconut juice, although he has indicated that he plans to open an organic grocery at that site.

Who *doesn't* know **Sylvia's** (328 Lenox Avenue, 212-996-0660), in business more than thirty years? The main entrance takes you to the original luncheonette counter but the place now fills most of the east-side block between 126th and 127th Streets, with separate dining rooms and a banquet hall (piled with tourists on weekends). I prefer the counter when I'm on my own, and to go during the week. I recommend their great breakfasts and the sweet-potato pie. Cookbooks by founder Sylvia Woods and Sylvia's sauces also are for sale here. And you'll know if Sylvia herself is in the restaurant if you spot a Rolls Royce with a license plate marked WOODS parked in a spot between the two buildings the complex occupies.

Stono (277 Malcolm X Boulevard/Lenox Avenue at 124th Street) is a homey, interesting place with excellent soul food. You can't miss it—the façade is covered with an attractive mural of African-American and Caribbean leaders. The name comes from a slave revolt in 1739. Inside, it's a quiet restaurant with tables adorned by placemats designed by Elizabeth, the owner (who wouldn't give me her last name). The placemats include photographs and biographies of famous African-American leaders and are really terrific. I asked if she had plans to produce these en masse—they'd surely sell! She said no. The entrées here are typical Southern American: chopped barbecue pork, chicken, or spare ribs; whiting fish; smothered steak; chicken; and breakfast including waffles and so on. The most expensive of these meals is $12 and they include two side dishes, a salad, and cornbread. It's a real down-home feast, but you also have to be prepared to wait some down-home time because everything is made to order and no one appears to be in a particular rush. Around the corner, at 100 West 124th Street (212-316-0607), is a take-out operation run by the same family. The offerings are essentially the same but the prices are lower.

At 2331 Frederick Douglass Boulevard at 125th Street is the original **Manna's** (212-749-9084; closed Sunday). Here, in addition to the self-service salad bar, you can order hearty and inexpensive prepared meals. They come with two side orders (chosen from macaroni and cheese, candied yams, peas and rice, greens, potato salad, or cole slaw) and most cost no more than $7.95. Thursday is West Indian Dinner Day and features jerk chicken, pork, or curried goat.

Markets   The only food market of note in this area is **Young Spring Farm** (62 West 125th Street), which has an excellent selection of fresh, packaged, and bottled goods (beverages and sauces) catering to Caribbean and African tastes. Salted and dried fish are among the products available here.

■ Elsewhere in Harlem . . .

This stretch of 125th Street has some interesting shops. **Enchanted Harlem** (1 West 125th Street) specializes in high-end gifts and clothing with African, Caribbean, and African-American themes. **Sambuya** (16 West 125th Street), which opened in mid-2002, is Gambian-owned and has some beautiful African textiles, carvings, and jewelry. It's typical of the shops opening in this area, catering not only to African residents but to

African-Americans and others interested in African culture. Further down, **Djema Imports** (60 West 125th Street) has a magnificent window display of African fabrics and sells the same types of goods you'll see at Sambuya. Djema has been around longer—the owner started as a stall vendor with the Malcolm Shabazz Market group (see pages 217–218) and eventually saved up to buy the low-rise building his shop now occupies.

■ Harlem Sites & Landmarks

There's no way to adequately summarize the many historic sights in this small area of Harlem. So bring a good guidebook, such as *Blue Guide New York* by Carol Von Pressentine White (New York: W. W. Norton, 1991, 2nd ed.) or the excellent *Touring Historic Harlem* by Andrew S. Dolkart and Gretchen S. Sorin (see page 306), which includes four detailed walks. I found a free mini-guide version from a kiosk in Harlem staffed by Uptown Ambassadors and sponsored by the Upper Manhattan Empowerment Zone. You can buy a copy of the full book in Harlem at the Harlemade gift shop on 174 Lenox Avenue at 119th Street, call the New York Landmarks Conservancy at 212-995-5260, or check local bookstores.

There are several places you will pass as you visit the markets and eateries described in the previous pages. **Graham Court** (1923-1937 Adam Clayton Powell Boulevard at the northeast corner of 116th Street) was designed by the architects of the landmark Apthorp at Broadway and 79th Street and features many of the same lush elements including a two-story arch leading to an inner courtyard. The building could use a good cleaning and the courtyard, from what you can see from the street, looks seriously neglected. **First Corinthian Baptist Church** (see page 215) at the southwest corner of 116th Street opened in 1913 as the Regent Theater, a movie palace with an exterior and interior than give you an inkling of its early grandeur. It's possible to go in during Sunday services. As at any church, dress conservatively.

One block east, at Lenox Avenue and 116th Street, you'll see Malcolm Shabazz Mosque (see page 217), which also serves as an anchor for local economic development. **The Mount Morris Historic District** runs from 120th to 124th Streets between Lenox and Madison Avenues and contains a trove of gorgeous churches and private homes as well as **Marcus Garvey Park,** an important gathering place during the 1920s for the followers of the charismatic black nationalist leader. The **Ethiopian Hebrew Congregation,** 123rd Street at Mt. Morris Park West, houses one of the oldest congregations of Ethiopian Jews. **Studio Museum in Harlem** (144 West 125th Street, 212-864-4500) exhibits historic and contemporary African-American, Caribbean, and African art. Its classy book and gift shop includes quality products for children. **Theresa Towers** (Adam Clayton Powell Boulevard and 125th Street) was better known in its earlier incarnation as a hotel (built in 1912) and the place Fidel Castro chose to stay in 1961 during a UN session rather than a midtown hotel. It's now an office building with a White Castle on the ground floor. **Apollo Theater** (253 West 125th Street), built in 1914 as the Harlem Opera house, is famous as a performance venue for African-American musical artists and for its amateur nights. (Black audiences were first admitted in 1934.) Ella Fitzgerald was discovered here at age sixteen.

■ Green Space

There are few really nice places for outdoor noshing in this area. I recommend **Morningside Park** from 110th to 114th Streets—a magnificent renovation includes a lovely willow-framed lake and lots of seating. Other possibilities are the Malcolm Shabazz Harlem Market (see pages 217–218), which has seats for snacking; Marcus Garvey Park (see page 223), with picnic tables at Madison Avenue at 124th Street; and an uninviting cluster of benches on a shady triangle where 116th Street crosses St. Nicholas Avenue and Adam Clayton Powell Boulevard.

• • •

Harlem's Renaissance Area

135th Street and Nearby

Once you head north of 125th Street in central Harlem you're moving in the direction of where it all began. Black Harlem originally was centered around 135th Street and Lenox Avenue, where the famous **Schomburg Center for Research in Black Culture** is located (515 Lenox Avenue, also known as Malcolm X Boulevard), along with several other major community institutions including Harlem Hospital, the Harlem YMCA, and the 369th Armory a little further east at Fifth Avenue and 143rd Street.

This area is where Harlem's black community took root. When the subways first reached Harlem in 1904 an enterprising African-American realtor named Philip Payton launched a marketing campaign to lure black New Yorkers here as other neighborhoods further south (such as San Juan Hill, where Lincoln Center now stands) were being gutted for new construction. Histories of Harlem (check Gilbert Osofsky's *Harlem: The Making of a Ghetto* [New York: HarperCollins, 1963] or Jervis Anderson's wonderful

This Was Harlem [New York: Farrar, Straus & Giroux, 1983]) describe the process by which the in-migration of African-Americans from the South and new immigrants from the Caribbean slowly transformed the community—and also prompted white flight. The Harlem Renaissance of the 1920s emanated from this neighborhood; the **Harlem YMCA** at 180 West 135th Street played a seminal role as the artistic and spiritual home for some of Harlem's great creative minds, including Langston Hughes, Countee Cullen, James Weldon Johnson, Romare Bearden, Aaron Douglas, and Zora Neale Hurston. Works of some of the great visual artists can be seen in Harlem Hospital, the Schomburg Center, and the YMCA. (The Schomburg Center has a stunning book and gift shop, and the Studio Museum of Harlem on 125th Street is also an excellent resource; see page 223.)

As part of your visit to this area, make sure to walk the blocks of West 138th and West 139th Streets between Adam Clayton Powell Boulevard and Frederick Douglass Boulevard. Nicknamed Striver's Row because this is where many of Harlem's upwardly mobile professionals bought homes in the early twentieth century, it contains some of the area's finest architecture and retains a regal presence. The northern block of 139th Street was designed by Stanford White of McKim, Mead, and White, the architects of many of Columbia University's finest buildings. Dolkart and Sorin's *Touring Historic Harlem* guidebook provides the history and details of Striver's Row and includes the names of some of the famous people who lived here.

This area, as elsewhere in Harlem, is undergoing major change. On the southwest corner of 135th Street and Adam Clayton Powell Boulevard, the sparkling new Thurgood Marshall Academy signals a new educational powerhouse in the area. It's a charter school backed by an economic development corporation sponsored by the nearby Abyssinian Baptist Church. Once the site of the famous jazz club Small's Paradise, its designers have preserved the original façade. Food-wise, at this writing there is not yet a critical mass of good restaurants and just a handful of markets worth mentioning, but you still can feed yourself well!

Getting There   The best way is to take the #2 or #3 train to 135th Street and Lenox Avenue. There's a parking lot near Harlem Hospital at Lenox Avenue and 136th Street.

Eateries   Here are a few places you should check out with pleasure. Yet again, there's a Manna's—this one is called **Manna's Too!!** (486 Lenox Avenue at 134th Street, 212-234-4488) and is similar to the other two I've mentioned (see page 221 and page 222). It has a self-service salad bar for $3.99 a pound. Divided into two large sections, one has the healthy, familiar dishes—fresh fruit, raw vegetables, and salads (plus one "cheat"—banana pudding), while the more popular section has the traditional Southern offerings that draw the crowds—collard greens, candied yams, spare ribs, curried or jerk chicken, and pork chops. It is almost always packed—the proximity to Harlem Hospital helps, but I also attribute it to the variety, economy, self-service, and lovely setting. The place is new, neat, well set up, and comfortable (but with a sign setting a twenty-minute limit for seating). The walls are adorned with framed posters of famous African-Americans: Rosa Parks, Sojourner Truth, Muhammad Ali, and others.

For take-out food, I was delighted to find that **Lowe's Restaurant** at 164 West 116th Street had opened a new branch in 2002 on 101 West 136th (212-491-2808), offering its popular *rotis,* patties, curries, and other West Indian specialties in this restaurant-starved area. The new place is very small, but I imagine this is just a foothold and that they'll eventually expand since there's a captive customer base across the street at Harlem Hospital and at the Schomburg itself—not to mention tourists!

Miss Maud's Spoonbread (527 Lenox Avenue at 137th Street, 212-690-3100) is an offshoot of Miss Mamie's Spoonbread on 366 West 110th Street; they serve the same quality seafood, stews, and desserts for which Miss Mamie's is well known. **Jimmy's Uptown** (2207 Adam Clayton Powell Boulevard at 130th Street, 212-491-4000) is a dining venue that also includes Sunday brunch, but be prepared for some downtown prices: brunch will set you back about $30.

I like **Gary's Jamaican Hot Pot** (2260 Adam Clayton Powell Boulevard, 212-491-5270), which has been around for more than twenty years. In this homey place, decorated with West Indian artwork and photographs or paintings of various leaders from Marcus Garvey and Malcolm X to Bill Clinton, you can get lunch specials including a main dish and two sides for just $6, and most other entrées are no more than $8 or $9. The selection is typical Jamaican—goat, beef, lamb curries, and oxtail stews, for example. **Home Sweet Harlem Café** (270 West 135th Street, 212-926-9616) is a relative newcomer to Harlem, with some traditional Southern fare—waffles on weekends and sweet potato pie—but the menu also includes lots of vegetarian dishes, including sandwiches served on various organic breads with fillings such as hummus and avocado; roasted vegetables with goat cheese; and a "sunshine" burger made of carrots, brown rice, sunflower seeds, and sea salt. It's made up like a country place in the middle of the city. (This block is interesting to walk on—further east, on the same side of the street, you'll pass the Harlem Walk of Fame, which features plaques embedded in the sidewalk honoring Harlem's great performers, such as Billie Holliday, Dizzy Gillespie, and Machito.)

Markets   There are two markets of note here. **Sea & Sea** (2391 Adam Clayton Powell Boulevard) is owned by the same folks who run the other Sea & Sea at 60-62 West 116th Street (see page 216). As with that one, this store is physically huge and they have a large steam oven where they can steam your selection of seafood and vegetables on the spot, and season it, too. Just one block south is a very interesting market called **H & H Produce** (2363 Adam Clayton Powell Boulevard). Don't look for a sign on the store—there isn't one. But in good weather you'll see tables outside piled with fresh collard greens, whatever fruit is in season, and jars of *scuppernong* jelly (made from a type of wine grape) and *mayhaw* jam (from a Georgia berry), as well as sorghum, chowchow (relish), and cans of green peanuts. These are all brought up to Harlem from Georgia and the Carolinas, and you won't see them in too many other places. On weekends you can also buy homemade pies and get fresh barbecue prepared on an outdoor grill. You'll have to know to ask, but H & H also carries frozen raccoon and possibly other wild game typical of the South.

Bakeries   For years, the northwest corner of 139th Street and Adam Clayton Powell Boulevard was occupied by Better Crust Bakery, ensconced in one of the corner Striver's Row buildings. Better Crust went out of business some years back but, happily, a new bakery, **Make My Cake,** has filled the void (2380 Adam Clayton Powell Boulevard, 212-234-2344) with their carrot cakes, coconut cakes, sweet-potato pies, apple pies, and other mouthwatering dishes. The owners have a large adjacent room that looks perfect for a sit-down café, which this neighborhood badly needs. The owners claim they use it to plan the many parties they cater, but I keep hoping they'll go one step further—it surely will be packed if they do! (There's a larger branch of Make My Cake at 103 West 110th Street, facing Central Park, near the beautiful Harlem Meer and the Science Discovery Center.)

Side Trip

West Harlem

While central Harlem is in the midst of a major culinary and development renaissance, the area west of St. Nicholas Avenue, which is the eastern border of the Harlem valley, has been relatively dormant in terms of good new food (although there are a handful of exceptions). It is a northern continuation of Morningside Heights, where Columbia University is located (between 110th and 125th Streets) and where Broadway dips before rising again. For the purposes of this section, the southern border is 125th Street and the northern border is 155th Street. It includes an area that was dubbed Sugar Hill because of its relative affluence compared to the rest of the Harlem community (decades before gentrification!), and its significant landmarks include the **City College of New York** and the **Hamilton Grange**, a former residence of Alexander Hamilton. But while this site (now a federal monument) is tucked among some of the nicest brownstones and churches in Harlem, you have to remember that it once was a lone building surrounded by farmland! **Riverbank State Park**, built above a pollution control plant, is an important community amenity. Its amazing facilities, which stretch over the Hudson River (and the plant) from 138th to 145th Streets, give families a real opportunity to escape the oppressive summer heat without having to travel far away, and its river vistas are spectacular.

Visiting this area after many years, I was struck by a number of changes. Superficially it looked the same. The stretch of Broadway from 135th Street to 155th Street is loaded with beautiful brownstones and pre-war apartment buildings punctuated by a few housing projects. As elsewhere in Harlem, the brownstones gradually are being upgraded as well-to-do African-Americans and people of other backgrounds are moving into the area. The overall architecture is remarkable: since there has been so little new construction, you can get a sense of how other Manhattan neighborhoods of this vintage, such as the Upper West Side, looked before postwar high-rises began to proliferate along the avenues. Just don't look at the ground-floor façades, many of which have been ruined to create bland storefronts. But from the second floor on up, the architecture of many has not been touched.

Getting There   The #1 and #9 subway lines run through this area. Exit at 137th or 145th Street. You can also take either the M4 or M5 bus along Broadway; the M4 runs uptown along Madison Avenue from 34th to 110th Street before heading west and up Broadway to Fort Tryon Park and the Cloisters Museum (see pages 258–261). The downtown route goes along Fifth Avenue. The M5 heads up Avenue of the Americas to Central Park and then weaves west uptown toward Riverside Drive, returning to Broadway at 135th Street. If you have the luxury of time, it's a lovely bus ride.

Restaurants   Most of the eateries here are informal, family-friendly places, including lots of Dominican and Cuban restaurants. One of my favorites is **El Castillo del Rey** (3451 Broadway at 141st Street, 212-926-0319), which is very family friendly and has great chicken and Caribbean specialties. You can get away with a hearty meal for very little; on a budget, the soups—*sopas*—are an amazing deal. For $4.50 you can get a large soup that is usually packed with meat and vegetables and will keep you going for much of the day. You'll get a crusty bread and butter with it. Daily specials start at less than $4; seafood dishes, especially *paella* and lobster, are the only items that could break your budget. If you can get to **Mi Floridita** (3219 Broadway at 129th Street, 212-662-0090), it's worth seeing for both its size and scene as well as the food. There often are lots of children here, as this place tends to attract families. Despite the cross street number, it's only one block north of 125th Street, but it's a bit out of the way unless you're shopping at the huge Fairway Uptown Supermarket nearby on 12th Avenue at 131st Street. **Largo** (3387 Broadway, 212-862-8142) is a newish place with a very pleasant atmosphere that is particularly convenient for City College students and faculty because it's so close to the 137th Street subway entrance. It's the type of place that would fit in well near NYU or Columbia—its a relatively inexpensive eatery that meets a student's budget (well, maybe a graduate student on a modest splurge). The cuisine is adapted Mexican, with *empanadas,* quesadillas, *ceviche* platters, wraps, and so on, and you can manage for $15 or less if you don't drink.

I couldn't resist checking out **El Toro Partido,** a new Mexican and Ecuadorian restaurant at 3431 Broadway between 139th and 140th Streets (212-281-1587). A sign on an outdoor chalkboard highlighted the daily special of *sopa de pollo con matzoball!* This small restaurant—there are just five little tables, each seating two or three people—feels almost like someone's eat-in kitchen. You can watch all the cutting and cooking from the counter and you'll get excellent dishes in return. The *mole rojo* (red mole) chicken offered a rather surprising (and, to me, welcome) sweet and fiery taste. You also can get Mexican breakfasts and all sorts of tacos, as well as a *grande huarache,* an Ecuadorian *tamale* with a number of different fillings (chicken, beef, or sausage) and toppings (beans, onions, and avocados) for just $4. The arrival of Mexican and Ecuadorian places in this part of Harlem is relatively recent but their numbers are bound to increase.

Calvin Copeland has been operating in Harlem since 1961, when he opened a catering service; he then opened a cafeteria in 1975. The upscale **Copeland's Restaurant** followed in 1981, and both the cafeteria and restaurant share the same address and phone number (549 West 145th Street, 212-234-2356). Copeland has quite quickly made a name for himself, not only for the great Cajun, Southern, and continental food he offers and for the jazz (you can hear it at Sunday brunch and most weeknights) but also for the fact that he filled a real neighborhood void. (Even now, there's no place comparable in this part of Harlem.) The cafeteria is truly no-frills—you're more likely to hear rap music from a boom box than jazz—but the restaurant is gracious and you'll want to dress appropriately. A small serving of gumbo is heaped with shellfish, while Copeland's special barbecue is spicy, and servings are generous. Main dishes come with two vegetables and you may, as I did, find that there's no space for dessert. This is not a nosher's paradise, however—prices are appropriately higher for the service and dishes, and while most main dishes average $12 to $18, a few (such as surf and turf and seasonal seafood) are substantially more. It's worth it—but the cafeteria is fun, too. I had the smothered chicken with sides of collards and potatoes, and the food was great. You can get away with a full meal for $6 or less.

Another non-nosher's eatery in this area is the elegant **Sugar Hill Bistro** (458 West 145th Street, 212-491-5505), which is unique in New York City, as far as I know, in occupying an entire brownstone—it's a combination restaurant, music venue, and art gallery. Even though it's just a block from Copeland's, it's fair to say that it's in a different neighborhood—it's more connected to the landmark Convent Heights area than the gritty Broadway of West Harlem, which is Copeland's closest link. The Bistro, which opened in 2001, serves only dinner and drinks during the week (it opens at 5 P.M.), so for daytime folks like me, the all-you-can eat Sunday gospel brunch, for $20, is, well, a godsend, and it includes one drink. The cuisine is eclectic, to say the least, with some Southern-style and Caribbean dishes—blackened catfish, Cuban-style Cornish hen, and *ropa vieja* (shredded beef) Napoleon—but the range of dishes includes fancy raviolis, lobster pot pie, and other great touches. (I was tempted by vanilla whipped sweet potatoes, a side dish that costs $6.) Be prepared to spend far more than a nosher's budget here, too—an early-bird special (5 P.M. to 6:15 P.M.) gets you a three-course meal for $29.

Markets   Most markets in this area specialize in produce and packaged goods from the Caribbean. None is particularly impressive. See the Washington Heights Side Trip (pages 258–261) for some good markets nearby.

Bakeries   La Rosa Bakery (3395 Broadway at 137th Street, 212-281-1500) has been serving delicious Dominican baked goods (including elaborate birthday cakes, flan, bread puddings, and pastries filled with fruits such as guava and pineapple) for years. Check out the playfully decorated cakes in the storefront: one shows a soccer team and the flags of the Dominican Republic and Germany; another shows a busty woman in a see-through outfit and some beer bottles (a bachelor party, no doubt); and another, for a baby shower, has a pregnant woman in the center.

Also . . .   While you're in this area, check out **Hamilton Palace,** a mini-department store on the northeast corner for Broadway and 146th Street, which occupies a former movie palace and still has many of its original baroque adornments. Also note the **Nova Cinema** on Broadway at 147th Street, which was once called the Bunny. You still can see the name Bunny etched into the façade—and you'll also see two sculptures of rabbits flanking the roof.

■ A Ramble Along Frederick Douglass Boulevard

The forty-plus blocks of Frederick Douglass Boulevard, starting at 110th Street to its northern terminus at about 155th Street, used to be marked by vast empty lots and a generally depressing appearance. But this important Harlem avenue—an extension of Central Park West—began to change in the mid-1990s, and now it has been significantly transformed: most vacant lots have been replaced with new housing and many existing buildings have been restored. At major intersections there are new institutions, including the Magic Johnson cinemas and shopping center at 125th Street. With all these changes have come new restaurants and markets—and they're still coming! Below is a sampling of a few places on Frederick Douglass Boulevard—and one popular old place, too.

Tropical Fresh Brew Café (2194 Frederick Douglass Boulevard between 118th and 119th Streets, 212-531-2880) is an attractive coffee shop and bakery owned by Stephen Tebid, originally from Cameroon. Here you can get all sorts of freshly squeezed juices and smoothies as well as fabulous fresh Cameroonian coffee. Stephen claims that his beans are the freshest you'll get because he has them shipped directly to his shop. His cakes come from Pozzo Bakery (on Ninth Avenue) and elsewhere in Manhattan. It's a lovely new place (opened in mid-2002) and, to me, signals where much of this neighborhood is going. (Indeed, shortly before this book went to press, Fresh Brew had a new neighbor, **Les Ambassades** [2200 Frederick Douglass Boulevard, 212-666-0078], a French-style bakery and café in a lovely, large space, with various coffees and teas, cold beverages, fresh bread, and pastries. Owner Gorgui Ndoye hails from Senegal. This neighborhood is in bloom!)

Revival (2367 Frederick Douglass Boulevard at 127th Street, 212-222-8338) is one of the freshest, nicest places in Harlem. I particularly appreciate its wonderful Sunday brunch buffet, for just $15.99, which includes a generous selection of ready-to-eat, all-you-can-eat selections of fruit, grits, bacon, sausage, hash, muffins, and grilled tomatoes and other vegetables *plus* made-to-order omelets *and* waffles. Coffee and soft drinks are included in the price; alcoholic beverages are not. Revival, which opened in 2001, also serves full lunches and dinners with a focus on Cajun and Southern cooking. I love its decor—the interior is brick and wood and the windows are large and welcome the sun (and the neighborhood).

Further north, toward the Striver's Row area, one of my favorite places is **Yvonne Yvonne** (301 West 135th Street, 212-862-1223; closed Sunday), a cute take-out Jamaican eatery on a pretty block near St. Nicholas Park. In warm weather, a few chairs and tables are set up outside and you can look west and see some of the landmark buildings of the City College campus overlooking the park. Opened in 2002, Yvonne Yvonne got its start out of a mobile Jamaican jerk truck that serves hospital workers at the Cornell Medical Center on the Upper East Side. This is the owner's first stationary place. (The truck still operates.) Fried fish and chicken plus barbecue and jerk dishes are the staples here. I like the descriptions of the serving sizes (one entrée plus two sides): a full meal called "Not So Hungry" is $4.50; "Diet Size" is $5.50; "Big Strong Healthy Man" is $6.50, and "Charming, Polite Little Girl" is $8.66. Sides include rice and peas, macaroni and cheese, potato salad, yams, friend plantains, collard greens, steamed cabbage, and mashed potatoes. Desserts include bread pudding, sweet potato pudding, carrot cake, black wine cake, and pineapple coconut cake.

Across from Striver's Row are two popular supper places that I didn't visit since my focus is on lower-cost eateries with a lively lunch trade—but you may want to investigate them for yourself. **Sugar Shack** (2611 Frederick Douglass Boulevard at 139th Street, 212-491-4422) is known for attracting a younger chic crowd for late-night dinners and drinks and has special nights including one for poetry, a gay and lesbian night, and a DJ on weekends.

Londel's (2620 Frederick Douglass Boulevard at 140th Street, 212-234-6114) caters to an upscale, slightly older crowd and is known more as a jazz club than restaurant. It does have lunches, and it's a good place if you want a quiet business lunch because the crowds mostly come at night. When I went there during the day I found an attractive, mellow place—a bit slow (everything is made to order)—with good food (continental and Southern cuisine) and entrées ranging from $8 for grilled chicken salad to $20 for T-bone steak, but most are less than $10. Dinners are another story—expect to pay $14 to $20, and more, for entrées. There's jazz on weekend evenings; you should call ahead to double-check on cover charges.

Charles Southern Style Kitchen (1837 Frederick Douglass Boulevard between 151st and 152nd Streets, 212-926-4313) is a homey place that I first found out about from an ad in a community newspaper I picked up in Harlem. What I didn't know at the time was that Charles's fame had spread quite wide and I had missed out on it. What you get here is heaping dinners with two sides and delicious corn bread for just $6 or $7, and sandwiches are just $2.50 to $4, and they're the equivalent of two meals. Most people, though, love the lunch buffet—all you can eat, literally (and this is dangerous) for $6.99. But this is only from Tuesday through Friday from 1 P.M. to 4 P.M., so you might have to sneak away from work for a midday splurge or schedule a meeting here, although the premises are as plain as they get. Dinner buffet is $9.99, Tuesdays through Saturdays from 4 P.M. until closing and Sundays from 1 P.M. to 7 P.M. (Charles is open seven days, by the way. Many of the local West Indian places are closed Sundays.) Another great deal is Charles's Southern-style breakfast. There aren't too many places anymore where you can get waffles *and* chicken *and* beef, pork, or turkey sausage, *and* home fries or grits, and a cup of coffee for just $3.50. A key drawback is that Charles's is out of the way for many people. None of the Harlem landmarks are in this area, either (although it's close to the old Polo Grounds stadium—now a housing project). By subway, take the B or D train to 155th Street and walk four blocks south, or take the M10 bus, which heads straight up Frederick Douglass Boulevard; it's certainly an experience worth trying. (I rode my bicycle to get there. It was quite a thrill to observe how Frederick Douglass Boulevard is being made over. Hope truly springs eternal!)

There's lots of retail activity animating Frederick Douglass Boulevard, particularly in the Striver's Row neighborhood. Check out **Africart Moth-**

erland (2478 Frederick Douglass Boulevard at 134th Street, 212-368-6802), owned by Papa and Aida Diagne. It's a lovely shop that specializes in Senegalese clothing and features textiles and African carvings from West and East Africa. Its Web site is www.Africartmotherland.com. **Moshood** (2533 Frederick Douglass Boulevard) is the third boutique owned by Nigerian designer Moshood, who started in Brooklyn, expanded to Atlanta, and then landed in Harlem in late 2002. **Harlem Collective** (2533 Frederick Douglass Boulevard near 135th Street) is a cooperative artists' gallery.

. . .

Lower East Side

The Lower East Side, a fellow foodie alerted me, is more than pickles and pastrami. Well, I knew that. What I didn't know was that of all the neighborhoods I've written about, this would be the most dissonant. On one hand, you still have the old-timers—Russ & Daughters, Katz's Deli, and others now into the fourth generation of family ownership—still drawing customers, partly from nostalgia, partly to get food they can't get elsewhere in the unique ambiance of New York City. On the other hand, you have the newcomers—upscale health food stores, *tapas* bars, expensive sushi, and a row of French shops charging Upper East Side prices for their fare. (A *croque monsieur*—a grilled cheese-and-ham sandwich that is street food in Paris—costs $8.50 here.) On the *third* hand, there is the growing encroachment of Chinatown. And on the *fourth* hand—often overlooked—you have the bodegas, Mexican eateries, and Dominican bakeries that challenge gentrification. If you find yourself doing a double take during much of your journey here, don't be surprised. There's much that requires a second look.

Who would have imagined a few years back that Orchard Street would draw fashionistas seeking tenement-chic? Nowadays, boutiques and galleries line block after block. Yet a chunk of Orchard Street is still a bargain-hunter's paradise. For me, the most jarring change is the ethnicity of many store owners: many European Jews have been replaced by Muslims from Bangladesh. And then if you segue to Chinatown, you don't have to segue far, because Chinatown's borders have steadily seeped into the Lower East Side. I still remember how people gaped in disbelief when the original East Broadway headquarters of the Yiddish newspaper the *Forward* were sold to Chinese people in the 1970s and became a church. Now it's onto its next phase of development, as market-rate condos are appearing in a neighborhood that's become very desirable. The landmark Eldridge Street Synagogue is now completely surrounded by Chinese businesses.

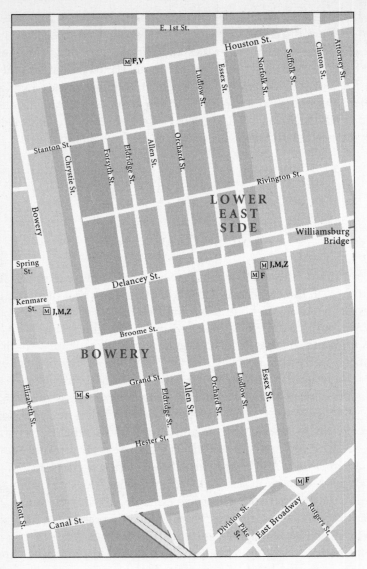

▪ Tips for Touring

The Lower East Side is rich in history and walking opportunities. Several organizations offer regular tours of the area.

The Lower East Side Business Improvement District (see page 240) offers free tours (with an emphasis on shopping opportunities). The Lower East Side Tenement Museum (see page 240) hosts hour-long neighborhood tours.

Green Space is in short supply in this area, probably because of the ongoing demand for housing. But it's there. Tree-filled **Seward Park**, where

Essex Street meets East Broadway, has been fixed up and is lovely for outdoor eating. The once-bedraggled **Sara Delano Roosevelt Park**, which occupies several islands between Forsyth and Chrystie Streets, is being renovated. At its entrance on Rivington Street, the luxurious **M'finda Kalunga Community Garden**—open to the public Wednesdays, Thursdays, and Sundays—is named for a nearby site that used to be an African burial ground. The section at Delancey Street is now being rebuilt and should be lovely when its done.

By the way, the Lower East Side has New York City's only accordion shop: **The Main Squeeze** (19 Essex Street), which sells and repairs accordions.

▪ Getting Oriented

The Lower East Side is defined here as the area south of Houston Street, bordered on the west by Chrystie Street and the south by Canal Street, but it now includes areas that overlap with Chinatown, as Chinatown's borders keep expanding (see pages 186–196).

BY SUBWAY

The F and V trains follow the old IND (Sixth Avenue/Avenue of the Americas) subway line to two key stops in this area: Second Avenue (where the V terminates) and Delancey Street, which is known as the Essex Street stop on the J, M, and Z lines, linking Queens and Brooklyn with a few stops in lower Manhattan.

BY BUS

Bus lines to the area include the M15, which heads south on Second Avenue (which becomes Chrystie Street when it crosses Houston Street) and north on First Avenue (which is Allen Street below Houston Street). The J, M, and Z trains also stop at the intersection of Delancey Street and the Bowery (it's one of the grimmest subway stations in New York City). The M14 bus traverses 14th Street; take the eastbound one marked Essex Street, which turns south on Avenue A (which becomes Essex Street when it crosses Houston Street). Make sure the bus says Essex Street (M14A) because the M14D goes too far east (down Avenue D, which becomes Columbia Street).

BY CAR

Take the FDR Drive to Grand Street and follow it to Essex Street. There are two municipal parking facilities in the area: a large garage at Essex Street between Rivington and Delancey Streets and outdoor parking at Broome and Ludlow Streets at Essex Street.

Markets   Most East Side mavens know **Russ & Daughters** (179 East Houston Street, 212-475-4880) for the quality Eastern European–style fish, cheeses, and appetizers (such as dried fruit and chocolates) sold here since 1914. Mark Russ Federman, who co-owns the store with his wife, Maria, credits neighborhood gentrification with bringing younger shoppers to complement the aging stalwarts who have been their mainstay. With two members of the fourth generation on board—Federman's daughter, Niki, and nephew, Josh Tupper, Russ & Daughters is poised to expand as a growing percentage of its business takes place on line. Note the bagel pudding—Russ & Daughters's answer to what to do with day-old bagels!

Along one wall near the ceiling at **Economy Candy** (108 Rivington Street, 212-254-2606; www.economycandy.com) is a shelf packed with antique gumball machines. Owner Jerry Cohen assiduously collects them—and will sell them "for the right price." You can spend much less buying the goodies that pack the store—old-fashioned chocolates, jelly beans, and bins of penny-candies plus spices, jams, cookies, teas, and other condiments. The City of New York established the **Essex Street Market** (120 Essex Street between Rivington and Delancey Streets; open Saturday, closed Sunday) in

SALMON TARTARE

Courtesy of Russ & Daughters on the Lower East Side, Manhattan

2 ½ pounds smoked salmon (preferably a mild variety such as Gaspé Atlantic)
1 red onion, finely chopped
½ cup scallions, finely chopped
1 tablespoon parsley, finely chopped
1 ½ teaspoons olive oil
2 tablespoons red vinegar

1. Cut the salmon into very small pieces and place it in a large bowl.
2. Stir in the onion, scallions, and parsley.
3. Add the olive oil and vinegar.
4. Keep refrigerated until ready to serve.

the 1930s to provide a sanitary centralized location for street vendors. Renovated in the mid-1990s, it's now a delightful microcosm of the Lower East Side, housing a Caribbean produce stall; a Chinese dumpling bar; an Uzbek barber (who has forty-seven clocks in his small space); a *botanica*; a fish market; a Latino nostalgia stand; an art gallery; a tailor; a used clothing store; and the Tralala Juice Bar, which also sells cookies and muffins along with orange butterscotch balls (75 cents each) and Irish potato peanut butter candies (50 cents each). City ownership keeps rents low, so food prices are too, according to Jeffrey Ruhalter of **Jeffrey's Meats** (Essex Street Market), a shop that Ruhalter's immigrant great-grandfather established in the 1930s. (Most of Ruhalter's business comes from a food- wholesaling operation that he runs from a small desk at the market; the actual butcher business represents a fraction of his income.) By the way, the one thing Essex Street Market *doesn't* have is a kosher store of any type.

Earth Matters Health Food (177 Ludlow Street, 212-475-4180) opened in December 2001 and looks remarkably entrenched. It's an organic market with an upstairs café and an outdoor area where yoga classes are sometimes held, and it provides an antidote to the cholesterol-laden platters around the corner at Katz's.

You'll find several kosher places south of Delancey Street. **Kossar's Bialys** (367 Grand Street, 212-473-4810), famous for sixty-plus years for its onion disks, garlic knots, bagels, and, of course, bialys, which often sell out by early afternoon. One Sunday I arrived to see one of the bakers hastily preparing dozens of bialys for the next baking cycle, which lasts just about six minutes. It's quite a sight—and smell! Overall, it's a very plain place, though, and you're not meant to spend much time there unless you know the owner well enough to schmooze. Also kosher are **East Broadway Kosher Bakery on Grand** (363 Grand Street); **Gertels** (53 Hester Street), known for its great breads and *babkas,* found at gourmet shops all over New York City; **Kadouri & Sons** (51 Hester Street, 212-677-5441), a gorgeous market that specializes in sweets, nuts, dried fruit, and condiments from Israel and elsewhere in the Mediterranean (with fabulous gift platters) plus a large selection of coffees and teas; and **The Sweet Life** (63 Hester Street, 212-598-0092), a candy shop where I found Bernie Bott's Flavour Beans for my daughter, who is a Harry Potter fan.

On the same block as Kossar's, by the way, is the famous (and non-kosher) **Doughnut Plant** (379 Grand Street, 212-505-3700), whose founder, Mark Isreal, drew on a recipe from his grandfather, using natural ingredients only, to start his business in 1994. Now he supplies major gourmet stores as well as selling retail from his own, which is open every day except Monday. There are daily fruit, nut, chocolate, and vanilla glazes, as well as about two dozen other donut flavors, including seasonal specialties such as rosewater and pumpkin, which you can see listed at www.donut-plant.com. When I chatted with Mark, he said he was also selling Mexican-style *churros,* a cruller-type doughnut that he says started out in Spain and was brought here. You can sometimes see Mexican vendors selling sugar-soaked *churros* on subway platforms, but Mark says his are less oily. Doughnuts here don't come cheap, though: expect to shell out $1.75 for each one.

Guss' Pickles (85 Orchard Street, 917-701-4000) and **The Pickle Guys** (49 Essex Street, 212-656-9739) peddle pickles, peppers, pickled veggies, olives, and related goodies. Guss', located on the Lower East Side for decades, has had to relocate twice in recent years because of rent hikes; its first relocation was at the Tenement Museum for a brief period until its current space opened up. The Pickle Guys, whose founder, Alan Kaufman, was previously with Guss', opened in 2002 and has a nice-looking, well-located space near what remains of the old Jewish Lower East Side and not far from the Henry Street Playhouse, which is at 466 Grand Street.

Eateries   The knishery **Yonah Schimmel's,** founded in 1910, is still around at 137 East Houston Street (212-477-2858), selling baked, not fried, knishes. Most are about $2; they also have a $3 knish of the day. There's ample seating, and the menu also includes salads and sandwiches. Someone has repainted the outdoor sign at **Katz's Delicatessen** (205 East Houston Street, 212-254-2246) to change the opening year from 1898 to 1888. I don't know why that matters, but inside the decor appears not to have changed for decades, which I find both amusing and mildly depressing. The overstuffed pastrami sandwiches and other cold cuts remain a draw at this kosher-style deli, the last of its kind in the area. **Bereket** (203 East Houston Street) is a fast-food Turkish place with an appealing, low-cost selection of salads, dips, and kebabs. Vegetarians will do well here. I had a tasty shrimp burrito platter at **El Sombrero** (108 Stanton Street, 212-254-4188), a friendly, if bedraggled, Mexican place, with most entrées $7 to $10. I avoided hangouts like Pink Pony (176 Ludlow Street) and 99 Riv (99 Rivington Street) because they are pro-smoking. The French newcomer **L'Epicerie** (168 Orchard Street, 212-420-7520) has a smoke-free café/bistro that really looks like a neighborhood café-and-grocery in Paris, and a bar, **Café Charbon,** where you can smoke Gauloises to your heart's content. Prices are on the high side—you're paying for the right to linger. Between the bar and the restaurant is a miniature Tabac, a cigarette-and-magazine store modeled on Parisian shops—and, as in Paris, it's closed from about noon to 2 P.M. **Grilled Cheese NYC** (168 Ludlow Street, 212-982-6600) tends to draw twenty-somethings in the neighborhood and offers grilled cheese sandwiches with various types of bread and combinations of fillings. **Teany** (90 Rivington Street) is an attractive vegan teahouse, co-owned by rocker Moby, offering more than ninety teas (some prepared with pieces of fruit, which remind me of the Korean teas I tasted in Flushing), salads, and snacks. It's not too expensive and it's popular with European tourists.

Perhaps **Sammy's Roumanian** (157 Chrystie Street, 212-673-0330) didn't once seem so out of the way, but its current location places it among wholesale shops and service stores. Like Katz's, its walls are adorned with photographs and news clippings of customers past and just a handful of customers present. Come here for all the *schmaltz* you can get (you will gape at the serving sizes—you might OD if you clean your plate). It's most fun with a group.

Shalom Chai Pizza (357 Grand Street, 212-598-4178) is one of the area's few kosher sit-down places, offering dairy entrées, Israeli dips, and pita sandwiches. The offbeat **Good World Bar and Grill** (3 Orchard Street, 212-925-9975) is a Swedish restaurant whose specialties include seafood and Swedish meatballs. The interior is dark and heavy, as if prepared for a permanent winter (I visited in the summer but it felt oddly cold). Most entrées are $7 to $12, except for grilled fish and roasted lamb ($18). The owners have retained the canopy and barber pole of the previous tenant, a Chinese barber shop. **Happy Shabu Shabu & Café** (54 Canal Street, 212-226-8868) is a nifty new Chinese hot pot place located in the historic Jarmulovsky Bank building. They have a $4.50 lunch special. This location is not yet officially identified as Chinatown, but it's certainly making inroads. Happy Shabu Shabu is one of the prettiest new places I've seen—it has large windows overlooking the sidewalk and beautiful decor. The folks I've met there are very friendly. Shabu Shabu's dishes are cooked at the table in a spicy or plain (usually chicken-based) broth—you can choose from different combinations of meats, greens, and seafood to cook in the broth. **Il Laboratorio del Gelato** (95 Orchard Street, 212-343-9922), opposite the Tenement Museum, opened in 2002 and serves homemade gelato, coffee, and milk shakes. Its young owner is the founder of a successful line of sorbets called Ciao Bella.

Several blocks east of Essex Street you'll see an enclave of markets, cafés, and galleries that feel quite different from the rest of the Lower East Side, and I think I know why. For one thing, they are quite a bit further from the subways—and thus from tourists who don't know this is a hip place to be. For another, the north-south streets end at Delancey Street because the Williamsburg Bridge meets land here. So the atmosphere is quieter and somehow more neighborly—and very interesting. You'll find a number of new and attractive places that signal the arrival of upscale eating. Some of these serve dinner only. One of these *isn't* **Clinton Street Baking Company** (4 Clinton Street, 646-602-6263), which serves its own products with its breakfast, lunch, and brunch menus of mostly light meals including eggs, granola, brioches, grilled chicken, burgers, and salads. Three places share the same owner and a retro feel: **aKa Café** (49 Clinton Street, 212-979-6096), **71 Clinton Fresh Food** (212-614-6960), and **Alias** (76 Clinton Street, 212-505-5011). Only aKa serves lunch, which is mostly fancy sandwiches. I didn't try the dinners, but appetizers run $6 to $9 and nouvelle Américaine fish and poultry entrées are $15 to $18. **Azul** (152 Stanton Street at Suffolk Street), 646-602-2004) offers Argentinian entrées, including some great seafood dishes. **Tonic** (107 Norfolk Street, 212-358-7503), mainly a late-night music club, draws all ages to its Sunday klezmer brunches.

Don't miss **Streit** Matzoh Company (148-154 Rivington Street, 212-475-7000), which has sold matzoh and other kosher products since 1916. A new product is Mediterranean matzoh, made with sun-dried tomatoes, basil, garlic, and olive oil. Prices are low—a box of matzoh is just $1.50 to $1.75. Fourth-generation Streitses now run the place!

■ Museums and Cultural Centers

There's plenty to do and see on the Lower East Side beyond eating and food shopping. The **Clemente Soto Velez Cultural Center** (107 Suffolk Street) houses several arts organizations. My favorite is TEATRO SEA at Los Kabayitos Puppet & Children's Theatre (see sea-ny.org for more information), which claims to be the only bilingual (Spanish-English) puppet theater in the United States. I've seen several shows here, and the puppetry is fun for adults as well as kids. Even if you don't speak Spanish, you'll understand the stories. **Henry Street Settlement** has been a Lower East Side mainstay since 1893, providing a vast range of social and cultural services, and it operates the wonderful art and theater complex at 466 Grand Street. For details, see its classy Web site, henrystreet.org. **Eldridge Street Synagogue** (12 Eldridge Street, 212-219-0903), built in 1886, is being restored and hosts many programs and tours. It's somewhat startling to visit now, since virtually every other business on its block is Chinese. Though still relatively new, the **Lower East Side Tenement Museum** (97 Orchard Street, 212-431-0233; www.tenement.org) has become a neighborhood mainstay, helping to revive the area as a tourist and shopping destination (although not without controversy: its plan to buy a tenement adjacent to one of its buildings has stirred some community opposition). Its book and gift shop is terrific. The **Lower East Side Conservancy** (www.nycjewish tours.org) has information on the various synagogues of the Lower East Side including those that have been put to other uses. You can use the site to create your own tour of local Jewish history. The **Lower East Side Business Improvement District** (www.lowereastsideny.com) has put together a good brochure that lists markets and cultural venues, it also has a very good map.

. . .

Ninth Avenue

Heaven in Hell's Kitchen

It's hard today to imagine that the area known as Hell's Kitchen was a haven for gangs. It's even harder—except maybe on a hot summer day—to understand why this neighborhood was once called Hell's Kitchen. Amid the high-rises that now necklace this area, Ninth Avenue/Hell's Kitchen is dense with stores and apartments. Named for a mid-nineteenth century gang that terrorized the area—said to be the most dangerous and poorest in New York City—it's now the calm eye of a development storm. Having won designation as a preservation district, Ninth Avenue is exempt from overbuilding, but new high-rises have sprouted to the east and west, particularly in the low 40s. These buildings bring more affluent residents, and thus more business, to local stores. But they come at a cost, making some of the smaller, family-owned businesses vulnerable. As I was first writing about this neighborhood toward the end of 2001, the decades-old Alps Pharmacy, located in an old tenement on the northeast corner of 42nd Street and Ninth Avenue, closed, and the building was replaced by a high-rise. I was sad to see it go—it was one of the few old-fashioned family pharmacies left in this area. It appears, however, that some of the older, small service businesses and food shops have managed to survive because their owners also own the buildings they occupy.

The challenge of writing about food on Ninth Avenue is knowing when to stop—there's so much to cover. There's also a fair amount of turnover. I've chosen to cover a relative handful of places that offer something unique in character, history, and/or cuisine that you'd have a hard time finding elsewhere.

■ Getting Oriented

This tour spans 34th to 54th Streets along Ninth Avenue. I've divided the area into three sections: 34th to 40th Streets, 40th to 48th Streets, and 48th to 54th Streets. Each section starts with markets, followed by bakeries and restaurants. I've *omitted* Restaurant Row (46th Street between Eighth and Ninth Avenues) and most Asian places because I've covered those extensively in my chapters on Flushing, Sunset Park, Curry Hill, and Manhattan's Chinatown.

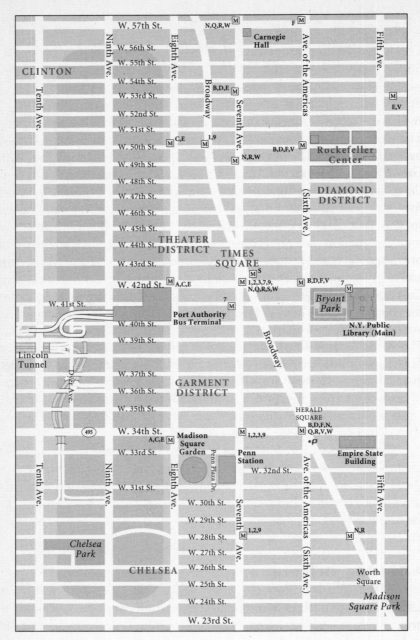

BY SUBWAY

The closest subways are the A, C, and E lines which stop at Eighth Avenue and 34th, and also 42nd, Streets. The C and E stop at 50th Street and the A and C trains stop at Columbus Circle where Broadway meets Eighth Avenue.

BY BUS

Crosstown buses include the M34 and M16 (34th Street); the M42 (42nd Street); the M49 (on 50th Street heading east and 49th Street heading west); and the M57 (57th Street). Uptown, take the M10 on Eighth Avenue or the M104, which heads west on 42nd Street and turns north on Eighth Avenue, or the M11 on 10th Avenue. The M11 goes south on Ninth Avenue. The Port Authority Bus Terminal straddles Eighth and Ninth Avenues between 40th and 42nd Streets.

Green Space   There's not much of it around here. One of the few spots is the **Clinton Community Garden** on 48th Street between Ninth and Tenth Avenues, which allows limited public access. In 1984 it became the first such space in New York City to win permanent parkland status (see www.clintoncommunitygarden.org for details). You can also go to the attractive but brick, not green, pedestrian space at **Worldwide Plaza,** which spans Eighth and Ninth Avenues between 49th and 50th Streets and has tables and chairs.

Cultural Highlights   Ninth Avenue restaurants are popular destinations for theater-goers, as Broadway, Off-Broadway, and Off-Off-Broadway theaters are close by. The **Irish Arts Center** is at 553 West 51st Street (212-757-3318) and the **Caribbean Cultural Center** is at 408 West 58th Street (212-307-7420). The **Alvin Ailey School** will be relocating to new headquarters on Ninth Avenue and 55th Street.

· · ·

34th to 40th Streets

Markets   I like **Mexican King Deli** (464 Ninth Avenue, 212-629-7579), which has a few tables for a quick meal as well as a line of Mexican and Colombian products. The menu includes Puebla-style chicken and beef with a type of Colombian sauce.

Followers of New York City neighborhood lore know about the feud between factions of the Manganaro clan who own adjacent, competing stores (both with restaurants) specializing in Italian food on Ninth Avenue. They allegedly haven't spoken to each other in decades. A local cynic remarked that it wasn't true, but that the publicity was brilliant for both shops. The stores are **Manganaro's Gourmet Foods—Grosseria and Ristorante** (488 Ninth Avenue, 212-563-5331 or 800-4SALAMI) and **Manganaro's Hero Boy** (492-494 Ninth Avenue, 212-947-7325), named for the ultra-long, ultra-thick cold cut sandwich that is the family trademark—and the focus of the dispute. The Grosseria, with its pressed tin ceilings and unrenovated interior, is clearly the more old-fashioned and traditional of the two. It's also the quieter. **Hero Boy,** on the other hand, has been modernized and looks like a huge family restaurant one would see in a shopping mall or an airport, and it's often packed.

Giovanni Esposito and Sons Meat Shop (500 Ninth Avenue at 38th Street, 212-279-3298) has been at its current site for some sixty years but was founded more than a century ago by Giovanni, an immigrant from Naples. These days its business is divided equally among retail customers and restaurants, says owner Robert Esposito, one of Giovanni's grandsons. Prices stay reasonable (and customers loyal) in part because the family owns the building it occupies. **Michael and Sons Meat Market** (516 Ninth Avenue at 38th Street) is more a grocery than a meat market, specializing in Ecuadorian and Peruvian packaged products, although it has a large meat counter. **West African Market** (533 Ninth Avenue near 40th Street) has been at this location for at least fifteen years and offers ingredients for West African cooking including dried fish, palm oil, canned goods from Ghana and The Ivory Coast, super-hot peppers and pepper sauces, and many other products plus videos and housewares. It's a colorful and interesting place to visit.

Bakeries   Cupcake Café (522 Ninth at 39th Street) has been around for ages; it's a bedraggled but popular bakery-café where you can gets soups, quiche, and sandwiches in addition to their famous, elaborately decorated cupcakes and cakes. Just looking at their cakes adds calories!

Restaurants   Soul Fixins' (371 West 34th Street, 212-736-1345) is around the corner east of Ninth Avenue and makes a good starting point for the tour. In the neighborhood since the early 1990s, this small soul food place offers a rich menu of ready-to-serve Southern-style dishes. Lunch specials are $4.95 but for a little more ($7.95 to $9.95) you'll get two side dishes and a roll and corn bread—enough food for two. I enjoy the atmosphere at **Celia's** (450 Ninth Avenue, 212-563-1245), a Dominican place that's open from 6 A.M. to 4 P.M., catering to local factory and postal workers. Tasty, inexpensive Caribbean dishes are ready to eat; most entrées are $5, slightly more for seafood stews or salads. Breakfast is served here all day. The caterer **Mitchel London Foods** (458 Ninth Avenue, 212-563-7750) has opened a new kitchen and café. The space is large, attractive, and informal and the sandwiches and all-day breakfasts are reasonable. **Los Dos Rancheros Mexicanos** (507 Ninth Avenue, 212-868-7780) is perhaps the only truly authentic Mexican restaurant on Ninth Avenue, owned and run by Mexicans. They also have a grocery next door. The chicken with *pipian* (pumpkin seed) sauce is terrific, and platters, which come with six tortillas, rice, and beans, are $7 and $8. **Supreme Macaroni/Guido's Restaurant** (511 Ninth Avenue, 212-564-8074), here more than fifty years, has a pasta shop in the front of the store that sells unusual pasta shapes and

MICHAEL'S CHAMPAGNE CHICKEN

*Courtesy of Giovanni Esposito and Sons Meat Shop
on Ninth Avenue, Manhattan*

2 whole boneless chicken breasts
½ pound mushrooms
Flour
Salt
Pepper
Butter, margarine, or light oil for sautéing
Juice of 1 lime
¾ cups champagne (remember, don't use a wine for cooking that
    you wouldn't drink!)
Nutmeg

1. Cut chicken breasts in half and trim the fat.
2. Slice the mushrooms in half.
3. Dredge the chicken breasts in a mixture of flour and salt and pepper to taste.
4. Heat the butter or oil in a large skillet and brown the chicken over medium heat for about 5 minutes total or until both sides are golden brown.
5. Squeeze the lime juice over the chicken—enjoy the sizzle and aroma!
6. Add the champagne and mushrooms, sprinkle the top with ground nutmeg, and reduce the heat to a simmer.
7. Cook, covered, for 20 minutes; if more gravy is needed, add some chicken stock mixed with flour. Serve over rice or couscous.

a busy restaurant offering lovely pastas, veal, chicken, shrimp, and eggplant entrées. It's one place that still bustled even during the dark days after 9/11. A newcomer, **Pomodoro Italian Express Food** (518 Ninth Avenue, 212-239-7019) offers a happy alternative to typical Italian fast food (pizza): salads, thick sandwiches on baguettes or focaccia, and pastas. **Chez Gnagna Koty's—Senegalese Cuisine** (530 Ninth Avenue, 212-279-1755) has a fusion menu that includes Moroccan couscous dishes along with traditional West African entrées. The decor is pleasant, with colorful tablecloths and napkins with African patterns. I tried the African patties in hot sauce. **Café Andalusia** (533 Ninth Avenue, 212-736-9411) is a simple place with a counter and a few tables, but it has an impressive menu of *tapas,* some Argentinian steak dishes (including *gaucho* burger), and seafood. My choice was a tasty *camarones verde*—shrimp in green sauce. **Tagine Dining Gallery** (537 Ninth Ave at 40th Street, 212-564-7292) is more than a restaurant. Toni Gallo and Hamid Idrissa are partners in life as well as business, and Tagine reflects their love of world cultures. The downstairs houses a performance space that hosts a range of programs. Meals are prepared or overseen by Idrissa, who used to run a catering business, and you can order their *tagines* (named for the clay bowl in which they're pre-

MAAQUDA
(MOROCCAN POTATO CROQUETTES)

Courtesy of Hamid Idrissa of Tagine Dining Gallery on Ninth Avenue, Manhattan

2 Idaho potatoes
1 teaspoon ground cumin
1 tablespoon chopped cilantro
1 egg
½ tablespoon all-purpose flour
Cayenn pepper to taste
Salt to taste
Vegetable oil for frying

1. In a medium pot, boil the potatoes for about ½ hour or until soft for mashing.
2. Remove the potatoes immediately from the hot water and leave them to dry and cool.
3. Peel and mash the potatoes with a hand masher—don't add anything!
4. Mix in the remaining ingredients.
5. Heat the vegetable oil in a large skillet.
6. Form little patties out of the mixture. Either deep-fry or fry lightly; if not deep-frying, cook on both sides until they are dark brown.

pared), which often combine contradictory flavors. I had lamb with prunes—amazing! Others combine preserved lemons, olives, or a hot relish called *chamoula,* made with garlic, lemon juice, olive oil, cumin, cayenne, cilantro, and vinegar.

. . .

40th to 48th Streets

Markets   **Sea Breeze Fish Market** (541 Ninth Avenue) has been here for sixty years, according to co-owner Vincent Dimino (who owns another Sea Breeze, with partner Angelo Bono, on 85th Street and 18th Avenue in Bensonhurst). **International Grocery** (543 Ninth Avenue at 40th Street) has a vast selection of spices, flours (at least ten different types including rice, corn, soy, chickpea, rye, pastry, whole wheat, and some organic ones), legumes (four types of lentils, for instance), and other grains and ingredients for baking and cooking, along with cooking utensils and some prepared foods—mostly Greek appetizers, dips, and pastries—as well as halvah and chocolate. It's heaven for folks who cook or bake from scratch. **Empire Coffee and Tea Company** (568 Ninth Avenue, 212-262-5908) is a New York old-timer—founded in 1908—and for years was a low-key but popular shop with an exceptional inventory of quality coffee beans and loose tea at reasonable prices. Now it's an upscale coffee and tea boutique, with an espresso bar and its own catalog. Across the street, Tom Saat, originally from Turkey, operates **Just Pickles,** a stand in front of **Stiles Farmer Market** (both at 569 Ninth Avenue), one of three Stiles markets in the area. (The others are at 472 Ninth Avenue at 36th Street and West 53rd Street, east of Ninth Avenue.) A pint of assorted pickles is $3; a quart is $5. Stiles, meanwhile, offers produce at steep discounts compared to local markets; they also sell coffee beans for $3.99 a pound. **Ninth Avenue Cheese Market** (615 Ninth Avenue at 44th Street) has been around for years, but its current owner has made it spiffier and has expanded, with a branch called **Kashkaval** at 856 Ninth Avenue north of 55th Street and outlets at Grand Central Station. But before you get to the cheese, you're likely to be seduced by the aroma of top-notch coffee beans. You'll also find many dips, appetizers, breads, and packaged imports. Try the variations of *skordalia,* a Greek dip usually made of mashed potatoes, garlic, olive oil, and spices; theirs are made with more ingredients and flavors such as sun-dried tomato, beet, roasted pepper, curry, and spinach, but the results vary. Roasted pepper *skordalia* is delicious; beet *skordalia* is boring. **Mazzella Market** (692-696 Ninth Avenue) is perhaps best known for being around: this large wholesale and retail produce market has been on Ninth Avenue for decades.

Bakeries   Poseidon Bakery (629 Ninth Avenue between 44th and 45th Streets) has been at this site for about eighty years! Now run by the third generation of the founding family, it offers marvelous Greek cookies and pastries including strudels, baklava, and spinach and cheese pies baked with hand-made phyllo dough, a rarity these day since most Greek bakeries now use machines. (The current phyllo experts are from Puerto Rico and Mexico; owner Lili Fable says her son also knows how to make phyllo dough.) Nearby, **Amy's Bread** (672 Ninth Avenue between 46th and 47th Streets) is a relative—and welcome—area newcomer with a lovely selection of breads, muffins, and cakes, plus tables where you can enjoy your food with coffee. (Amy's also has shops in Chelsea Market and on the Upper East Side.) **Pozzo Pastry Shop** (690 Ninth Avenue between 47th and 48th Streets) is another old-timer, and feels it—in a good way. Enjoy their large selection of biscotti and old-fashioned cookies and cakes. When I first found **Leon Bakery** (695 Ninth Avenue, near 48th Street) it was a cluttered Mexican grocery with an equally cluttered bakery area. Just before *el Día de los Muertos* (Day of the Dead, observed November 1), Leon sells traditional miniature sugar skulls and skeletons for the holiday. You can also find delicious *tamales* and *picaderos* (spicy tortilla wraps). When I visited just before finishing this book, I was delightfully surprised to see that Leon had had a complete makeover and it is now a beautiful sit-down Mexican café with groceries in the rear. The owners have opened up the back part of the store, creating an entirely new and beautiful experience. I love seeing success stories like this, and Leon is a real treat for this neighborhood (and for you—go!).

Restaurants   Bali Nusa Indah (651 Ninth Avenue, 212-974-1875) is one of two Indonesian restaurants I know of in New York City. It features *rijstaffel* (Indonesian buffet) at dinner. Go with friends. A fish mousse in spicy peanut sauce was unexciting; a vegetable curry was slightly better. My best choice was *es teler,* an Indonesian iced dessert drink made with fruits from Southeast Asia.

■ ■ ■

48th to 54th Streets

Markets   The only significant one in this stretch is the spacious gourmet-quality **Amish Market** (731 Ninth Avenue), oddly named since the owners and many employees are Turkish and there are no Amish dishes in evidence, though it has everything else.

Restaurants **El Deportivo** (701 Ninth Avenue at 48th Street, 212-757-0819) offers a large menu of reasonably-priced Caribbean dishes. Their $6.45 ample daily specials include a fine codfish salad. **Costa del Sol** (369 West 50th Street Street at Ninth Avenue, 212-541-8382) offers fine Spanish meals at reasonable prices; many entrées with rice and vegetables are under $15, and I enjoyed chicken in almond sauce for under $12. **Grand Sichuan** (745 Ninth Avenue at 50th Street, 212-582-2288) gets raves from Chinese friends. Its vast menu features dishes adapted from a TV series popular in China, Hong Kong, and Taiwan. The menu also explains why few Chinese in the United States order chicken: because the poultry is rarely as fresh as the backyard chickens they are used to. To compensate, Grand Sichuan lists dishes it makes from newly slaughtered chicken. Greek food fans will enjoy the huge menu at **Uncle Nick's** (747 Ninth Avenue, 212-245-7992) including their combination plates. A personal favorite is shrimp *saganaki* (baked cheese), here served over tomatoes with a few pieces of grilled shrimp. Two small Brazilian places add a nice flavor to this section of Ninth Avenue. When I first encountered **Café Brasil** (746 Ninth Avenue, 212-247-5500), it was primarily a bakery and most of the baked goods were Italian. A Brazilian chef appears to have been hired and the café now specializes in Brazilian *churrasco* (grilled chicken and beef) and is open for lunch and dinner. Dishes are no more than $12 and most are $8 to $10. It's a sweet, friendly place. Not quite next door, although it has a next-door address, **Rice & Beans** (744 Ninth Avenue, 212-265-4444), which specializes in Brazilian *feijoada* (spicy bean stew with seafood and chicken) but has other traditional dishes as well. **Old San Juan** (765 Ninth Avenue at 52nd Street, 212-262-7013) was opened a few years ago by the founders of La Milonga, an Argentine place that occupied this spot for decades. The owners retired, then got restless and re-opened with Argentinian grill and *empanadas* alongside Caribbean pork, beef, and seafood. The most expensive entrées are just under $20; most are a lot less. **Ariana Afghan** (787 Ninth Avenue at 52nd Street, 212-262-2323) is one of two Afghan eateries on Ninth Avenue. (The other is **Afghan Kebab #1**, 764 Ninth Avenue at 51st Street, 212-307-1612.) The excellent menu features kebab and *tandoori* entrées, but you also can make a meal with appetizers such as *bolanee* (turnovers) filled with pumpkin and potatoes, which are light and perfect, and eggplant *buranee*—fried with spices, garlic, yogurt, and mint, which is outstanding. **Island Burgers and Shakes** (766 Ninth Avenue, 212-307-7934) is a fifties-type place with fifty-plus types of burgers and a chicken *churrasco* (grilled chicken breast sandwich) specialty. **New York Popover** (789 Ninth Avenue, 646-746-0315) brought a whole new take on fast food to Ninth Avenue when it opened in 2001, offering entrée popovers (basically sandwiches in popover bread) plus vegetable, meat, and cheese popovers and dessert popovers with all sorts of toppings. Apparently it's working—the place is still there more than a year later. One explanation might be that prices are very reasonable; the entrée popovers, like gourmet sandwiches, are no more than $7, and most are less. **Pita Grill** restaurant (790 Ninth Avenue, 212-765-1100), which opened here in 2002, offers typical Middle Eastern specialties with a twist: some of the thick, creamy dips are low-fat (hummus) or fat-free (*babghanoush*) and salad dressings include fat-free or light choices. It's a pleasant, healthy option. The last stop on Ninth Avenue is one that I especially recommend: **Rinconcito Peruano** (803 Ninth Avenue at 53rd Street, 212-333-5685). It's a small and plain-looking family-run place with a handful of tables and minimal (but not minimalist) decoration. I had a fabulous *aji de gallina,* a shredded chicken casserole with walnuts, Parmesan cheese, *mirasol* hot peppers, potatoes, hard-boiled eggs, olives, and rice. Sometimes the plainest-looking places offer the most delicious meals!

Manhattan Side Trip

Curry Hill

There's no hill in Curry Hill, the name someone (I couldn't figure out who) gave to a three-block cluster of South Asian markets and eateries along Lexington Avenue. But there's no hill, either, in Murray Hill, the neighborhood where it's located. Go figure. In any case, you'll see an amazing number of eating places and markets packed into these blocks. It's one-stop shopping and eating if you love curry! (NOTE: Be aware that many restaurants in this neighborhood—kosher and not—close from 3 P.M. to 5 P.M., although not the fast-food places. Udipi Palace is an exception.)

Getting There   The #6 train stops at Park Avenue and 28th Street; walk one block east to Lexington Avenue. Crosstown buses are the M23 on 23rd Street and the M34 or M16 on 34th Street. Downtown buses M101, M102, and M103 run on Lexington Avenue and uptown on Third Avenue.

Green Space   The closest green space is Madison Square Park between Madison and Fifth Avenues from 23rd to 26th Streets. It's a schlep, but it's worth it if it's a beautiful day to eat outside.

Markets   **Kalustyan's** (123 Lexington Avenue, 212-685-3451), founded in 1944, is the granddaddy and the FAO Schwarz of Curry Hill markets. It's great fun to visit. Almonds coated in edible gold and silver sparkle in a jar near the entry (and they'll cost you—$5.99 a quarter pound—no samples!) and the variety of nuts, rice of different colors and sizes from around the world, multicolored couscous, spices, legumes, teas, dried

fruit, and other good-
ies are simply over-
whelming. You'll enjoy
visiting the second-
floor deli, where head
chef Apiar Afarian
doles out good humor
along with his Medi-
terranean concoctions.
Although the place
started as a vendor of
Indian foods exclu-
sively and then added
Middle Eastern prod-
ucts, it's now truly

Apiar Afarian dishing up specialties at Kalustyan's in Curry Hill.

international as co-owners Sayedul Alam and Aziz Osmani, cousins originally from Bangladesh, have identified a larger market for their wares
including many professional chefs.

No idea how to use the ingredients? Then buy one of the dozens of
cookbooks with recipes from around the world, along with some cookware, for sale. The back refrigerator is packed with the condiments
Kalustyan's prepares in-house. I adore *mohammara,* a Syrian-Lebanese
relish made with Aleppo peppers, pomegranates, walnuts, molasses, olive
oil, and pignoli nuts. As with other stores of this type, Kalustyan's does a
chunk of business (about 25%) by mail and, increasingly, the Internet (see
www.kalustyan.com and www.forspice.com).

Up the street, **Spice Corner** (135 Lexington Avenue at the southeast corner of 29th Street) has an inviting inventory of products not just from India
but elsewhere in Southern Asia and from other places such as Jamaica and
Israel. Its many non-food items include toiletries and cooking utensils. **Foods
of India,** next to Kalustyan's at 121 Lexington Avenue, sells just what its name
implies and is an efficient alternative for South Asian cooking needs. The
aroma of incense engulfs you as you enter **Little India** (128 East 28th Street);
it has a bit of everything (but produce): packaged foods, spices, periodicals,
incense, housewares. Upstairs, **Little India Emporium** sells saris and jewelry.
Restaurants   There's a cluster of kosher vegetarian Indian restaurants in
the neighborhood. I've eaten at two: **Udipi Palace** (formerly New Madras
Palace, 101 Lexington Avenue, 212-889-3477) and **Pongal** (81 Lexington
Avenue, 212-696-5130). The kosher vegetarian menus offer similar dishes:
dosas (crepes), *utthapam* (rice pancakes, which look like mini-pizzas),
iddlies (rice lentil cakes), and curries. The others are **Saravana Bhavan
Dosa Hut** (102 Lexington Avenue, 212-725-7466) and **Madras Mahal** (104

Lexington Avenue, 212-684-4010). **Curry Leaf** (99 Lexington Avenue, 212-725-5558), owned by the folks who own Kalustyan's, features regional cuisines of South India and is a few notches above many others in the area, and it's in a newer, nicer setting. Every dish is made-to-order, so be patient.

Curry in a Hurry (119 Lexington Avenue, 212-683-0900), on the other hand, offers lower-cost Indian fast food. There's a free salad bar plus seating in a relatively quiet setting upstairs (although Indian videos are sometimes shown). The place—in Curry Hill since 1976, but not always at this location—is rather frayed at the edges, but I had a satisfying dinner of chicken *tikka* and *saag paneer* (spinach and cheese) with rice, *nan* (a grilled bread), and enjoyed a salad bar (about $10, with free soda refills).

Most Pakistani places, such as **Chatkhara** (103 Lexington Avenue, 212-779-2889) and **Niamat Kada** (124 Lexington Avenue, 212-683-6207), have dishes ready to go and the settings are more informal with lower prices. I like these places; you can get your money's worth in ample servings of various curries and have the chance to try different dishes.

Curry Hill's first glatt kosher meat restaurant, **Baruch Kosher Deli & Grill,** opened in early 2001 at 115 Lexington Avenue at 28th Street (212-686-5400). The owners are none other than Alam and Osmani of Kalustyan's, but their partner is an observant Jew. It offers both Mediterranean and South Asian specialties.

Wander through Curry Hill and you'll find much more than curry. Some new, upscale restaurants are opening near the boutique hotels that are now proliferating. But some old-timers continue to draw customers. A lovely and charming one is the French **La Petite Auberge** (116 Lexington Avenue, 212-689-5003), which offers a $15.95 prix fixe lunch (a reliable soup or starter, a fish or meat entrée, and dessert). Another cute place is **Chez le Chef** (127 Lexington Avenue, 212-685-1888), which sells home-baked pastries and has large breakfast and lunch menus (including sandwiches and lots of soups—their pumpkin ginger soup is delicious) and an eclectic selection of entrées. Prices are somewhat steep for the area—only one sandwich is less than $6—but their excellent bread is baked on the premises.

Also . . . The playhouse for **Repertorio Español,** a theater troupe that performs plays in Spanish or by Spanish-language playwrights, is located at 138 East 27th Street. For more information, call 212-889-2850.

Manhattan Side Trip

Little Italy

Knowing the great Italian markets in Belmont and Bensonhurst, I'm rarely tempted to visit Manhattan's Little Italy. But I decided to check it out for this book because of its fame, its proximity to other neighborhoods I've covered in more detail—the Lower East Side and Chinatown—and for its economic importance to New York City. The annual St. Gennaro Festival, held in September, continues to attract huge crowds, yet it's almost an anomaly, surrounded by growing numbers of Chinese enterprises.

Getting There   Take the #6, J, M, N, R, Q, W, or Z train to Canal Street. The exits are at Broadway and Lafayette—and Centre—Streets. Mulberry Street, Little Italy's "Main Street," is east of these exits, stretching north from Canal to Kenmare Streets. (There also are a few places remaining on the side streets, but their numbers are dwindling.) Here you'll see at least a dozen restaurants and cafés, along with souvenir shops. I didn't sample the eateries and cafés, but I did visit its four markets. Three are just off of Mulberry Street. **Italian Food Center** (186 Grand Street, 212-925-2954) has a reasonable selection of prepared and packaged Italian food and ingredients, as well as a catering business. I did find the sugar-free version of Manhattan Special, an espresso-flavored soda that I love. The "Manhattan" in the name, by the way, refers to Manhattan Avenue in Williamsburg, where the company is based. **Alleva Dairy** (188 Grand Street, 212-226-7990), founded in 1892, claims to be the oldest Italian cheese store in America, and they still make their own excellent mozzarella and also sell many other cheeses and some prepared foods. Next door, **Piemonte Food Products** (190 Grand Street, 212-226-0475) sells its own brand of fresh and dried pastas and a selection of imported pastas. They have many different types of ravioli and tortellini, including tofu-stuffed whole wheat vegetarian ravioli and fresh garlic or basil fettuccine.

Go one block east, past Mott Street, to find **Di Palo Fine Foods** (200 Grand Street, 212-226-1033), which has been making *latticini fresci* (fresh cheese) since 1925. They have a little of everything, and they also have the most character and draw the biggest crowds. "It's a diamond in the rough," one shopper told me as he waited for his prosciutto to be sliced. And "waiting" is a key word here because that's what you have to do much of the time. It's not just that so many people want to buy there, but the Di Palos— siblings Luigi, Marie, and Salvatore, grandchildren of the founder—actually enjoy talking to customers (especially Luigi, who knows everything). They always have special cheeses and other products just flown in from Italy, so you should ask what's new each time. Di Palo also has some branded products including sauces and some pastas, and they prepare all sorts of special salads and other goodies such as roasted vegetables in their kitchen. In late 2002 the store relocated into significantly larger quarters from its old, packed space at 206 Grand Street. In making this move, it replaced a Chinese market—a reversal of the usual pattern. After shopping at Di Palo, I often head to the Chinese "market row" on Mott Street between Grand and Hester Streets, where you can get all sorts of fabulous produce, fish, and other goods at bargain prices—it's some of the most interesting (and most fun) food shopping in New York City.

Manhattan Side Trip

Little Seoul

West 32nd Street Between Fifth Avenue and Broadway

Korean immigration to the United States dates back to the 1920s but, as with other immigrant groups, their numbers weren't significant until immigration laws were relaxed in 1965 and many more Koreans came to this country. In the early 1970s the first Korean greengrocers opened in New York City, introducing twenty-four-hour access to fresh produce, which in those days was revolutionary. These markets rapidly sprouted throughout many neighborhoods and are now entrenched within the fabric of New York City commerce, as are three other businesses in which Koreans are especially prominent: dry cleaners, fish markets, and nail salons. A number of neighborhoods in Queens—Bayside, Woodside, Elmhurst, Flushing, and Sunnyside—now have critical masses of Korean residents and Korean stores, while in Manhattan an astounding number of Korean businesses clog the block of West 32nd Street between Fifth Avenue and Broadway, with spillover in all directions. Within this one block are at least twelve restaurants (several of which are open twenty-four hours), one supermarket, a big bookstore, and two bakery-cafés. There are also several hotels on the block that house Korean restaurants and cafés. The colors, textures, and tastes of Korean food are as diverse and stimulating as this 24/7 neighborhood itself.

This tour focuses on this remarkable block, which is sometimes known as Little Seoul or Koreatown. But in fact, Little Seoul extends in all directions within this neighborhood.

Getting There   Nearest subways are the B, D, F, N, Q, R, V, and W at 34th Street and Avenue of the Americas/Broadway. Sit in the southern-most car and exit at 32nd Street. (Double-check maps for route changes during ongoing subway construction.) Little Seoul is one block east of Penn Station and a short walk from the 33rd Street PATH stop.

You also can take the bus downtown on Fifth Avenue (M2, M3, M5) or Broadway (M6 or M7) or uptown on Avenue of the Americas (M5, M6, M7). The M4 goes down Fifth Avenue but turns West on 34th Street, so if you take this bus get off at 34th Street.

Bakeries   There are two here: **Café Metro** (2 West 32nd Street) and **Pari-**

pariko (49 West 32nd Street), which I prefer. It's a cute, bright place with Korean rap music playing, a young crowd, and an interesting dessert menu of ice cream (including Asian bean ices with fruit), pastries, flavored juice drinks, and popular *boba* (bubble) tea made with chewy tapioca beads. But they're pricey: you'll pay $4 to $5 for beverages and the same for desserts, so go when you have time to linger! I like Paripariko's faux Chagall murals and bright lights. You can also buy cakes and pastries—many of them European style—to take home.

Snackeries   I love **Woorijip** (12 West 32nd Street, 212-244-1115), which has a salad bar ($4.99 a pound) where you'll have an ample selection of *kimchee* (cabbage), sprouts, noodles, chicken, fish, vegetables, sautéed tofu, and more. A popular dish is *bibimbop,* a rice-based platter with fried eggs and shredded vegetables including lettuce, sprouts, seaweed, spinach, carrots, and cabbage sautéed in sesame oil along with bite-size pieces of chicken. I love the range of flavors and textures in this dish; it's a bargain at $6 and it comes with miso soup. Usually *bibimbop* is prepared in a stone bowl and it's served that way in fancier restaurants, sometimes with beef or seafood. Here you get it in a fast-food aluminum container.

Restaurants   The range starts with the simple and popular **Mandoo Bar** (2 West 32nd Street, 212-279-3075), which specializes in small dumplings (which you can see the chefs forming in the window), and goes to fancier places suitable for business lunches. I like Mandoo because it's smaller and the setting is attractive. Many places are big and bustling: **Kangsuh** (1250 Broadway, entrance on 32nd Street), for example, resembles a mall. Most of these places have lunch specials for $7 to $9, including an all-you-can-eat buffet at **Café Zen-X** (34 West 32nd Street); complete dinners here easily exceed $25. Many, such as **Kum Gan Sam** (49 West 32nd Street) offer Korean barbecue, Japanese specialties, and Chinese dishes, but the teriyaki and sushi I've had were mediocre so I suggest you stick with the Korean food. Some places, such as **Seoul Garden** (34 West 32nd Street, 2nd floor), have mini-grills at the table so you can make your own barbecue. The **Dae Dong** chain, one of the first Korean eateries in New York City, has a place at 17 West 32nd Street. **Kunjip Restaurant** (9 West 32nd Street, 212-946-3028) has one of the nicest settings—no kitsch here—and a $6.95 lunch menu.

EAST OF FIFTH AVENUE

A very special place for many fans of Korean food is **Hangawi** (12 East 32nd Street, 212-203-0077; www.hangawirestaurant.com), known for its vegetarian, non-dairy dishes (and thus its attraction for kosher customers). It's also known for its high prices; the dinner menu includes a prix fixe Matsutake Feast for $69.95, which includes soup, appetizers, and entrées using *matsutake* mushrooms, and dessert. Less costly takeout meals are available at lunchtime. Appetizers and salads are $3 and $9; entrées are $12 and $16. I ordered pumpkin porridge, mini-pancakes, and avocado salad ($18 total). The setting aims at Zen: dimly lit with Asian instrumental music and low tables with cushions and rugs. Although the take-out presentation was impressive, the food lacked the zest I love in mainstream Korean cuisine; the porridge was dull, the pancakes just okay. To my surprise the after-dinner sweets were artificially flavored Jolly Rancher candies!

Markets   There's only one, the huge **Han Ah Reum** (25 West 32nd Street), where you'll find ingredients for Korean cooking along with prepared dishes. Han Ah Reum has its flagship in Flushing (see page 34) and a second in Woodside (see page 76).

Green Space   There isn't much green space in this area but it's nice to know there's a place where you can sit and read quietly amid the bustle of Herald Square. It's in the form of a triangular park—its southern tip is one block west of Little Seoul where Broadway and Avenue of the Americas cross. It's called **Greeley Square** (not Greeley Triangle!), named for the journalist and social reformer who was founding editor of the *New York Herald*. The park was beautifully renovated in 1999 and now has an almost Parisian look, with green folding chairs, little green round tables, big planters, and kiosks selling magazines and coffee. Traffic patterns have been modified, so the area is far less chaotic, and pedestrian spaces have been increased around the park, so a once-forbidding space has become a great success. There's also a corresponding triangle to Greeley's north at Herald Square.

Also . . .   Don't miss **Koryo** bookstore (35 West 32nd Street, video store at 7 West 32nd Street), packed with books, magazines, CDs, dolls, and other items. I bought *Vignette of Korean Cooking* by Jae Ok Chang (Daegu, Korea: Maeilwonsaek Press, 2000) for $20. It's a fine English-language cookbook with clear explanations of how to use Korean ingredients and excellent photographs accompanying most recipes. Ms. Chang says she wrote the book to help American-born Koreans maintain their traditions.

Manhattan Side Trip

Tastes of Persia

Heading west from the Curry Hill area (see pages 250–252) will take you into York City's rug district and toward two Persian restaurants and two Persian markets.

Getting There   The closest subway lines are the N and R at 28th Street and Broadway, and the #6 train at 28th Street and Park Avenue. From the West Side you can also take the #1 and #9 trains to 28th Street.

The menu at **New Nader Restaurant** (48 East 29th Street, 212-683-4833) offers fascinating combinations of ingredients such as pomegranates, mint and other herbs, assorted nuts, rice, and spices in its alluring range of appetizers and entrées. On my first visit I sampled a fluffy rice dish with barberries (similar to currants), almonds, and pistachios, and *mirza ghasemi* (smoked eggplant with garlic and fried tomatoes), which was complex and yummy! On a second visit I tried a chicken *koresh* (a chicken and rice stew) with fluffy basmati rice. It was just okay—I've had a better *koresh* at Kabul Kebab in Flushing (see page 37), which specializes in Persian dishes.

Ravagh Grill, located in the Rug Center at 11 East 30th Street (212-696-0300) is smaller than Nader but offers many of the same wonderful Persian dishes including *Khoresh Fesenjan,* a mixture of crushed walnuts and boneless chicken cooked in pomegranate paste. It's only $10 and comes with basmati rice. A typical Persian soup is *ash reshteh,* made of vegetables, chickpeas, kidney beans, nottodes, fried onions, yogurt, garlic, and meat. It's very easy with a soup like that and many of the meat-free appetizers to create a satisfying vegetarian meal. Slightly beyond the rug district is a glatt kosher Persian placed called **Colbeh** (43 West 39th Street, 212-354-8181).

Both **Nader Food Market** (1 East 28th Street) and the larger **Pars International Market** (145 West 30th Street; www.pars.com; closed Sunday) have an ample selection of dried fruit and nuts (try lemon-roasted pistachios!), spices and herbs, and pistachio butter, as well as Iranian imports and cookbooks. Nader is older and looks it—the store is drab and the inventory more standard. Pars is gorgeous and has lots of housewares, along with Iranian soaps and self-care items. They also sell creamy Persian ice cream and lemon licorice, which my daughter loves! At Nader, which is open seven days, I bought *A Taste of Persia* by Najmieh K. Batmanglij (Mage, 2000), which has a recipe for pistachio soup that I've since made and others I used to create a New Year's Eve dinner. (I've also found great Persian recipes at www.ee.surrey.ac.uk/Personal/F.Mokhtarian/recipes.)

Manhattan Side Trip

Washington Heights and Hudson Heights

During the Revolutionary War, this area played a strategic role because of its geographic elevation, and three forts—Fort George, Fort Washington, and Fort Tryon—were built here. But nowadays many folks refer to this neighborhood of Manhattan, bordered approximately on the south by 155th Street and on the north by 190th Street, as Quisqueya Heights because of the large population of people from the Dominican Republic who live here. (Quisqueya refers to the indigenous people of the island.) In reality it's much more varied, with distinct communities from the Dominican Republic, Mexico, Puerto Rico, and other Caribbean and Latin American countries, not to mention people of European and other roots who also call Washington Heights home.

Washington Heights also has a healthy dose of local history. Key landmarks include the Audubon Ballroom, where Malcolm X was shot; Audubon Terrace, a complex of cultural institutions located on the west side of Broadway from 153rd to 155th Streets; and Columbia-Presbyterian Hospital, which occupies a big chunk of local real estate. Further north, Yeshiva University occupies several blocks of land and is a very self-contained community with a bare handful of kosher places for faculty and students. The community of Hudson Heights (see pages 262–263), an enclave of prewar apartment buildings west of Broadway from 181st Street to Fort Tryon Park, is a growing subset of Washington Heights that includes refugees from the Upper West Side, Russian Jews, an older community of German Jews, and a generally eclectic mix of musicians, academics, and other professionals.

I recommend two side trips to Washington Heights, one along a twelve-block stretch of Broadway (including some blocks of St. Nicholas Avenue) that includes the Audubon Ballroom, Columbia-Presbyterian Hospital, and the famous Christian Universal Church of Reverend Ike, and a second through the restaurants and cafés of Hudson Heights, including a lovely place in Fort Tryon Park, followed by a magnificent dessert: a visit to the Cloisters Museum.

▪ Side Trip #1: Washington Heights

Getting There   Take the #1, A, or C train to 168th Street, which lets you out at the busy intersection of 168th Street, Broadway, and St. Nicholas Avenue. Several bus lines head up to Washington Heights, but the trip can be long. The three I recommend are the M3, M5, and M100. The M3 runs north along Madison Avenue and eases west at 110th Street, turning north on St. Nicholas Avenue, where it rides all the way uptown. The M5 moves north on Avenue of the Americas, eases over to Broadway after Central Park South, and eventually heads up Riverside Drive and then north onto Broadway from 135th Street. The M100 begins at Second Avenue and 125th Street, then heads west toward Amsterdam Avenue, where it turns north until about 163rd Street, at which point it veers onto Broadway, one block south of where the Washington Heights tour begins. The walking on this tour spans 163rd to 176th Streets.

Although the 168th Street subway has several exits, I recommend the main one at 168th Street and Broadway. You'll be on the west side of Broadway at the hospital site. (The medical complex occupies many buildings and in recent years it has expanded east of Broadway.) Head south. On this tour your first stop will be **Carrot Top Pastries** (3931 Broadway at 165th Street, 212-927-4800), which has been a neighborhood fixture for years. Carrot Top started out as a cake café specializing in carrot cake but is now a full-fledged restaurant with pastas and sandwiches—it's a great haven for medical staff!

Cross the street to 163rd Street. Here you'll see a pair of Dominican markets, including **Liberato** (3900 Broadway at 163th Street) and **La Rosa** (3910 Broadway, a few doors up). Liberato, which has had a plastic helicopter suspended from its canopy for years, is the quintessential Dominican market—a bit frayed at the edges, with bins full of the roots, tropical fruit, greens, peppers, and other vegetables used in Caribbean cooking, along with cookware and canned goods—and loud music. La Rosa is a smaller, newer place with an extensive selection of fresh fish and meat— perhaps the nicest-looking Dominican market I've seen in New York City. On the same block is **Parrilla,** an Argentinian Restaurant (3920 Broadway, 212-543-9500) that features pastas and traditional mixed grill (the grill is in the front of the store) and live music on weekends. **El Presidente** (3938 Broadway, 212-927-2965) is a large Dominican place that's been in Washington Heights for years but recently had a complete makeover. The main dining area is almost stately, and much of the menu is pure diner fare but you can also order a *desayuno Hispano* (Spanish breakfast) of *mondongo con pan* (tripe with bread) and various combinations of plantains, yucca, fried eggs, and oatmeal (they average $5). House platters—Dominican specialties—include variations of tripe, grilled or sautéed chicken, and roast pork, and still the price is reasonable, from $5 to $10.75 for *mofongo* (mashed green plantain) with shrimp scampi. The menu also offers Italian pastas and seafood. If you're looking for a more homey atmosphere, go to **El P Café**—the entrance is just to the right of the main restaurant entrance. Here you'll find counter service (and the identical menu) and, more likely than in the other setting, someone to chat with.

Crossing 165th Street, you'll come to the historic **Audubon Ballroom.** Years ago the community fought to save the building when Columbia University wanted to develop it for medical purposes. A compromise was struck: the façade was saved and a permanent display devoted to Malcolm X was given a dramatic space within the building. Attached to it is a new scientific research and technology facility. The ground floor has several shops—a café, a bookstore, a busy Dallas BBQ restaurant, and a pizzeria. The building spans several addresses; 3940 Broadway brings you to the Malcolm X Memorial, which was not yet accessible to the public as I was preparing this book, but you can see some of the work in progress through the large glass windows on the second floor.

Heading north, you'll hit the busy intersection with St. Nicholas Avenue. Keep to the right (east). The east side of Broadway will become St. Nicholas Avenue. Check out **El Salvadoreño/El Rincón Centroamericano** (1229 Saint Nicholas Avenue at 172nd Street, 212-927-3898), a lively Salvadoran place that offers music on weekends. You can stick to Salvadoran (and some Honduran) *antojitos* (appetizers and snacks) such as *pupusas* and *tamales* or order full meals of chicken, steak, or pork with rice, refried beans, cream, and *chimol* (a mixture of onions, peppers, tomatoes, and parsley). You also can buy snacks and sodas from El Salvador here. I happen to like this place a lot. Continue to 175th Street. Within just a few blocks you'll get a flavor of the community, especially if you visit on a busy weekend.

Across the street you might want to take a look at **Antillana #2** (1274 St. Nicholas Avenue), a new and predominantly Dominican and Mexican market that features a large meat counter and produce. It epitomizes what the neighborhood shops looks like now, with a nice combination of products for both cuisines and loud music (Mexican the day I visited) in the background.

The block of 175th Street between St. Nicholas and Broadway has been dubbed **Placita de las Americas** and is a flea market during the day. Overlooking la Placita is the church of Reverend Ike, the flamboyant minister and television evangelist whose "prosperity theology" made news in the 1970s as worshipful followers subsidized his ascent to wealth. His church occupies a former Loews movie palace at 175th Street and Broadway, and when it's not a church it doubles as **Taquilla de United Palace**, a performance venue for Latino singers.

El Malecón I (4141 Broadway at 175th Street, 212-927-3812) is one of the best Dominican restaurants I've ever eaten in. I often patronize the smaller El Malecón II at 764 Amsterdam Avenue at 97th Street (212-864-5648) on the Upper West Side, close to my home, but this one is the flagship—almost three times larger with a bigger menu, a lovely setting, and spectacular food. Let me start with the rotisserie chicken, which you can smell from the street—it lures you in—and then the *café con leche,* which (at just $1) is among the best Latin coffee you'll get. The menu has everything—oxtail, beef, chicken, pork, and goat plus lots of seafood dishes—and in many combinations. It's fun to come to Malecón during a busy weekday evening when families pack the place and they do a brisk take-out business. The acrobatics of preparing and serving food is almost elegant here—they've got it down to a formula.

Restaurant El Ranchito (4129 Broadway, 212-928-0866), a second Salvadoran place in this area, is smaller than El Salvadoreño and has a more basic menu of *platos típicos*. It has a homier feeling, too. **International Food House Restaurant** (4071 Broadway between 171st and 172nd Streets, 212-740-1616) is a twenty-four-hour Dominican-style buffet place. It's a newcomer to this area of Washington Heights but it has a more established predecessor on Dyckman Street in Inwood. You can pile on *"todo lo que pueda comer"* (all you can eat) with $3.95 breakfast specials starting at 6 A.M., lunch at $5.95, and dinners at $6.95 during the week (more on weekends). I saw four different types of rice—yellow or white, with pigeon peas or green peas—red and black beans, several chicken combinations, plantains and yucca, several different salads, and various stews of fish, beef, pork, or poultry in the great sauces that make Dominican cooking so delicious. Not great for folks watching their weight!

Two nice eateries near the Columbia-Presbyterian hospital complex are **Aqua Marina** (4060 Broadway, 212-928-0070), a small, moderately priced Italian restaurant with pastas and other entrées costing no more than $13, and **Coogan's Restaurant** (4015 Broadway, 212-928-1234), a large and animated Irish restaurant and pub, which doubles as a local meeting place. I doubt either would be here if the hospital were not, but they do offer a clue to the great diversity of this area of Washington Heights. Plus the overall infrastructure around here has improved a great deal—a few messy traffic intersections have been filled in with small garden plazas and many of the graceful older buildings have been cleaned, so it's a lot nicer for exploring than it used to be. You'll also see lots of lovely churches as you explore.

After these visits, the tour is over—but perhaps your appetite has been whet for more. You can explore St. Nicholas Avenue further—it's the true Broadway of Dominican Washington Heights—and check out the panoply of markets and restaurants that dot the avenue including the many sidewalk vendors who animate the area.

By the way, there's a tradition of Dominican *chimichurri* trucks similar to the Mexican taco trucks you'll find on the Upper West Side and in other neighborhoods with a critical mass of Mexicans. You'll also find *roti* trucks that serve West Indian food; some park by hospitals that have West Indian staff. The Dominican trucks sell *empanadas* (patties stuffed with chicken, potato, meat, and other fillings) and various *cuchifritos* (fried specialties) and also *batidos*, the wonderful tropical fruit shakes that can be almost a meal.

▪ Side Trip #2: Hudson Heights

I don't know when it began, but the northwestern corner of Washington Heights is now known as Hudson Heights, probably as a convenience to real estate agents who market this area as an even-further-uptown version of the Upper West Side. It is geographically separated from the rest of Washington Heights by the geological rise of the terrain west of Broadway—you even can see some boulders jutting out from the west side above Bennett Avenue—while 181st Street, to the south, dips toward the valley of the rest of Washington Heights. The Hudson River is its scenic western border and Fort Tryon Park, home to the gorgeous Cloisters Museum, is the northern border.

Getting there   Take the A train to 181st or 190th Streets. The 190th Street stop leaves you just south of Fort Tryon. The #4 bus, which originates at Penn Station and moves north on Madison Avenue before heading west on 110th Street to Broadway, ultimately goes north on Fort Washington Avenue, directly to this neighborhood; it terminates at the Cloisters.

This area has a fairly good number of worthy destinations for food lovers, considering the fact that the commercial area is pretty small. You can combine a nice meal with a visit to the park and the Cloisters. The most notable eatery is **New Leaf Café** (1 Margaret Corbin Drive, 212-568-5323), operated by the New York Restoration Project (www.nyrp.org), Bette Midler's initiative to redevelop upper Manhattan parks and community gardens. (A boathouse on upper Broadway is another of NYRP's projects.) New Leaf is a non-profit eatery that has restored the building in which it operates and all profits go to helping the organization. The menu is modestly priced nouvelle cuisine, offering salads and light meals, and there's a bar. (Expect to pay $12 to $18, without drinks.) An outdoor patio during warm weather is one of its greatest draws and it's just a short walk from the 190th Street subway stop (when you take the elevator to Fort Washington Avenue) and from the #4 bus. Lunch is served Tuesday through Saturday from noon to 3 P.M.; dinner is served Tuesday through Sunday from 6 P.M. to 9:30 P.M. You can hear live jazz Thursday nights from 8 P.M. to 11 P.M. and savor a Sunday brunch from 11 A.M. to 4 P.M.

The main food drag in Hudson Heights is the short block of West 187th Street between Fort Washington and Pinehurst Avenues. With one exception, there's nothing particularly ethnic about them, but they offer a lot more variety for eating out than folks in this immediate area have had in years, so I'll summarize them briefly. **Bleu Evolution** (808 West 187th Street, 212-928-6006) could just as well be in Woodstock or a New England country inn with a touch of Victorian whimsy. Its setting is eccentric—the owners seem to have raided antique shops and attics to furnish the place with stuffed chairs, couches, and tables—and it's complemented by an eclectic menu that I would dub New Lower East Side, with its mixture of creative salads and Mediterranean and fusion entrées including lots of seafood, pasta, chicken, and some meat dishes. A really nice feature is the way-uptown menu price: dinner entrées range from $8 (for pasta) to $16 (for sirloin steak), so this a great place for budget-conscious eaters wanting a good meal who don't mind the trek up-uptown. By the way, Bleu Evolution has a neat little courtyard that it shares with Café Capo Verde (see below). **107 West at 187th Street** (811 West 187th Street, 212-923-3311) is an Upper Upper West Side version of a West Side Cajun favorite. **Gideon's Bakery** (810 West 187th Street, 212-927-9262) is a kosher place that has been attractively renovated and includes some seating and great traditional coffee cakes, rugalach, and fancier confections. **Café Capo Verde** (589 Fort Washington Avenue, 212-543-9888) shares the same backyard (and owners) as Bleu Evolution around the corner and serves up magnificent desserts and all sorts of coffees and teas. The setting is also eclectic Victorian—it's the type of place to finish a novel or play a quiet game of chess. **Kismat** (603 Fort Washington Avenue at 187th Street, 212-795-8633) is a very decent Indian restaurant. I can't say that it offers anything you wouldn't find in Curry Hill or Jackson Heights, but it does serve its community well just by being there. **Frank's Market** (807-809 West 187th Street) calls itself "Uptown's First Real Gourmet Market," and it is. It has a great selection of, well, everything—cheeses, meats, crackers and cakes, produce, packaged goods, dairy products, and so on—from almost around the world.

You'll find a handful of interesting places on West 181st Street, west of Fort Washington Avenue (including the area's first Starbucks). **Gruenebaum's Bakeries** (725 West 181st Street, 212-781-8813) shares the same owner as Gideon's and has been in the neighborhood for decades selling traditional kosher breads, cakes, rugalach, and cookies. What's different is a new sit-down café toward the rear of the bakery, which meets a real need in this community where there aren't enough places to simply sit and sip. **Smart Choice Russian Market** (801 West 181st Street) is a small Russian deli. Its presence alone indicates the existence of a customer base for its products, but it doesn't compare to what you'd find in Brighton Beach!

Manhattan Side Trip

Yorkville

By 1990, it was still possible to describe the Yorkville area of the Upper East Side as having a significant German, Hungarian, and other Eastern European presence. As the years have gone by, though, this heritage has slowly eroded as long-established markets and cafés have shut their doors or merged with others. A few old family businesses hang on, although some are no longer in the founding family.

So this side trip is a short and somewhat melancholy one. The type of ethnic and cultural continuity or renewal one sees in other areas is not taking place here. On the other hand, the Upper East Side has many truly extraordinary markets. To some extent, the sophisticated gourmet markets have taken the place of the local ethnic markets, providing unusual products from around the world. But the sense of rootedness that the old markets offered is practically gone from here.

Yorkville was, like many upper Manhattan neighborhoods, a rural settlement until the first train and stagecoach lines arrived in 1848 and the first mass housing was developed. Further home building followed when elevated rail lines reached Yorkville in the late 1870s. The first subway lines arrived about twenty-five years later. Among the early mass settlers were Germans, some fleeing political or religious persecution, others seeking economic opportunity. Still others, already living in New York, were seeking their way out of Kleine Deutschland—Little Germany—in what is now Tompkins Square and the East Village, for better places to raise their families. At its peak, the population of New York City's German community was 600,000.

Irish, Hungarian, Czech, and other immigrants also found homes here and eventually established fraternal organizations, religious institutions, newspapers, and other small businesses. World wars, revolutions, and economics were the key drivers for immigrant expansion; the Hungarian presence ballooned after the thwarted 1956 revolution and at one point, according to travel agent Barbara Bollok, who has headed Molnar Travel Agency in Yorkville for over thirty years, 300,000 Hungarians called New York City home. She now estimates that the number is closer to 40,000.

In the last twenty to twenty-five years, rising real estate values plus the effects of assimilation have forced some of the old establishments out of business, while others have closed because their owners retired and there was no younger generation willing to replace them.

Although it can be difficult to write about a neighborhood in the throes of so much change, Yorkville does still retain much of its early heritage and its beautiful historic architecture, and it's worth preserving.

Getting There   The #4, #5, and #6 trains go to 86th Street and Lexington Avenue. The #6, which is a local, also goes to 77th Street and Lexington Avenue. The M101, M102, and M103 buses go uptown on Third Avenue and downtown on Lexington Avenue. The M15 bus goes uptown on First Avenue and downtown on Second Avenue. Crosstown buses linking the east and west sides are the M79 along 79th Street and the M86 along 86th Street.

Markets   Two old-time markets stand out here: **Schaller & Weber** (1654 Third Avenue, 212-879-3047), which opened in the neighborhood in the 1950s, is a glistening meat market that specializes in German sausages and German imports but also has a wide range of meats and other products. (Many of its products are sold by other retailers.) I've seen cheeses from all over Scandinavia and elsewhere in Eastern Europe and their packaged products—chocolates, jams, seasonings, cookies, and more—come from all over. Schaller & Weber also has a wonderful selection of beer steins in the store window—and all, of course, are for sale. A package of assorted sliced salamis for $9.99 a pound is nice to buy. (The packages are usually a half pound or less.) These assortments give you a good sampling of what's available. **Yorkville Meat Emporium** (1560 Second Avenue) also has the names Hungarian Meat Shop and Yorkville Packing House on its sign. There once were, in fact, two such markets, but they have merged. Here you'll also find a wonderful selection of Hungarian and other Eastern European sausages but you can also buy home-baked strudel and other cakes and breads, as well as packets of crushed poppy seeds, walnuts, and almonds for your own baking. There's also a wonderful Hungarian cream cheese with paprika, onions, and caraway, as well as Hungarian syrups and other products you won't find elsewhere. **Crown Wine & Liquors** (1587 Second Avenue) is a Hungarian-owned shop that, in addition to having a mainstream inventory also has a good selection of Hungarian wines and liqueurs. **Likitsakos Market** (1174 Lexington Avenue at 80th Street) is not precisely in Yorkville, and it doesn't represent the Eastern European tradition I've been harping on; yet for the dozen or so years it has been in business it has made its mark, offering superb Greek dips, yogurts, and fresh salads as well as an overall wonderful choice of gourmet food. I like the fact that the Greek heritage of the owners gets so much attention!

Restaurants   **Heidelberg Restaurant** (1648 Second Avenue, 212-628-2332), which opened in 1939, is a traditional German place serving schnitzels (fried fingers of veal, pork, or chicken), pot roast, sausages, paprika chicken, and other specialties, with sides such as dumplings, sauerkraut, and red cabbage. It's possible to create a light meal with salads and so-called "nature schnitzel," which is a term for plain veal cutlet or assorted cold cuts. Heidelberg's $8.95 lunch special includes a German pancake or apple pancake; a ham or tuna salad platter or cold pot roast; and a side dish. The desserts are rich, and pricey: Asbach coffee (Asbach brandy and coffee topped with fresh whipped cream and chocolate shavings) will set you back $6.25. The other desserts cost less but are just as rich: a concoction called *rote gruetz* ($5.95)—raspberry, strawberry, and cherry compote topped with vanilla sauce—is just one example! **Mocca Restaurant** (1568 Second Avenue, 212-734-6470) opened around 1980 but I was sure that it was much older based on the presence of old pressed-tin ceilings, some pressed tin on the wall, and an old tile floor. My waitress explained that Mocca, which serves Hungarian food, replaced an older German place known as H&H, and that the owners didn't do any redecorating! A popular $7.95 lunch includes soup or salad (take the wonderful, hearty Hungarian soup), an entrée, which can include goulash, meat, or breaded chicken, and a Hungarian pastry for dessert. You also get delicious Hungarian bread and a beet salad with your meal. **Totonno's Pizzeria** (1544 Second Avenue, 212-327-2800) has been in Yorkville just a few years. It's a branch of the very famous Totonno's in Coney Island (see page 176), which opened its doors in 1924. Like its parent, Yorkville's Totonno's serves only whole pizzas and uses a coal-fired oven. Unlike its parent, its setting is a lot nicer and it's open every day. (Coney Island's Totonno's is only open Wednesday through Sunday.)

Bakeries, Cafés, and Desserts   **M. Rohr's House of Fine Teas** (303 East 85th Street) is a tea and coffee shop with a small café—and an insurance company in the back. As long as Rohr's has been in business (it opened in 1896) it has also shared operations with an insurance firm run by the same family. These days a big chunk of its tea and coffee business is on line, although there is seating if you want to have a cappuccino and some cookies or biscotti here. **Orwasher's Handmade Bread** (308 East 78th Street), which opened in 1916, still uses a brick oven to produce its many delicious types of bread—plain, seeded, rye, and more. Although the founding family was Jewish and the bread is kosher, the bakery is open seven days. **Elk Candy Co.** (1628 Second Avenue) was opened in 1933 by a German family, but since around 1987 it has been run by an Albanian family. Its spectacular marzipan specialties and many of its chocolates are still made in-house but the novelty chocolates that also are famous at Elk are purchased elsewhere.

Also . . .   While you're in Yorkville, you might want to check out a few local landmarks that are within a block of the shops. **Zion St. Mark's Lutheran Church** at 339 East 84th Street has been landmarked; it was built in 1888 and it's the only church that are still holds services in German. **St. Elizabeth of Hungary** (211 East 83rd Street) is an important neighborhood anchor. A couple of doors down you'll find **Hungarian Books** at 225 East 83rd Street; the store sells about a half dozen English-language Hungarian cookbooks. **Molnar Travel Agency** at 245 East 81st Street has traditional Hungarian clothing and knickknacks in its window. **Leon Lascoff Pharmacy** (1209 Lexington Avenue at 82nd Street)—one block north of Likitsakos—is always wonderful to visit. It was founded in 1899 and it's now located in the same marvelous space it first occupied in the 1930s.

Check out the shop windows showing photos of the original Lascoff preparing prescriptions and the old tools that were used to make them.

A bit off the beaten—and eaten—track, at 78th and 79th Streets between York Avenue and the FDR Drive, is an apartment complex called **City & Suburban Homes.** These landmarked apartments were developed in the early twentieth century to provide humane living space for working-class people. These nice-looking six-story walkup apartments remain moderate in rent (and hard to get into). The apartment complex with the fascinating balconies facing City & Suburban on 78th Street is called the **Cherokee Apartments.** They were originally built as part of a treatment center for tubercular patients; the balconies were meant to give people easy access to clean air.

Bronx

BELMONT
PELHAM PARKWAY AREA (LYDIG AVENUE)
CITY ISLAND

SIDE TRIPS

- *Afro-Caribbean Bronx*

- *Cambodia in the Bronx (and more!), with a Visit to Poe Cottage*

- *Morris Park*

...

Bronx Notes

Archival photographs of the Bronx show sylvan images of tree-lined boulevards with handsome apartment buildings and lush parks. For many immigrants, moving to the Bronx was a critical step up and out of "the city" to more space and clean air. The borough's layout was designed for this: the Grand Concourse Boulevard leads to many large parks and the borough has more green space per person than any of the other four.

But during the past forty years the Bronx has experienced a roller coaster of exhilarating ups and calamitous downs. Now-familiar images of neighborhood devastation—a process some attribute to middle-class flight from poorer neighborhoods when the enormous Co-op City complex opened—only expedited the process. Yet the Bronx also contains Wave Hill, one of New York City's environmental treasures, as well as the Wildlife Conservation Society (the Bronx Zoo) and the exquisite New York Botanical Gardens just north of the zoo.

Many positive changes have reshaped the Bronx in the last twenty years, many in neighborhoods that have been rebuilt after years of neglect, and they have been further strengthened by immigrants from Latin America, Africa, and Eastern Europe. If you take one of the elevated trains that goes to the Bronx—the #2, #4, #5, or #6 train—you'll see dozens, no, hundreds of new housing units that have filled in formerly empty spaces or the lots where burned-out buildings once stood. You'll see gardens and shopping centers. And you'll see new markets and restaurants revitalizing once-vacant areas. At the famous Charlotte Street site, visible at a glance from the train window between the Freeman Street and 174th Street stops, you'll see an inner-city suburb of single-family homes, some with boats in their backyards. The homeowners are South Bronxites who persevered through the bad old days and had enough faith to invest their savings in this community. Today, as the lawns and trees have grown in, they're a sight to behold.

Two Bronx neighborhoods are often featured in guidebooks: Belmont, also known as Little Italy of the Bronx, and City Island, a breath of New England just off Pelham Bay. These neighborhoods are the easiest to describe and the most obviously appealing to visitors and, yes, I've profiled them here.

But in my own wanderings, I've identified a few other neighborhoods that are interesting to visit because of the way they mirror borough dynamics. In the future, I think we'll see even more interesting developments in

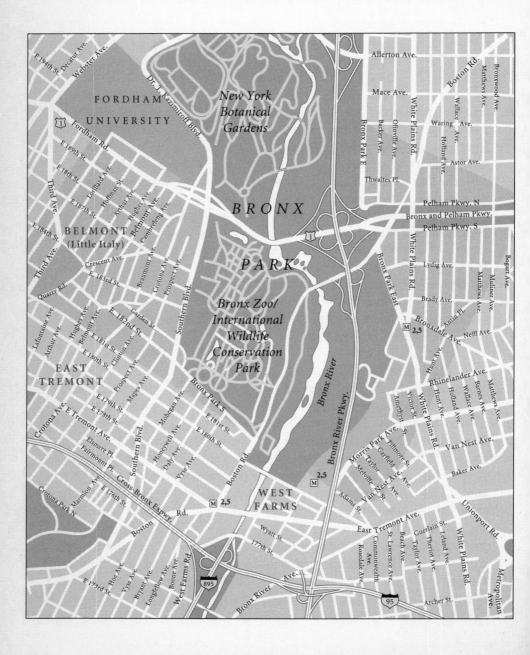

this changing borough. An emerging middle-class community of anglo-phone West Africans, many from Ghana and Nigeria, is having economic impact through the creation of small businesses including restaurants, markets, and services. They also are creating churches and other institutions. Their presence adds a wonderful new dimension of diversity to New York City and I was curious to know more myself, so I took a look around and designed a side trip to several Ghanaian places (see pages 296–297). Similarly, I created a side trip to a neighborhood with a small cluster of African and Asian markets (see pages 298–299) including one specializing in food from Cambodia because it highlights the fact that the Bronx is truly a global borough!

While researching the Bronx, I found two Web sites by former Bronx-ites who are obsessed with their birthplace. One of them, www.backtothe-bronx.com, includes a trivia quiz and a monthly magazine. Cofounder Stephen Samtur, with his wife, Susan, and Martin Jackson, has also cowritten *The Bronx: Lost, Found and Remembered* (Scarsdale, New York: Back in the Bronx, 1999). The other site, www.bronxboard.com, features a busy interactive discussion group and has links to books and videos on the Bronx. Founder Larry Bermel, a software developer married to another Bronxite (but now living in Westchester), started a Web site in 1996 to help Bronxites find old friends. Within a month it was getting 2,500 hits a day—and now it gets many thousands more. Bermel has since created similar boards for Manhattan, Brooklyn, and Queens.

Another Web site that indulges nostalgic memories of the Bronx is www.bronxview.com/memories/index.html, which provides an affectionate sampling of what it was like to grow up there in the 1940s, fifties, and sixties.

- - -

Belmont

Who *doesn't* know Arthur Avenue by now? Food lovers in New York City and beyond know it almost as a brand name—the hub of Little Italy of the Bronx, often associated with great restaurants and markets. With roots nearly a century old, Belmont, as the neighborhood is called, manages to combine old-world tradition—some family businesses date back eighty years and more—with cutting-edge marketing strategies. It now even has its own Web site.

When I first visited Belmont in the early 1980s, it was striving to stave off the decay that plagued surrounding areas. Native son Joe Cicciu, executive director of the Belmont Arthur Avenue Local Development Corporation (LDC), explained how merchants organized to save the neighborhood. The LDC was formed in 1981 to market Belmont's tourist potential and rebuild its infrastructure. Community leaders launched a new cultural center, revived the famous indoor market, and promoted links to neighborhood institutions such as the Bronx Zoo, the New York Botanical Gardens, and Fordham University. A concurrent revival of gourmet cooking and interest in eclectic cuisines has spurred even more people to check out Belmont.

But Belmont has something else that few guidebooks mention: a growing number of Albanians from Kosovo, Mexicans, and other new immigrants who are gradually transforming the texture of the residential and retail community—just as all neighborhoods evolve over time. (There's even a new mosque, which operates in an old house just two blocks north of Mt. Carmel Church and which serves a growing population of Muslims from West Africa and regions of the Middle East living in the Bronx.) Strolling through, you will see wonderful Italian cafés, markets, restaurants, and gift shops. Since the Albanians in this area have opened many shops and a number of restaurants, I've also listed some of these.

▪ History

Belmont takes its name from an estate owned by the Lorillard family that covered the area that now includes the New York Botanical Gardens and St. Barnabas Hospital. The family auctioned off the estate in 1870. In the 1880s the City of New York began laying down streets and developers built the first housing. Three streets bear the Lorillard legacy: Lorillard Place, Belmont Avenue, and Arthur Avenue, which was named for Catherine Lorillard's favorite president, Chester Alan Arthur.

Belmont's transformation into an Italian community started at the beginning of the twentieth century as Sicilian immigrants—many of them landscapers and stonemasons—flocked here to build the Bronx Zoo, the New York Botanical Gardens, the Bronx reservoir, and the Third Avenue elevated train. Our Lady of Mount Carmel Church, Belmont's religious anchor, was established in 1906.

Pushcart peddlers and small shops dominated the retail scene until 1940, when the Arthur Avenue Retail Market was created to bring the pushcarts indoors. In the 1950s and 1960s, as the people in the community became increasingly affluent, and into the 1970s, as the South Bronx spun into decline, many Belmont families joined the middle-class flight to suburbs for better schools and more space. (The construction of Co-op City, a complex of thirty-five apartment towers, hastened the fall of the South Bronx.) A core of older Italians did remain in the area.

Albanians and Yugoslavians began arriving in the 1960s and opened businesses, markets, and social clubs. As they prospered, many also moved out (but kept their businesses here) so that residentially Belmont these days is mostly Latino and West Indian, with other new groups making inroads. (For instance, the Musa Mosque, catering to a significant population of West Africans, opened in early 2002 at 633 East 189th Street on the corner of Belmont Avenue.) There are Jamaican and Mexican markets immediately beyond Belmont's Italian hub.

■ Getting Oriented

Belmont sits south of Fordham University, west of the Bronx Zoo, a few blocks east of the Grand Concourse, and north of the Cross-Bronx Expressway. St. Barnabas Hospital, one of the borough's larger health care facilities, sits southwest of the neighborhood and its employees are among the neighborhood's regular weekday lunch customers.

I've divided this tour into two parts: Arthur Avenue and East 187th Street. No mass transit plunks you in the middle of Belmont, but there are many subway and bus combinations that will take you within a few blocks. On a good day, you can get there from midtown Manhattan in forty-five minutes; on a bad day, allow yourself an hour or more. Driving is much faster—in non-rush-hour traffic!

BY SUBWAY AND BUS

The fastest route: Take the D train to Fordham Road and any eastbound bus to Arthur Avenue. Make sure the bus is *not* marked "Limited," or it will skip the stop. You're almost there when you see the White Castle on the right. At Arthur Avenue (at an Amoco gas station) turn right (south) for three long blocks to the main intersection at 187th Street.

I also recommend the two travel options listed below because they allow you to ride an elevated train and see what the Bronx looks like now!

The easiest connection: take the #2 train to Pelham Parkway and the BX12 westward bus to Arthur Avenue (marked Fordham Center or Sedgwick Avenue). Exit at the north (front) end of the subway station and walk back one short block to the bus stop at Pelham Parkway. The BX12 runs often. Make sure it's *not* marked "Limited." Arthur Avenue is the first stop after the major intersection at Southern Boulevard. (You'll see the New York Botanical Gardens on your right and the Bronx Zoo on your left.) Cross Fordham Road at Hoffman Street.

My favorite route: I prefer a combination of the #2 or #5 train and the

BX9 bus, which brings you closer to Belmont than the other options and is quite fast. Exit at the East Tremont stop. Cross Boston Road to East Tremont (there's a Montefiore Medical Group clinic on the corner) and cross again (a busy two-way street—be careful!) to a bus stop in front of a beige brick school building. The bus line starts here. Get off at Southern Boulevard and 187th Street and you're three short blocks to the first Belmont shops. To return, walk back on East 187th Street to Southern Boulevard and turn right, where you'll see the BX9 bus stop. In this direction, the bus goes directly to the East Tremont subway stop. It's the last stop on the line, so you don't have to think too hard. Turn right and go upstairs or *carefully* cross Boston Road (where the bus stops) and you'll find an elevator to the tollbooth.

BY CAR

From the east or west take the Bruckner Expressway or Cross-Bronx Expressway to the Bronx River Parkway. Head north to Exit 7W (Fordham Road), go under the overpass, and make your first left onto Arthur Avenue. From the north take the Sprain Brook or Bronx River Parkway south to Fordham Road, go under the overpass, and make your first left onto Arthur Avenue. Parking can be tricky on weekends. There's a municipal lot located between Arthur Avenue and Hoffman Street just south of 186th Street. Some restaurants have valet parking.

Many car services operate in the Bronx and you usually can hail one near your subway stop to go directly to Belmont. Prices are $4 to $6, but always ask the driver first. In Belmont, Flash car service can pick you up quickly with a call to 718-365-8888. Many restaurants use this service.

BY TRAIN

Belmont is convenient to any Metro-North train that stops at Fordham. On exiting, cross Fordham Road and take any eastbound bus, or walk; it's just two bus stops away.

▪ Tips for Touring

- ▪ Saturdays in Belmont are very busy—avoid driving if possible, or go early. Best overall shopping times are early in the week and before lunch.
- ▪ If you're on a budget but want a great meal, check out the delis on 187th Street, which have great prepared dishes. You can take a terrific picnic to the New York Botanical Gardens.

- From mid-July through mid-August many shops close for vacation. If you have your heart set on a particular place, call ahead to make sure it's open!
- Combine your visit to Belmont with either the Bronx Zoo (718-367-1010; www.wcs.org; free on Wednesday) or the New York Botanical Gardens (718-817-8700; www.nybg.org).

■ ■ ■

Arthur Avenue

One of the challenges of trying to cover Belmont is that there are so many great places packed into a small area. If you visit any that I missed, send me your impressions.

Restaurants   Since most of my visits were at lunchtime, I often ordered a couple of appetizers and took an entrée home for supper so I could taste several dishes per place. I didn't order wine. Some restaurants will serve appetizer-size pastas for those who might not want a full entrée. **Ann & Tony's** (2407 Arthur Avenue, 718-933-1469) specializes in Neapolitan cuisine. I enjoyed both the delicious eggplant rollatini appetizer (served with a delicious *pane di campana*—country bread) and ravioli entrée, and also the ambiance: recorded classical guitar set the tone I needed that day. Service was prompt and friendly. The bill came to $22. You get a 10% discount if you're coming from or going to a Yankees game—show your ticket stub. **Dominick's** (2335 Arthur Avenue, 718-733-2807; closed Tuesday) retains its reputation as a menu-less, family-style restaurant that offers several set dishes on a given day, but they will accommodate your tastes if they have the ingredients on hand. One noon I stopped in and asked if they had anything "light." "Water," said the host. I went elsewhere. At **Pasquale's Rigoletto** (2311 Arthur Avenue, 718-365-6644), my waiter bore an eerie resemblance to Massimo Troisi, the (deceased) star of *Il Postino*. (I kept waiting for him to quote Neruda.) The place is busy, pretty, and bright, with large windows looking onto Arthur Avenue and dressed-up waiters, but it's casual dress for customers. I was quickly seated and almost immediately a waiter brought a plate with *bruschetta* and a fantastic Argentinian *reggianati* cheese (sold at Mike's Deli in the Arthur Avenue Retail Market). I almost made a meal of it, as my empty dish was quickly replenished. Seeing that the entrées at nearby tables were enormous, I opted for two appetizers, *mozzarella caporese* (a salad of mozzarella, tomatoes, and sweet red peppers) and a stuffed artichoke special (which frankly I found less special than the mozzarella salad). Between the appetizers and the bread and cheese, I was quite full, but I stayed for an espresso with amaretto. My bill for the appetizers, a soda, and coffee came to about $24. Across the street, I saw tour groups line up for **Mario's** (2342 Arthur Avenue, 718-542-1188) and I tried it myself a few days later. Over eighty years old, Mario's sustains a great reputation, but my experience was mixed. Large and impersonal, its service seemed dour, although my pasta in Napolitana sauce ($12) was fresh and accomplished and I'm told they'll make pizzas on request even though they're not on the menu. The desserts looked tired. The regular menu at **Emilia's** (2331 Arthur Avenue, 718-367-5915; closed Monday), a warm and intimate place, has a nice selection of chicken, veal, and pasta entrées, but I opted for one of the daily specials. (The lunch special—pasta and salad or a meat or fish entrée with one vegetable—is just $9.95. Dinner specials are a few dollars more.) The arugula and ricotta ravioli with walnut sauce and the linguini in pesto with shrimp and sun-dried tomatoes were delicious.

Eateries   As you walk down Arthur Avenue from Fordham Road, the first eatery you'll see is **Tony & Tina's** (2477 Arthur Avenue), a pizzeria. In large neon letters, you'll also see the word "burek." Tony & Tina's is Albanian, and in addition to pizza, they make *bureks*—pastries stuffed with spinach, cheese, or meat (similar to the *bourekas* you'll find in shops selling Mediterranean food). The pizzas here are just okay. **Giovanni's** (2343 Arthur Avenue, 718-933-4141) also owned by Albanians, is a full-fledged restaurant but more informal than the others. It's popular for its brick oven pizza. The considerable menu and child-friendliness are major draws (if you have kids). It's one of few Belmont eateries open seven days.

Bakeries   **Addeo Bakers** (2352 Arthur Avenue, 718-367-8316) specializes in Italian standards—lard breads, semolina breads, *pane di casa,* breadsticks, and biscotti, although it also touts its "4-way bread": no salt, no sugar, no fat, and added fiber (it's found next to the lard loaves). Addeo's main shop is one block away at 2372 Hughes Avenue. **Madonia Brothers** (2348 Arthur Avenue, 718-295-5573) has taken a more creative twist. Peter Madonia took over the store in 1988 after his brother, Mario, died. This represented an abrupt career change—Peter was trained as an urban planner and was then first deputy fire commissioner in the administration of New York City's Mayor Edward Koch. When we met in 2000, he described the satisfaction of being his own boss in a place he knows well. Over time he has expanded the business, recruited a head baker, and diversified his products. Rye bread and Jewish-style challah didn't sell, but he's had success with Mexican-inspired jalapeño cheese bread and Cajun-spiced-bread. Two absolute winners are Madonia's olive bread, which swims in olives, and the fenugreek-raisin bread, which is so savory that you don't need to embellish it to make it tastier. In 2002 Peter Madonia returned to public life as chief of staff for New York City's newly elected mayor, Michael Bloomberg.

Markets   Teitel Brothers (2372 Arthur Avenue, 718-733-9400) opened in 1915 and this bustling grocery is now owned by the founders' grandsons, Gil and Ben, with great-grandson Eddie on board. How did Austrian Jews end up in this Italian neighborhood? "They took the wrong turn," said Gil. On the contrary, they took the right turn: the packed store thrives on a huge turnover of cheeses, vinegars, high-end olive oils, syrups, legumes, and appetizing goods, cookies, and other imports. A three-year-old Parmesan cheese that would sell for almost $13 a pound elsewhere costs $7 here. The company also has a growing mail-order and Web-based business. Try to go during the week and early in the day if you want to avoid the crowds. Smartly, they have a lot of folks behind the counter, so turnover is fast.

Belmont's two seafood markets are **Randazzo's** (2327 Arthur Avenue, 718-367-4139) and **Cosenza's** (2354 Arthur Avenue, 718-364-8510). Both have clam bars ($4 a half dozen) and both are closed Mondays. Randazzo's has been redone and currently is spiffier than Cosenza's. Brothers Frank and Joe Randazzo, now in their forties, are the third generation to run it. Specialties include *alici* (Italian anchovies), *latrigglia* (a bony red snapper–like fish preferred by Greek, French, and Spanish cooks), and *seppia* (a type of calamari). Catering to more sophisticated customers, Randazzo's markets a tuna as sushi quality and also offers a Cajun-spiced fish.

If you love meat, you'll love Belmont! Its many pork stores and butchers prepare sausage in-house. You'll find almost everything at bustling **Biancardi** (2350 Arthur Avenue, 718-733-4058) with its large selection of Italian specialties and some unusual products (such as quail and chicken sausage with broccoli rabe) plus kebabs ready for grilling and stuffed chicken breast. (Note that there is rabbit and goat in the store window; if you're vegetarian, stay away! And if you aren't, the sight of these might make you one.) Biancardi also sells cheeses and hot sauces.

Calandra's Cheese (2314 Arthur Avenue, 718-365-7572), an old-timer, has sold homemade mozzarella, ricotta, and other fresh cheeses for decades. The founders are for the most part retired to their home (and dairy) in Nazareth, Pennsylvania, leaving management and cheese preparation to the Alcocer family, originally from Bolivia. Current manager Maria Alcocer carves mozzarella elephants, pigs, and giraffes in her spare time, an old folkloric tradition. (You also can see a mozzarella menagerie at Di Palo's Fine Foods at 200 Grand Street in Manhattan's Little Italy; see pages 253–254).

PUMPKIN CHEESECAKE

Courtesy of Calandra Cheese in Belmont, Bronx

Yield: One 8" cake

1 1/2 pounds ricotta cheese
2 eggs, separated (set aside the whites)
1 cup sugar
1 heaping teaspoon cinnamon
1 1/2 cups mashed pumpkin
1 teaspoon baking powder
1 teaspoon vanilla
1/2 teaspoon allspice

1. Preheat the oven to 350°F.
2. Using an electric mixer, beat all the ingredients together except the egg whites.
3. When well blended, fold in the egg whites.
4. Pour the batter into a greased 8" springform pan and bake for 1 hour, or until center appears firm.
5. Turn the oven off and leave the cake in the oven for another hour.

• • •

Arthur Avenue Retail Market

Joe Libertore still sells plants and seeds at the entrance of the **Arthur Avenue Retail Market** (2344 Arthur Avenue) as he has done since 1936, when he was seventeen. In 1940 he was among dozens of pushcart peddlers moved indoors by the LaGuardia administration.

Starting in the 1960s the market went into slow decline. One of the key reasons, Joe Cicciu of the Belmont Arthur Avenue LDC told me, was the tension between area shop owners and the market merchants, whose low monthly fees enabled them to sell their products for less than the individual stores. Some stall-owners themselves—and then shoppers—deserted the market and it began to look decrepit. In the early 1980s an association of stall-owners organized to redevelop the market, and a revamped market, with new lighting and an updated interior and a new exterior was dedicated in 1983. The market now is well maintained and it is an important engine for the local economy.

On a busy day the market can be packed and you may hear banter in Italian. If you dislike crowds, go early in the week and early in the day, when it is less crowded. You'll find great prices and quality on produce and other products here.

Sit-Down Meals   Informal sit-down meals are available at two places. The popular **Café al Mercato** serves salads, pastas, and frittatas, as well as combination sandwiches with amusing names such as "Bronx Tail" (with mortadella, provolone, and mozzarella) and "The Right Stuff" (grilled vegetables in balsamic vinegar). **Mike's Deli** (718-295-5033) is a bustling place with an earthy appearance that belies its sophisticated inventory. They have a huge assortment of sandwiches, stuffed breads, salads, pasta, and grilled specialties, not to mention meats, cheeses, and other ingredients that I keep finding òn each additional visit. There are several tables for lunch, which often are crowded. You can buy a very nice cookbook here called *Festa del Giardino* by Sally Maraventano (Stony Brook, New York: Center for Italian Studies, State University of New York at Stony Brook, 1999), who grew up in Belmont; it has recipes for vegetarian pastas, sauces, salads, and soups.

Mount Carmel Gourmet Foods (718-933-2295) complements Mike's Deli, with an excellent selection of packaged Italian products and some prepared products such as an outstanding homemade black olive paste. A specialty is balsamic vinegar from Modena, where the owners are from. There's a gorgeous selection of olive oils—the bottles alone are sensational and make nice gifts. The shop sells baskets and will help you put together gift baskets.

Italian cookware isn't missing at the market! Go to **Nick's Place,** to the right of the main entrance, for a full range of serving bowls and utensils that Nick Marchese sells. He covers just about every budget from, inexpensive inventory from China and Korea to quality merchandise from Italy and elsewhere in Europe.

■ ■ ■

East 187th Street

Along this east–west boulevard in Belmont you'll find an amazing number of shops packed into a few blocks, including pastry shops, gift shops, and the street's centerpiece, Our Lady of Mt. Carmel Church.

Restaurants   **Carmela's** (620 East 187th Street), which shares owners with Egidio's pastry shop (see page 282), is more like a bistro, serving salads and sandwiches and chicken, fish, and veal entrées. Less expensive than the other restaurants, it's good for a quick and solid meal but has few of the extra touches that add to the appeal (and price) of the others.

Eateries   Full Moon (600 East 187th Street, 718-584-3451; closed Sundays) is a basic, busy pizzeria on Belmont's best corner, but I believe we can anticipate an expansion since the owners have sold the restaurant next door and will expand the pizzeria into a larger adjacent space on the other side along Arthur Avenue.

Cafés   Although there are several on 187th Street, I'm drawn to two: **Di Lillo** (606 East 187th Street, 718-367-8198) and **Egidio** (620 East 187th Street) for a simple reason—they have tables and serve cappuccino and espresso in addition to terrific cannoli, cheesecake, and other cream-laden pastries. Both are neighborhood old-timers and sell Italian gelato in season.

Bakeries   The editor of an Italian food magazine and other foodies I know call **Terranova** (691 East 187th Street, 718-367-6985) Belmont's most authentic Italian bakery, citing its crusty breads, focaccia, and *taralli*. There's a modest selection of cookies and many imports, as well as home-baked products, but go there for the bread! On a weekday, you might even get to see the huge baking area in the back with bread dough on wooden shelves slowly rising before being baked.

Markets   There are several delis on the street, but I particularly like **Tino's** at 609 East 187th Street (I've tried their ziti and roasted sweet and hot peppers) and **Joe's** (685 East 187th Street). Both have excellent prepared foods. Tino's has one table with two chairs outside the store, but these places are great if you *don't* have time for a sit-down meal but do want excellent, inexpensive dishes that are ready to go.

Borgatti (632 East 187th Street, 718-367-3799; open Tuesday through Saturday from 9 A.M. to 6 P.M., Sunday from 8 A.M. to 1 P.M.; closed Mondays) is more than a store; it's also a gathering place to share gossip and good news. I was stunned to learn that Mario Borgatti, spry, warm, and funny, is in his mid-eighties. He and his brother, Larry, some years younger, are there most days, as are various Borgatti offspring and friends who make and sell the flat egg noodles and ravioli that are the store's specialty. (The third generation—Mario's son, Chris, and his wife, Karen—have taken on much of the daily responsibilities, and if you catch Chris when things aren't too hectic he might demonstrate how the dough is mixed, processed, and made into different widths of pasta.) Check out the domestic and imported sauces including Rao's, Sclafani, and Cucina Antica.

The **Amalfi** produce stand (576 East 187th Street) will make you think that either you're in an Italian village or you're in Belmont in the 1950s, except that they now stock jalapeño peppers and other produce for the many Mexicans who now live in Belmont. Check out the squash flowers, small white eggplants, cherry peppers, and other produce used in traditional Italian recipes.

Mt. Carmel Wine & Spirits (612 East 187th Street, 718-367-7833) has been in Belmont since 1935 and offers one of New York's largest selections of Italian wines, including sixty chiantis. Raymond Polanco, who bought the store in 1996 when the previous owner retired, stocks specialties such as Bertani Amarone (bottles are $100 to $300), sweet *recioto* wines, a large selection of *grappas* (including a glass chess set with pieces filled with *grappa*—it's yours for $1,300), and Amari bitters. They also sell a variety of lemon-flavored liqueurs such as a kosher liqueur made from etrog, a cousin of the lemon used in the Jewish Sukkot ceremony, which Polanco started buying at a customer's request. The display is beautiful to behold. On Saturday afternoons Polanco holds wine tastings with Madonia's bread and Calandra's cheese (and sometimes cheese from **La Casa della Mozzarella,** 604 East 187th Street, 718-364-3967).

GRANDMA'S PASTA PISELLI CON PANCETTA

Courtesy of Filomena de Palma of Borgatti in Belmont, Bronx

½ cup extra-virgin olive oil
1 medium yellow onion, chopped
¼ pound sliced pancetta
2 cans small sweet peas
2 cups water
1 pound papardella pasta (pasta noodles cut 1" wide)
Salt and ground pepper to taste
Grated Parmesan cheese
Fresh basil leaves (4 to 5 for each serving)

1. In a large saucepan heat the olive oil over medium heat and add the onion. Cook until the onion is translucent.
2. Add the pancetta, reduce the heat to low, and cook 3 to 4 minutes.
3. Add the peas and water. Raise the heat to medium and cook for 20 minutes, stirring occasionally.
4. Boil the pasta in salted water until *al dente* (Borgatti's pasta takes 4 minutes).
5. Drain the pasta in a colander, transfer it to a serving bowl, and toss with the pancetta sauce. Serve with a garnish of pepper, Parmesan, and basil.

Coffee and Gifts   Follow the aroma of freshly-ground coffee and you'll land at **Cerini's** (662 East 187th Street), which sells coffee and everything you need to make and drink it. A fun place to visit is **Capri Universal** (617 East 187th Street), an Italian gift and kitchenware emporium with goods ranging from tchotchkes of questionable taste to fine imported bread-boards, coffee makers, dishes, and decorative items. Check out the CDs, including an anthology of "Mob Hits." In addition to religious items at the **Catholic Goods Center** (630 East 187th Street), you'll find the *From the Monastery* cookbook series by Brother Victor-Antoine D'Avila-Latourette (New York: HarperCollins, 1989), which offers gorgeous recipes featuring ingredients you'll find in the neighborhood. The books are great for vegetarians and cooks looking for something different.

■ And Around the Corner . . .

One of Belmont's best restaurants is on neither Arthur Avenue nor East 187th Street. You'll have to walk two blocks east along 186th Street to find **Roberto's Restaurant** (632 East 186th Street, 718-733-9503; closed Monday), where Belmont Avenue meets Crescent Street. From the outside I'd often wondered if the place was even open. Finally going in one day, I found that it *was* open and I felt as though I'd just stepped into an Italian village eatery. It was my biggest surprise in Belmont, but apparently I'm a latecomer to this delight. Opened in 1992 by Roberto Paciello, from Salerno, Roberto's has a gorgeous menu that offers northern and southern cuisine and Paciello's interpretation of Italian nouvelle cuisine. All pastas are homemade and the servings are big and gorgeous—and are meant to be shared. (Roberto's doesn't serve half-sizes, so don't bother asking for one!) There are also many chicken, veal, beef, and seafood entrées. I had a delicious pasta with truffle sauce, shrimp, and scallops and a plate of "grandmother's cheesecake," made with ricotta cheese and dried fruit. Roberto recommends the pasta: "Anyone can make veal and chicken," he said, but "not anyone can make good pasta." I spent more than $25 for lunch (without wine)—a bit pricey for a nosher, I thought, until I remembered that my serving was really for two. The surroundings and service are warm and solicitous (Ann & Tony's offers a close equivalent)—and on weekends folks line up to get in. In 2002 Roberto's added outdoor seating to accommodate the demand.

Also in 2002, **Café Maggiolino** (2374 Belmont Avenue) opened across the street from Roberto's, serving coffee, tea, and alcohol, sweet cold beverages, and desserts including Bindi pastries from Italy. Both Roberto's and the new café face a three-way intersection creating something like a plaza. The café has ample outdoor seating. (The owner told me that nearly half of his weekend patrons come after eating at Roberto's.) The two places are beautifully complementary and together provide the feel of a miniature Italian piazza. It's interesting to note how one place can make such a difference—but it does, adding real new charm to this part of Belmont.

▪ Cultural Highlights

Our Lady of Mt. Carmel Church at 619 East 187th Street was established explicitly to reach out to Belmont's Italian community. It opened in a storefront in 1906, and the lower church was built in 1907, the upper church in 1917. Priests from Mt. Carmel used to go to Ellis Island to bring new arrivals to the neighborhood.

At its height, from the 1940s to 1960s, Monsignor John Ruvo told me Belmont had 40,000 residents of Italian origin and Mt. Carmel held nineteen masses each Sunday, spread out in various spaces. Nowadays, he says, there are about 5,000 Italians in the area. Although Mt. Carmel still caters to Italian Catholics and has members on Long Island and in Westchester, many members are Spanish-speaking and some newer members are from African countries including Nigeria, Ghana, and Uganda. (The parochial school students mirror the membership.) The church is busy the second Sunday of the month with baptisms in Spanish, but baptisms in Italian, held the fourth Sunday, are rare.

Italian-centered celebrations remain important and the church sponsors annual feasts to honor St. Anthony and Our Lady of Mt. Carmel.

• • •

Other Faces of Belmont

"Little Albania"

If there were such a thing as a Little Albania in New York City, the cluster of Albanian markets, cafés, and social clubs in Belmont is it. Walking in the area you'll see the Kosova Photo studio, as well as a travel agency, a printing company, and other shops that cater to Albanians. Lojom, a discount store on Arthur Avenue, and Giovanni's Pizzeria are Albanian-owned.

Albanians have been immigrating steadily to the United States since the end of World War II, but their numbers have ballooned after each of the periodic crises in the Balkans, most notably within the last few years as violence in Kosovo province escalated. Mt. Carmel Church has helped to house and clothe some Kosovo refugees.

Because of Albania's proximity to Italy, many Albanians grew up speaking Italian, and in Belmont many Albanians work in the Italian markets, restaurants, and other shops. They have also opened many of their own in various neighborhoods of the north Bronx including the Pelham Parkway area (see pages 287–289) and Norwood (not profiled in this book).

Several Albanian restaurant-cafés now operate in Belmont. They include **Drini Café-Restaurant** (2328 Arthur Avenue, 718-367-3917), which has an English-language menu **Gurra Café** (2325 Arthur Avenue) across the street, and **Restaurant Shqipitar** (660 East 187th Street). Albanian cuisine is meat based—heavy on steak, veal, chicken, sausage, and goulash—but usually includes some pasta dishes, too. Don't be surprised if you find a lot of smoking—this is a culture in which it's pretty much entrenched (among men—and you won't see many Albanian women eating out). Several Albanian markets specialize in food products and other goods from the Balkans including CDs and videos, newspapers, and greeting cards. These include **Kosova Commerce Corp.** (2326 Arthur Avenue), **Briska Grocery** (2333 Arthur Avenue), **Mergimtari** (565 East 187th Street), and **Scalinada** (667 East 187th Street). You'll find interesting sweets, preserves, juices, and syrups from the Balkan region and elsewhere in Eastern Europe.

▪ Virtual Belmont

Belmont's merchants, led by businessman Lou Izzo, have created a Web site for the entire retail community: www.arthuravenuebronx.com. Considering the push to increase tourism here, this is no surprise.

What *has* been a surprise, says Izzo (whose son-in-law designed the site), is the traffic: 30,000 hits a month, including 1,200 for its recipes and 2,000 to its message board. The reason Izzo didn't register the site as ArthurAvenue.com is that Mike's Deli, based in the Arthur Avenue Retail Market, beat him to it.

Local businesses such as Teitel Brothers and Mt. Carmel Liquors report significant mail order and Web business.

▪ Arthur Avenue on Film

Keep alert for a documentary called *Arthur Avenue—from Generation to Generation,* which tracks several generations of families that maintain Arthur Avenue's traditions.

Richard Picker made the film for home viewing with support from the

National Italian American Foundation. Mario Borgatti and Mike Greco are among the old guard interviewed, while Peter Madonia and Sal Biancardi are forty-something members of the younger generation who returned to Belmont after pursuing careers elsewhere (Madonia in city government, Biancardi on Wall Street).

For details, call FilmRite at 914-946-5262 or send an e-mail to richard@filmrite.com. You can also write to the FilmRite Entertainment Group, 399 Knollwood Road, White Plains, New York 10603. The fifty-eight-minute video costs $19.95; add $3.99 for shipping and handling.

Belmont also has a cultural past: Dion DiMucci of Dion & the Belmonts grew up here. Joe Pesci was "discovered" in a local restaurant, and actor Chazz Palmienteri is a native son. (But his movie *A Bronx Tale* was decried as inaccurate and demeaning by several folks I talked to.)

■ The August Festival

See Nero in the flesh! And Christopher Columbus, Lucrezia Borgia, and Leonardo (da Vinci) himself! Since 1997 merchants in Belmont have hosted the annual **Ferragosto**—August—**Festival,** modeled after a Roman harvest festival that dates back to 300 B.C. Originally organized by the Belmont Italian American Playhouse, a theater group that closed in 2001, Ferragosto uses actors to portray key personalities from Roman and Italian history. It's a lot of fun. You'll see them stroll through the neighborhood as local vendors offer product samples, and you'll enjoy Italian-style vaudeville, opera, puppet shows, and a thirty-piece mandolin and guitar band. Local hero "Uncle" Floyd Vivino—also known as the Italian Soupy Sales—is the host. Ferragosto draws thousands of people each year. Check the Web site, www.arthuravenuebronx.com for information on this and other events related to Belmont.

■ ■ ■

Pelham Parkway Area/Lydig Avenue

"Fifteen years ago there were ten, maybe fifteen kosher stores here," said Harvey Starr, owner of H. Starr & Son at 732 Lydig Avenue, when I interviewed him for *NoshNews*. The store had then been in the area for more than thirty years. "Now there are just three." "These days," added his wife, Judy, who has worked with him here for more than a dozen years, "the customers are mostly elderly and don't bring their kids or grandchildren"—

who live elsewhere. That's one side to the Lydig Avenue neighborhood south of Pelham Parkway.

The other side is the new: the influx of immigrants from Albania, Russia, the Caribbean, and East and Southeast Asia, who have made this small Bronx enclave a true melting pot. Twenty years ago, when I began scouting neighborhoods for Hungry Pedalers Gourmet Bicycle Tours, I was fascinated by the old-world atmosphere of Lydig Avenue. It felt like a shtetl in New York City. Today, the old world strikes a fragile balance with the new, yet the neighborhood still has the air of a village where people of many backgrounds interact. On one of my visits to Starr's, the only customers were a Muslim family—a mother with three children, the only children I've seen there—buying kosher meat because it's prepared according to the Muslim halal requirements.

This side trip to Lydig Avenue highlights how a small but dynamic neighborhood can support a myriad of small businesses. I find this area particularly interesting for two reasons. First, the Pelham Parkway area has a rich history. The Bronx and Pelham Parkway (its original name, now never used) was one of the first of a series of tree-lined parkways in the Bronx designed to link the borough's many parks. Completed in 1911, it was located in an area of estates; inadequate transport and housing made it difficult for most city dwellers to get to it. In 1912 the Pelham Parkway station was added to the existing railroad network and soon the estates were being auctioned off to developers; working-class families would flock to the new apartment buildings that had sprouted all over. By the 1950s and 1960s the area was primarily a Jewish and Italian middle-class community (with a critical mass of Italian families living further east, in Williamsbridge and Morris Park).

In addition to the history, I'm fascinated with how rapidly the Pelham Parkway area is changing. In the early 1980s the neighborhood still had many Jewish families and kosher eateries, but Russians were becoming a significant presence as well. By the time I wrote about Lydig Avenue for *NoshNews* in 1999 just a handful of kosher places remained, serving mostly elderly customers. Although several Russian stores are still there, a new wave of immigrants from the Balkans appears to be supplanting many of the older shop owners, and a growing number of markets and bakeries are now owned by Albanians, who also own shops in the neighborhoods just north of Pelham Parkway. In addition, new Asian shops appear to be making inroads.

If you can't justify going to this place on its own because it occupies such a small area, you can combine it with a visit to the Bronx Zoo, just a ten minute walk away, or the New York Botanical Gardens, which can be reached quickly by car or bus. I recommend that you use your visit to put together a great picnic lunch or go shopping; despite the availability of great food, local eateries are rather unexciting.

▪ Getting Oriented

The tour covers just over three blocks. White Plains Road is the main commercial artery.

BY SUBWAY

Take the #2 or #5 train to the Pelham Parkway stop. Get on the last (rear) car. You'll see a down escalator if you exit on the downtown side. If you walk a bit north, you'll come to Pelham Parkway itself, a busy boulevard with two three-lane roads separated by a wide, tree-filled grassy area and service roads in each direction. The walk to Lydig Avenue is one long block south. Turn left (east) at Lydig.

BY CAR

From the Cross-Bronx Expressway, head north on the Bronx River Parkway and turn east onto Pelham Parkway. Lydig Avenue is one block south of Pelham Parkway. You'll have to find parking on area streets; I'm aware of no local lots.

BY TRAIN

Take the Metro-North train to Fordham Road and then catch the BX12 bus due east. Ask the driver to stop at White Plains Road.

You can easily integrate your tour here with a visit to the Bronx Zoo, a short, easy walk from Pelham Parkway or Lydig Avenue. From Pelham Parkway, turn west and head down Boston Road. You'll soon see signs leading to the Bronxdale entrance to the zoo. You can also walk from Lydig Avenue: head west instead of east (the direction toward the shops) until it ends at Bronx Park East. Cross the street to the park and follow the path around the Ben Abrams playground. As you follow the path, you'll see the zoo entrance. For more information, including driving directions, call 718-367-1010 or check www.Bronxzoo.com.

. . .

Lydig Avenue

All but one shop profiled here is on Lydig Avenue east of White Plains Road, and all but one of these is on the south side of Lydig Avenue. It's not a busy street overall, but when you cross, do be careful.

White Plains Road to Cruger Avenue is a bit dull. A bland bakery is followed by **710 International Buffet** (710 Lydig Avenue), a fast-food Tex-Chinese place, where you can get burritos, tacos, and diced chicken with peanuts and other Chinese dishes, as well as a salad bar. But clean your plate: the restaurant will assess a 20% surcharge if you leave salad bar selections behind. At 720 Lydig Avenue you'll find the attractive **European Meat Market,** an Albanian-owned place that specializes in products from Eastern Europe, particularly the Balkans, so you'll see smoked meats, poultry, cheese, chocolates, preserves, soup mixes, and other packaged goods from countries including Slovenia, Macedonia, Croatia, and Poland. The butcher is crowded into the back area. Sarajevo Delight, the Slavic version of Turkish Delight, is an interesting product. You can also buy Albanian audiotapes here. (I purchased one of Albanian wedding music.)

Cross Cruger Avenue and you'll soon come to **H. Starr & Son** (732 Lydig Avenue, 718-892-5355). Although it's the area's last kosher butcher, most sales these days are for the traditional Eastern European specialties Harvey Starr and an assistant prepare Tuesday through Friday, which include stuffed cabbage, noodle pudding, potato *latkes,* mushroom barley soup, and other ready-to-eat dishes. Starr does lots of deliveries, which is a big favor for his loyal customers who aren't as mobile as they used to be. "We know most of our customers by name," Judy Starr told me, "and we see them all the time. So if someone doesn't show up one week, I write it down and then call." (Younger Orthodox families generally want glatt kosher meat, which the Starrs don't sell, so they usually go to Riverdale, in the west Bronx, for it.) **Premier Food European Delicatessen** (738 Lydig Avenue, 718-829-3760) is a lovely Russian place selling, literally, soup to nuts, Eastern European style (with a big meat counter in between). You'll find chicken, beef, and veal *vareniki* (a Russian version of ravioli); an amazing selection of Russian-style breads; Russian soft drinks (*kvas,* apple soda, and others); cheeses and blintzes (including the Red Square brand); plus meat, oozy pastries, preserves, and chocolate. It helps to speak Russian here! **D&L Kosher Food & Bakery** (746 Lydig Avenue, 718-239-5455), four doors down, is a stark, somewhat sad place with three tables and curt service. Come for the kasha knishes and the other traditional Ashkenazic kosher specialties. Next door, at the corner of Holland Street, is **White Sails Fish Market** (748 Lydig Avenue). It's operated by an Italian-American family and has been in the neighborhood for over forty years. They sell shrimp and crab, but there's a kosher section, too.

Cross Lydig Avenue on this block and you'll see **Asian Market** (737 Lydig Avenue), which at first glance seems like an anomaly here. It opened in early 2002 in a cramped space; its shelves are chock full of products from Vietnam, Thailand, China, and the Philippines, and other East and Southeast Asian countries. I saw containers of hard-to-find fresh lemon-grass as well as cans of basil seed drink with honey, a popular Thai bever-age that I think might catch on in the United States!

Sadly, one of my favorite Lydig Avenue stores, Jack's Kosher Dairy, which was on the same block, is no longer in business. I went there as much to take in the aroma of herring and pickles—the Jewish girl's equivalent to Proust's madeleines—as to buy their delicious kosher rugalach and fresh pot cheese. Jack's was managed by a Russian fellow named Abe who ran the place for nearly twenty years. I miss it!

Crossing Holland Avenue, on the south side of the street you'll see a cluster of Albanian-owned businesses including a social club, a real estate agency, and a travel agency. **Dkakjini Burek** (758 Lydig Avenue) is the name of a small café that sells *bureks* (phyllo pastry stuffed with meat, cheese, or potato—very similar to the *bourekas* sold in Sephardic markets). They're just $3 each, and you can chase them with a cup of cappuccino or a soft drink. This place seems geared for Albanian-speaking customers but they won't turn you away, and a good *burek* can keep you going for a while. A few doors down you'll find **Gina's Bakery** (766 Lydig Avenue, 718-792-4037). Although the sign says it's Italian the owners are Albanian, and their breads come from a bakery they own in Norwood, a neighborhood west of the Botanical Gardens.

■ Picnic Sites and Parks

A wide, grassy, tree-filled expanse separates the two sides of Pelham Park-way; it's a natural park that is often crowded with families on weekends. **Bronx Park** also offers a nice setting for a picnic.

■ ■ ■

City Island

Who said there was a New England fishing village in "Da Bronx"? But just past Pelham Bay Park and over a drawbridge you'll find New York City's own City Island, a collection of mostly prewar single-family homes (most

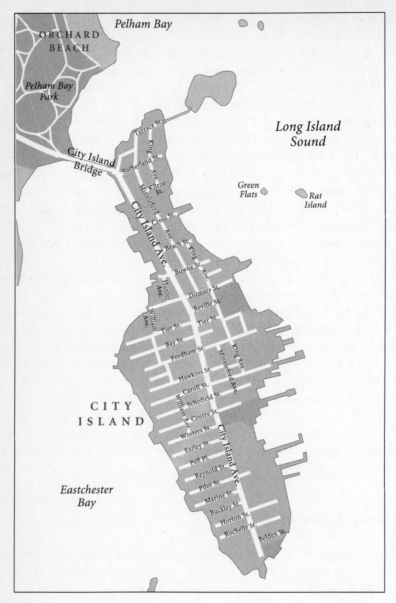

of cottage proportions) surrounded by boats and with spectacular views of the Long Island Sound. The island has been drawing seafood mavens for years, along with folks wanting a change from the rough and tough city without actually having to leave it. Rich in nautical history, City Island is one of New York City's gems. My only caveat is that traffic (and yes, noise) can get ridiculous in summer; you would do well to consider a weekend visit in the spring or fall, when many restaurants are open but the crowds aren't there. (Quite a few restaurants are open year-round, too; call to check.)

■ History

Known as Minnewits by the Siwanoy Indians who first lived there, and then as Minneford Island by the British settlers who came in 1685, it was renamed City Island in 1761 after it was purchased by one Benjamin Palmer. Fishing and clamming became a source of income, as did salt refining. City Island was part of Westchester County until a local referendum in 1896 joined it to New York City. It was a shipbuilding and yachting center during the eighteenth and nineteenth centuries and a parking lot for the yachts owned by many financiers and industrialists. In the twentieth century, during wartime, it became the site for building submarine chasers and military patrol boats, landing crafts, and mine sweepers. After the war, local yacht builders won fame for building several prize-winning yachts that defended the Americas Cup. Although the last boatyard closed in 1982, yacht clubs, sailing schools, marinas, and fishing boats remain an attraction today, as do sail makers and marine supply and repair shops—along with restaurants and antique shops. There's also a very good nautical museum, open Sunday afternoons only (pages 295–296). There's no public beach.

■ Getting Oriented

BY MASS TRANSIT

You will need to catch the BX29 bus marked City Island. It makes a loop between the island and Pelham Bay, which can be reached in several ways. The easiest is by taking the #6 subway (from the east side of Manhattan) to the last stop, Pelham Bay Park, where you can make the connection. From the West Side of Manhattan it's a little trickier; you will need to take a subway and then two buses. You can take the D train to Fordham Road or the #2 train to Pelham Parkway and catch the BX12 bus due east (the bus runs on Fordham Road for the D train and along Pelham Parkway for the #2); confirm with the driver that it stops at Pelham Bay Park, where you can connect to the BX29. During the summer, some BX12 buses go straight to City Island, but make sure that's how the bus is marked because many other summer BX12 buses head to Orchard Beach.

BY CAR

Take Route 95 North to Exit 8B, marked City Island. Turn right after the drawbridge (you'll see a sign for City Island) and take the second turn at the traffic circle. Once you're over the bridge you're there. But be prepared for snarls if you're visiting on a warm-weather weekend.

OTHER TRANSPORTATION

There's a well-paved bicycle path that runs through the north Bronx including Gun Hill Road and Pelham Parkway, and it eventually goes to City Island. For exact directions you can access the excellent New York City bicycle map at www.ci.nyc.ny.us/html/dot/pdf/2003bikemapfront.pdf.

· · ·

City Island Avenue

City Island restaurants cater to all budgets and tastes and most have parking lots. I've listed a few examples. The tour starts at the far end (southern end) of the island.

Starting with the most basic, there's the Nathan's-like **Johnny's Reef Restaurant** (2 City Island Avenue, 718-885-2086; open March through November; closed Friday) at the far end of the island, a cavernous fluorescent white space with a cafeteria format and no personality. It has ample outdoor seating on a deck overlooking the Long Island Sound; there's also a lot of indoor seating. People flock here for the good prices on fish and it's great for large families with kids. **The Lobster Box** (34 City Island Avenue, 718-885-1952) offers a total contrast. Its uniformed wait staff and the interior decor, with old paintings and wood paneling, give the air of an exclusive country club that you should get dressed up for before you go. The main dining area includes a huge picture-window view of the water. Non-lobster entrées range from about $18 to $24, while lobster dishes will set you back $30 to $40. Lobster boxes combine lobster with steak or other seafood such as fried shrimp, scallops, or fillet of sole. There are also pastas and a children's menu that includes a whole broiled or steamed lobster for $17.95.

Tito Puente's (64 City Island Avenue, 718-885-3200) specializes in Caribbean-style seafood as well as Latin cuisine in general and offers live jazz on Fridays and Saturdays and a Latin jazz brunch on Sundays for $19.95

(reservations are recommended). Every few Thursdays they have a Comedy Night. If you call ahead, you save $3 for the evening's dinner and show ($37 instead of $40).

In the middle of the island eateries mix with antique shops and gift shops and the cuisine is more Upper West Side. The places tend to be smaller and more intimate. At **The Black Whale** (279 City Island Avenue, 718-995-3657), seafood dishes are in the minority. Count on wraps, Caesar salads, quesadillas, grilled chicken, pastas, and the like; entrée salads and pastas range from $11 to $16. Seafood entrées ($16 to $18) include lobster pot pie, sesame-crusted tuna, and Maryland crab cakes. If you're in an Italian mood, **The Tree House** (273 City Island Avenue, 718-885-0806) specializes in northern Mediterranean cooking, with several specialty pastas (lobster ravioli in vodka sauce and a vegetarian lasagna made with feta cheese and spinach, as well as more traditional ones). Entrées range from $9.95 (for the least expensive chicken dish) to $22.95 (for steak). A popular old-timer here is **The Crab Shanty** (361 City Island Avenue, 718-885-1810), an informal place that has a children's menu and a very reasonable lunch menu (fish entrées range from about $9.95 to $15.95).

You'll find one of City Island's biggest surprises and charmers soon after you cross the bridge. **Le Refuge Inn** (620 City Island Avenue, 718-885-2478) calls itself New York City's only real French inn. Located in a nineteenth-century former captain's residence, it has fabulous harbor views and includes a bed and breakfast in addition to its French meals. (Its owner, Pierre Saint-Denis, also operates Le Refuge at 166 East 82nd Street in Manhattan.) They have a prix fixe $19.50 Sunday brunch and $45 dinner. You can walk through the kitchen to a porch area in the back if you prefer a setting less formal than the main dining room. Postcards of Le Refuge are smartly designed to give the impression you're on an island near the French Riviera rather than in the Bronx.

Also . . . If you happen to visit City Island on a Sunday afternoon, you'll do well to visit the **City Island Nautical Museum**, which is located in an historic former public school built in 1897. In 1986, when the school building was sold for development, a portion was reserved for use by the City Island Historical Society and a community center, and now several old schoolrooms serve as museum galleries. (Condominiums were built on the rest of the school area.) Exhibits in these schoolrooms include paintings of City Island during the 1930s; a library of books, magazines, newspapers, and scrapbooks; and memorabilia highlighting City Island's history as a shipbuilding community. The museum also recreates a schoolroom of the 1930s, and a community room contains personal heirlooms—jewelry, clothing, toys, and other objects—donated by island residents. One of the most fun exhibits is of photographs of movies that were shot on location on City Island. The museum is located in the middle of the island at 190 Fordham Street. You'll find more information at www.cityislandmuseum.org/.

Bronx Side Trip

Afro-Caribbean Bronx

I'm not sure if anyone has dubbed the area of the Bronx north of Yankee Stadium "Little Accra" as yet. I've read many articles about Ghanaians in the Bronx, and every time I find an African market in Manhattan or Brooklyn I look for copies of the newspaper *African Abroad,* which often carries advertisements from African markets and restaurants, a good deal of which seem to be in this neighborhood.

Taking a careful look at a map, though, it becomes clear that the markets and restaurants are relatively scattered. No one area contains just these markets. But I found a few by riding the #4 train and taking a quick bus ride up Burnside Avenue. If you're an explorer who shares an interest in Africa and how immigration from Africa is having an impact on the neighborhoods of New York City, you might want to take the side trip described below.

First, though, read the section on Central Harlem that describes the francophone African community that has grown up around West 116th Street (see pages 214–216). In the East Harlem chapter (see pages 196–211), you'll also read about a few West African markets that have been established in this neighborhood. These are run mostly by people from Senegal, the Ivory Coast, and nearby countries where French is an important language.

Getting There   Take the #4 train to Burnside Avenue and then take the BX43 bus west up Burnside Avenue (and it's quite "up") to University Avenue. It's a short distance but a steep uphill.

One of the first places you'll see is **African & American Restaurant** (1987 University Avenue, 718-731-8595). The decor isn't much, but the food is great and the prices are cheap. A soul food meal of jerk chicken and collards, macaroni and cheese, or other sides will set you back about $5 or $6, depending on how many sides you want. Everything here is ready-made. The African dishes include spicy chicken and fish stews with a starch—usually *gari*—which is used to absorb the sauces. Next door is **One Stop African Caribbean Market** (1985 University Avenue, 718-583-8283), which sells clothing, cosmetics, shoes, and packaged foods.

The immediate area, by the way, is rather attractive, with a nice-looking public school and some classic prewar buildings that appear to have been upgraded. **Bronx Community College** is a few blocks north on University Avenue and contains the Hall of Fame, which overlooks the East River. Few people remember that New York University used to have its Bronx campus on this site. As a community college, it reflects the international nature of the Bronx as it is now with its large Latino, African, Caribbean, and Asian student body.

Head back down Burnside Avenue—you might want to walk it this time—and you'll pass a terrific Jamaican place called **Food Hut** (52 West Burnside Avenue, 718-294-9455), which has seating but also very good take-out chicken stew, oxtail, peas, jerk chicken, curries (goat and chicken), stew fish, and so on. They also have patties, breads, and lots of cakes— carrot, spice, rum, and "Jackass Corn"—and plaintain tarts. The servings here are either small, medium, or large—and the large, in most cases, is no more than $9 (for the stew fish), and most are less. You can also get hearty breakfast porridges (corn, banana, peanut, or oats), which come with yam or banana; the large is $7 and the small is $4.75. A block closer to the subway you'll pass the terrific **La Junquera Bakery** (20 West Burnside Avenue, 718-583-1857), a Dominican place that is one of the nicest I've seen. They make a beautiful display of their pastries, patties, and cakes. In addition to baked goods, La Junquera also serves Dominican main dishes.

Now take the #4 train two stops south to Mount Eden Avenue. There are two fine Ghanaian stores in this neighborhood. First, walk up Mount Eden Avenue to **Eddie's Place—African American Food Market** (32 Mount Eden Avenue, on the corner of Walton Avenue, 718-731-3100). Here you'll find cookware, fabrics, and CDs, along with shelves of canned and boxed food from Ghana, jasmine rice from Thailand, corned beef from Argentina, sardines from China, and Heinz ketchup. There are also soft drinks from Ghana (ginger beer and lemonade) and Ghanaian beer. Walk one block north on Walton to 174th Street and turn left (west) to **Unity Market** (60 East 174th Street, 718-466-0160). This also is a very attractive store, selling fabrics and cookware as well as lots of food. I saw clay African trading beads in a display case, and I noticed a hot sauce called *shitor din* (also known as *shito* or *sheeto*), made of prawn powder, dried shrimp, hot pepper, tomato paste, ginger, onions, and oil. I also found homemade peanut butter, African ginger, and African pepper, used to make herbs and to spice dishes. There are also lots of African music CDs in these stores; you can ask the owner to recommend the best music.

As an aside, Unity is located next door to a non-profit organization called **Rocking the Boat** (rockingtheboat.org), a boat building and educational project that works with schools. It's sponsored by New Settlement, a Bronx housing program that also sponsors community outreach projects.

We hear about these projects but rarely see them. In the window here, you'll actually see the boat-in-progress that community children and some adults have been building.

Also... If you're interested in learning more about African cooking so you can try out some of the ingredients at these stores, check out this fabulous recipe Web site: www.safarimkt.com/african-food-recipes.htm.

Bronx Side Trip

Cambodia in the Bronx (and More!), with a Visit to Poe Cottage

Every so often I stumble on an unexpected treasure in my urban journeys.

This happened at 194th Street in the Bronx when I took a bus heading south from Norwood toward Fordham Road along Valentine Avenue. I spotted a sign reading "Cambodian market" and couldn't contain my curiosity. I got off at the next stop and walked back.

I found myself in a rather remarkable part of the Bronx. I'd heard of **Poe Park**, which contains a cottage that was Edgar Allan Poe's last residence (see page 299). The park has a wonderful playground and it's surrounded by the type of prewar apartment buildings that would make realtors salivate if they were located on the Upper West Side. But this is a polyglot immigrant neighborhood of upwardly mobile strivers, complemented (and made somewhat more complex) by a new Mormon church nearby. At times you'll see the young, clean-cut, usually white missionaries from the church scattered around, dressed in short-sleeved white button-down shirts, dark slacks, and the ever-present name tags on their shirt pockets. I was in a nearby pizzeria one day when two of them came in to order two dozen pizzas (and asked if they could be ready in a half hour!).

Getting There Take the D train to Kingsbridge Road and walk south on the east side of the Grand Concourse to Poe Park. Cross the park on the lane in front of Poe Cottage. At Valentine Avenue you'll see the markets. East Kingsbridge Road winds around the park and meets Valentine Avenue at a somewhat confusing intersection (at first I thought all the markets were on Valentine Avenue) and ends at Fordham Road. On Fordham Road, by the way, you can take any eastbound bus to Belmont (see pages 275–276). Ask the driver to drop you off at Arthur Avenue, and turn right (south). The hub is at 187th Street. You can walk there from this area in fifteen to twenty minutes. Most eastbound buses go to the Bronx Zoo; the BX12 goes to Pelham Parkway.

(By the way, when I first reported on the Cambodian markets in 1999,

Bronx's only Starbucks was located nearby at 312 Fordham Road. Although this area of Fordham Road near the Grand Concourse is terrifically busy, the Starbucks closed in 2002. It just didn't fit in!)

I was amazed to find that the Cambodian place on 194th Street was just one among a cluster of stores selling food products from Asia, Africa, the Caribbean, and Latin America. If you're looking for hard-to-find ingredients for these regional cuisines, you need go no farther! Following the curve along the park you'll find the Cambodian shop, **Neighborhood Oriental Market** (229 East Kingsbridge Road), which has products from Thailand as well as Cambodia. That shop shares an address with **Naveen International** (229 East Kingsbridge Road, 718-733-6200), a store specializing in products from Guyana and Southeast Asia. Next door is **Medina Grocery & Halal Meat** (239 East Kingsbridge Road, 718-365-1990), whose owner is from Bangladesh. From store to store you'll find a vast selection of produce and packaged goods from Thailand, Vietnam, China, India, Pakistan, Bangladesh, Egypt, Ghana, Guinea, Mexico, the Caribbean, and Guyana. I found an exquisite extra-hot sauce from Guyana under the Chatak brand. All three stores stock audio and video cassettes and cooking utensils. Places like this are an interesting mirror of the neighborhoods they serve.

It's often hard to find good sit-down meals in these neighborhoods, but I found two. The bustling **Bronx BBQ**, just north of Fordham Road (305 East Kingsbridge Road, 718-584-0050), is the area's nicest restaurant, with a large menu of Southern and Caribbean dishes. It also has a busy take-out business. One block south, **Mr. Taco** (281 East Kingsbridge Road) is an attractive, smaller alternative with a terrific Mexican menu and modest prices.

Also . . .   A bonus to your food safari to this neighborhood is **Poe Cottage**, Edgar Allan Poe's last residence (before Bronx was part of greater New York City), across the street from the markets. The cottage is now a museum owned by the City of New York and administered by the Bronx County Historical Society. The park also has a great playground. The address is 3309 Bainbridge Road, a street that curves around the park and meets East Kingsbridge.

Poe moved here in 1846 from crowded New York City to what was then the village of Fordham, hoping that his ailing wife, Virginia, would recover from tuberculosis. She did not, and, upon her death, Poe reportedly fell into a deep depression, during which time he wrote the classic poems "Annabel Lee," "Ulalume," and "The Bells" while living here. (He died in Baltimore in 1849.) Poe Cottage is open Saturdays from 10 A.M. to 4 P.M. and Sundays from 1 P.M. to 4 P.M. Admission is $2. For information call 718-881-8900.

Bronx Side Trip

Morris Park

When you reach the Italian enclave in Morris Park you'll have the sensation of being transported a few decades back in time. Unlike Belmont, Morris Park does not draw tourists and it comes across as a very inwardly focused community. Its location near a cluster of hospitals draws a ready clientele for its trattarias, cafés, and excellent bakeries, and other folks come simply because they *know* about it.

In contrast to the gritty setting of Belmont, with its bedraggled six-story apartment buildings and houses that have clearly seen better days, Morris Park is a spiffier, well kept community of attached and some detached red brick homes, with garages, small front lawns with flower beds, and, if you peek through on some of the side streets, ample (for the city) backyards, some with hardy vegetable gardens and above-ground pools. While some business owners admit that they commute from suburbs, others remain close by; it's a nice enough place to live and there's less of a compulsion to leave.

As for Morris Park itself, well, there is no Morris Park. But there used to be a Morris Park Race Track, located south of Pelham Parkway South between Williamsbridge Road and what was then called Bear Swamp Road (and is now more innocuously known as Bronxdale Avenue). Built in the 1880s, it was a popular draw through the early 1900s, made easier by the fact that the New Haven Railroad built a rail line specifically to transport patrons to the track. (I suspect there's an interesting story about this!) Apparently owner John A. Morris went through hard times and the track went bankrupt in 1904.

What then followed is a curious niblet of history, which I found too irresistible to skip when I found this story on line in the *Bronx Times*. Apparently some eighty rich members of the Aeronautic Society negotiated a lease from the city for the racetrack land. Stables for 700 horses were turned into what, when you think about it, was probably one of the first incubators for new technology. Three Swiss engineers with familiar last names—Walter Chrysler and brothers Louis and Gaston Chevrolet—developed what were then some of the best examples of high-speed cars, including a Fiat that won a mile record of 52.8 seconds. The success of their efforts drew wealthy backers, who funded the launch of the Chevrolet Motor Company in 1911. Gliders were built in the former stables, as were monoplanes, hybrid biplanes, triplanes, and even weird helicopters by enthusiasts who didn't know how to fly them! A dirigible also was launched from Morris Park, and there also were balloon ascents in which courageous passengers were taken aloft for the first time in aviation history. Bronxites can claim to having sponsored the first airport. There were other inventions such as "wind wagons," which were bicycles that became airborne (in theory); some accidents—but no deaths—were reported.

Two disastrous fires eventually led to the demise of the embryo airport. After 1910, the avenues we know today were laid out and homes were built on what was once the Morris Park Race Track.*

Getting There   Take the #2 or #5 train to 180th Street and then take the BX21 bus marked Westchester Square. The area around the subway station doesn't look very nice (although the building housing the train station is a landmark). But don't be deterred: the bus stop is in front of a large, modern transit police facility and the bus runs fairly often because its end destination is several hospitals. Get off at Haight Avenue and then walk back in the direction you came. This is the beginning of a four-block stretch of bakeries, cafés, and small markets ending at Colden Street.

But if you're one of those folks who *has* to see it all, keep walking until you reach an older Italian section—I've listed the main places. These older shops give you a hard-to-find feel for the atmosphere of an earlier era of the Bronx, which I don't think will last much longer. You can then catch the BX21 bus back toward 180th Street.

Be prepared for outstanding pastries and breads in this area, as well as excellent Italian coffee! Be prepared, as well, for people to be smoking in some of these establishments.

▪ Haight Street to Lurting Street

Patricia's Brick Oven Pizza & Pasta (1080 Morris Park Avenue, 718-409-9069) is a comfortable neighborhood trattaria with red-and-white checked tablecloths and an appealing collection of vintage photographs of the Morris Park area. The menu is not bad—there's a good selections of pastas, chicken and veal dishes, and some seafood. It's a very comfortable, homey place. Patricia's opened around 1994, which makes it a relative newcomer to this community, where some stores are now being managed by members of the third generation of the founding family.

In fact, just next door to Patricia's is **Scaglione Bakery** (1078 Morris Park Avenue), whose manager, Danny Scaglione, told me that his grandfather founded it in the 1930s on East 114th Street between First and Second Avenues in East Harlem, one block west of Rao's Restaurant. Grandpa moved to Morris Park in the 1950s. Danny's father lives above the bakery (the family owns the building) and still comes in frequently, although

*http://www.bxtimes.com/News/2000/0720/Columns/09. html

Danny and his family now live in Westchester. While they sell typical Italian breads, they also have specials Tuesday through Saturday—cheese and olive on Tuesdays and jalapeño and cheddar on Thursdays, for instance—and they also serve great sandwiches on focaccia bread.

▪ Lurting Street to Hone Street

Enrico's Pastry and Caffe (1057 Morris Park Avenue, 718-823-7207; closed Monday) is a wonderfully old-fashioned place serving hot and iced espresso and cappuccino, delicious pastries, and, in the summer, twenty-two flavors of gelato including peanut butter chocolate swirl, banana royale, and something called "the kitchen sink." One flavor I've seen at a number of Italian ice places is called "lily with nuts." I have yet to find someone who can explain to me just what that means! Enrico's was extensively renovated in 2002 to more closely resemble a traditional Italian café, with terra-cotta floors and murals. You can get all the traditional pastries—*sfinge* filled with cannoli cream, fruits, nuts, and chocolate chips, and *zeppole* filled with a custard pastry with maraschino cherries, for example.

▪ Hone Street to Paulding Street

La Casa del Caffe (1036 Morris Park Avenue) not only serves an incredible cup of espresso but also sells and repairs Italian espresso makers. If yours needs fixing, you can call Domenico or Anna Agovino at 718-931-7816.

▪ Paulding Avenue to Colden Street

The Chocolate Place (1008 Morris Park Avenue) is owned by Angela DaBeninga, who is annoyingly thin ("Good metabolism," she says). She opened her first chocolate shop elsewhere in the Bronx in 1987 and relocated to this much larger space in the early 1990s. Walk in and you'll be hooked by the aroma of chocolate and all the things you can do with it. This chocolate-lover's paradise offers not just ready-made chocolates but all the fixings—molds, decorations, and other ornaments—to make your own. (She used to hold classes, and says she's too busy now—but ask.) They sell bags of meltable chocolate in twelve colors (including purple, turquoise, yellow, and pink) in addition to standard milk, dark, and white chocolates. Did I mention the old-fashioned candies? You can find gigantic Pixie Sticks, candy dots, bubble gum crayons, and chocolate cigarettes. You can also buy gifts here—puzzles, dolls, and jewelry—and in warm weather the shop sells ice cream and slush.

Russo Brothers Bakery (980 Morris Park Avenue) could easily be your last stop. The breads here are spectacular—seeded round breads and long breads and also "Sicilian fries" (herbed croutons cut like French fries) and *tostini,* twice-cooked flatbreads seasoned with herbs, a very nice accompaniment to a salad or cheese. A container of either is just $2.

■ If You Want to Keep Going . . .

A few blocks further you'll come to a busy intersection with Bronxdale Avenue, where you'll find a cluster of shops at 900 Morris Park Avenue, including **Café Dion** and **Mamma Mia Trattoria** (718-430-7066), where you can get a great $5.50 pasta lunch special with salad.

The area becomes slightly drearier as you proceed, but then you will come to St. Dominic's Church and a handful of older Italian markets. An old-timer here is **Riviera Ravioli** (643 Morris Park Avenue at Union Port Road, 718-823-0260), where you can buy homemade pasta and fresh cheese and sausage. It's only open weekdays from 8 A.M. to 4 P.M.

Resources

■

Each issue of *NoshNews*—and each chapter of this book—is packed with supplementary information about the neighborhoods you'll be visiting. However, I thought it would be helpful to assemble some additional information to supplement your experiences.

It was tempting to try to build a comprehensive list of books and Web sites and places to follow up on all of your adventures. But I decided to focus on the best materials I found—and the ones I used the most. Let me know if I've missed critical resources that would enhance future editions of this book.

▪ Bibliography

This is a sampling of the books that have helped me put together issues of *NoshNews* and this book. Also, many neighborhood chapters make reference to local resources. I always pick up community newspapers when I'm wandering through neighborhoods. Although they're not slick or fancy, they often contain useful information on local trends, including new markets and restaurants, and they occasionally provide very valuable insights. Community newspapers that I've found in East Harlem, Greenpoint, and Flushing have been especially helpful.

Asia Society, *Asia in New York City: A Cultural Travel Guide* (New York: Balliett & Fitzgerald and Emeryville, California: Avalon Travel Publishing, 2000). This book covers many aspects of the visual and performing arts, foods, religion, and other traditions and trends among different Asian communities throughout New York City.

Alliance for the Arts, *Kids Culture Catalog: A Cultural Guide to New York City for Kids, Families and Teachers* (New York: Harry N. Abrams, Inc., 1996). Despite the title, I find this book a valuable resource for adults—it really delves into detail on interesting cultural landmarks throughout New York City and complements many of my food explorations.

Boggs, Vernon, Gerald Handel, Sylvia Fava, et al., *The Apple Sliced* (South Hadley, Massachusetts: Bergin & Garvey, 1984). This book has helpful sociological essays on New York City neighborhoods and trends.

Citizens Committee for New York City, *The Neighborhoods of Brooklyn* (New Haven: Yale University Press, 1998). This is a wonderful resource for anyone curious about Brooklyn, and I hope similar books will be published on the other boroughs! It has terrific maps, history, photographs, and current commentary on forty-five discreet Brooklyn neighborhoods. (What fun it must have been to write, too!)

Dolkart, Andrew S. and Gretchen S. Sorin, *Touring Historic Harlem: Four Walks of Northern Manhattan* (New York: New York Landmarks Conservancy, 1987). Dolkart (whom I took a course from many years ago) is one of the most dedicated architectural historians in New York City. This book provides terrific details on Harlem's history and architectural features and is divided into four neighborhood walking tours. (See page 223.)

Federal Writers Project, *New York Panorama—A Companion to the WPA Guide to New York City* (New York: Random House, 1938 and New York: Pantheon, 1982). I have the 1982 paperback, which has an introduction by Alfred Kazin. This wonderful and fun book provides terrific and detailed histories of many New York City neighborhoods. It's particularly useful when you want to get background information on places that have clearly changed, such as Yorkville, Chinatown, or Manhattan.

Harlow, Ilana, *The International Express: A Guide to Ethnic Communities along the 7 Train* (booklet and video) (Queens Council on the Arts, 79-01 Park Lane South, Woodhaven, NY 11421-1166). Folklorist Harlow chronicles the traditional life that flourishes in the communities along the route of the #7 elevated train in Queens, with an introduction to ethnic neighborhoods and listings of restaurants, shops, houses of worship, and festivals. The video focuses on the art and culture of four of the communities along the train route.

Jackson, Kenneth T., ed., *The Encyclopedia of New York City* (New Haven, Connecticut: Yale University Press, 1995). This formidable volume, amply illustrated, provides good background on neighborhoods, institutions, and individuals who contributed to the making of New York City.

Kahn, Robert, ed., *City Secrets: New York City* (New York: The Little Bookroom, 2002). This guide contains a wealth of cultural, historical, and culinary information on the five boroughs provided by writers, artists, and other professionals—including yours truly—on their favorite places in New York City.

Queens Council on the Arts, *Queens Cultural Guide.* This booklet provides basic information on the cultural resources of Queens. Your best bet to learn more about Queens is to follow up directly with the council (see the address listed above under Ilana Harlow, or refer to www.queenscouncilarts.org).

Stern, Zelda, *The Complete Guide to Ethnic New York* (New York: St. Martin's Press, 1980). This is the first guide I'm aware of that chronicles the ethnic communities in New York City, including the food and shops. (The book I cowrote with Mark L. Clifford, *The Food Lover's Guide to the Real New York,* New York: Prentice-Hall, 1987, is the second). Long out of print and, of course, outdated, Stern's book, which is divided into ethnic groups, remains valuable for the ethnic histories it provides. It can be a wistful read, too, when you follow its descriptions of neighborhoods (such as Yorkville) where their main institutions are now long gone! Unfortunately, it's very short on the culture of the boroughs, where much of the most interesting activity can be found.

Ultan, Lloyd and the Bronx County Historical Society, *The Beautiful Bronx (1920–1950)* (New York: Arlington House, 1979). This is a lovely pictorial history of the Bronx during one of its several golden ages. Ultan has been the official Bronx historian for years and has written and edited several other excellent Bronx histories.

White, Norval and Elliot Willensky: *AIA Guide to New York City: The Classic Guide to New York's Architecture* (Fourth Edition) (New York: Three Rivers Press, 2000). This is a great book to take with you as you walk (although it's bulky!) but it can be frustrating, too, because of its heavy emphasis on Manhattan and a few neighborhoods in Brooklyn. I have seen so many amazing buildings throughout the city and wish someone had information about them!

A great one-stop resource for books on New York City, including architecture and history, is Urban Center Books, located at the the Municipal Arts Society (457 Madison Avenue at 51st Street, 212-935-3960, www.mas.org).

▪ Food References

There are many excellent books to guide you through the more exotic foods that you will encounter in your journeys. Here are four favorites that have helped me, but be aware that some are huge and not meant for lugging around in a neighborhood!

Ferguson, Clare, *Street Food* (Alexandria, Virginia: Time-Life Books, 1999). This breezy, colorful book explains a lot of the so-called "street food" that you can find on travels around the globe—or in the neighborhoods of New York City's boroughs. It includes fifty recipes.

Lau, Anita Loh-Yien, *Asian Greens* (New York: St. Martin's Press, 2001). This volume is slim but nonetheless full of information on Asian produce, with beautiful photographs and sixty nice recipes.

Schneider, Elizabeth, *Vegetables from Amaranth to Zucchini* (New York: William Morrow, 2001). This formidable volume, seven years in the making and with hundreds of recipes, is the food explorer's answer to "What's that?" Schneider has done an amazing job!

Solomon, Charmaine, *Encyclopedia of Asian Food* (North Clarendon, Vermont: Periplus Books, 1998). I saw an odd-looking citrus fruit on East Broadway in Chinatown and didn't know how to ask what it was, nor could anyone completely answer when I tried. (I finally asked two Chinese high school girls and they provided an explanation but not the English name.) I looked in Solomon's book, and without too much cross-referencing discovered it was a pomelo; the book also included a description of the pomelo's ritual use. (It's commonly used during the annual harvest festival.)

As I mentioned in the introduction, you can find dozens (no, hundreds!) of food titles, at both Kitchen Arts & Letters (1435 Lexington Avenue) and at Kalustyan's (123 Lexington Avenue).

▪ Organizations

Two groups stand out for the ways in which they promote and advocate for the preservation of New York City's outstanding local cultures:

Center for Traditional Music and Dance (www.ctmd.org)
200 Church Street, Suite 300
New York, New York 10013

Since its founding in 1968, CTMD has played a critical role in supporting and preserving the music and dance heritage of New York City's multitude of immigrant groups. It works in partnerships with musicians and dancers to promote and preserve their cultural heritage and to support research that documents individuals and groups practicing the musical and dance traditions of their homelands. CTMD organizes or co-sponsors festivals all over New York City—many in the neighborhoods in which people of a common ethnic group live—and in larger venues to bring people of many backgrounds together. Its annual FolkParks presentation at Lincoln Center provides several hours of performances representing cultures from around the world. CTMD also sells recordings of these groups.

City Lore (www.citylore.org)
72 East 1st Street
New York, New York 10003

CityLore, founded in 1986, is made up of folklorists who prefer the term "cultural activists" because of their "[commitment] to the principles of cultural equity and democracy." Through publications, exhibits, and programs, CityLore does a phenomenal job of highlighting the complex and intimate folk cultures that make up New York City. An annual People's Hall of Fame awards ceremony, launched in 1993, honors grassroots heroes who have contributed in special ways to New York City's culture; it's accompanied by a multimedia exhibit at the Museum of the City of New York.

▪ Web Sites

In the course of researching both *NoshNews* and this book, I've spent considerable time surfing the Internet for helpful Web sites. I've found quite a spectrum, from excellent to well-meaning to inaccurate to awful.

Some of the most amusing sites were created by individuals who lived in neighborhoods I profiled (particularly in the Bronx and in Greenpoint, Brooklyn), and although these folks may have moved away physically, they never left in spirit! These nostalgia sites are a good place to learn about neighborhood history: famous folks who lived in those neighborhoods and famous landmarks that are now long gone. Some sites also have bulletin boards where current and former neighborhood residents trade information and gossip. Many of these are mentioned in the neighborhood chapters of this book.

Here are some Web sites I've found during the course of my research:

www.nycitystore.com/subcat.asp?sid=21. Includes a list of books about New York City, and

www.mcny.org/answers.htm. This "Just for Fun" site, hosted by the Museum of the City of New York, answers all sorts of questions about New York City.

Information on the Bronx is available from the Bronx Tourism Council at www.ilovethebronx.com/ and through a site called Bronx Mall at www.bronxmall.com/cult/ that will link you not just to information and events but also to articles about the neighborhoods and culture of the Bronx.

For Brooklyn, www.brooklynx.com (BRIC—Brooklyn Information & Culture Service) is a main source of tourism information in Brooklyn, but it relies heavily on advertising. I recommend it for some neighborhood information but advise users that it is limited. The Web page on Bay Ridge makes absolutely no mention of the rich Arabic (Christian and Muslim) presence in the neighborhood.

The Queens Council on the Arts (www.queenscouncilarts.org) does a superb job of capturing the life and culture of New York City's neighborhoods and institutions. It's a great portal to this complex and exciting borough.

For Manhattan, the Museum of the City of New York (www.mcny.org) is a great entry to New York City's culture and history, although it isn't so much broken down into neighborhoods.

Demographic and population data on New York City is available from the Department of City Planning Web site, www.ci.nyc.ny.us/html/dcp/pdf/census/demonyc.pdf.

For street fair information, here are two sites I found: www.nycstreetfairs.com/sched.html and www.nycstories.com/places/getout/streetfest.html, which highlights fairs throughout the boroughs.

For information on New York City parades, see www.carnaval.com/cityguides/newyork/parades.htm.

For information on major New York City events, see www.ci.nyc.ny.us/html/cau/html/major.html.

Index